U.S. HISTORY

A Document-Based Skillbook

Beverly Vaillancourt

Publisher: Tom Maksym

Executive Editor: Steven Jay Griffel

Vice President, Production and Manufacturing: Doreen Smith

Art Director: Eric Dawson

Creative Director/Assistant Vice President: Amy Rosen

Production Manager: Jason Grasso

Marketing Manager: Kathy Wanamaker

Project Manager: Steven Genzano

Production Editor: Carol Deckert

Designer: Pronk & Associates

Cover Design: Pronk & Associates

Cartographer: Sharon MacGregor

Proofreader: Pat Smith

Copy Editor: Dee Josephson

Permissions Manager: Kristine Liebman

Photo Researcher: Robert E. Lee

Grateful acknowledgments are made to the following reviewers:

David Moon has a Master of Arts Degree in Education from Viterbo University and teaches Advanced Placement courses in government and U.S. History at Reedsburg Area High School, Reedsburg, Wisconsin.

Peter Shrake holds a master's degree in history from the University of Wisconsin-Eau Claire and since 1999 has served as Executive Director of the Sauk County Historical Society, Sauk County, Wisconsin.

This book is dedicated to the resourceful teachers and students involved in the national Center for Civic Education *We the People* program. In particular, it is dedicated to Dee Runaas, Tim Moore, and Beth Ratway for their inspiration.

ISBN 1-4138-0722-4

TABLE OF CONTENTS

Foreign Policy

Expansion

INVENTIONS

CIVIL RIGHTS

DOMESTIC POLICY

A CHRONOLOGICAL APPROACH

PREFACE

U.S. HISTORY: A DOCUMENT-BASED SKILLBOOK is a compilation of the most significant documents that shaped our nation's story. The documents were chosen through a project called *The People's Vote*, sponsored by the National Archives and Records Administration, National History Day, and *U.S. News and World Report*. As part of this project, almost forty thousand people cast their votes, via the Internet or on paper ballot, for the documents they felt were most important in shaping American history. The documents considered ranged from the colonial days through the Voting Rights Act of 1965. Among the top ten documents were the Social Security Act, Civil Rights Act, the Thirteenth and Nineteenth Amendments, and the Emancipation Proclamation. The document considered most significant was the Declaration of Independence, followed by the Constitution and the Bill of Rights.

Through the study of these one hundred most significant documents, you will gain a better understanding of how important they were in shaping American domestic and foreign policy. Collectively, through reading about the events and personalities that shaped the documents, you will better understand how bias, debate, and compromise have defined American politics and laws.

Inquiry

Questions that provide opportunities for critical thinking follow each document excerpt. You will be asked to draw conclusions, determine point of view, or assess the significance of the document within its historical context.

Research

Each lesson concludes with three distinct research activities that allow you to further explore the document and/or historical events related to the document. Some lessons provide a *Link to the Past* where you will be able to investigate relationships between events that span many years. Each of the many research activities can be accomplished individually or as group projects.

Liberty

"Where liberty dwells, there is my country."
–BENJAMIN FRANKLIN (1706–1790)

Prologue

o Thomas Jefferson, liberty was a "boisterous sea . . . never without a wave." Franklin Delano Roosevelt defined liberty as "the air that we Americans breathe." John F. Kennedy resolved that "We shall pay any price, bear any burden, meet any hardship, support any friend, oppose any foe, in order to assure the survival and the success of liberty." The framers of America's government believed liberty to be an "unalienable right," the heart of the new nation. For the sake of liberty, Americans have been called to arms at home and across the seas, believing as Thomas Paine did: "He that would make his own liberty secure must guard even his enemy from oppression." Throughout America's history the meaning of liberty has been used by different groups to attain different goals, to define the value of one culture over another, to restrict the freedom of some for the greater freedom of others. Liberty gained. Liberty lost. In this first unit, you will be introduced to some of those who championed the cause of liberty.

1776   Lee Resolution

*"We are in the very midst of a revolution the most complete,
unexpected and remarkable of any in the history of nations."*

–JOHN ADAMS

HISTORICAL BACKGROUND

IN early 1763 relations between England and the colonies appeared fairly cordial. With the exception of New Orleans, all land from the Atlantic to the Mississippi River was under the control of England. With solid allegiance to the British Crown, the colonies looked forward to a time of unparalleled growth and prosperity. However, just thirteen short years later, many colonists were calling for a break with England and for an independent United States. What had happened?

One of the foremost problems faced by England in the 1760s was how to manage the vast lands it now claimed in the name of King George III. British forts located from the Great Lakes to western Pennsylvania proved difficult to protect against Native American uprisings. Restive colonists, eager to move west of the Appalachian Mountains, resented the English king's proclamation that prohibited such settlement. It appeared to England that the only option to protect and manage the land it claimed was to keep an army in America. But who would pay for such a huge expense?

The French and Indian War (1754–1763) proved to be a costly conflict, leaving England with an enormous debt of almost £130 million. The English government needed a source of revenue to pay past debts and to maintain British soldiers in America. The solution was to impose taxes on the English colonists. The Sugar Act of 1764 placed duties on sugar, indigo (used for dying cloth), coffee, wine, molasses, syrup, and many other items. Imports from Great Britain, such as linen and silk, also were taxed. With the Sugar Act, the British Parliament imposed duties on virtually every item needed for maintaining a household in the colonies.

The Stamp Act of 1765 went beyond the scope of the Sugar Act by imposing a tax on all items requiring paper, from legal documents to calendars to almanacs to playing cards. Even dice, though not made of paper, bore the brunt of the Crown's taxing authority. The Stamp Act crossed economic lines, uniting the social classes in their ire against the taxing dictates of Parliament. Moreover, the Stamp Act was an attempt to raise money for England instead of a means to regulate commerce, something the colonists found particularly offensive.

The Tea Act of 1773 exacerbated colonists' resentment toward British-imposed taxes. Arguments against taxation intermixed economics with the rationale that England had no right to tax the colonists without their consent. Britain's attempt to reap shillings from the colonists was met by several demonstrations of resistance, including the Boston Tea Party, boycotts of English goods, and outright civil disobedience. Unrest grew over Britain's imposition of laws that colonists viewed as unjust and detrimental to their economic prosperity. The result was a colonial rebellion that England viewed as tantamount to treason.

Many colonists, known as "patriots," rallied against British rule. One patriot, Richard Lee, was a Virginia delegate to the Second Continental Congress. On June 7, 1776, Lee introduced a resolution calling for separation from England, a directive to form alliances with foreign governments, and a call for the colonies to form a confederation. The *Lee Resolution* provided the core wording that later became the major tenets of the Declaration of Independence. The first section of the *Lee Resolution* was adopted by delegates from twelve colonies on July 2, 1776, with New York withholding its approval until July 9, 1776. Approval of the second section would wait until September 1776. Congressional action creating a confederation of states occurred in November 1777.

Resolved, That these United Colonies are, and of right ought to be, free and independent States, that they are absolved from all allegiance to the British Crown, and that all political connection between them and the State of Great Britain is, and ought to be, totally dissolved.

That it is expedient forthwith to take the most effectual measures for forming foreign Alliances.

That a plan of confederation be prepared and transmitted to the respective Colonies for their consideration and approbation. ✳

A STAMP

Left: A royal stamp required on all legal documents.

Below: A document showing the stamp.

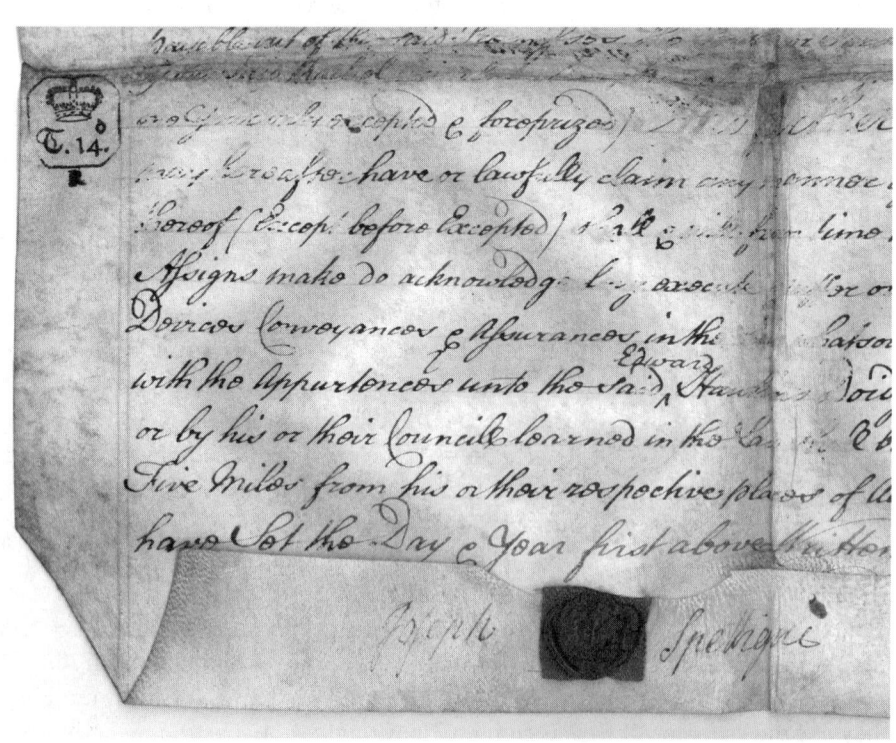

Critical Thinking

Determine Point of View
Reread John Adams's quote on page 3. The words come from a letter written by John Adams to William Cushing on June 9, 1776. What do you think he means by "unexpected and remarkable"?

Assess Significance
On June 11, 1776, Congress appointed three concurrent committees to respond to the three parts of the Lee Resolution: to write a declaration of independence, to form alliances with foreign governments, and to create a confederation of states. In your opinion, which committee had the most significant purpose? Why?

Draw Conclusions
The British government considered acts of rebellion to be acts of treason. Why would individuals such as Richard Lee, Patrick Henry, or Samuel Adams risk the dire consequences of being charged with treason?

Research and Writing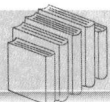

Relating Events
Research the Royal Proclamation of October 7, 1763. Explain the events that led to the establishment of the Proclamation Line. What points in the proclamation do you think colonists found inflammatory? Why was such a plan not feasible to enforce? What future events were prompted by the enactment of the Royal Proclamation of 1763?

Historical Interpretation
In 1774, King George III wrote to Lord North, "The die is now cast; the colonies must either submit or triumph." Research the four Coercive Acts passed in the spring of 1774. What did they involve? How did the colonists react? Why was the English government so unwilling to compromise with the American colonists? In what way did King George's words set the stage for the American Revolution?

Link to the Past
Research the protest movement surrounding the Vietnam War during the late 1960s and early 1970s. Research the civil disobedience of the colonists, such as the tarring and feathering of tax collectors. Describe the civil actions of the colonists in the 1760s and early 1770s and the civil actions associated with the Vietnam War protests 200 years later. Compare and contrast the purpose, actions, and result of the events in each time period.

1776 Declaration of Independence

"Where liberty dwells, there is my country."

–BENJAMIN FRANKLIN

HISTORICAL BACKGROUND

BY 1776 American colonists had endured years of strife between themselves and the English government. They had been taxed without being duly represented in Parliament. They had seen their ports closed, their public meetings restricted, and their trade regulated by a distant government that seemed all too unyielding to the protests of the colonists. To some, independence from England was the unthinkable. To others, it was an absolute necessity caused by the actions of a tyrannical English government. Influenced by the writings of English philosopher John Locke, Thomas Jefferson and others viewed independence as a natural right. The Declaration of Independence was the bold assertion of that right.

On June 11, 1776, the Second Continental Congress appointed the "Committee of Five" composed of Thomas Jefferson, John Adams, Benjamin Franklin, Robert R. Livingston, and Roger Sherman to collaborate on a statement declaring American independence from England. The task of writing fell to Thomas Jefferson who was considered the most eloquent writer of the group. Jefferson set upon the difficult task of drafting a carefully worded document that, once signed, would be the equivalent to an act of treason against the English crown.

In the Declaration of Independence, Jefferson argued that government is a contract between the people and those who govern the people. He asserted that governments derive "their just powers from the consent of the governed." It was a radical premise wholly discarded by King George III of England.

Perhaps even more offensive to King George III was the lengthy list of grievances the colonials personally held against him.

He has called together legislative bodies at places unusual, uncomfortable, and distant from the depository of their public Records, for the sole purpose of fatiguing them into compliance with his measures. . . .

He has made Judges dependent on his Will alone, for the tenure of their offices, and the amount and payment of their salaries. . . .

He has erected a multitude of New Offices, and sent hither swarms of Officers to harass our people, and eat out their substance. . . .

He has kept among us, in times of peace, Standing Armies without the consent of our legislatures. . . .

For cutting off our Trade with all parts of the world:

For imposing Taxes on us without our Consent:

For depriving us, in many cases, of the benefits of Trial by Jury:

For transporting us beyond Seas to be tried for pretended offences. . . .

The Declaration of Independence was originally signed by John Hancock, president of the Second Continental Congress, and Charles Thomson, secretary. It was sent to state assemblies and commanding officers of the Continental Army. On July 19 the Continental Congress directed that a copy of the Declaration of Independence be handwritten on parchment with the new title, "The unanimous Declaration of the thirteen united States of America." Formal signing by 56 members of the Continental Congress began on August 2, 1776.

The Declaration of Independence begins with a bold statement of independence. The document continues with a litany of transgressions enacted by King George III against the colonies. It makes reference to the colonies existing under "absolute Despotism."

National Archives Document

IN CONGRESS, July 4, 1776
The unanimous Declaration of the thirteen united States of America,

When in the Course of human events, it becomes necessary for one people to dissolve the political bands which have connected them with another, and to assume among the powers of the earth, the separate and equal station to which the Laws of Nature and of Nature's God entitle them, a decent respect to the opinions of mankind requires that they should declare the causes which impel them to the separation.

We hold these truths to be self-evident, that all men are created equal, that they are endowed by their Creator with certain unalienable Rights, that among these are Life, Liberty and the pursuit of Happiness.—That to secure these rights, Governments are instituted among Men, deriving their just powers from the consent of the governed,—That whenever any Form of Government becomes destructive of these ends, it is the Right of the People to alter or to abolish it, and to institute new Government, laying its foundation on such principles and organizing its powers in such form, as to them shall seem most likely to effect their Safety and Happiness. . . . ✳

Below: The Committee of Five (from left to right): Benjamin Franklin (1), Thomas Jefferson (2), Robert R. Livingston (3), John Adams (4), and Roger Sherman (5).

Critical Thinking

Determine Point of View

The Declaration of Independence embodies a sense of fortitude, determination, and purpose. On what basic principles was the Declaration of Independence founded? How did the colonists justify their actions? By signing the Declaration of Independence, what did the delegates indicate about the sovereign will of the people?

Draw Conclusions

Why do you think Thomas Jefferson included the following statement of principle in the Declaration of Independence?

> … a decent respect to the opinions of mankind requires that they should declare the causes which impel them to the separation

Analyze Cause and Effect

In adopting the Declaration of Independence, what prompted the inclusion of "it becomes necessary for one people to dissolve the political bands which have connected them with another"?

Research and Writing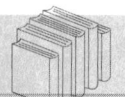

Historical Interpretation

The Lee Resolution and the Declaration of Independence were formulated in response to several acts passed by Parliament that were viewed as unfair and oppressive by many colonists. These included the Stamp Act, Tea Act, and Coercive (Intolerable) Acts. Research the cumulative effect of these acts. Which groups were economically impacted by the acts? How cohesive were the colonists in their discontent with England? How did those who favored rebellion champion their cause among the colonies?

Analysis

Access and read the entire Declaration of Independence. Identify the main points of the document. What justification did the colonists give for separation from England? What are identified as the rights of the people? Which grievances listed do you feel are the most egregious? Write a summary analyzing the most significant points made by Jefferson.

Link to the Past

The Declaration of Independence was a bold step taken by a fledgling nation. In signing the Declaration of Independence, the delegates pledged "to each other our Lives, our Fortunes and our sacred Honor." Many of the delegates paid dearly. Lewis Morris from New York, for example, lost his property and most of his wealth in the ensuing American Revolution. All who signed were considered rebels by the English government. Research the dissolution of the Union of Soviet Socialist Republics in 1991. What parallels can be drawn between the principles fought for in the American Revolution and the issues surrounding the break up of the USSR? What general conclusions can be made?

1782 The Great Seal of the United States

"Honor est premium virtutis."
(Honor is the reward for virtue.)

–MARCUS TILLIUM CICERO (106–43 B.C.)

HISTORICAL BACKGROUND

Soon after the Continental Congress ratified the Declaration of Independence, it appointed John Adams, Benjamin Franklin, and Thomas Jefferson to design a seal for the United States. Plans called for the seal to appear on all official documents, treaties, and proclamations. The design committee was charged with creating a seal that symbolized the independence of the new nation.

It took three committees and five designs before the final design for the Great Seal was accepted by the Continental Congress. The final design incorporated ideas from the earlier designs. On the obverse, or principal side, of the first design was written *E Pluribus Unum*, or "Out of Many, One." This motto continued to appear throughout the design process. The olive branch, a constellation of 13 stars, and the red, white, and blue shield survived scrutiny. Later, the imperial eagle was replaced with the nation's symbol, the bald eagle. The final design tipped the eagle's wings upwards, as if in flight. Also added were thirteen arrows.

The final design for the reverse of the Great Seal showed a thirteen-step pyramid, which symbolized strength and duration. At the foot of the pyramid was placed the year 1776 in Roman numerals in honor of the Declaration of Independence. An Eye of Providence surrounded by rays of light was placed above the pyramid. Added was the motto *Annuit Coeptis (He [God] has favored our undertakings,)* which alluded to the delegates' belief that there had been divine intervention in the American cause for independence. The Latin words *Novus Ordo Seclorum*, meaning a new American era, completed the design.

Congress approved the final design on June 20, 1782. It was first used on September 16, 1782, to seal a document granting General Washington the power to negotiate an agreement with the British for improved treatment and subsequent exchange of prisoners of war. Today the obverse of the Great Seal authenticates the signature of the president on official documents. Only after the president signs a document, and it is countersigned by the secretary of state, is the seal affixed.

Left (far): Original design for seal presented to Jefferson, Franklin, and Adams by designer Du Simitiere.

Left (near): Lawyer William Barton's design submitted to the third committee.

"The Escutcheon [shield] is composed of the chief [upper part of shield] &
pale [perpendicular stripes], the two most honorable ordinaries [symbols].
The Pieces, paly, represent the several states all joined in one solid compact
entire, supporting a Chief, which unites the whole & represents Congress. The
Motto alludes to this union. The pales in the arms are kept closely united by
the Chief and the Chief depends on that union & the strength resulting from it
for its support, to denote the Confederacy of the United States of America &
the preservation of their union through Congress.

"The colours of the pales are those used in the flag of the United States of
America; White signifies purity and innocence, Red, hardiness & valour, and
Blue, the colour of the Chief signifies vigilance, perseverance & justice. The
Olive branch and arrows denote the power of peace & war which is exclusively
vested in Congress. The Constellation denotes a new State taking its place and
rank among other sovereign powers. The Escutcheon is born on the breast of
an American Eagle without any other supporters to denote that the United
States of America ought to rely on their own Virtue.

"Reverse. The pyramid signifies Strength and Duration: The Eye over it &
the Motto allude to the many signal interpositions of providence in favour of
the American cause. The date underneath is that of the Declaration of
Independence and the words under it signify the beginning of the New
American Æra, which commences from that date." ✳

Below: Present seal.

Critical Thinking

Classify Information

Create a chart that explains the meaning of each symbol depicted in the original design of the Great Seal.

Assess Significance

The Continental Congress intended for the design of the Great Seal to signify the independence, valor, and virtue of the new nation. Do you feel this was accomplished in the final design? Why or why not?

Draw Conclusions

In all, it took six years and the design efforts of fourteen people before a final design for the Great Seal was approved by the Continental Congress. Why do you think it took so long? How might compromise have entered the discussions surrounding the final design's approval?

Research and Writing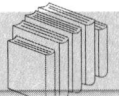

Relating Events

By 1841 the brass die cut for the original design of the Great Seal was worn. It is surmised that the new die cutter, John Peter Van Ness Throop, used the worn brass die as a guide instead of referring to the original descriptions of the design. Mistakes occurred. Research the designs for the Great Seal. What were these mistakes? How does the 1841 die differ from those before and after it?

Historical Interpretation

The use of seals has been a critical component of official documents for many centuries. Research the history of official seals. Where were official seals first used? Why were they used? Why is the United States seal called a Great Seal? How does the United States Great Seal differ from the Presidential Seal?

Biography

Research the life of Du Simitiere, Francis Hopkinson, William Barton, or Charles Thomson. How did their experiences, involvement in the American cause for independence, and/or colonial craft influence their designs? Why were they chosen to assist in creating the Great Seal? What part of each individual's original design continues in the design used today?

1783 The Treaty of Paris

"The only maxim of a free government ought to be to trust no man living with power to endanger the public liberty."

–JOHN ADAMS

HISTORICAL BACKGROUND

THE Treaty of Paris concluded America's quest for independence. At the negotiating table in Paris, France, were John Adams, Benjamin Franklin, and John Jay, all skilled orators and avid patriots. Representing the British was David Hartley. At stake was not only British recognition of the independence of the United States, but also the economic possibilities of westward expansion in tandem with fragile alliances with other European countries. In all, the stage was set for a most ambitious and lively series of negotiations.

The precursor to the Treaty of Paris had been crafted five years earlier on February 6, 1778, when the United States signed a Treaty of Alliance with France. In this 1778 treaty, France and the United States agreed to fight together until American independence was won. Secondly, it was agreed that neither country would conclude a "truce of peace" without the consent of the other. Lastly, both governments agreed to protect each country's possessions in America against "all other powers."

When Adams, Franklin, and Jay finally met to negotiate America's independence in 1783, two crucial points were made clear: (1) that the United States was an independent nation free from England's control and (2) that its territory should include not just the thirteen colonies but all the land held by England, west to the Mississippi River. Reluctantly, British officials agreed. On November 30, 1782, Franklin, Jay, and Adams signed a preliminary agreement with England. As a means to maintaining the integrity of the Treaty of Alliance, the American delegation informed the French minister of the impending treaty one day prior to its signing. The Treaty of Paris was signed on September 3, 1783. The Continental Congress ratified the treaty on January 14, 1784.

The Treaty of Paris began with a long reference to King George III. It referred to the American Revolution as "past misunderstandings and differences." It also made lengthy reference to the qualifications and appointments of Hartley, Franklin, Adams, and Jay.

Article 1 acknowledged that "said United States . . . to be sovereign and independent states, that he . . . relinquishes all claims to the government, propriety, and territorial rights of the same and every part thereof."

Article 2 defined land boundaries. The Mississippi River became the territorial boundary between the United States and the vast land held by Spain. Florida reverted from England to Spain.

Article 3 granted fishing privileges off Newfoundland and in the Gulf of St. Lawrence as well as the use of "unsettled" coasts of "Nova Scotia, Magdalen Islands, and Labrador" to "dry or cure fish."

Article 4 stated that there would be "no lawful impediment to the recovery" of pre-Revolutionary War debts owed to British merchants.

In Article 5, the United States agreed to "recommend"

- that state legislatures provide restitution for damages to estates belonging to British Loyalists;
- that Loyalists would have twelve months to return to the states to attempt to receive compensation for damage to their estates;
- that any confiscated estates be "restored" to the Loyalists.

The other five articles of the Treaty of Paris provided for an end to all "hostilities both by sea and land," free navigation of the Mississippi River by both "subjects of Great Britain and citizens of the United States," and a mutual agreement to return any conquered lands.

NATIONAL ARCHIVES DOCUMENT

It having pleased the Divine Providence to dispose the hearts of the most serene and most potent Prince George the Third, by the grace of God, king of Great Britain, France, and Ireland, defender of the faith, duke of Brunswick and Lunebourg, arch-treasurer and prince elector of the Holy Roman Empire etc., and of the United States of America, to forget all past misunderstandings and differences that have unhappily interrupted the good correspondence and friendship which they mutually wish to restore. . . .

Article 1:
His Brittanic Majesty acknowledges the said United States, viz., New Hampshire, Massachusetts Bay, Rhode Island and Providence Plantations, Connecticut, New York, New Jersey, Pennsylvania, Maryland, Virginia, North Carolina, South Carolina and Georgia, to be free sovereign and independent states, that he treats with them as such, and for himself, his heirs, and successors, relinquishes all claims to the government, propriety, and territorial rights of the same and every part thereof.

Article 2:
And that all disputes which might arise in future on the subject of the boundaries of the said United States may be prevented, it is hereby agreed and declared, that the following are and shall be their boundaries. . . .

Article 5:
It is agreed that Congress shall earnestly recommend it to the legislatures of the respective states to provide for the restitution of all estates, rights, and properties, which have been confiscated belonging to real British subjects. . . .

D. HARTLEY (SEAL)
JOHN ADAMS (SEAL)
B. FRANKLIN (SEAL)
JOHN JAY (SEAL) ✳

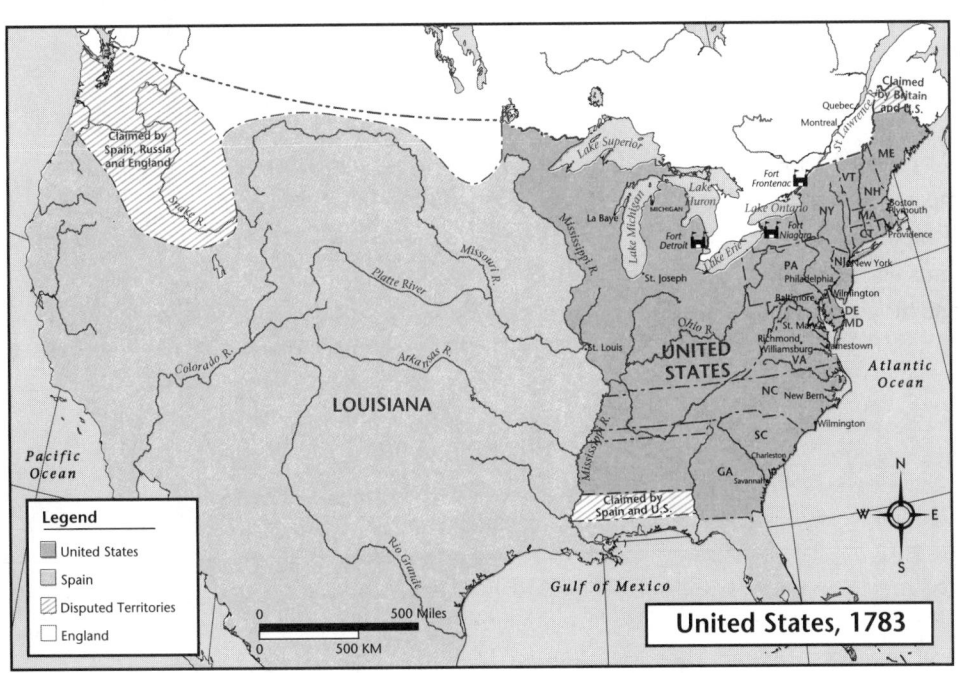

Left: Land to the Mississippi River, once held by Great Britain, was ceded to the United States as the result of the Treaty of Paris.

Critical Thinking

Determine Point of View

Consider the issues of independence, land, and compensation for damage to Loyalists caused during the American Revolution. On which points do you think Franklin, Adams, and Jay would have been most willing to make concessions or strike compromises? On which issues do you think they would have been resolute?

Draw Conclusions

The French had been strong allies during the American Revolution. Why do you think Franklin, Adams, and Jay were willing to compromise the 1778 Treaty of Alliance, as well as risk the good will of France by signing a preliminary agreement with England with barely a day's notice given to the French minister?

Assess Significance

Reread the beginning of the Treaty of Paris. Think of the power of words. Why do you think England referred to the American Revolution as "past misunderstandings and differences"?

Research and Writing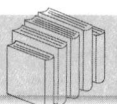

Counterpoint

The Treaty of Paris included many significant concessions by the British, specifically in the area of debt recovery. Read the articles pertaining to the recovery of property and debts. Take the role of Franklin, Adams, and Jay and create a counterpoint for the British argument that all debts and properties owed to Loyalists should be fully compensated or recovered. Why do you think the term "recommend" was used in Article 5 instead of "must"?

Biography

Reread the quote on page 12 by John Adams. What wisdom did he attempt to impart? Research the life of John Adams. Draw a relationship between his life and his words. Do you feel his words were specific to the time or do they extend beyond his years to future generations? Explain.

Historical Interpretation

Study the map on page 13 as well as Article 2 of the Treaty of Paris. Research the political events of the time. What boundaries were set by the treaty? How and why did Florida become a boundary line? How was the northern boundary defined? Why did the British want to keep the Mississippi River open to British subjects? How did the newly established border affect Native Americans living east of the Mississippi River?

1791 The Bill of Rights

"A bill of rights is what the people are entitled to against every government on earth."

–Thomas Jefferson

Historical Background

Out of the turmoil of the American Revolution a structured new government evolved. The ratification of the United States Constitution marked the culmination of years of debate on centralized versus decentralized government. Yet, concern was voiced about the lack of a written declaration of rights for the ordinary citizen, for nowhere in the newly ratified Constitution were the rights of the people defined.

From the local town tavern to the halls of state legislatures, the merits of the Constitution were debated. The central question was how the federal government would protect the people from its own potential tyranny. In fact, five of the states that ratified the Constitution included a list of rights they felt were necessary. In all, 210 amendments to the Constitution were recommended by the state legislatures. On October 4, 1787, Richard Lee wrote the following to Samuel Adams:

> . . . In a government therefore, when the power of judging what shall be for the *general welfare*, which goes to every object of human legislation; and where the laws of such Judges shall be the *supreme Law of the Land*: it seems to be of the last consequence to declare in most explicit terms the reservations above alluded to. So much for the propriety of a Bill of Rights as a necessary bottom to this new system . . .

Not everyone agreed. Some representatives felt there were far more pressing issues before Congress than a written declaration of rights. James Madison, for example, once argued that rights were far more protected by a system of checks and balances built into the organization of the government than by a written declaration of rights. However, in response to Jefferson's incontrovertible belief to the contrary and to fulfill a promise he made when elected to Congress, in June 1789 Madison proposed that a "declaration" of rights be "prefixed to the constitution." Its beginning words echoed those found in the Declaration of Independence:

> . . . all power is originally rested in, and consequently derived from, the people . . .

In September 1789 Congress approved twelve amendments for ratification by the states. The first two amendments, one concerning the number of constituents per congressional representative and a second clarifying compensation for members of Congress, failed ratification. However, on December 15, 1791, with three-fourths of the states having ratified the third through twelfth proposed amendments, Congress approved the Bill of Rights.

With ratification of the Bill of Rights, the persistent effort by the states to attach a written statement of citizens' rights to the United States Constitution was realized. As America's history unfolded, the strength of the Bill of Rights would be challenged from state courts to the United States Supreme Court. In *Texas v. Johnson* (1989), for example the U.S. Supreme Court ruled that burning an American flag in protest of government policies was an extension of Gregory Johnson's freedom of speech and thus protected by the First Amendment. In a much earlier case, *Presser v. Illinois* (1886), the U.S. Supreme Court ruled that the right to bear arms, guaranteed by the Second Amendment, applied only to the federal government but did not prohibit states from limiting an individual's ownership of guns. The Presser decision was cited to support the Court's ruling almost one hundred years later in a case questioning the constitutionality of an ordinance in Morton Grove, Illinois, which banned handgun possession within the city.

The Preamble to The Bill of Rights 1791
Congress of the United States

begun and held at the City of New-York, on
Wednesday the fourth of March, one thousand seven hundred and eighty nine.

THE Conventions of a number of the States, having at the time of their adopting the Constitution, expressed a desire, in order to prevent misconstruction or abuse of its powers, that further declaratory and restrictive clauses should be added: And as extending the ground of public confidence in the Government, will best ensure the beneficent ends of its institution. . . .

Below: James Madison

Article the third . . . Congress shall make no law respecting an establishment of religion, or prohibiting the free exercise thereof; or abridging the freedom of speech, or of the press; or the right of the people peaceably to assemble, and to petition the Government for a redress of grievances.

Article the fourth . . . A well regulated Militia, being necessary to the security of a free State, the right of the people to keep and bear Arms, shall not be infringed.

Article the fifth . . . No Soldier shall, in time of peace be quartered in any house, without the consent of the Owner, nor in time of war, but in a manner to be prescribed by law.

Article the sixth . . . The right of the people to be secure in their persons, houses, papers, and effects, against unreasonable searches and seizures. . . .

Article the seventh . . . No person shall be held to answer for a capital, or otherwise infamous crime, unless on a presentment or indictment of a Grand Jury. . . .

Article the eighth . . . In all criminal prosecutions, the accused shall enjoy the right to a speedy and public trial. . . .

Article the ninth . . . In Suits at common law, where the value in controversy shall exceed twenty dollars, the right of trial by jury shall be preserved. . . .

Article the tenth . . . Excessive bail shall not be required. . . .

Article the eleventh . . . The enumeration in the Constitution, of certain rights, shall not be construed to deny or disparage others retained by the people.

Article the twelfth . . . The powers not delegated to the United States by the Constitution, nor prohibited by it to the States, are reserved to the States respectively, or to the people. ❈

Critical Thinking

Assess Significance

Which amendment do you feel is most significant? Why?   3rd

Classify Information

Which amendments address the rights of citizens in their homes? Which amendments address the rights of citizens in the courts? Which amendments address property rights? Create a chart and write an explanation of your reasoning.

Draw Conclusions

Reread the Preamble to the Bill of Rights. What reasons were given for including a Bill of Rights in the Constitution? Why did Congress believe the Bill of Rights would extend "public confidence in the Government"?

└ prevent abuse of powers

└ more clear

└ so to protect from tyranny

Research and Writing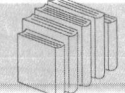

Counterpoint

Those arguing against including a bill of rights in the Constitution postulated that because the Constitution did not allow the federal government to *restrict* rights, amendments *granting* rights were not necessary. Others felt the granting of rights should be a power reserved for the states and not the responsibility of the federal government. Reread the quote at the beginning of this lesson. Research the writings of Thomas Jefferson or George Mason. Then write an essay countering each of these two arguments. Use primary source quotations to strengthen your counterpoint.

Link to the Past

Research James Madison's original twelve amendments to the Constitution. Though Madison's second amendment concerning compensation of members of Congress failed to win approval, his concerns were revisited two hundred years later when, in 1992, the required number of states finally agreed to the 27th Amendment. Research the debate surrounding the 27th Amendment. Compare and contrast arguments for and against Madison's proposed *Article the Second* with those of the 27th Amendment?

Relating Events

Choose one of the first eight amendments. Research a United States Supreme Court decision that used the tenets of the amendment as a basis for the case. What were the issues of the case? How was the amendment interpreted in this case? How were the rights granted by the amendment used to support the opinion of the Court in either upholding the decision of a lower court or overturning it? What is your opinion of the Court's decision and how it applied the amendment?

1820 The Missouri Compromise

"All legislation is founded upon the principle of mutual concession."

–HENRY CLAY

HISTORICAL BACKGROUND

THE origin of the political controversy surrounding the Missouri Compromise is found in another compromise that framed the United States Constitution. In 1787 delegates to the Constitutional Convention were deadlocked over the issue of a state's representation in Congress. To break the stalemate, on July 12, 1787, Congress accepted the Three-fifths Compromise. This compromise allowed for three of every five slaves to be counted in a state's population for the purpose of assigning seats in the House of Representatives. The issue of slavery would continue to dominate national politics as the country entered the nineteenth century.

In 1819 the Missouri Territory applied for admission to the Union. Missouri's southern settlers fully expected the territory to enter the Union as a slave state. The controversy that ensued exemplified how divided Congress had become over the humanitarian and political ramifications of slavery. Northern politicians expressed concern that Missouri would be the first slave state created from land acquired in the Louisiana Purchase, thereby setting an alarming precedent for land west of the Mississippi River. Southerners viewed the debate as an attempt to restrict slavery, especially in light of New York representative James Tallmadge's earlier proposal to forbid the importation of slaves and emancipate existing slaves in Missouri, and similar proposed legislation affecting the Arkansas Territory. Moreover, many Congressional members believed allowing Missouri to enter as a slave state would upset the balance of slave and free states in Congress.

Only when Maine, a state carved from Massachusetts, petitioned for statehood as a free state, was the stalemate over Missouri resolved. The Missouri Compromise allowed the Missouri Territory to enter as a slave state, and Maine as a free state. An amendment attached to the compromise excluded slavery thereafter in all remaining lands in the Louisiana Purchase above the 36°30'N parallel. Because the northern lands in question seemed of little economic consequence, southern politicians were willing to exchange those lands to assure the perpetuation of slavery in the Arkansas Territory. Moreover, the Missouri Compromise maintained the delicate balance of slave and free states in Congress. President Monroe signed the Missouri Enabling Bill into law on March 6, 1820.

In 1820 the South had 89 members in the House of Representatives to the North's 116. It appeared as if the balance of political power was, indeed, tipping in the North's favor. The South viewed Missouri's entrance to the Union as a slave state as an opportunity to gain representation in Congress while preserving the institution of slavery in Missouri. However, as the country expanded, the stage was set for future sectional conflict. An aging Thomas Jefferson likened the Missouri Compromise to a "firebell in the night" whose solemn sound warned of the dire consequences of sectionalism.

NATIONAL ARCHIVES DOCUMENT

An Act to authorize the people of the Missouri territory to form a constitution and state government, and for the admission of such state into the Union on an equal footing with the original states, and to prohibit slavery in certain territories.

Be it enacted by the Senate and House of Representatives of the United States of America, in Congress assembled, That the inhabitants of that portion of the Missouri territory included within the boundaries herein after designated, be, and they are hereby, authorized to form for themselves a constitution and state government, and to assume such name as they shall deem proper; and the said state, when formed, shall be admitted into the Union, upon an equal footing with the original states, in all respects whatsoever. . . .

SEC. 3. And be it further enacted, That all free white male citizens of the United States, who shall have arrived at the age of twenty-one years, and have resided in said territory: three months previous to the day of election, and all other persons qualified to vote for representatives to the general assembly of the said territory, shall be qualified to be elected and they are hereby qualified and authorized to vote, . . .

SEC. 8. And be it further enacted. That in all that territory ceded by France to the United States, under the name of Louisiana, which lies north of thirty-six degrees and thirty minutes north latitude, not included within the limits of the state, contemplated by this act, slavery and involuntary servitude, otherwise than in the punishment of crimes, whereof the parties shall have been duly convicted, shall be, and is hereby, forever prohibited: Provided always, That any person escaping into the same, from whom labour or service is lawfully claimed, in any state or territory of the United States, such fugitive may be lawfully reclaimed and conveyed to the person claiming his or her labour or service as aforesaid.

APPROVED, March 6, 1820. ❋

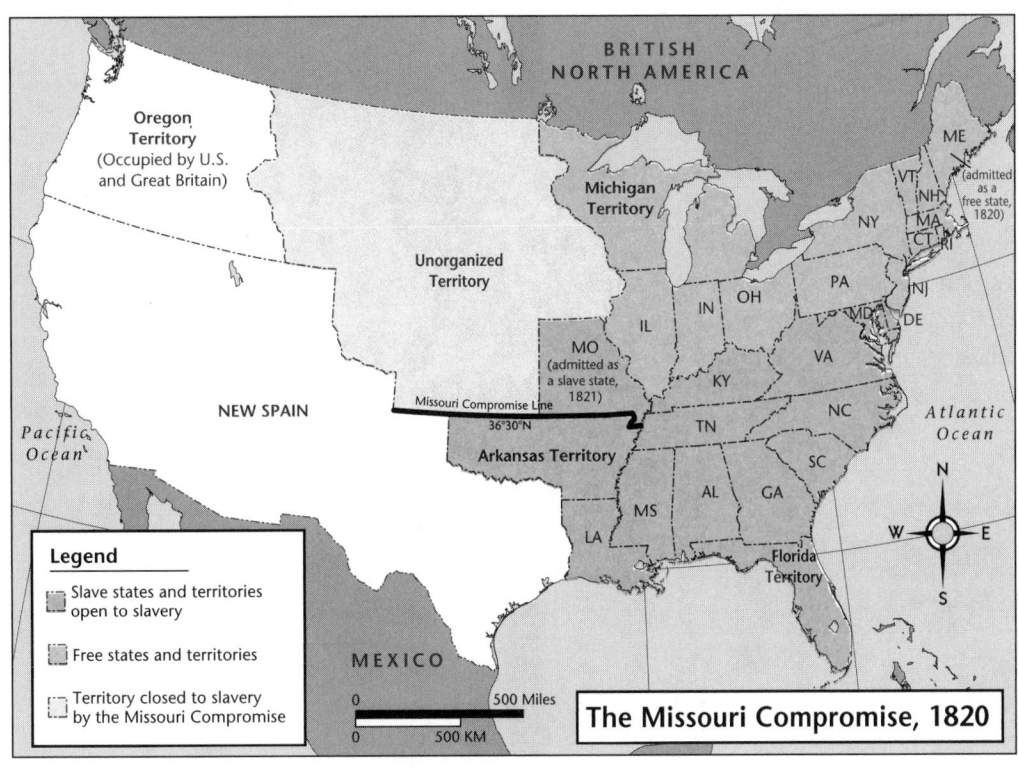

The Missouri Compromise, 1820

Critical Thinking

Analyze Cause and Effect
How did the Missouri Compromise limit future political clout for slave-holding states?

Determine Point of View
Massachusetts Senator Charles Sumner (1811–1874) once said, "From the beginning of our history, the country has been afflicted with compromise. It is by compromise that human rights have been abandoned." How do Sumner's words reflect on the Missouri Compromise?

Assess Significance
How did the Missouri Compromise strike a balance between free and slave states? How important was it for the northern section of the Louisiana Purchase to remain free?

Research and Writing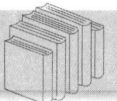

Analysis
Read the Three-fifth's Compromise found in Article I, Section 2 of the United States Constitution. How did the Three-fifths Compromise predestine the conflict over political representation in Congress? Why did the statistics for slave-holding in southern states make it critical for the South to include slaves in population counts?

Historical Interpretation
In 1793 Congress passed a fugitive slave law that allowed for the arrest and return of escaped slaves. Those accused did not have the right to trial by jury, nor could they provide evidence on their own behalf. Missouri's state constitution allowed slavery, as well as restricted the immigration of free African-Americans to the state. In what way did the Missouri Compromise continue to erode the liberty of African-Americans? How did the Missouri Compromise appease northern legislators while ensuring the continuation of slavery?

Link to the Past
James Madison wrote:

> …I believe there are more instances of the abridgement of the freedom of the people by gradual and silent encroachments of those in power than by violent and sudden usurpations.

Research the USA Patriot Act of 2001. Can Madison's quote be applied to the provisions in that act? In your view, did the war on global terrorism at the time justify the provisions inherent in the Patriot Act?

The Compromise of 1850

"I wish to speak today, not as a Massachusetts man, not as a Northern man, but as an American . . . I speak today for the preservation of the union."

–DANIEL WEBSTER, SPEAKING TO CONGRESS 1850

HISTORICAL BACKGROUND

BY 1850 the balance of free and slave states held at fifteen each. In 1850 California applied for admission to the Union as a free state. Southern states were outraged once more that admission of a free state would threaten the political balance of free and slave state representation in Congress, a balance that had existed since before the Missouri Compromise. Greater yet was the concern that other western states would enter the Union as free states.

Resolution of the dispute fell to the "Great Compromiser," Henry Clay. At 73 years old and ill, Clay returned to Washington after a seven-year absence because he feared the fabric binding the Union would soon be torn apart by growing sectionalism. He constructed a compromise that sought to placate both the South and the North. Clay presented his proposal to members of Congress, beseeching them to place the Union above sectional loyalties. Known for his eloquence, Daniel Webster rose to speak in favor of Clay's proposal. What followed was Webster's famous three-hour Seventh of March Speech. He began with,

> Mr. President, I wish to speak today, not as a Massachusetts man, nor as a Northern man, but as an American, and a member of the Senate of the United States. . . . I speak for the preservation of the Union. Hear me for my cause.

The speech and proposed compromise caused a fury in Congress. Seven long months of discussion in Congress finally culminated in the Compromise of 1850. Though the Compromise of 1850 allowed California to enter the Union as a free state, it did not restrict slavery in the Utah or New Mexico territories. It promised that slavery would not be abolished in the District of Columbia or in Maryland without the consent of its citizens. The Compromise abolished the buying and selling of slaves in the District of Columbia. It also gave assurance that Congress would not interfere with the slave trade elsewhere in the South. Finally, it strengthened the Fugitive Slave Act by providing for penalties of up to $1000 and six months in jail for anyone interfering with the recovery of a runaway slave.

Sectionalism, distrust, and anger fueled congressional debate in 1850. For the South, the outcome seemed apparent: the North was intent on eliminating slavery through the passage of state laws restricting both local courts and law enforcement from aiding slave catchers and through the admission of new free states into the Union. Southern legislators hoped for an extension of the Missouri Compromise line to the Pacific Coast. When this hope faded, talk of secession grew. In his last speech to Congress, South Carolina senator John C. Calhoun warned that

> . . . the agitation of the subject of slavery would, if not prevented by some timely and effective measure, end in disunion. . . . The agitation has been permitted to proceed with almost no attempt to resist it, until it has reached a point when it can no longer be disguised or denied that the Union is in danger. You have thus had forced upon you the greatest and gravest question that can ever come under your consideration: How can the Union be preserved?

Calhoun's dire warning helped spur passage of the Compromise of 1850, a compromise that would soon unravel. It would not be long before war waged between the northern and southern states. Central to the conflict was the very definition of liberty.

CLAY'S RESOLUTIONS January 29, 1850

Adopted as part of the Compromise of 1850

. . . 1. Resolved, That California, with suitable boundaries, ought, upon her application to be admitted as one of the States of this Union, without the imposition by Congress of any restriction in respect to the exclusion or introduction of slavery within those boundaries. . . .

5. Resolved, That it is inexpedient to abolish slavery in the District of Columbia whilst that institution continues to exist in the State of Maryland, without the consent of that State, without the consent of the people of the District, and without just compensation to the owners of slaves within the District. . . .

6. But, resolved, That it is expedient to prohibit, within the District, the slave trade in slaves brought into it from States or places beyond the limits of the District, either to be sold therein as merchandise, or to be transported to other markets without the District of Columbia.

7. Resolved, That more effectual provision ought to be made by law, according to the requirement of the constitution, for the restitution and delivery of persons bound to service or labor in any State, who may escape into any other State or Territory in the Union. And,

8. Resolved, That Congress has no power to promote or obstruct the trade in slaves between the slaveholding States; but that the admission or exclusion of slaves brought from one into another of them, depends exclusively upon their own particular laws. ✳

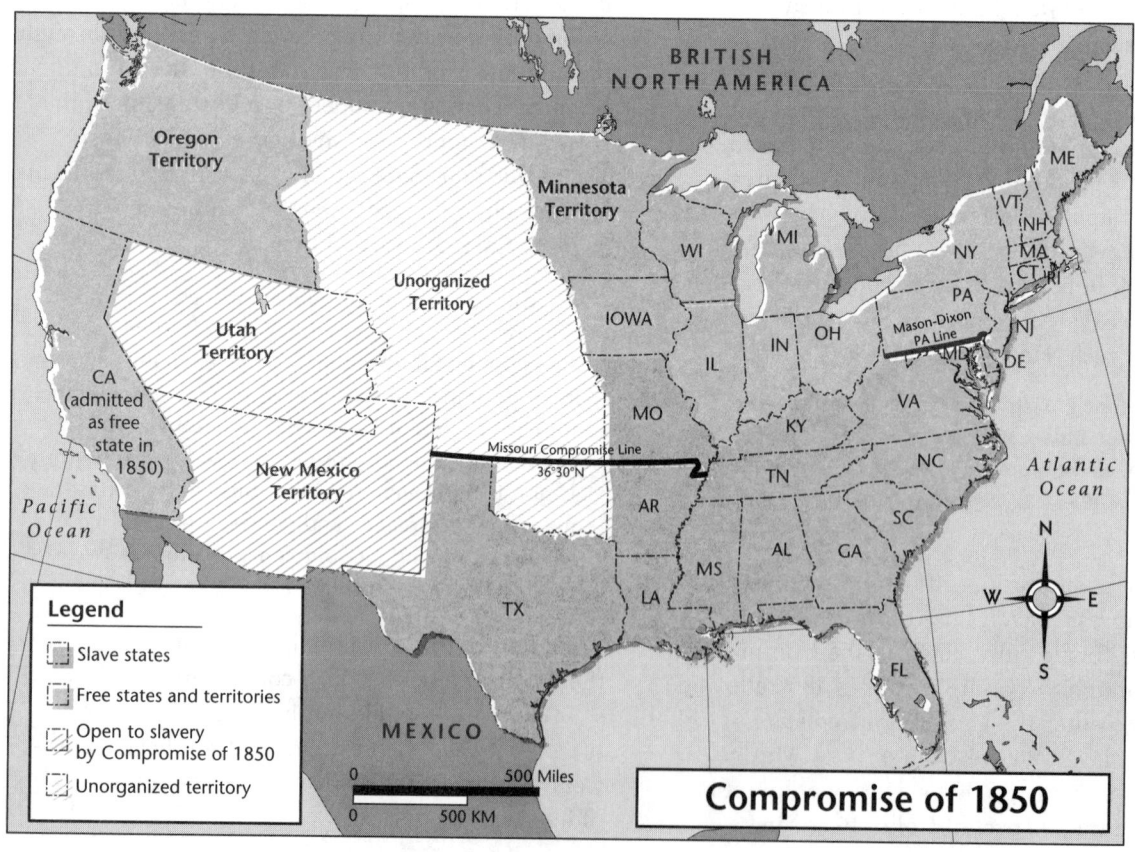

Compromise of 1850

Critical Thinking

Draw Conclusions

The South felt its liberty was at stake. The North argued for liberty. Was the definition of liberty in conflict? Explain.

Determine Point of View

On July 22, 1850, Henry Clay stated, "I owe a paramount allegiance to the whole Union—a subordinate one to my own State." What was Clay attempting to convey to members of Congress?

Assess Significance

Reread Clay's fifth and sixth resolutions. What is the significance of the conciliatory nature of these two resolutions? How is the issue of slavery both inexpedient and expedient?

Research and Writing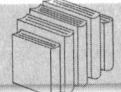

Analysis

As part of the Compromise of 1850, the Fugitive Slave Act strengthened the power of slave holders and slave catchers. Access and read the entire Compromise of 1850 and the Fugitive Slave Act. How did the laws threaten the liberty of escaped and freed African-Americans? Why did the Fugitive Slave Act spark such literary works as Harriet Beecher Stowe's *Uncle Tom's Cabin* in 1851? What parallels can be drawn between the Compromise of 1850 and the Fugitive Slave Act?

Historical Interpretation

In response to Clay's resolutions, Senator John C. Calhoun responded,

> It is time, senators, that there should be an open and manly avowal on all sides as to what is intended to be done. If the question is not now settled, it is uncertain whether it ever can hereafter be; and we, as the representatives of the States of this Union regarded as governments, should come to a distinct understanding as to our respective views, in order to ascertain whether the great questions at issue can be settled or not. If you who represent the stronger portion, can not agree to settle them on the broad principle of justice and duty, say so; and let the States we both represent agree to separate and part in peace.

Who was Calhoun referring to as the "stronger portion"? What was he intimating? What was his meaning of "justice and duty"? Access the Compromise of 1850. Which resolutions seemed to consider Calhoun's warning?

Biography

Research the lives of John C. Calhoun, Henry Clay, and Daniel Webster. Write a short biography of each individual. Draw parallels between their lives while highlighting their intense differences.

1854   The Kansas-Nebraska Act

"I think we must get rid of slavery or we must get rid of freedom."

–Ralph Waldo Emerson

Historical Background

Although the Missouri Compromise held the fragile bonds of unity together for over three decades, it, along with the Compromise of 1850, unraveled in the short span of two years. The precursor to the Civil War, aptly called Bleeding Kansas, exemplified the fractionalized country. As Abraham Lincoln stated in 1858,

> A house divided against itself cannot stand. I believe this government cannot endure permanently half-slave and half-free.

In 1854 Congress passed the Kansas-Nebraska Act. This law, contrived and relentlessly advocated by Senator Stephen Douglas of Illinois, created the Kansas Territory west of Missouri and the Nebraska territory west of Iowa and Minnesota. Rather than require both territories to enter the Union as free states, as stipulated by the 1820 Missouri Compromise, it rather allowed for popular sovereignty to determine the destiny of the two territories. Douglas postured that the people's vote, not an act by Congress, should decide if a territory entered the Union as a free or slave state. Once signed into law by President Pierce, the rush was on to extend slavery north of the Missouri Compromise line into the Kansas Territory.

Election day arrived in Kansas in 1855. Preceding it was an influx of settlers, mostly from Missouri, who were resolute that elections would favor proslavery candidates. Election day brought a second influx of hundreds of Missouri men who crossed into Kansas in order to cast illegal, proslavery votes. The newly elected proslavery legislature convened, though its legality was certainly in question. The governor of Kansas called for new elections in areas where fraudulent voting was suspected. This time the free-soil candidates prevailed, resulting in the establishment of two state legislatures. Meanwhile, the proslavery legislature was busy enacting ominous legislation including slave codes, harsh penalties for anyone assisting runaway slaves, and a validation of all votes cast by nonresidents. The anger that had festered in the country for years soon erupted in Kansas.

The first major confrontation occurred in the free-soil Kansas town of Lawrence. In the spring of 1855, hundreds of Missourians crossed the border, ostensibly to serve warrants on local leaders for treason. The onslaught left Lawrence a burned and looted town. Staunch abolitionist John Brown vowed revenge. On May 24, 1856, Brown and a small group of men hacked to death five men from the proslavery settlement of Pottawatomie. Chaos in Kansas followed the sacking of Lawrence and the Pottawatomie Massacre, leaving hundreds dead, including John Brown's son, and over $1 million in property damage. Thousands of settlers fled "Bleeding Kansas" in the wake of the violence.

Federal troops were brought in to maintain the peace and a renewed attempt was made to create a state constitution. Following seven years of political maneuvers, strife, and conflict, Kansas entered the Union as a free state in January 1861. The country, however, was on the brink of its own Civil War.

NATIONAL ARCHIVES DOCUMENT

An Act to Organize the Territories of Nebraska and Kansas
Approved, May 30, 1854

SEC. 20. *And be it further enacted,* That the executive power and authority in and over said Territory of Kansas shall be vested in a Governor. . . .

SEC 22. *And be it further enacted,* That the legislative power and authority of said Territory shall be vested in the Governor and a Legislative Assembly. . . .

SEC. 23. *And be it further enacted,* That every free white male inhabitant above the age of twenty-one years who shall be an actual resident of said Territory, and shall possess the qualifications hereinafter prescribed, shall be entitled to vote at the first election. . . .

SEC. 28. *And be it further enacted,* That the provisions of the act entitled "An act respecting fugitives from justice, and persons escaping from, the service of their masters," approved February twelfth, seventeen hundred and ninety-three, and the provisions of the act entitled "An act to amend, and supplementary to, the aforesaid act," approved September eighteenth, eighteen hundred and fifty, be, and the same are hereby, declared to extend to and be in full force within the limits of the said Territory of Kansas. . . . ✳

Below: This mural on the wall of the Kansas State Capitol Building shows John Brown in the midst of the confrontations that framed Kansas statehood.

Critical Thinking

Draw Conclusions

Read Section 23 of the Kansas-Nebraska Act. How did this provision impact the controversy surrounding the proslavery vote in Kansas?

Classify Information

Study the painting on page 25. What groups are pictured in the painting? What doctrines are identified? Why is John Brown painted as a central figure looming over the others?

Assess Significance

How did the Kansas-Nebraska Act perpetuate fugitive slave laws?

Research and Writing

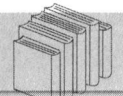

Point of View

When Stephen Douglas introduced the Kansas-Nebraska Act, his underlying intent was to secure the western lands for the eventual building of a transcontinental railroad. Douglas had introduced several railroad bills into Congress without success. Encouraged by industrialists in his native Chicago, Douglas persevered. The resulting Kansas-Nebraska Act appeared to barter the liberty of African-Americans in Kansas in exchange for Southern support of a bill designed to promote the railroad industry.

However, Douglas prefaced the Kansas-Nebraska Act with these words:

> It is the true intent and meaning of this act not to legislate slavery into any State or Territory, or to exclude it therefrom, but to leave the people thereof perfectly free to form and regulate their domestic institutions in their own way, subject only to the federal constitution.

Research Douglas's efforts to gain support for a transcontinental railroad. What is your point of view in regard to the true intent of the Kansas-Nebraska Act?

Biography

Research the life of John Brown. Who was he? What motives inspired his rampage in 1856 and again in 1859? What happened at Harper's Ferry? How did events at Harper's Ferry create a sense of martyrdom? How did John Brown impact the abolitionist movement? What was his impact on southern resolve?

Historical Interpretation

Research the Lincoln-Douglas debates. Access and read the first Lincoln-Douglas debate that occurred in Ottawa, Illinois on August 21, 1858. What was the purpose of the debate series? How do the Missouri Compromise of 1820, the Compromise of 1850, and the Kansas-Nebraska Act enter into the debate? What is the position of Douglas? What is the position of Lincoln? Whose position was more tenable? What was the outcome of the debates?

1887   The Dawes Act

"Let me be a free man, free to travel, free to stop, free to work, free to trade where I choose, free to choose my own teachers, free to follow the religion of my fathers."

—CHIEF JOSEPH

HISTORICAL BACKGROUND

THE late 1800s saw a change in policy toward Native Americans. The oppressive Indian policies of the past were replaced with a paternalistic approach to Native American people, traditions, and cultures. Native Americans, it was reasoned, would fare much better if they lived as whites, adopted the religion of whites, and went to white-run schools. Reform-minded legislators believed the most benevolent approach to preserving the Native American race was to make Native Americans wards of the government. To that end, the federal government planned to provide the land, education, and the Christian values needed for Native Americans to assimilate into the white culture.

The government assimilation program focused on the education of Native American youth. Native American children were sent to Christian-based schools. Here they were dressed as white children, taught to read and write, and prompted to cast off their traditions and religion and assume the ways of the white man.

In attempting to explain the plight of Native Americans, on January 14, 1889, Chief Joseph spoke in Washington, D.C. with an appeal to Congress to honor the cultural ways of Native Americans.

Too many misinterpretations have been made; too many misunderstandings have come up between the white men and the Indians. If the white man wants to live in peace with the Indian he can live in peace. There need be no trouble. Treat all men alike. Give them the same laws. Give them all an even chance to live and grow. All men were made by the same Great Spirit Chief. They are all brothers. The earth is the mother of all people, and all people should have equal rights upon it. You might as well expect all rivers to run backward as that any man who was born

a free man should be contented penned up and denied liberty to go where he pleases. If you tie a horse to a stake, do you expect he will grow fat? If you pen an Indian up on a small spot of earth and compel him to stay there, he will not be contented nor will he grow and prosper. I have asked some of the Great White Chiefs where they get their authority to say to the Indian that he shall stay in one place, while he sees white men going where they please. They cannot tell me.

Long held prejudices, however, overshadowed the words of Chief Joseph. In 1887 Congress passed the Severalty Act, commonly called the Dawes Act. Introduced into Congress by Massachusetts Senator Henry L. Dawes, its intent was to further assimilate Native Americans into the white culture. The Dawes Act directed the president to grant 160 acres of land to individual Native Americans, with title and U.S. citizenship conveyed once the land had been lived on for twenty-five years. The land parceled by the Dawes Act was reservation land that had been set aside in past years for Native Americans to live on as tribal organizations. The law further permitted the federal government to sell to whites all remaining reservation land not parceled to Native Americans.

The results were devastating for Native Americans. Within a few short years, over half of all remaining reservation land was opened to white settlement and to the railroads. Moreover, most land granted to Native Americans was unsuitable for agriculture. With the tribal life of Native Americans broken, survival became difficult. In 1860 there were approximately 333,000 Native Americans. By 1900 the population had dwindled to 237,000. As a result of the Dawes Act, the federal government would remain in control of Indian land and Indian life for years to come.

An Act to provide for the allotment of lands in severalty to Indians on the various reservations, and to extend the protection of the laws of the United States and the Territories over the Indians, and for other purposes.

Be it enacted by the Senate and House of Representatives of the United States of America in Congress assembled, That in all cases where any tribe or band of Indians has been, or shall hereafter be, located upon any reservation created for their use, either by treaty stipulation or by virtue of an act of Congress or executive order setting apart the same for their use, the President of the United States be, and he hereby is, authorized, whenever in his opinion any reservation or any part thereof of such Indians is advantageous for agricultural and grazing purposes, to cause said reservation, or any part thereof, to be surveyed, or resurveyed if necessary, and to allot the lands in said reservation in severalty to any Indian located thereon in quantities as follows:

- To each head of a family, one-quarter of a section [160 acres];
- To each single person over eighteen years of age, one-eighth of a section;
- To each orphan child under eighteen years of age, one-eighth of a section; and
- To each other single person under eighteen years now living, or who may be born prior to the date of the order of the President directing an allotment of the lands embraced in any reservation, one-sixteenth of a section: . . .

And every Indian born within the territorial limits of the United States to whom allotments shall have been made under the provisions of this act, or under any law or treaty, and every Indian born within the territorial limits of the United States who has voluntarily taken up, within said limits, his residence separate and apart from any tribe of Indians therein, and has adopted the habits of civilized life, is hereby declared to be a citizen of the United States. . . .

That nothing in this act contained shall be so construed to affect the right and power of Congress to grant the right of way through any lands granted to an Indian, or a tribe of Indians, for railroads or other highways, or telegraph lines, for the public use, or condemn such lands to public uses, upon making just compensation. ✳

The Effects of the Dawes Act on Indian Land

Critical Thinking

Make Predictions

What effects do you think the Dawes Act had on Native American culture?

Assess Significance

Study the maps of Indian lands. What impact did the Dawes Act have on reservation land? Read the last paragraph of the Dawes Act as cited. Of what significance was the granting of "right of way"? How would this provision lead to the disruption of tribal lands?

Determine Point of View

What does the phrase "has adopted the habits of civilized life" found in the Dawes Act say about the white culture's perception of Native American culture during the late 1800s? How would this perception foster forced assimilation of Native Americans into the white culture?

Research and Writing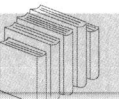

Point of View

Research the programs aimed at assisting Native American assimilation into white culture. Explain how such programs fractured Native American cultures and traditions. What were their effects? How did the focus of the assimilation programs change in the early 1900s? Explain this appeal made by the 1927 Grand Council of American Indians.

> The white people who are trying to make us over into their image, they want us to be what they call assimilated, bringing the Indians into the mainstream and destroying our own way of life and our own cultural patterns. They believe we should be contented like those whose concept of happiness is materialistic and greedy, which is very different from our way. We want freedom from the white man rather than to be integrated. We don't want any part of the establishment, we want to be free to raise our children in our religion, in our ways, to be able to hunt and fish and to live in peace. We don't want power, we don't want to be congressmen, bankers, we want to be ourselves. We want to have our heritage, because we are the owners of this land and because we belong here. The white man says there is freedom and justice for all. We have had "freedom and justice," and that is why we have been almost exterminated. We shall not forget this.

Relating Events

Native Americans were granted levels of citizenship in 1901 and again in 1924. Research legislation designed to grant citizenship to Native Americans. How did some states effectively disenfranchise Native Americans? Where did it happen? Why did it happen?

Analysis

On June 18, 1934, Congress passed the Wheeler-Howard Act (Indian Reorganization Act). In response to this legislation, Indian Commissioner John Collier wrote:

> Through 50 years of "individualization," coupled with an ever-increasing supervision over the affairs of individuals and tribes so long as these individuals and tribes had any assets left, the Indians have been robbed of initiative, their spirit has been broken, their health undermined, and their native pride ground into the dust. The efforts at economic rehabilitation cannot and will not be more than partially successful unless they are accompanied by a determined simultaneous effort to rebuild the shattered morale of a subjugated people that has been taught to believe in its racial inferiority.

Research this legislation. How did the Wheeler-Howard Act repeal the Dawes Act? What were its provisions? How did it affect federal assimilation programs? Did the Wheeler-Howard Act renew a spirit of liberty among Native Americans?

1941 The Four Freedoms

*"People who are hungry and out of a job
are the stuff of which dictatorships are made."*

–FRANKLIN D. ROOSEVELT

HISTORICAL BACKGROUND

AMERICAN life changed dramatically during the early 1900s. The Industrial Revolution, growth of cities, and thousands of immigrants seeking liberty in America would bring to the 20th century new economic and political challenges. During the tumultuous years of the Great Depression and World War II, Americans perceived a new threat to their life, liberty, and happiness. To that end, Franklin Delano Roosevelt, born into wealth, would be elected as a friend of the common man to four terms as president of the United States.

Franklin Delano Roosevelt's strong belief in the ideals of democracy and his proclivity for optimism in the American spirit, even in the most onerous times, inspired the resolve to accomplish formidable goals. When President Roosevelt took office in 1933, the country was in its fourth year of a depression. Unemployment in the cities had reached 50%. Nationwide, one of every four Americans was unemployed. Unable to pay their mortgages, almost a million people had lost their homes and farms. Thousands of banks failed, and the government lacked the means to protect the savings of millions of Americans. In response, Roosevelt put into place the New Deal. Hospitals, libraries, schools, roads, and parks were built through large-scale public works projects. A social security system gave hope that elder Americans would not be displaced. Federal funds were provided to assist home owners. To everyday Americans, Roosevelt's New Deal policies focused on preserving American freedoms for the downtrodden.

In his 1937 Second Inaugural Address, Franklin D. Roosevelt encouraged a country emerging from the devastating Great Depression with these words,

Our progress out of the depression is obvious. But that is not all that you and I mean by the new order of things. Our pledge was not merely to do a patchwork job with secondhand materials. By using the new materials of social justice we have undertaken to erect on the old foundations a more enduring structure for the better use of future generations. In that purpose we have been helped by achievements of mind and spirit. Old truths have been relearned; untruths have been unlearned. We have always known that heedless self-interest was bad morals; we know now that it is bad economics. Out of the collapse of a prosperity whose builders boasted their practicality has come the conviction that in the long run economic morality pays. We are beginning to wipe out the line that divides the practical from the ideal; and in so doing we are fashioning an instrument of unimagined power for the establishment of a morally better world. . . . We of the Republic are men and women of good will; men and women who have more than warm hearts of dedication; men and women who have cool heads and willing hands of practical purpose as well. They will insist that every agency of popular government use effective instruments to carry out their will. . . .

By the summer of 1940 war raged across Europe. Once again Roosevelt called upon Americans. Almost two centuries after the adoption of the Lee Resolution and the Declaration of Independence, President Roosevelt spoke of the "decent respect for the rights and the dignity of all our fellow men" in his State of the Union message to Congress. Roosevelt asked that additional dollars be appropriated for war munitions and supplies to aid European allies fighting Adolf Hitler. He also asked Americans for their willingness to make personal sacrifices to assist in the Allies' war effort. Roosevelt inspired Americans to gather their resolve once again, this time to fight for liberty on foreign shores, and ultimately, he argued, to fight for American liberty. In Roosevelt's plea, he highlighted "four essential human freedoms": freedom of speech, freedom of worship, freedom from want, and freedom from fear.

Excerpt from President Franklin Roosevelt's Annual Message to Congress
1941

. . . Let us say to the democracies: "We Americans are vitally concerned in your defense of freedom. We are putting forth our energies, our resources and our organizing powers to give you the strength to regain and maintain a free world. We shall send you, in ever-increasing numbers, ships, planes, tanks, guns. This is our purpose and our pledge. . . ."

If the Congress maintains these principles, the voters, putting patriotism ahead of pocketbooks, will give you their applause.

In the future days, which we seek to make secure, we look forward to a world founded upon four essential human freedoms.

The first is freedom of speech and expression—everywhere in the world.

The second is freedom of every person to worship God in his own way—everywhere in the world.

The third is freedom from want—which, translated into world terms, means economic understandings which will secure to every nation a healthy peacetime life for its inhabitants—everywhere in the world.

The fourth is freedom from fear—which, translated into world terms, means a world-wide reduction of armaments to such a point and in such a thorough fashion that no nation will be in a position to commit an act of physical aggression against any neighbor—anywhere in the world. . . .

Since the beginning of our American history, we have been engaged in change—in a perpetual peaceful revolution—a revolution which goes on steadily, quietly adjusting itself to changing conditions. . . .

This nation has placed its destiny in the hands and heads and hearts of its millions of free men and women; and its faith in freedom under the guidance of God. Freedom means the supremacy of human rights everywhere. Our support goes to those who struggle to gain those rights or keep them. Our strength is our unity of purpose. To that high concept there can be no end save victory. ✳

OURS...to fight for

Freedom of Speech

Freedom of Worship

Freedom from Want

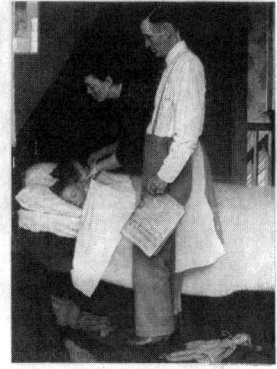

Freedom from Fear

Above: The celebrated painter Norman Rockwell created a series of paintings illustrating Roosevelt's vision. A national tour of Rockwell's paintings raised money for the war effort. The Charter of the United Nations, created after World War II, included Roosevelt's four freedoms.

Critical Thinking

Determine Point of View

What does Roosevelt mean by "the voters, putting patriotism ahead of pocketbooks, will give you their applause"?

Assess Significance

Look for similar themes between the ideals of the colonists and the words of Franklin Roosevelt 165 years following the adoption of the Lee Resolution and the Declaration of Independence. What common themes run through all three documents?

Analyze Cause and Effect

What was taking place in Europe and Asia at the time FDR made this speech? What events might have caused him anguish concerning the four freedoms?

Research and Writing

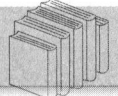

Point of View

Access and read a copy of President Franklin Roosevelt's 1941 Annual Message to Congress. Focus on the following excerpt:

> Since the beginning of our American history, we have been engaged in change—in a perpetual peaceful revolution—a revolution which goes on steadily, quietly adjusting itself to changing conditions....

Write an essay explaining what you believe Roosevelt means by "a perpetual peaceful revolution." Why does he connect his thoughts in 1941 with the events of early American history? What kind of revolution do you think Roosevelt contemplated?

Relating Events

On May 26, 1940, in one of Roosevelt's radio "fireside" chats, he expressed the following:

> It is the task of our generation, yours and mine. But we build and defend not for our generation alone. We defend the foundations laid down by our fathers. We build a life for generations yet unborn. We defend and we build a way of life, not for America alone, but for all mankind. Ours is a high duty, a noble task.

Research Roosevelt's fireside chats. What was the purpose of the chats? How did Americans respond to the chats? In what way did he interconnect his democratic ideals with his domestic and national policies? How did Roosevelt use his fireside chats to foster support for his policies?

Link to the Past

Arguments supporting Operation Iraqi Freedom defended the war in Iraq for two reasons. First, it would bring democracy to the oppressed people of Iraq. Second, the war was part of an international effort to combat global terrorism and thus preserve American liberty. Research President Bush's rationale for sending troops into Iraq. What was the outcome of Operation Iraqi Freedom? Were efforts to bring democracy to the country successful? What was the role of the United Nations? Can Roosevelt's words found in his Four Freedoms address be applied to events in Iraq? Why or why not?

Division of Powers

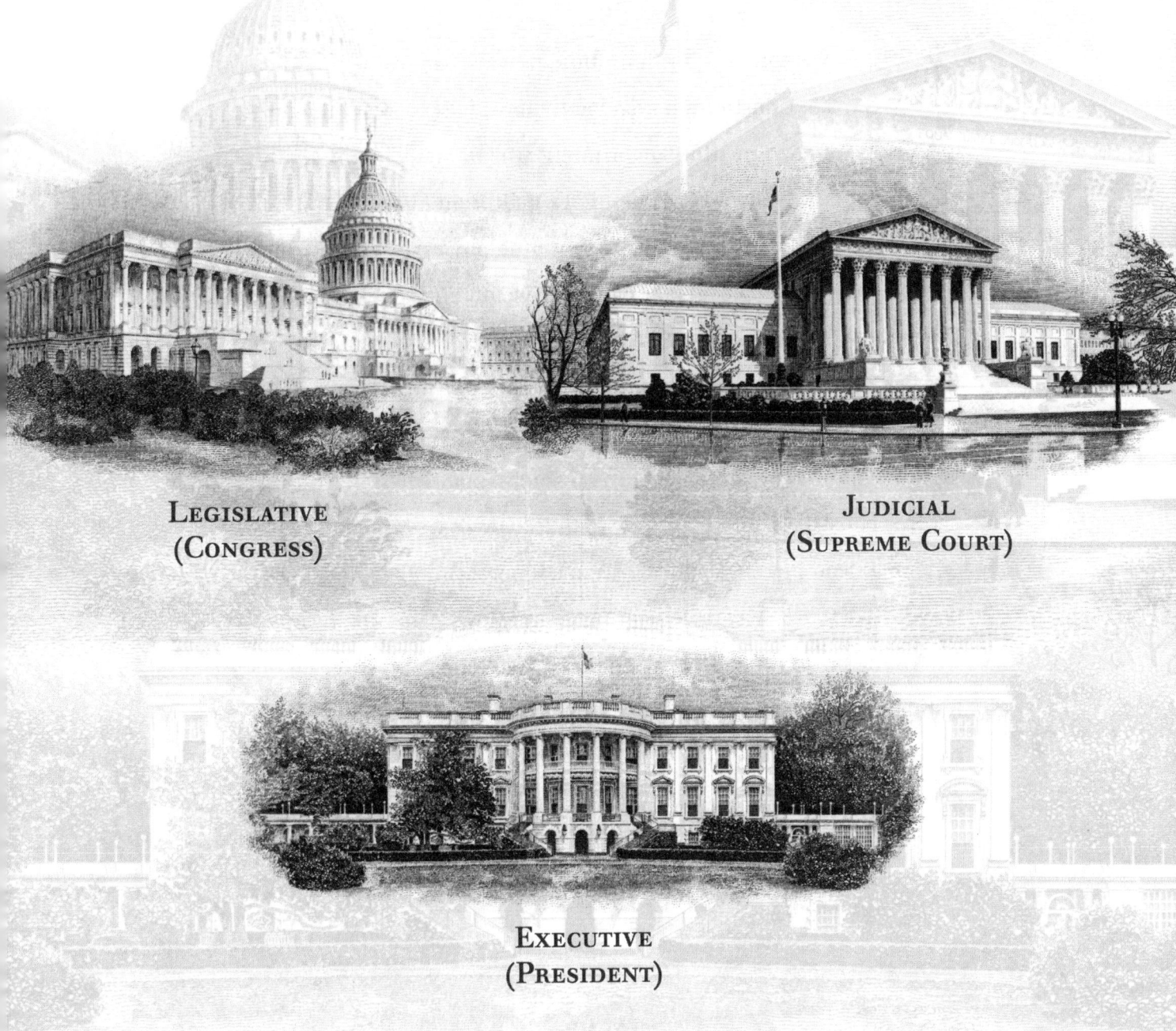

LEGISLATIVE
(CONGRESS)

JUDICIAL
(SUPREME COURT)

EXECUTIVE
(PRESIDENT)

"I know no safe depository of the ultimate powers of the society but the people themselves."

–THOMAS JEFFERSON (1743–1826)

Prologue

Government is, by definition, power. The framers of the U.S. Constitution decided the best way to avoid the abuse of power within government was to divide it among the stakeholders. The framework of the Constitution, then, is a system of checks and balances woven throughout the powers granted to three distinct branches of government. The division of power also extends to the relationship between the federal and state governments. The final element is the power granted to the people, popular sovereignty—the ultimate power within a democracy. Woodrow Wilson captured the essence of the framers' plan when he stated, "Power consists in one's capacity to link his will with the purpose of others, to lead by reason and a gift of cooperation." The division of powers is a tug-of-war, a constant ebb and flow of opinion over where the power of one government entity begins and where it ends. In this second unit, you will have the opportunity to learn how others have viewed the importance and function of the division of political power within American government.

1777 Articles of Confederation

"It is not by the consolidation, or concentration, of powers, but by their distribution that good government is effected."

–Thomas Jefferson

Historical Background

Just days after America declared its independence from Great Britain, the Continental Congress began work on a plan for a new government in America. It was an audacious task. How could such a diverse country in the throes of rebellion possibly reach agreement about how it should be governed? The answer was a loose confederation of states under the umbrella of a federal government.

The Continental Congress formed a committee and chose John Dickinson as the principal writer to draft a constitution for an independent nation. On November 15, 1777, Congress agreed to the committee's plan for a new government. The plan was called the Articles of Confederation. It would be America's first lesson in self-governance. Central to the Articles of Confederation was the philosophy that little government intervention into the affairs of state governments was preferable to a strong centralized government. Moreover, in drafting the document, several critical issues had been raised:

- How much representation should each state have in the new government?
- Should states with a greater population have greater representation?
- How should the issue of western land be handled? Six states claimed land west of the Appalachian Mountains, based on the clause "from sea to sea" in their original land grants from the English crown.
- Would it be possible to design a republic that could possibly govern such a large area as the emerging United States?

- Would the states be willing to concede power to a federal government?
- Should there be just one law-making branch of government?
- Would states retain their individual powers within the framework of a national government?

Having lived under the rule of an oppressive British monarch, the delegates to the Second Continental Congress were leery of establishing an executive branch. The solution was to avoid having a chief executive and to concentrate power in the Congress instead. The Articles of Confederation established a "firm league of friendship" between the states. Each state would have one vote in Congress regardless of its population. Each state would retain its independence and sovereignty. All powers not specifically designated to the federal government would continue to be held by the states. The division of power, then, was simply a division between the powers held by the states and the power vested in a representative Congress.

Ratification by all thirteen states was required before the Articles of Confederation could become the governing document for the new nation, a process that took four years. Maryland, the last of the thirteen states to ratify, finally approved the plan on March 1, 1781. Though the Articles of Confederation would be replaced by the United States Constitution within the decade, they carried the fledgling nation through the years of the American Revolution and provided the foundation for establishing the United States as a republic.

. . . Articles of Confederation and perpetual Union between the states of New Hampshire, Massachusetts-bay Rhode Island and Providence Plantations, Connecticut, New York, New Jersey, Pennsylvania, Delaware, Maryland, Virginia, North Carolina, South Carolina and Georgia.

I.

The Stile of this Confederacy shall be **"The United States of America."**

II.

Each state retains its sovereignty, freedom, and independence, and every power, jurisdiction, and right, which is not by this Confederation expressly delegated to the United States, in Congress assembled.

III.

The said States hereby severally enter into a firm league of friendship with each other, for their common defense, the security of their liberties, and their mutual and general welfare. . . .

V.

. . . Freedom of speech and debate in Congress shall not be impeached or questioned in any court or place out of Congress, and the members of Congress shall be protected in their persons from arrests or imprisonments, during the time of their going to and from. . . .

XIII.

Every State shall abide by the determination of the United States in Congress assembled, on all questions which by this confederation are submitted to them. And the Articles of this Confederation shall be inviolably observed by every State, and the Union shall be perpetual. . . . ✳

Below: Zechariah Fowle printed the Articles of Confederation in 1777. Zechariah was the younger brother of printer and British loyalist Robert Fowle.

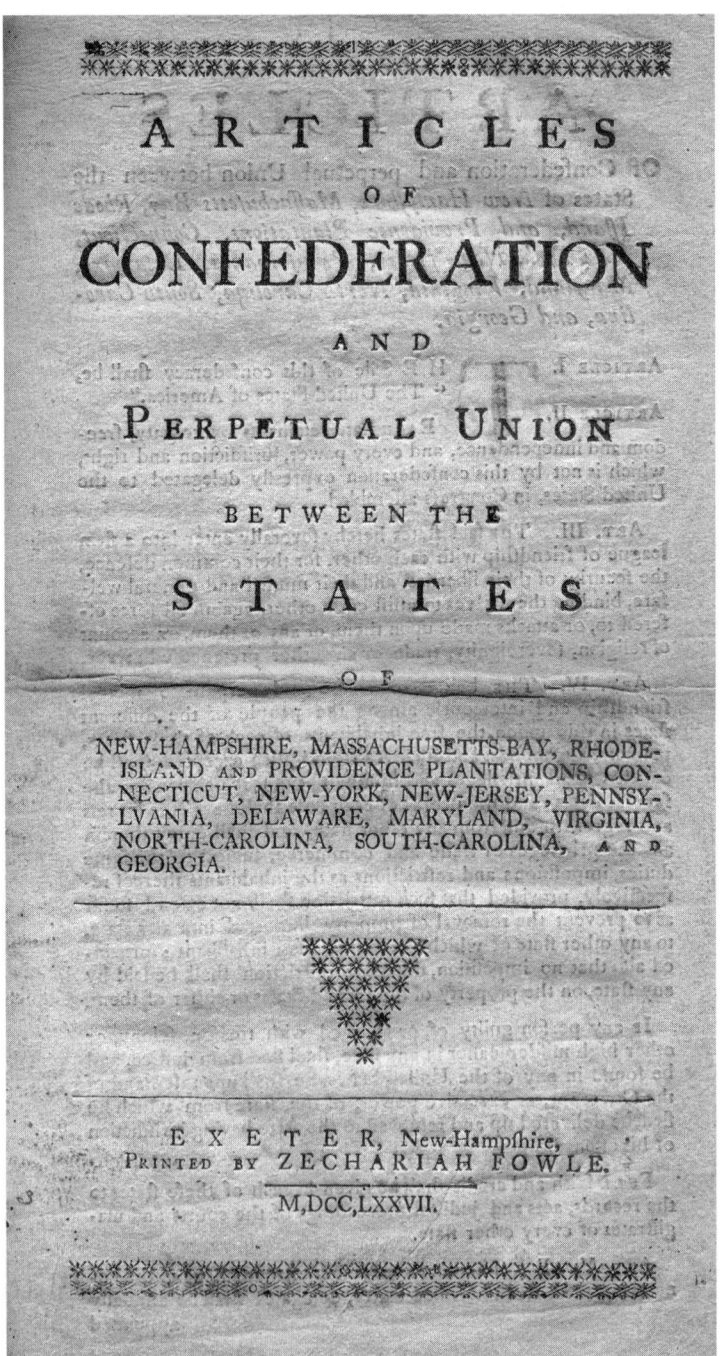

Critical Thinking

Draw Conclusions

Why did the states define their political accountability as a "firm league of friendship"?

Determine Point of View

Read the quote by Thomas Jefferson on page 35. What does Jefferson mean? How does the quote apply to the structuring of a federal government?

Compare and Contrast

Reread the excerpt from Article V. Why do you think such liberties as "freedom of speech and debate" were embodied in the Articles of Confederation?

Research and Writing

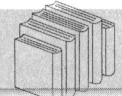

Biography

John Dickinson served in Congress, representing both Delaware and Pennsylvania. Loyal to the British crown, yet incensed by oppressive acts perpetuated on the colonists, Dickinson found himself in the perplexing position of hoping for reconciliation with Britain while organizing protests against the actions taken by Parliament. Written collaboratively with Thomas Jefferson, on July 6, 1775, Dickenson expressed his exasperation in *Declaration Of The Causes And Necessity Of Taking Up Arms:*

> A declaration by the representatives of the united colonies of North America, now met in Congress at Philadelphia, setting forth the causes and necessity of their taking up arms....
>
> In our own native land, in defence of the freedom that is our birthright, and which we ever enjoyed till the late violation of it —for the protection of our property, acquired solely by the honest industry of our fore-fathers and ourselves, against violence actually offered, we have taken up arms. We shall lay them down when hostilities shall cease on the part of the aggressors, and all danger of their being renewed shall be removed, and not before ...

Research the life of John Dickinson. Access and read the *Olive Branch Petition* dated July 8, 1775, also authored by Dickinson. What might account for why Dickinson's political philosophy evolved from this position to the point where he agreed to draft the Articles of Confederation?

Counterpoint

The intent of the Articles of Confederation was to establish a working friendship among states, a friendship that would allow for state governments to function independently yet still legislatively respond to the needs of the entire country, when identified and when deemed necessary. Read the Articles of Confederation. Research the arguments surrounding ratification of the Articles. Why did it take four years for the plan to be ratified? What were the arguments against ratification? How were those arguments countered? What prevailing argument convinced Maryland to ratify the Articles of Confederation?

Relating Events

Article XI of the Articles of Confederation allowed for "Canada acceding to this confederation, and adjoining in the measures of the United States, shall be admitted into, and entitled to all the advantages of this Union; but no other colony shall be admitted into the same, unless such admission be agreed to by nine States...." Research the political relationship between Canada and the United States in 1777. Provide an explanation for Article XI.

1787 The Virginia Plan

> *"A government composed of such extensive powers should be well organized and balanced."*
>
> –James Madison in a letter to George Washington, April 1787

Historical Background

THE lamplight of the American Revolution was the political ideal of a "representative" government, the definition of which was as diverse as the delegates engaged in its debate. The very essence of democracy was central to the discussion. How would government govern? Who would be represented in the government?

The Articles of Confederation exacerbated the debate between those striving to maintain power within the states and those calling for a strong federal government. To that end, in May 1787 a Constitutional Convention was convened. On May 29, 1787, Edmund Randolph stood to speak to the delegates of the Constitutional Convention. First he gave due respect to the authors of the Articles of Confederation, stating that they had done their very best given the immediate concerns of the Continental Congress in 1777. Randolph argued, however, that the Articles of Confederation no longer addressed the needs of the country. As a corrective approach, he presented the Virginia Plan. This plan provided for a centralized government made up of three branches, with the ability of each branch to check the power of the others. The idea was considered radical by some and visionary by others.

Written by James Madison, the Virginia Plan proposed two legislative houses. One house would be comprised of members elected by the people for three-year terms, while the other house would have members elected to seven-year terms by state legislatures. Representation in each house would be proportional to a state's population. Because Virginia was the largest state, the plan drew immediate criticism from the other, smaller states.

Other aspects of Madison's Virginia Plan also generated considerable discussion:

- The combined legislature would choose the chief executive and federal judges;
- A division of federal powers between three branches: "Supreme Legislative, Judiciary, and Executive";
- The legislature would have the power of taxation;
- The legislature could veto state laws.

With the Virginia Plan, each branch would have the ability to check and balance the power of the other two. This, Madison reasoned, would prevent an abuse of power by any one branch.

The Constitutional Convention debated and voted on each resolution of the Virginia Plan. Madison, for example, argued for the popular election of one branch of the legislature, believing such elections were "essential to every plan of free Government." Others opposed elections by the people. Roger Sherman from Connecticut felt that people "immediately should have as little to do as may be about the Government." Others, such as Pierce Butler from South Carolina, thought "election by the people an impracticable mode." On a different point, Benjamin Franklin agreed with the need for a chief executive. He felt, however, the individual should not be compensated, believing that the combination of power and money "have in many minds the most violent effects."

Several days were spent debating the principles found in the Virginia Plan. It became a springboard for compromise after compromise, eventually leading to the adoption of the Constitution of the United States.

NATIONAL ARCHIVES DOCUMENT

1. **Resolved.** that it is the opinion of this Committee that a national government ought to be established consisting of a Supreme Legislative, Judiciary, and Executive.

2. **Resolved.** that the national Legislature ought to consist of Two Branches. . . .

7. **Resolved.** that the right of suffrage in the first branch of the national Legislature ought not to be according to the rule established in the articles of confederation: but according to some equitable ratio of representation— namely, in proportion to the whole number of white and other free citizens and inhabitants of every age, sex, and condition including those bound to servitude for a term of years, and three fifths of all other persons not comprehended in the foregoing description, except Indians, not paying taxes in each State.

9. **Resolved.** that a national Executive be instituted to consist of a single person to be chosen by the National Legislature for the term of seven years.

10. **Resolved.** that the national executive shall have a right to negative any legislative act: which shall not be afterwards passed unless by two third parts of each branch of the national Legislature.

Below: Benjamin Franklin

11. **Resolved.** that a national Judiciary be established to consist of One Supreme Tribunal. The Judges of which to be appointed by the second Branch of the National Legislature.

18. **Resolved.** that the Legislative, Executive, and Judiciary powers within the several States ought to be bound by oath to support the articles of Union. . . . ✳

Critical Thinking

Assess Significance
What was the political significance of the delegates' willingness to abandon the Articles of Confederation?

Compare and Contrast
How did representation of the people in the Virginia Plan differ from that found in the Articles of Confederation?

Determine Point of View
Why do you think Roger Sherman of Connecticut, Elbridge Gerry of Massachusetts, and others opposed election by the people?

Research and Writing

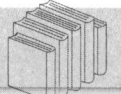

Counterpoint
William Patterson offered the New Jersey Plan as a counter to the Virginia Plan. The New Jersey Plan suggested a careful revision of the Articles of Confederation. Patterson argued for more efficient ways for Congress to raise revenue and regulate trade. He asserted that the national legislature should be maintained with equal representation for each state, representation without regard to size or population. Research the New Jersey Plan. Write an essay explaining the reasoning behind the ideas proposed in the New Jersey Plan. Explain how the New Jersey Plan countered the Virginia Plan.

Analysis
Considerable controversy surrounded whether the "National Executive" should be one individual or a group of several persons. Read the *Debates in the Federal Convention of 1787* for June 1–4, 1787, available through the Avalon Project at Yale Law School (www.yale.edu/lawweb/avalon/debates/601/htm). How did Madison report the debate? What was of great concern? Who spoke for a single executive? Why? Who believed the "National Executive should be structured as a council? Why? How was the debate resolved?

Biography
The American poet Philip Freneau (1752–1832), friend of Jefferson and Madison, wrote a poem in tribute to Benjamin Franklin following his death on April 17, 1790. Research the life of Benjamin Franklin. Explain why, at the age of 81, Franklin's words at the Constitutional Convention drew such regard and respect.

ON THE DEATH OF DR. BENJAMIN FRANKLIN

Thus, some tall tree that long hath stood
The glory of its native wood,
By storms destroyed, or length of years,
Demands the tribute of our tears.

The pile, that took long time to raise,
To dust returns by slow decays:
But, when its destined years are o'er,
We must regret the loss the more.

So long accustomed to your aid,
The world laments your exit made;
So long befriended by your art,
Philosopher, 'tis hard to part!—

When monarchs tumble to the ground,
Successors easily are found:
But, matchless Franklin! what a few
Can hope to rival such as you,
Who seized from kings their sceptered pride,
And turned the lightning darts aside.

1787 The Constitution of the United States

"The happy Union of these States is a wonder; their Constitution a miracle; their example the hope of Liberty throughout the world."

–JAMES MADISON

HISTORICAL BACKGROUND

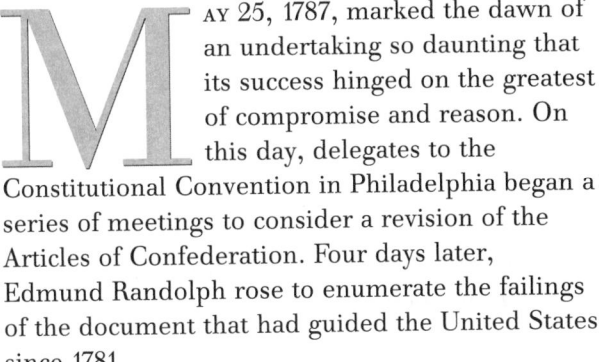

MAY 25, 1787, marked the dawn of an undertaking so daunting that its success hinged on the greatest of compromise and reason. On this day, delegates to the Constitutional Convention in Philadelphia began a series of meetings to consider a revision of the Articles of Confederation. Four days later, Edmund Randolph rose to enumerate the failings of the document that had guided the United States since 1781.

According to notes taken that day by James Madison, Randolph warned of "the prospect of anarchy from the laxity of government everywhere" if changes and additions were not made to the Articles. Among the failings noted by Randolph was the inability of Congress to protect the country from foreign invasion or even settle differences between the states. He noted in particular that the Articles were "not even paramount to the state constitutions." Perhaps most imposing was the provision that amendments to the Articles of Confederation required the unanimous consent of all the states, something difficult to achieve.

A grave question faced the delegates of the Constitutional Convention as they met in the summer heat behind closed doors. How could a document be crafted so that it addressed the needs of a growing country, provided equity in representation for both the larger and smaller states, and most importantly, created a division of powers that seemed prudent and benign, yet was capable of managing the country's affairs? It seemed an insurmountable task. At times the Convention appeared deadlocked, yet the delegates pressed on, reaching compromise after compromise.

On September 17, 1787, thirty-nine delegates signed the newly affirmed Constitution of the United States. Three delegates—Edmund Randolph, George Mason, and Elbridge Gerry—refused to add their signatures. In the end, few delegates were completely satisfied with the document. Some feared that it granted the federal government far too many powers, diluting those of the individual states. Some thought the document was so filled with political error that it was doomed to failure. In the end, Benjamin Franklin's wisdom sealed the discussion. He told his fellow delegates,

> I agree to this Constitution with all its faults, if they are such; because I think a general Government necessary for us. . . . I doubt too whether any other Convention we can obtain, may be able to make a better Constitution. For when you assemble a number of men to have the advantage of their joint wisdom, you inevitably assemble with those men, all their prejudices, their passions, their errors of opinion, their local interests, and their selfish views. From such an assembly can a perfect production be expected? It therefore astonishes me, Sir, to find this system approaching so near to perfection as it does. . . .

The Constitution begins with a Preamble. These few but significant words state the reasons for establishing the Constitution. It begins with "We the People," in effect firmly establishing that government receives its power and authority from the people. This concept of popular sovereignty, embodied in those three powerful words, became the keystone for the republic.

The seven articles that form the Constitution established the basic organization of the government of the United States, its relations with the state governments, and its fundamental powers. The Constitution's first three articles divided the national government into three branches, each with distinct powers. Difficult discussions surrounded the establishment of an executive branch. Long-held fears of creating another monarchy pervaded the discussions. Ultimately, the executive branch was created in response to the concern that without it the legislative branch would become too powerful. However, the chief executive, the president, would have limited powers and a limited term of office.

Article IV established the rights of individuals in states. It addressed the issue of runaway slaves and also provided for the establishment of new territories and states. Article V established an amendment process, requiring a two-thirds vote by Congress or the states to initiate any amendment to the Constitution, followed by three-fourths of the states ratifying the amendment before it could take effect. This established the delicate balance between making the amendment process difficult enough to protect the Constitution from being changed on a whim, while acknowledging that unanimous decisions are hard to achieve. Articles VI established the supremecy of the Constitution and U.S. laws over those of the states, while Article VII set forth the process for ratification of the Constitution.

NATIONAL ARCHIVES DOCUMENT

We the People of the United States, in Order to form a more perfect Union, establish Justice, insure domestic Tranquility, provide for the common defense, promote the general Welfare, and secure the Blessings of Liberty to ourselves and our Posterity, do ordain and establish this Constitution for the United States of America.

Article. I. Section 1. All legislative Powers herein granted shall be vested in a Congress of the United States, which shall consist of a Senate and House of Representatives. . . .

Article. II. Section 1. The executive Power shall be vested in a President of the United States of America. He shall hold his Office during the Term of four Years. . . .

Article. III. Section 1. The judicial Power of the United States shall be vested in one supreme Court, and in such inferior Courts as the Congress may from time to time ordain and establish. . . .

Article. VII. The Ratification of the Conventions of nine States, shall be sufficient for the Establishment of this Constitution between the States so ratifying the Same. ✳

Left: Painting of George Washington at the Constitutional Convention.

Critical Thinking

Assess Significance

Prior to signing the Constitution, Benjamin Franklin, Alexander Hamilton, and others expressed the desire that approval of the document appear as unanimous, even though three delegates held to personal principles and refused to sign. Yet, the Constitution reads, "by the Unanimous Consent of the States …" How was this possible? Why do you think the delegates were so concerned about approval appearing unanimous?

Determine Point of View

Reread Madison's words on page 41. Express his viewpoint in your own words.

Draw Conclusions

Why do you think the delegates agreed to include the following provision in Article IV?

> No Person held to Service or Labour in one State, under the Laws thereof, escaping into another, shall, in Consequence of any Law or Regulation therein, be discharged from such Service or Labour, but shall be delivered up on Claim of the Party to whom such Service or Labour may be due.

Research and Writing

Historical Interpretation

The Connecticut Compromise, or Great Compromise, finally broke the impasse over representation in Congress. It proposed a Senate, where representation would be equal among states, and a House of Representatives, where representation would be proportional to each state's population. It also addressed the sensitive issue of population versus property. If slaves were property, an opinion held by southern delegates, how then, northern delegates asked, could they be counted when determining the population of a state? The answer was the Three-Fifths Compromise. Research the Three-Fifths Compromise. When was it introduced? Who wrote it? How did it answer the debate of population versus property? Compare the Three-Fifths Compromise with Resolution 7 of the Virginia Plan.

Link to the Past

Several delegates feared placing too much power in the hands of a chief executive. Thus, John Dickinson proposed the idea of placing a power of impeachment in the hands of the "National Legislature," just in case a strong executive misused the powers of the executive branch. In 1968, and again in 1972, Richard M. Nixon was elected president of the United States. On Saturday, July 27, 1974, the first of three articles of impeachment against President Nixon were passed by the House Judiciary Committee. Nixon resigned from the presidency, the only United States president to do so, on Friday, August 9, 1974. With his resignation, Nixon avoided the possibility of losing an impeachment vote in the full House of Representatives and subsequent trial in the Senate. Research the events surrounding the 1974 Articles of Impeachment. Write an essay describing the events leading to and following the Articles. Do you think the impeachment process provides an effective way to address an abuse of power by the Executive Branch?

Biography

The delegates to the Constitutional Convention included men of great stature and intelligence. George Washington reluctantly agreed to attend, concerned that his absence would undermine the Convention in the people's eyes and thus reduce its chances for success. James Madison, the architect of the Constitution, defined the inadequacies of the Articles of Confederation and advanced solutions. Most of the delegates had some knowledge of law. Most had served in colonial and state legislatures. All staked their reputations and honor on the outcome of the Convention. Review the names of the delegates who signed the Constitution. Choose and research one delegate, accessing primary resources when possible. Write a biography about your chosen delegate.

1787–1788 The Federalist Papers

*"Every individual of the community at large has
an equal right to the protection of government."*

–ALEXANDER HAMILTON

HISTORICAL BACKGROUND

WITH four long summer months of debate and compromise behind them, the great challenge ahead for the delegates to the Constitutional Convention was ratification of the Constitution by special ratification conventions held in each state. One of the Constitutional Convention's last actions was an attempt to convince all delegates to speak well of the document once they returned to their respective states. The Constitutional Convention had been held in secret. The delegates had agreed to keep its record locked away in the care of the president of the Convention for fear that knowledge of the delegates' debates and compromises might hinder ratification. An extraordinary public relations venture was underway.

The Federalist Papers were a set of eighty-five lengthy essays written by James Madison, Alexander Hamilton, and John Jay and published in New York newspapers under the anonymous pen name "Publius." Their purpose was to extol the virtues of the proposed Constitution in hope of obtaining New York's ratification of the document. The newspaper essays of "Publius" examined in detail the reasoning behind the provisions in the Constitution in an attempt to sway public opinion. Ratification in New York was by no means assured. Two of the state's delegates had left the Convention in protest during its proceedings. New York's governor, George Clinton, also opposed the Constitution. However, on July 26, 1788, New York followed Virginia and became the eleventh state to ratify the

Constitution. Eventually, the essays of Publius were compiled under the title of "The Federalist."

Two essays in particular, Federalist 10 and 51, became hallmarks in the ratification debate. The concern of Federalist 10 was the ability of government to protect the country from insurrection. Madison wrote, "The instability, injustice, and confusion introduced into the public councils, have, in truth, been the mortal diseases under which popular governments have everywhere perished." The concern was real. Two years before, Daniel Shays, a former captain in the American Revolution, had led hundreds of farmers in rebellion against the government of Massachusetts. The federal government had been powerless to deal with the situation. In Federalist 10, Madison advanced the argument that a representative government protected the people against rule by misguided factions because representation extended across economic, geographic, and religious bounds. A centralized representative government, he reasoned, thus was an effective protection against rebellion.

Federalist 51 explained the importance of dividing the powers of government among the three branches. Considering the cynicism surrounding an executive branch, it was critical to convince people that such a division of powers would ensure a free government. Dividing power, argued Federalist 51, would check its abuse. Moreover, in arguing for a federal system of government, Hamilton or Madison postulated that a centralized government would unite the separate interests of the country.

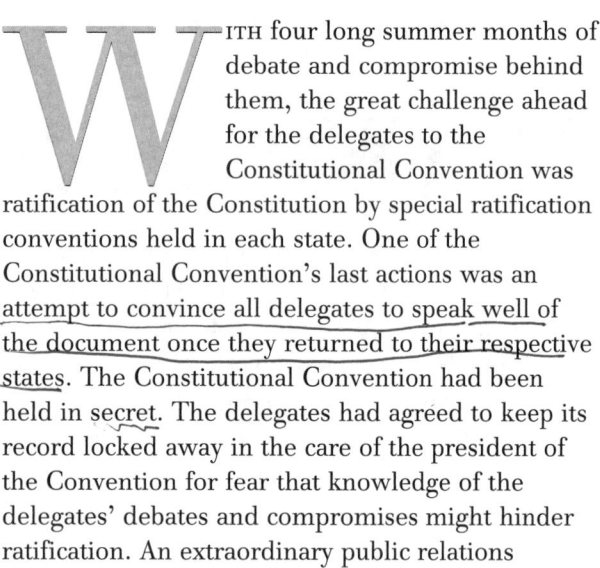

The Federalist Paper No. 10

The Same Subject Continued: The Union as a Safeguard Against Domestic Faction and Insurrection

To the People of the State of New York:

AMONG the numerous advantages promised by a well constructed Union, none deserves to be more accurately developed than its tendency to break and control the violence of faction. The friend of popular governments never finds himself so much alarmed for their character and fate, as when he contemplates their propensity to this dangerous vice. . . .

There are again two methods of removing the causes of faction: the one, by destroying the liberty which is essential to its existence; the other, by giving to every citizen the same opinions, the same passions, and the same interests.

It could never be more truly said than of the first remedy, that it was worse than the disease. Liberty is to faction what air is to fire, an aliment without which it instantly expires. . . .

The second expedient is as impracticable as the first would be unwise. As long as the reason of man continues fallible, and he is at liberty to exercise it, different opinions will be formed. . . .

From this view of the subject it may be concluded that a pure democracy, by which I mean a society consisting of a small number of citizens, who assemble and administer the government in person, can admit of no cure for the mischiefs of faction. . . .

A republic, by which I mean a government in which the scheme of representation takes place, opens a different prospect, and promises the cure for which we are seeking.

Below: Daniel Shays and other farmers in rebellion kept the Court of Common Pleas at Northampton and other courts from convening as a way to stop the trial and imprisonment of debtors.

The Federalist Paper No. 51

The Structure of the Government Must Furnish the Proper Checks and Balances Between the Different Departments

To the People of the State of New York:

. . . In order to lay a due foundation for that separate and distinct exercise of the different powers of government, which to a certain extent is admitted on all hands to be essential to the preservation of liberty, it is evident that each department should have a will of its own; and consequently should be so constituted that the members of each should have as little agency as possible in the appointment of the members of the others. . . .

. . . In framing a government which is to be administered by men over men, the great difficulty lies in this: you must first enable the government to control the governed; and in the next place oblige it to control itself. . . .

. . . It is of great importance in a republic not only to guard the society against the oppression of its rulers, but to guard one part of the society against the injustice of the other part. Different interests necessarily exist in different classes of citizens. If a majority be united by a common interest, the rights of the minority will be insecure. ✳

Critical Thinking

Cause and Effect
Why do you think Hamilton, Madison, and Jay wrote under the pen name of Publius?

Determine Point of View
Explain Madison's point when he states, "Liberty is to faction what air is to fire."

Draw Conclusions
In Federalist 51, Madison wrote, "What is government itself, but the greatest of all reflections on human nature." How is government a reflection on human nature?

Research and Writing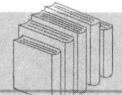

Counterpoint
At the end of the Constitutional Convention, James Madison noted in his record of the proceedings that

> Doctr. FRANKLIN looking towards the President's Chair, at the back of which a rising sun happened to be painted, observed to a few members near him, that Painters had found it difficult to distinguish in their art a rising from a setting sun. I have said he, often and often in the course of the Session, and the vicisitudes of my hopes and fears as to its issue, looked at that behind the President without being able to tell whether it was rising or setting: But now at length I have the happiness to know that it is a rising and not a setting Sun.

As the delegates left the Constitutional Convention they well understood that a new day had dawned in the history of the United States. Yet they also understood that ratification of the Constitution might prove more difficult than drafting it. Access and read Federalist 10 and 51. Then, research the 1787–1788 arguments against ratification of the Constitution found in the Antifederalist Papers. With Madison, Hamilton, Washington, and the well-respected Franklin solidly behind ratification of the Constitution, why was ratification so difficult in New York?

Relating Events
Research the economic and political reasons behind Shays's Rebellion in Massachusetts, an uprising that started with a petition to the government and ended in insurrection. What would prompt Jefferson to say in a letter to James Madison shortly thereafter,

> I hold it that a little rebellion now and then is a good thing, and as necessary in the political world as storms in the physical. Unsuccessful rebellions, indeed, generally establish the encroachments on the rights of the people which have produced them?

Read Federalist 10. How does Madison answer Jefferson?

Analysis
The Federalist Papers define in great detail each provision of the Constitution. Read in full one of the eighty-five Federalist Papers. Explain its purpose, and analyze its meaning in an essay. Relate the explanations it presents to the controversies of the time. Take the stance of a Federalist or Antifederalist in your essay's final comments.

1789 Washington's Inaugural Address

*"The preservation of the sacred fire of liberty and the destiny
of the republican model of government are . . . staked on the experiment
entrusted to the hands of the American people."*

—GEORGE WASHINGTON,
FIRST INAUGURAL ADDRESS, APR. 30, 1789

HISTORICAL BACKGROUND

"I do solemnly swear that I will faithfully execute the office of President of the United States, and will, to the best of my ability, preserve, protect, and defend the Constitution of the United States."
With those words, George Washington became the first president of the United States on April 30, 1789. Robert Livingston, chancellor of the State of New York, administered the oath of office on the balcony of Federal Hall in New York City. With great fanfare, Washington arrived at Federal Hall in the president's coach followed by a contingent of dignitaries and common folk. A congressional committee had decreed that the president's oath of office should be proclaimed "in the most public manner." Thus, with a crowd below, George Washington pledged to defend the country he had led into war against Britain. He also pledged to defend the Constitution in which he had played a central role. Yet, Washington's inaugural was not without controversy.

Great consternation had been expressed over creating an executive office with power placed in the hands of one individual. For some, the resemblance between president and king was far too similar. For others, however, great pomp and circumstance was not only appropriate but essential for an individual of such great stature. Washington, humbled by the magnitude of what the office of president would require of him, dressed in a simple brown suit for his inaugural. He had asked that all appearances of royalty be discarded, yet ties to royalty seemed to pervade the ceremony. Following Washington's oath of office, Livingston turned to the crowd to pronounce, "Long live George Washington, President of the United States." It had the familiar resonance of "Long live the King," heard in bygone days.

How the president should be addressed on Inauguration Day had been a point of contention in Congress. "His highness the President of the United States of America," suggested by the Senate, was undercut by objections from the House of Representatives. The president, some representatives reminded Congress, was a man of the people, not a ruler deserving of a royal title. In the end, Congress agreed on the formal title of "President of the United States" used by Livingston in introducing Washington to the New York crowd.

The division of power in government, and the Constitution's well-placed balance of those powers, was of paramount concern to Washington. The overwhelming task of creating a functioning government out of the much-debated republican concept embodied in the Constitution would prove to be a formidable task. How best to structure an executive department without creating the appearance of the authoritative rule given to kings would be critical. It was a pivotal point on which the future of the government hinged.

Congress had unanimously elected Washington. He began his presidency as a reluctant chief executive whose intentions had been for a quiet retirement after years of faithful service to his country. Yet, he took to his new role with dedication and passion. Deftly mediating differences that easily could have caused the great republican experiment to fail, in two terms as president Washington firmly established the executive branch as critical to the success of the federal government.

Fellow-Citizens of the Senate and of the House of Representatives:

. . . By the article establishing the executive department it is made the duty of the President "to recommend to your consideration such measures as he shall judge necessary and expedient." The circumstances under which I now meet you will acquit me from entering into that subject further than to refer to the great constitutional charter under which you are assembled, and which, in defining your powers, designates the objects to which your attention is to be given. It will be more consistent with those circumstances, and far more congenial with the feelings which actuate me, to substitute, in place of a recommendation of particular measures, the tribute that is due to the talents, the rectitude, and the patriotism which adorn the characters selected to devise and adopt them. In these honorable qualifications I behold the surest pledges that as on one side no local prejudices or attachments, no separate views nor party animosities, will misdirect the comprehensive and equal eye which ought to watch over this great assemblage of communities and interests, so, on another, that the foundation of our national policy will be laid in the pure and immutable principles of private morality, and the preeminence of free government be exemplified by all the attributes which can win the affections of its citizens and command the respect of the world. . . .

Besides the ordinary objects submitted to your care, it will remain with your judgment to decide how far an exercise of the occasional power delegated by the fifth article of the Constitution is rendered expedient at the present juncture by the nature of objections which have been urged against the system, or by the degree of inquietude which has given birth to them. . . . ✳

Below: Washington taking the oath of president, April 30, 1789, at Federal Hall (later the U.S. Subtreasury Building), Wall Street, New York City.

Critical Thinking

Determine Point of View

What does Washington believe to be the most critical purpose before Congress? Why does he caution Congress about Article V of the Constitution?

Analyze Cause and Effect

Washington requested that his eight-day journey from his home at Mount Vernon, Virginia, to New York be uneventful and free from the pomp afforded a monarch. Why do you think this was important to Washington?

Draw Conclusions

George Washington declined any payment for his services as president, limiting costs of the executive branch to "actual expenditures as the public good may be thought to require." Do you think this decision helped or impaired the public's perception of the executive branch and its leader?

Research and Writing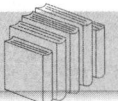

Link to the Past

Read Washington's First Inaugural Address in full. Then read the inaugural speech of the current president of the United States. What was the focus of Washington's speech? What was the focus of the current president's inaugural address? Explain any comparisons and/or contrasts in the way each individual perceives the role of president of the United States.

Relating Events

Washington's executive branch began with a foreign office and a treasury board. The country had a huge federal debt, the financial remnant of the American Revolution, and plenty of cynics who were convinced the federal government was sure to fail. Within months, Congress established a Department of State, a Department of War, and a Department of the Treasury. Research the history behind each department. Who did Washington choose to head each department? Why? What were their differences? How were the differences resolved? What did they ultimately accomplish?

Analysis

Prior to Washington's journey to New York, he confided the following in a letter to General Henry Knox,

> …for in confidence I tell you, (with the world it would obtain credit,) that my movements to the chair of government will be accompanied by feelings not unlike those of a culprit who is going to the place of his execution. So unwilling am I in the evening of life, nearly consumed in public cares, to quit a peaceful abode for an ocean of difficulties, without that competency of political skill, abilities and inclination, which are necessary to manage the helm. I am sensible that I am embarking the voice of the people, and a good name of my own, on this voyage, but what returns will be made for them, Heaven alone can foretell. Integrity and firmness are all I can promise. These, be the voyage long or short, shall never forsake me, I may be deserted by all men; for of the consolations which are to be derived from these, under any circumstances, the world cannot deprive me.

Research the life of George Washington. Write an essay that provides a background for Washington's decision to assume the role as first president of the United States.

1789 The Federal Judiciary Act

"Civil liberty . . . consists in an equal right to all citizens to have, enjoy, and do, in peace, security and without molestation, whatever the equal and constitutional laws of the country admit to be consistent with the public good."

–JOHN JAY, FIRST CHIEF JUSTICE OF THE SUPREME COURT

HISTORICAL BACKGROUND

ARTICLE V of the Constitution of the United States established a federal judiciary comprised of one Supreme Court and a set of inferior courts, allowed for a term of "good behavior" for all federal judges, gave the federal courts jurisdiction over laws arising from the Constitution, provided for trial by jury, and established the parameters of treason. The brevity of Article V allowed Congress the latitude to design for the federal judiciary. How many federal judges would there be? What would be their responsibilities? How many courts? Where would the courts be located? A myriad of questions needed to be answered.

One of the first actions of the First Congress was to organize the federal judiciary. One member from each state was assigned to the committee headed by Senators Ellsworth of Connecticut and Paterson of New Jersey. The resulting Federal Judiciary Act of 1789 established the essential framework for the federal judiciary. Though impacted by new laws over the years, and though certainly much larger than originally designed (today there are 94 district courts and 12 regional circuits), the federal court system established over two hundred years ago still functions as the basic structure of today's federal judicial system.

The 1789 Federal Judiciary Act legislated the following:

- The federal court system would be tiered;
- A Supreme Court would consist of a chief justice and five associate justices;
- The federal judiciary would further be divided into circuit and district courts;
- Members of both the Supreme Court and a district court would preside over circuit courts;
- State courts were granted original jurisdiction in most cases;
- Decisions from the highest state court could be appealed to the Supreme Court;
- The Supreme Court would have final jurisdiction over all constitutional issues;
- The Supreme Court would have the power to overturn the judgments of high state courts if a constitutional issue were involved.

Kentucky and Maine were not placed within a circuit but were district courts outside the ascribed three circuits. Under the provisions of the 1789 Federal Judiciary Act, each district would "consist of one judge, who shall reside in the district for which he is appointed, and shall be called a District Judge, and shall hold annually four sessions . . ." Additionally, two circuit courts were held annually within each district. Two Supreme Court justices plus one district court judge presided over each circuit court. Cases involving a jury trial originated in district courts with an appeal for redress at the circuit court level.

One provision of the 1789 Federal Judiciary Act was the establishment of an assessable court system. Thus, the Act delineated exactly where and when courts would be in session. Another important provision was the assurance of a jury of peers. To that end, the Act provided "That in cases punishable with death, the trial shall be had in the county where the offence was committed, or where that cannot be done without great inconvenience, twelve petit jurors at least shall be summoned from thence . . ."

THE FEDERAL JUDICIARY 1789

Supreme Court (6 justices)

A total of 13 district courts:

Connecticut, Delaware, Georgia, Kentucky, Maine, Massachusetts, Maryland, New Hampshire, New Jersey, New York, Pennsylvania, South Carolina, Virginia

11 of the district courts were then placed into 3 judicial circuits

SOUTHERN CIRCUIT	MIDDLE CIRCUIT	EASTERN CIRCUIT
South Carolina	New Jersey	New Hampshire
Georgia	Pennsylvania	Massachusetts
	Delaware	New York
	Maryland	Connecticut
	Virginia	

For many individuals, Section 25 of the 1789 Federal Judiciary Act caused significant consternation. This section gave federal courts the power to overturn state-court rulings in cases where a state law was in conflict with the Constitution, a federal law, or a treaty with another nation. For some, such oversight of state rulings was an encroachment on state powers. However, the 1789 Federal Judiciary Act was the country's first attempt at creating a fair and impartial federal court system. And, as with all legislation, future changes were inevitable.

NATIONAL ARCHIVES DOCUMENT

Congress of the United States,
begun and held at the City of New York on Wednesday the fourth of March one thousand seven hundred and eighty nine.

SECTION 1. Be it enacted by the Senate and House of Representatives of the United States of America in Congress assembled, That the supreme court of the United States shall consist of a chief justice and five associate justices. . . .

SEC. 2. And be it further enacted, That the United States shall be, and they hereby are divided into thirteen districts. . . .

SEC. 4. And be it further enacted, That the before mentioned districts, except those of Maine and Kentucky, shall be divided into three circuits, and be called the eastern, the middle, and the southern circuit. . . .

SEC. 24. And be it further enacted, That when a judgment or decree shall be reversed in a circuit court, such court shall proceed to render such judgment or pass such decree as the district court should have rendered or passed; and the Supreme Court shall do the same on reversals therein. . . .

SEC. 25. And be it further enacted, That a final judgment or decree in any suit, in the highest court of law or equity of a State in which a decision in the suit could be had, where is drawn in question the validity of a treaty or statute of, or an authority exercised under the United States . . . may be re-examined and reversed or affirmed in the Supreme Court of the United States. . . . ✳

Below: Early chambers of the United States Supreme Court.

Critical Thinking

Determine Point of View

Reread the words of John Jay on page 50. In your own words, restate what you think Jay means. Do you agree with John Jay? Apply his reasoning to a current issue.

Assess Significance

Why do you think Congress created a tiered system for the federal judiciary?

Draw Conclusions

One of the enunciated concerns of the Antifederalists prior to the Constitution's ratification was that justices would be granted a term of "good behavior." Antifederalist Paper No. 78, published in 1788, noted that "…there is no power above them [federal justices] that can control their decisions, or correct their errors. There is no authority that can remove them from office for any errors or want of capacity …" The Federalists countered that a lengthy judicial term would help to create an independent judiciary free from political winds. Today, many states elect, rather than appoint, their high court justices. Do you agree with the conclusion of the Antifederalists or the Federalists? What, if any, problems are created by this constitutional provision?

Research and Writing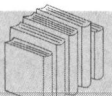

Link to the Past

Access and read the Federal Judiciary Act of 1789. Explain its provisions. Research the structure of the current federal court system. How does the current system compare with what was established in 1789?

Analysis

Though the United States Supreme Court, for the most part, spent its first two years on organizational matters, it wasn't long before the scope of the federal judicial system was challenged. Two cases, *Chisholm v. Georgia* (1793) and *Georgia v. Brailsford* (1794), involved unresolved debts from the American Revolution. At the heart of each case was the power of federal courts over state courts. In *Chisholm v. Georgia* (1793), for example, the Supreme Court held that an individual could use the federal courts to sue a state, even if the individual did not live in the state being sued. Research these two early Supreme Court cases. What were the issues involved in each case? How do they compare and contrast? How were they resolved? How did the Eleventh Amendment, ratified in 1798, clarify Article III, Section 2, Clause 1 of the Constitution?

Relating Events

The Judiciary Act of 1801 reduced the number of Supreme Court justices from six to five, and it replaced the circuit-riding duties of Supreme Court justices by providing for sixteen new judgeships divided among six judicial circuits. Circuit courts were given jurisdiction over constitutional issues. With less than two weeks left in his term as president of the United States, John Adams signed the legislation into law. Why was John Adams accused of packing the courts? Why were Adams's appointees termed "Midnight Judges"? What was President Jefferson's response to Adams's action? Research the Judiciary Act of 1801. How did it expand the scope of the federal judiciary? Why did Jefferson find the Act so adverse?

1803 Marbury v. Madison

*"It is emphatically the province and duty
of the judicial department to say what the law is."*

–John Marshall

Historical Background

ALTHOUGH the election of 1800 saw a majority of Jeffersonian Republicans elected to Congress, Federalists continued their hold on the federal courts. Of great insult to the Republicans was President John Adams's appointment in 1801 of John Marshall, then secretary of state, as Chief Justice of the Supreme Court. Marshall was a staunch Federalist and a political foe of Thomas Jefferson. In 1802 Congress passed yet another judiciary act. To many Americans, it must have appeared that the ideological battle between Republicans and Federalists in Congress was being waged on the steps of the federal judiciary.

The Federal Judiciary Act of 1802 reorganized the federal court system yet again. Although the Judiciary Act of 1801 eliminated circuit duties for Supreme Court justices, the Republican-controlled Congress reinstated that provision in the 1802 act. Renewed circuit duties for the justices eliminated the need for the sixteen new judgeships established by the 1801 act, thus returning the organization of the courts to an earlier structure. Crying foul, Federalists asserted that Congress did not have the authority to abolish the judgeships, since the Constitution required that federal judges, who are appointed for an unlimited term, cannot be removed from office except for bad behavior. Republicans responded that since the Constitution gave Congress the power to establish inferior courts, it also had the constitutional authority to dissolve them. Unquestionably, the battle line had been drawn. The case of *Marbury v. Madison* grew out of this political and ideological battle between Federalists and Republicans for control of the judicial branch.

William Marbury was one of several court appointments made by Adams before he left office. Though seemingly an insignificant appointment, Marbury sought the status and power associated with being a justice of the peace in the District of Columbia. When Jefferson, determined to rid the judicial branch of its Federalist bent, thwarted Marbury's appointment on a technicality, Marbury sought relief in the Supreme Court. In effect, Marbury asked the Court to uphold his appointment by issuing a *writ of mandamus*. This court order would, in effect, require Jefferson's secretary of state, James Madison, to deliver Marbury's commission. The case represented a political quagmire for the Court. If it ruled against Marbury, it would hand the Republicans a powerful political victory. If it ruled against Madison, Jefferson would likely ignore the ruling, leaving the Court insignificant in the grand scheme of the federal government. To resolve this dilemma, Chief Justice Marshall crafted a brilliant solution.

The Supreme Court's ruling in *Marbury v. Madison* was twofold. In an opinion written by Marshall, the Court agreed that Marbury had a right to his commission and that Madison should have delivered it to him. However, the Court ruled that Section 13 of the Judiciary Act of 1789, which gave it the power to issue the court order Marbury requested, exceeded the authority granted the Court by Article III of the Constitution, and thus was unconstitutional. So, in effect, the Court agreed with Marbury but said it was powerless to force the Republican administration to commission him because it lacked the constitutional authority to do so.

What appeared to be a victory for Jefferson was, ironically, a fortuitous victory for the Federalist-dominated Court. The ruling established the

Supreme Court as the ultimate authority on the Constitution. In addition, it secured for the Court the power to declare acts passed by Congress and signed into law by the president to be unconstitutional. This power of "judicial review"— the authority to declare "a law repugnant to the Constitution[to be] void"—was thus secured by the *Marbury v. Madison* ruling, giving the Court an expanded role in government that it continues to exercise today.

NATIONAL ARCHIVES DOCUMENT

Chief Justice Marshall delivered the opinion of the Court.

It [is] decidedly the opinion of the court, that when a commission has been signed by the president, the appointment is made; and that the commission is complete, when the seal of the United States has been affixed to it by the secretary of state. . . .

To withhold his commission, therefore, is an act deemed by the court not warranted by law, but violative of a vested legal right. . . .

The very essence of civil liberty certainly consists in the right of every individual to claim the protection of the laws, whenever he receives an injury. One of the first duties of government is to afford that protection. . . .

It is, then, the opinion of the Court [that Marbury has a] right to the commission; a refusal to deliver which is a plain violation of that right, for which the laws of his country afford him a remedy. . . .

Below: James Madison

Certainly all those who have framed written constitutions contemplate them as forming the fundamental and paramount law of the nation, and consequently, the theory of every such government must be, that an act of the legislature, repugnant to the constitution, is void. . . .

Thus, the particular phraseology of the constitution of the United States confirms and strengthens the principle, supposed to be essential to all written constitutions, that a law repugnant to the constitution is void; and that courts, as well as other departments, are bound by that instrument. . . . ✳

Critical Thinking

Assess Significance

How does the *Marbury v. Madison* ruling establish the Supreme Court as a third party in the Constitution's system of checks and balances?

Classify Information

What is the difference between original and appellate jurisdiction? Give an example of each.

Draw Conclusions

Article III, Section 2 of the United States Constitution states "In all Cases affecting Ambassadors, other public Ministers and Consuls, and those in which a State shall be Party, the supreme Court shall have original Jurisdiction. In all the other Cases before mentioned, the Supreme Court shall have appellate Jurisdiction...." Marshall argued that the *writ of mandamus* asked for by Marbury exceeded the court's jurisdiction because it lacked original jurisdiction in this case. Do you agree? Why or why not? Do you think Marbury would have prevailed if he had begun his lawsuit in a lower court?

Research and Writing

Relating Events

Marbury v. Madison is considered a landmark case because the opinion of the Court set a precedent upon which the decisions of other cases have been based. Marshall wrote almost half of the 1,100 opinions issued by the Court during his thirty-four years as Chief Justice. In another landmark case, *Cohens v. Virginia* (1821), the Court established the power of the federal courts to review decisions of high state courts. Speaking for the Court in this case too, Marshall wrote of the federal judiciary:

> It is authorized to decide all cases of every description arising under the Constitution or laws of the United States. From this general grant of jurisdiction, no exception is made of those cases in which a state may be a party.

Research this important case. What were the issues? How and why did this case reach the Supreme Court? Was this a case of appellate or original jurisdiction? How were the issues resolved? Why is *Cohens v. Virginia* considered a landmark case?

Historical Interpretation

The repeal of the Judiciary Act of 1801 was only the beginning of an effort by Republicans to purge the federal courts of Federalists. The next tactic was to target those judges who seemed most vulnerable to impeachment. First on the list was John Pickering, a federal district judge from New Hampshire. Next was a more formidable opponent, Supreme Court Associate Justice Samuel Chase. Research the impeachment efforts against Chase. Why was he targeted by Republicans for impeachment? What was the result of these impeachment efforts? How did Chase respond to his impeachment? How did Chase's impeachment affect later Supreme Court decisions?

Biography

Research the life of John Marshall. What part did he play in the formation of American government? Who were his political allies? What philosophical differences separated Marshall and Thomas Jefferson? In 1820 Jefferson wrote in a letter to William Jarvis, "To consider the judges as the ultimate arbiters of all constitutional questions [is] a very dangerous doctrine indeed, and one which would place us under the despotism of an oligarchy." How might Marshall have responded to Jefferson's comment?

1819 McCulloch v. Maryland

"In fashioning the bank, remember that it is to be made particularly instrumental in enriching and aggrandizing the elect few."

—PHILIP FRENEAU, IN OPPOSING ALEXANDER HAMILTON'S BID FOR A NATIONAL BANK

HISTORICAL BACKGROUND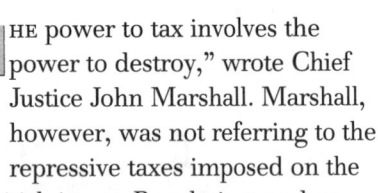

"THE power to tax involves the power to destroy," wrote Chief Justice John Marshall. Marshall, however, was not referring to the repressive taxes imposed on the colonists by the British in pre-Revolutionary days; rather, he was responding to issues before the Court in *McCulloch v. Maryland*. Central to the debate over the case was whether the state of Maryland had the power to tax the Second Bank of the United States, a federal bank chartered by Congress. Another question was whether the federal government even had the constitutional power to establish a national bank.

The idea of a national bank was controversial even before the first national bank, named the Bank of the United States, was chartered in 1791. Alexander Hamilton introduced the idea in 1790 as part of a three-fold plan to create a national system of finance. He believed a national bank would provide a safe place to deposit government funds, as well as allow for the regulation of bank practices across the country. Hamilton reasoned that since the Constitution granted Congress the power to borrow money, coin money, collect taxes, and "make all Laws which shall be necessary and proper for carrying into Execution the foregoing powers," that it had the authority to establish a system of finance, inclusive of a national bank. However, others held the idea in contempt, concluding that a national bank only served the interests of elite mercantilists and not those of the common man.

Opposition to the national bank continued into the next century. In 1803, Thomas Jefferson wrote to Albert Gallatin,

> I deem no government safe which is under the vassalage of any selfconstituted authorities, or any other authority than that of the nation, or its regular functionaries. What

an obstruction could not this bank of the United States, with all its branch banks, be in time of war! It might dictate to us the peace we should accept, or withdraw its aids. Ought we then to give further growth to an institution so powerful, so hostile?

Though the national bank closed in 1811, Congress established the Second Bank of the United States in 1816. Once again, the constitutionality of this action came under scrutiny.

In 1818 Maryland passed legislation to tax all banks that were doing business in the state but were not chartered by it. When James McCulloch, a cashier at the Baltimore branch of the national bank, issued bank notes on paper not stamped (and properly taxed) by the state, Maryland filed suit against him. The result was the landmark court case of *McCulloch v. Maryland*. While the impetus for the lawsuit was the unpaid tax, the core question was the ability of a state to tax an agency of the federal government and thereby exercise some degree of control over its operations. In effect, the sovereign power of the federal government was at stake. Another important but underlying issue was the constitutional authority of Congress to even establish a national bank in the first place.

The Supreme Court's ruling in *McCulloch v. Maryland* not only nullified Maryland's bank tax law, it affirmed the principle of the federal government's supremecy over state governments. Equally important was the Court's expansion of the legislative authority of Congress when it upheld the creation of a national bank through the "implied powers" granted Congress in the Constitution. The ruling did not subdue political tensions over a national banking system, however. Instead, the issue continued to fester, culminating in the Bank War of 1832–1833.

Chief Justice Marshall delivered the opinion of the Court. . . .

The first question made in the cause is, has Congress power to incorporate a bank? . . .

The power now contested was exercised by the first Congress elected under the present constitution. The bill for incorporating the bank of the United States did not steal upon an unsuspecting legislature, and pass unobserved. Its principle was completely understood, and was opposed with equal zeal and ability. After being resisted, first in the fair and open field of debate, and afterwards in the executive cabinet, with as much persevering talent as any measure has ever experienced, and being supported by arguments which convinced minds as pure and as intelligent as this country can boast, it became a law. . . .

Among the enumerated powers, we do not find that of establishing a bank or creating a corporation. But there is no phrase in the instrument which, like the articles of confederation, excludes incidental or implied powers; and which requires that everything granted shall be expressly and minutely described. . . .

Below: Marshall's handwritten opinion in *McCulloch v. Maryland.*

After the most deliberate consideration, it is the unanimous and decided opinion of this Court, that the act to incorporate the Bank of the United States is a law made in pursuance of the constitution, and is a part of the supreme law of the land . . .

. . . the States have no power, by taxation or otherwise, to retard, impede, burden, or in any manner control, the operations of the constitutional laws enacted by Congress to carry into execution the powers vested in the general government. This is, we think, the unavoidable consequence of that supremacy which the constitution has declared.

. . . this is a tax on the operations of the bank, and is, consequently, a tax on the operation of an instrument employed by the government of the Union to carry its powers into execution. Such a tax must be unconstitutional. *

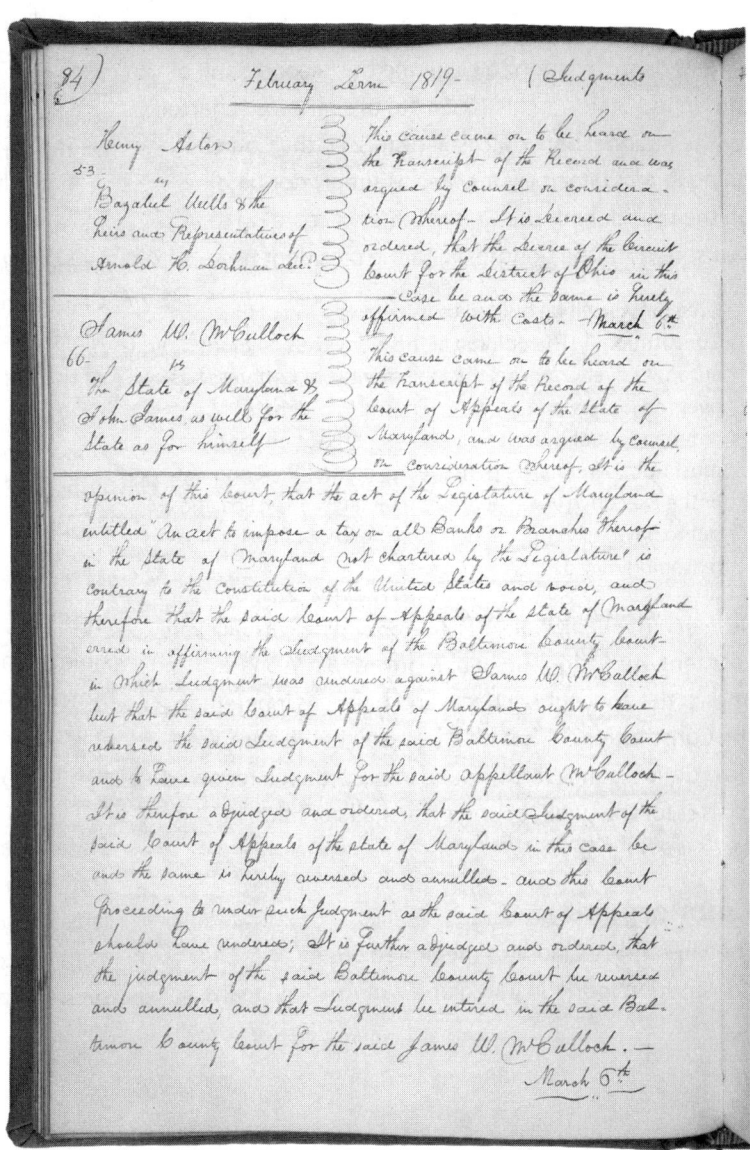

Critical Thinking

Classify Information
What is the difference between the *expressed* and the *implied* powers of Congress?

Draw Conclusions
In *McCulloch v. Maryland,* Marshall wrote, "This government is acknowledged by all to be one of enumerated powers. The principle, that it can exercise only the powers granted to it, [is] now universally admitted. But the question respecting the extent of the powers actually granted, is perpetually arising, and will probably continue to arise, as long as our system shall exist...." What is Marshall postulating in regard to *expressed* versus *implied* powers?

Analyze Cause and Effect
Why do you think *McCulloch v. Maryland* is considered a landmark case?

Research and Writing

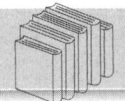

Relating Events
Andrew Jackson entered the presidency in 1828 with a fervent determination to eliminate the Second Bank of the United States. In his 1832 veto of a renewed charter for the national bank, Jackson dismissed the Court's ruling in *McCulloch v. Maryland* as simply not binding on the president of the United States. According to Jackson, both the Congress and the president must,

> ...each for itself be guided by its own opinion of the Constitution....The opinion of the judges has no more authority over Congress than the opinion of Congress has over the judges, and on that point the President is independent of both. The authority of the Supreme Court must not, therefore, be permitted to control the Congress or the Executive when acting in their legislative capacities, but to have only such influence as the force of their reasoning may deserve.

Research the Bank War of 1832–1833. Why was Jackson so intent on closing the bank? How do Jackson's words impact the concept of checks and balances inherent in the Constitution? What was the result of the Bank War? How do Jackson's words, found in his veto of a renewed charter for the bank, counter Marshall's opinion in *McCulloch v. Maryland*?

Counterpoint
The Supremacy Clause of the United States Constitution found in paragraph 2 of Article VI reads,

This Constitution, and the Laws of the United States which shall be made in Pursuance thereof; and all Treaties made, or which shall be made, under the Authority of the United States, shall be the supreme Law of the Land; and the Judges in every State shall be bound thereby, any Thing in the Constitution or Laws of any State to the contrary notwithstanding.

Research and read the entire opinion of John Marshall in *McCulloch v. Maryland.* How did the Supremacy Clause impact the Court's ruling? Excerpt the parts of Marshall's opinion that in particular speak to the weight of the Supremacy Clause. Given the Supremacy Clause, how could Jefferson and other Republicans believe unequivocally that Congress did not possess the constitutional right to establish a national bank with regulatory powers over state banks?

Historical Interpretation
In 1811, Congress refused to renew the bank charter granted in 1791 to the first Bank of the United States. The American economy then fell into a chaotic state. No national currency existed. Merchants often refused to accept payments made with paper currency from state banks, tender that was of questionable value. The United States Treasury, the collector of tax payments from the states, was in a similar quandary. Research the events that led to the charter of the Second Bank of the United States. With the country in economic disarray, why would states such as Maryland continue to oppose a national bank?

Gibbons v. Ogden

"On every question of construction, let us carry ourselves back to the time when the Constitution was adopted."

–Thomas Jefferson

Historical Background

ARTICLE I, Section 8 of the United States Constitution gives Congress the power to "regulate Commerce with foreign Nations, and among the several States. . . ." This provision, known as the Commerce Clause, was the basis of Daniel Webster's argument before the United States Supreme Court on behalf of his client, Thomas Gibbons, in the 1824 case of *Gibbons v. Ogden.* Following Webster's oratory, Chief Justice John Marshall delivered a unanimous decision for the Court. It was the last major decision handed down by Marshall, and like several other Marshall opinions, it set an important precedent upon which future cases would rest.

Thomas Gibbons was an entrepreneur who had procured a license under a 1793 federal law to allow him to operate two steamboats, the *Stoudinger* and the *Bellona*, between New York City and Elizabethtown, New Jersey. The only problem was that in 1808 Robert Fulton and Robert Livingston had established a steamboat line monopoly on New York's waters. The monopoly, granted by the New York state legislature, allowed Fulton and Livingston to sell licenses to individuals hoping to operate "boats moved by fire or steam" on waters running through the state of New York. Fulton and Livingston granted Aaron Ogden exclusive ferry rights to operate on the Hudson River in New York Harbor, waters that lie between New York and New Jersey. Ogden sought and was awarded an injunction to force Gibbons to cease his steamboat run into those waters, which Ogden contended were his sole purview.

Ogden took his case first to the Court of Chancery of New York, which ruled in his favor. Gibbons appealed to the Court of Errors of New York, which affirmed the lower court's ruling. With that, Gibbons appealed his case to the United States Supreme Court. The basis for Gibbons' appeal was that, because the Commerce Clause granted Congress the power to regulate commerce, Fulton and Livingston's state-granted monopoly should be null and void. Daniel Webster, acting as counsel for Gibbons argued before the Court that "the concurrent power of the States, concurrent though it be, is yet subordinate to the legislation of Congress; and . . . therefore, Congress may, when it pleases, annul the State legislation." Webster, an eloquent speaker, further argued that allowing individual states to regulate commerce would result in a myriad of conflicting laws, one to regulate New York Harbor, one for the Chesapeake Bay, another for Boston Harbor, and so on, until the intent of the Commerce Clause became meaningless.

The Court ruled that New York's actions conflicted with the federal Coasting Act, thus striking down the monopoly on navigation created by the state of New York. Marshall, ever the nationalist, reasoned the power to regulate commerce, "like all others vested in Congress, is complete in itself, may be exercised to its utmost extent, and acknowledges no limitation other than are prescribed in the Constitution." Thus, the Supreme Court's ruling in *Gibbons v. Ogden* firmly established federal authority over interstate commerce. Once again, the Marshall Court had clarified the supremacy of federal over state legislation.

Mr. Chief Justice MARSHALL delivered the opinion of the Court . . .

The appellant contends that this decree is erroneous because the laws which purport to give the exclusive privilege it sustains are repugnant to the Constitution and laws of the United States. They are said to be repugnant: first, to that clause in the Constitution which authorizes Congress to regulate commerce; second, to that which authorizes Congress to promote the progress of science and useful arts. . . .

The genius and character of the whole government seem to be that its action is to be applied to all the external concerns of the nation and to those internal concerns which affect the states generally; but not to those which are completely within a particular state, which do not affect other states, and with which it is not necessary to interfere for the purpose of executing some of the general powers of the government. The completely internal commerce of a state, then, may be considered as reserved for the state itself. . . .

But, in regulating commerce with foreign nations, the power of Congress does not stop at the jurisdictional lines of the several states. It would be a very useless power if it could not pass those lines. . . .

The power of Congress, then, whatever it may be, must be exercised within the territorial jurisdiction of the several states. The sense of the nation on this subject is unequivocally manifested by the provisions made in the laws for transporting goods by land between Baltimore and Providence, between New York and Philadelphia, and between Philadelphia and Baltimore. . . .

But the framers of our Constitution foresaw this state of things and provided for it by declaring the supremacy not only of itself but of the laws made in pursuance of it. The nullity of any act inconsistent with the Constitution is produced by the declaration that the Constitution is supreme law. . . .

Below: Chief Justice John Marshall

Decree

This court is of opinion that so much of the several laws of the state of New York as prohibits vessels, licensed according to the laws of the United States, from navigating the waters of the state of New York, by means of fire or steam, is repugnant to the said Constitution and void. . . . ✳

Critical Thinking

Assess Significance

Why do you think *Gibbons v. Ogden* is considered a landmark case?

Classify Information

Webster felt that it was critical for the federal government to regulate interstate trade, with state regulations only affecting commerce totally within a state. What type of commerce in your state comes under federal regulation? Is there any type of commerce in your state that might be affected only by state regulation?

Make Predictions

What do you think was the result of the ruling in *Gibbons v. Ogden* on commerce between New York and New Jersey in the 1820s? Do you think the ruling which dissolved the Fulton-Livingston monopoly increased or decreased competition among steamboat lines? Why?

Research and Writing

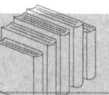

Historical Interpretation

Steam technology had a significant impact on commerce as the country moved into the nineteenth century. James Watt first patented his steam-powered engine in 1769. Steamboats made their debut during the time of the Constitutional Convention, when, in 1787, John Fitch navigated his forty-five-foot steamboat on the Delaware River. Robert Fulton expanded the commercial base of steam travel. Together with Robert Livingston, Fulton developed a successful passenger and freight steamboat line. Research the history of steam technology in the United States. How did it impact American commerce? In what way did it impact the growth of monopolies? How did the ruling in *Gibbons v. Ogden* affect interstate commerce in the expanding transportation market seen during the 1800s?

Analysis

Part of the debate surrounding the *Gibbons v. Ogden* case was whether the Constitution should be strictly interpreted word for word or whether there should be some latitude in its interpretation. "Strict constructionists" prefer the scope of the government to be limited, using a literal interpretation of the Constitution. A "loose constructionist," on the other hand, interprets the Constitution on a broader level.

Read Marshall's opinion in *Gibbons v. Ogden*. By what reasoning does Marshall include navigation in the definition of commerce? In what way does he interpret "among the several states"? How does he define the power to regulate? Is Marshall using a "strict constructionist" or a "loose constructionist" interpretation of the Constitution? Use excerpts from Marshall's opinion to support your thesis.

Link to the Past

Though the case of *Gibbons v. Ogden* occurred in 1824, its opinion regarding interstate commerce and the Court's interpretation of the Commerce Clause stood as precedent for future Supreme Court rulings that extended beyond the issue of navigable waters. In the case of *United States v. Lopez* (1995), the issue before the court was whether a student who had carried a concealed handgun into his high school could be charged with violating the Gun-Free School Zones Act of 1990. In deciding the case, the Supreme Court weighed the Commerce Clause, including citations from Marshall's interpretation of it in *Gibbons v. Ogden*. Research *United States v. Lopez*. What were the facts in the case? What was its outcome? How was the Commerce Clause used to structure the Court's opinion?

1913 Seventeenth Amendment

"When they call the roll in the Senate, the Senators do not know whether to answer 'Present' or 'Not guilty.'"

–THEODORE ROOSEVELT

HISTORICAL BACKGROUND

ALTHOUGH the Constitution specifically called for a division of powers between branches of government, it also provided for a division of power between the government and the people. The essence of the United States Constitution is how it begins. *"We the People . . . do ordain and establish this Constitution . . ."* Thus, philosophically at least, the Constitution's framers placed the power of the government in the hands of the people. The writers viewed the Constitution as a social contract. However, there was a bit of a catch, for those who actively participated in government were also those who had the advantage of wealth and property.

Once the delegates had decided on a bicameral legislature, the next step was to agree on how the members of each house of Congress should be selected. The result was Article I, Section 3 of the United States Constitution, which allowed that *"The Senate of the United States shall be composed of two Senators from each State, chosen by the Legislature thereof for six Years; and each Senator shall have one Vote."* The framers' decision to grant state legislatures the power to choose the members of the Senate proved a contentious one. Antifederalists were adamantly opposed to such an important office being insulated from the power of the people's vote. Though the framers of the Constitution acknowledged that the House of Representatives was closer to the people and the Senate more reflective of the country's "aristocracy," this did little to quell the concern of Antifederalists. In Antifederalist Paper 62, "Brutus" wrote,

Men long in office are very apt to feel themselves independent; to form and pursue interests separate from those who appointed them. And this is more likely to be the case with the senate, as they will for the most part of the time be absent from the state they represent. . . . It is probable that senators once chosen for a state will, as the system now stands, continue in office for life. The office will be honorable if not lucrative. The persons who occupy it will probably wish to continue in it and, therefore, use all their influence and that of their friends to continue in office. Their friends will be numerous and powerful, for they will have it in their power to confer great favors. . . .

Public perception in the late nineteenth century of a government controlled by wealth and special interests led to a cry for political reform. Progressive reformers termed the Senate a "Millionaires' Club." They charged its members as representing not the will of the people, but that of special interests and political machines. In 1903 President Theodore Roosevelt said,

The death-knell of the republic had rung as soon as the active power became lodged in the hands of those who sought, not to do justice to all citizens, rich and poor alike, but to stand for one special class and for its interests as opposed to the interests of others.

Moreover, due to political wrangling, the election of some senators had become deadlocked in state legislatures, leaving the Senate short of its full membership and "the people" thus unrepresented.

The precipitating event prompting passage of a constitutional amendment allowing for the direct election of U.S. senators occurred in 1911 when the *Chicago Tribune* reported that Illinois Senator William Lorimer had used bribery to attain his election by the state assembly. Lorimer was a political boss in Chicago and member of the Republican Party. The public, as well as several progressive-minded representatives in Congress, were outraged.

Beyond Washington, change was occurring at the state level. By 1912 over half of all states had adopted the "Oregon System." Initiated by the state of Oregon, the Oregon System established a procedure to appoint individuals who had been selected by popular vote to the Senate. With a gradual change at the state level for an elected Senate, a change in the Constitution seemed inevitable. The Seventeenth Amendment was passed by Congress on May 13, 1912 and, duly ratified, became law on April 8, 1913. It repealed portions of Article I, Section 3, Clauses 1 and 2 relating to the election of senators. The debate on representation in Congress, and the division of powers between government and the people, had certainly come full circle.

NATIONAL ARCHIVES DOCUMENT

Sixty-second Congress of the United States of America; At the Second Session,

Begun and held at the City of Washington on Monday, the fourth day of December, one thousand nine hundred and eleven.

"The Senate of the United States shall be composed of two Senators from each State, elected by the people thereof, for six years; and each Senator shall have one vote. The electors in each State shall have the qualifications requisite for electors of the most numerous branch of the State legislatures.

"When vacancies happen in the representation of any State in the Senate, the executive authority of such State shall issue writs of election to fill such vacancies: *Provided*, That the legislature of any State may empower the executive thereof to make temporary appointments until the people fill the vacancies by election as the legislature may direct. ✳

Below: A political reform movement to rid government of special interests resulted in passage of the Seventeenth Amendment in 1913.

A HUGE FEEDER, BUT A POOR MILKER.
UNCLE SAM (*loq.*). "If the beast cannot yield enough to fill that little pail, the sooner my stable is quit of her, the better."

Critical Thinking

Compare and Contrast

Compare the original Article 1, Section 3 with the Seventeenth Amendment. How do they differ?

Assess Significance

As had occurred some 120 years earlier, the method of electing senators encountered heated debate, especially from Southern Democrats who were not complacent about any further encroachment on what they viewed as their right to decide who could vote. What language in the Seventeenth Amendment allows states latitude in deciding who may vote?

Determine Point of View

Why might William Lorimer's ouster from the Senate have fueled political pressure to pass the Seventeenth Amendment?

Research and Writing

Link to the Past

Several efforts in the recent past have been expended on a proposal that would limit the terms of members of Congress. Research these efforts. Explain the reasoning behind the efforts to establish term limits. Why have efforts failed to achieve a constitutional amendment limiting terms in Congress?

Point of View

Read Antifederalist Paper 62 in its entirety. Read Federalist Papers 62 and 63. Explain the divergent points of view on the structuring of the Senate. On which points do both Publius and Brutus agree? Which view could be used to support the Seventeenth Amendment? Write an essay supporting either the Federalist or Antifederalist position.

Biography

Herbert Croly (1869–1930) was a political philosopher whose 1909 book, *The Promise of American Life*, influenced social thought and national politics in the early 1900s. Croly lived during a time of great change in America. The Industrial Revolution had transformed America from an agrarian to an urban society wrought with social ills, a highly visible and unequal distribution of wealth, and workers reduced to what Croly termed "wage slavery." Croly believed Americans needed to cast aside Jeffersonian ideals of individuality and a decentralized government and embrace the more Hamiltonian concept of a strong, centralized government. To Croly, individualism and *laissez-faire* government policies had allowed the industrialists of the Gilded Age to accrue great wealth at the expense of the working poor. Croly called for the federal government to institute political and social reforms through a series of federal regulations and social programs. Research the life of Herbert Croly. In what way does he expound on the writings of Hamilton and Jefferson? What influence did Croly have on the Progressives of the time? What reforms occurred? In what way was the reform movement, spurred by the Progressives, instrumental in passage of the Seventeenth Amendment?

1954 Senate Resolution 301

> *"McCarthyism is Americanism with its sleeves rolled."*
>
> –Joseph R. McCarthy

Historical Background

THE resolution in the Senate that led to the eventual censure of Senator Joseph McCarthy was precipitated by a fear of communism lurking on America's doorstep. It was a fear that seemed to fuel national politics and pervade discussions from the farm tables of his home state, Wisconsin, to the halls of Congress. The House Un-American Activities Committee (HUAC) had kept a close watch on the activities of "subversives" since 1938. However, it was the well-publicized "Hollywood Ten" that brought into America's living rooms just how well-orchestrated the Communist Party had been in subverting democracy, or so the HUAC claimed. The Hollywood Ten were among nineteen members of the Screen Writers Guild who were accused of subverting the government by injecting pro-communist propaganda into Hollywood movies. When asked to acknowledge their party affiliation, they refused to do so, claiming their politics to be a private matter. Held in contempt, they were sentenced to a year in jail and subsequently blacklisted by the movie industry.

With the nation in the midst of the Red Scare, McCarthy, a Republican senator, declared that he had a list of 205 federal officials who were known members of the Communist Party, though he refused to produce the list. Riding on the back of America's conflict with communist North Korea, McCarthy's trenchant remarks soon engulfed unsuspecting political foes. With his 1952 reelection campaign in full swing, McCarthy next turned his attention to exposing Communists in the Democratic Party, followed by a targeting of Secretary of Defense George C. Marshall.

As author, in 1948, of the post-World War II Marshall Plan to reconstruct Europe, Marshall was held in high regard within the Truman administration. Undeterred, McCarthy blamed Marshall for the communist take-over of China,

identifying Marshall as part of a greater conspiracy to promote the tenets of communism in America and throughout the world. It seemed as if McCarthy's tirades would never end, and neither would his trail of political victims. Of special note was the charge that J. Robert Oppenheimer, who was a leader in America's atomic weapons program, could not be trusted with the country's atomic secrets. Following an investigation by the United States Atomic Energy Commission, in 1954 President Dwight Eisenhower ordered all classified information withheld from Oppenheimer. To many, the division of power, with the people positioned as a check against the abuses of government, appeared at risk.

McCarthy stepped over the proverbial line when his accusations of Communist infiltration stretched into the United States Army. President Eisenhower, who by this time was privately skeptical of McCarthy's tactics and considered him "reckless," turned the tables on McCarthy by asking for a congressional investigation into McCarthy's governmental affairs. Yet, it was the power of the media that eventually brought McCarthy down. Hearings into the Army's so-called infiltration by subversives were broadcast on TV. What the public saw was a demagogic abuser of power, bent on the intimidation of witnesses in order to make a beleaguered point. When McCarthy even accused one of the Army's lawyers of consorting with Communists, implying that this man, too, was a member of a communist organization, the country had had enough. McCarthy was censured by the Republican-controlled Senate for conduct "unbecoming" a member of that body. Totally discredited, McCarthy died in 1957. However, the term *McCarthyism* lives on as a label for the behavior of those who recklessly degrade the character of others.

NATIONAL ARCHIVES DOCUMENT

Resolved, That the Senator from Wisconsin, Mr. McCarthy, failed to cooperate with the Subcommittee on Privileges and Elections of the Senate Committee on Rules and Administration . . . in stating to the press on November 4, 1954, that the special Senate session that was to begin November 8, 1954, was a "lynch-party" . . . and in characterizing the said committee as the "unwitting handmaiden," "involuntary agent" and "attorneys-in-fact" of the Communist Party and in charging that the said committee in writing its report "imitated Communist methods—that it distorted, misrepresented, and omitted in its effort to manufacture a plausible rationalization" in support of its recommendations to the Senate, which characterizations and charges were contained in a statement released to the press and inserted in the Congressional Record of November 10, 1954, acted contrary to senatorial ethics and tended to bring the Senate into dishonor and disrepute, to obstruct the constitutional processes of the Senate, and to impair its dignity; and such conduct is hereby condemned. ✳

Below: Senator McCarthy

Critical Thinking

Draw Conclusions

In its June 29, 1954, decision concerning J. Robert Oppenheimer, the Atomic Energy Commission concluded that

> …in respect to the criterion of 'associations,' we find that his associations with persons known to him to be Communists have extended far beyond the tolerable limits of prudence and self-restraint which are to be expected of one holding the high positions that the Government has continuously entrusted to him since 1942. These associations have lasted too long to be justified as merely the intermittent and accidental revival of earlier friendships.

How were McCarthy's accusations an affront to the First Amendment? Considering the above statement, what did the members of the Atomic Energy Commission assume?

Assess Significance

Though McCarthy may have correctly identified individuals affiliated with the Communist Party, he was not able to identify even one individual who was an agent for a communist government. Why, then, did it take so long before the Senate put a stop to McCarthy's personal indictments of so many individuals, including high-ranking officials in the government?

Determine Point of View

Although Eisenhower privately abhorred McCarthy's tactics, publicly he refused to rebuke him. In a letter to a friend, Eisenhower stated,

> With respect to McCarthy, I continue to believe that the President of the United States cannot afford to name names in opposing procedures, practices, and methods in our government. This applies with special force when the individual concerned enjoys the immunity of a United States Senator. This particular individual wants, above all else, publicity. Nothing would probably please him more than to get the publicity that would be generated by public repudiation by the President.

Do you agree with Eisenhower? Why or why not?

Research and Writing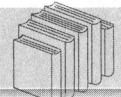

Historical Interpretation

President Truman, who preceded Eisenhower, was quick to hop onto the anti-communist bandwagon. In 1947 he signed an executive order establishing an employee loyalty program, which in part read "There shall be a loyalty [to the Unites States] investigation of every person entering the civilian employment of any department or agency of the executive branch of the Federal Government …" Reports of Communists lurking within his own administration proved an embarrassment to the president. Among those accused was Alger Hiss, an individual who had served in the government, including the State Department, and thereafter as president of the Carnegie Endowment for International Peace. Research the events surrounding the Hiss affair. Who was Alger Hiss? What was the basis for the claims against him? How did Truman respond to the charges against Hiss? How did the Hiss trial give rise to the career of future president Richard Nixon? What was the result of the trial? Do you think the preoccupation with communist infiltration of America had an impact on the allegations against Hiss? Why or why not?

Relating Events

Research the McCarran Internal Security Act. How did it define communism? From what did it bar registered communist members? Why did Truman consider the Act a threat to the Bill of Rights? What prompted Kansas Senator Pat McCarran to introduce the bill leading to the Internal Security Act? What was the law's result?

Biography

Write a biography of Joseph R. McCarthy. Explain what led to his rise in status and his eventual demise. Read Senate Resolution 301. What reasons are given for McCarthy's censure?

Foreign Policy

Prologue

ince it first declared itself an independent nation, the
United States has had some form of foreign policy. Much of
the country's foreign policy is led by the political
philosophy of the president. The U.S. Constitution grants the
president the power to make treaties and appoint ambassadors.
Additionally, the secretary of state, one of the most influential
positions in the Cabinet, serves as the president's liaison with other
nations. In 1796 President George Washington advised, "The great
rule of conduct for us in regard to foreign nations is in extending
our commercial relations, to have with them as little political
connection as possible." President Theodore Roosevelt, on the
other hand, believed that the United States should "speak softly and
carry a big stick." Though only Congress can declare war,
presidents in their constitutional role as commander-in-chief have
taken the country into war, both in response to aggression toward
America and its allies and preemptively. America has come to the
aid of countries in need. Its foreign policy decisions have at times
determined the destiny of distant nations. Far from the isolationist
thinking of Washington, America has become a pivotal voice in
international relations. In this third unit, you will gain an
understanding of the decisive role America's foreign policy has
played in international politics.

1778 Treaty of Alliance with France

"Humanity has won its battle.
Liberty now has a country."

—Marquis de Lafayette

Historical Background

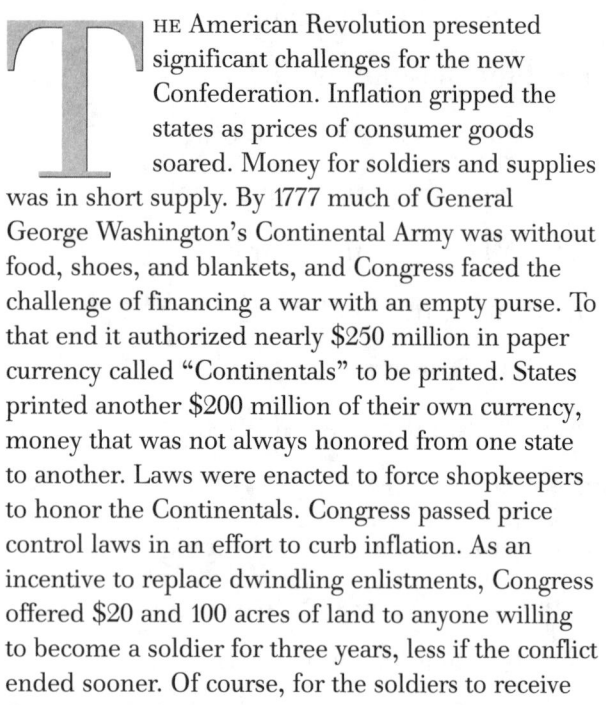

THE American Revolution presented significant challenges for the new Confederation. Inflation gripped the states as prices of consumer goods soared. Money for soldiers and supplies was in short supply. By 1777 much of General George Washington's Continental Army was without food, shoes, and blankets, and Congress faced the challenge of financing a war with an empty purse. To that end it authorized nearly $250 million in paper currency called "Continentals" to be printed. States printed another $200 million of their own currency, money that was not always honored from one state to another. Laws were enacted to force shopkeepers to honor the Continentals. Congress passed price control laws in an effort to curb inflation. As an incentive to replace dwindling enlistments, Congress offered $20 and 100 acres of land to anyone willing to become a soldier for three years, less if the conflict ended sooner. Of course, for the soldiers to receive that reward, the war first had to be won, and by the winter of 1777–1788 an American victory was by no means a certainty.

In fact, Britain frequently seemed to have the upper-hand in America's battle for liberty. With an ample supply of soldiers and arms, Native Americans and German mercenaries paid to fight, and a seemingly indomitable navy in control of the seas, British forces had succeeded in occupying every major colonial city, including New York, Philadelphia, Boston, and Charleston. Meanwhile, wintering in the bitter cold at Valley Forge, Washington's soldiers were in dire straits. In February 1778, Washington appealed to New York Governor George Clinton for help: "I mean the present dreadful situation of the army for want of provisions, and the miserable prospects before us is more alarming than you will probably conceive. . . .

For some days past, there has been little less, than a famine in camp."

Yet, while British forces excelled at sea, they found the rugged inland terrain with its thick forests more formidable. It was in such terrain that the Battle of Saratoga produced a major victory for the Americans. Here in upstate New York, British General John Burgoyne and nearly 6,000 of his troops surrendered on October 17, 1777, to General Horatio Gates. It was a much-needed success for the Americans and proved to be a turning point in the war. Although France had previously assisted the Americans by providing ships, provisions, and military supplies, the outcome at Saratoga renewed French interest in recognizing both American independence and the ultimate defeat of Great Britain.

On February 6, 1778, American envoys Benjamin Franklin, Silas Deane, and Arthur Lee signed three agreements with France. With the Treaty of Amity and Commerce, France recognized the independence of the United States. The treaty also granted mutual trade privileges. The second agreement, the Treaty of Alliance, created a military alliance between the United States and France. It committed France to military involvement in the American Revolution should war break out between itself and Britain. Once engaged in battle with the British, France pledged to continue America's fight for liberty until its independence was won. Territorial agreements were also a part of the Treaty of Alliance. France agreed not to annex any territory on the North American mainland but was permitted to seize the British West Indies, islands critical in international trade. In June 1778, British and French ships exchanged gunfire, and with that France became an active military ally of the United States

The final diplomatic agreement between France and the United States was a secret treaty that allowed

Spain to join their alliance. In 1779, following France's pledge to help the Spanish regain territories lost to the British in previous wars, Spain joined in the war against Great Britain. Meanwhile, the Dutch had been profiteering from trade agreements with America and France, much to Britain's disapproval. In response, the British declared war on the Netherlands. All this intrigue made the American Revolution an international conflict as well as a fight for one young nation's independence.

National Archives Document

The most Christian King and the United States of North America, to wit, New Hampshire, Massachusetts Bay, Rhodes island, Connecticut, New York, New Jersey, Pennsylvania, Delaware, Maryland, Virginia, North Carolina, South Carolina, and Georgia, having this Day concluded a Treaty of amity and Commerce. . . .

ART. 1.
If War should break out betwan [sic] france and Great Britain, during the continuance of the present War betwan the United States and England, his Majesty and the said united States, shall make it a common cause, and aid each other mutually with their good Offices, their Counsels, and their forces, according to the exigence [sic] of Conjunctures as becomes good & faithful Allies.

ART. 2.
The essential and direct End of the present defensive alliance is to maintain effectually the liberty, Sovereignty, and independance [sic] absolute and unlimited of the said united States, as well in Matters of Gouvernement as of commerce. . . .

ART. 6.
The Most Christian King renounces for ever the . . . part of the continent of North america which before the treaty of Paris in 1763. . . .

ART. 8.
Neither of the two Parties shall conclude either Truce or Peace with Great Britain, without the formal consent of the other first obtain'd; and they mutually engage not to lay down their arms, until the Independence of the united states shall have been formally or tacitly assured by the Treaty or Treaties that shall terminate the War. . . .

ART. 10.
The Most Christian King and the United states, agree to invite or admit other Powers who may have received injuries from England to make common cause with them. . . .

Done at Paris, this sixth Day of February, one thousand seven hundred and seventy eight.

C. A. GERARD
B. FRANKLIN
SILAS DEANE
ARTHUR LEE

Below: The *Bonne Homme Richard* was commanded by John Paul Jones. In 1779 it engaged the British frigate HMS *Serapis* in the North Sea off Famborough Head, England. With his ship heavily damaged, Jones responded to a demand from the *Serapis* that he surrender, "I have not yet begun to fight!" Jones eventually won the battle, though the *Bonne Homme Richard* was lost.

Critical Thinking

Determine Point of View

Reread Washington's words on page 70. What opinion do you think Washington had of the American Revolution in the winter of 1777–78? What do you think Washington felt was critical to the success of the Revolution at that point?

Assess Significance

One week after learning of the Treaty of Alliance with France, Washington issued an order by which his men were required to assemble and "Upon a signal given, the whole army will huzza, 'Long Live the King of France.' The artillery then begins again and fires thirteen rounds; this will be succeeded by a second general discharge of musketry, in running fire, and a huzza, 'Long Live the Friendly European Powers.' The last discharge of thirteen pieces of artillery will be given, followed by a general running and huzza, 'The American States.'" Of what significance was the intervention and support of France in the American Revolution?

Analyze Cause and Effect

The entrance of France, Spain, and subsequently the Dutch required the British to defend their empire in the Caribbean and elsewhere. What impact do you think the involvement of these other countries had on Britain's ability to wage war against the United States?

Research and Writing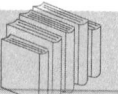

Biography

In 1777 the Marquis de Lafayette crossed the Atlantic to support the Patriot cause by becoming a part of the American Revolution. As a member of French nobility offering to serve without pay as a Continental soldier, Lafayette imparted a sense of strong foreign support for the Revolution. On July 31, 1777, Congress commissioned Lafayette as a Major General, and he served as a trusted member of Washington's staff. The two men forged a close friendship that lasted for the rest of Washington's life. Research the life of the Marquis de Lafayette. What role did he play in the American Revolution? Why did Benjamin Franklin consider him a hero? How did Lafayette participate in the alliance between France and the United States? Write a biography of Lafayette, focusing on his impact on the American Revolution.

Relating Events

In 1781 British General Lord Cornwallis, along with 7,000 soldiers, succeeded in securing a hold on Yorktown, Virginia. Cornwallis relied on the Royal Navy to reinforce and supply his troops. Washington, who at that time was stationed in New York with 9,000 troops of his own, saw a chance to trap Cornwallis at Yorktown. He relayed a message to Rear Admiral J. P. Compte de Grasse of the French Fleet for assistance. Soon de Grasse was moving his ships to the scene while Washington marched his men south to Virginia. Research the Battle of Yorktown. How was this battle definitive in securing American independence? In what way was the Franco-American alliance crucial to the defeat of the British at Yorktown? How did the French Navy play a pivotal role in the American Revolution?

Analysis

Concerned with the Franco-American alliance and worried about the possibility of defeat, in the spring of 1778 Britain attempted to reconcile with the Americans by promising to repeal the Tea and Coercive Acts. The British sent a peace commission led by the Earl of Carlisle to negotiate a peace settlement with Congress. However, the United States was in no mood to bargain away the American Revolution. Research the British government's efforts to broker a peace agreement. What other concessions was Parliament willing to make to secure a settlement? What was the response of Congress to the Carlisle Commission? How did financial assistance by France bolster America's resolve to continue its war effort?

1796 Washington's Farewell Address

"The greater part of our happiness or misery depends upon our dispositions, and not upon our circumstances."

–MARTHA WASHINGTON

HISTORICAL BACKGROUND

AFTER eight years of dutifully serving the country as president, George Washington was ready to return to his beloved Mount Vernon for a well-deserved retirement from public office. At his side was Martha Dandridge Custis Washington. She had served as a devoted wife during the American Revolution, joining and providing emotional support for Washington and his beleaguered troops at Valley Forge. As First Lady, Martha Washington took on the duties of entertaining guests and managing the president's lavish quarters located near Federal Hall in New York City. Over the years they had suffered a series of personal tragedies, including the deaths of Martha's children. Washington was sixty-four years old and tired. It was time to go home.

As the election of 1796 drew near, speculation surrounded the possibility of Washington's retirement. Meanwhile he was hard at work on his Farewell Address to the nation. Washington actually had begun the address when he first contemplated retirement from the presidency four years earlier. A hearty thirty-two pages in length, the completed address was published in the *Daily American Advertiser* on September 19, 1796. It began with "I should now apprise you of the resolution I have formed, to decline being considered among the number of those out of whom a choice is to be made." It was the definitive answer on whether Washington would seek a third term as president.

Washington's Farewell Address was a conscientious thesis on the intricacies of an ideal government. Written as a compilation of the wisdom gained by an individual who had spent his life immersed in the toils of conflicting doctrines

and ideals, it reflected the advice of a sage statesman. Washington's administration had not been without its trials and tribulations. Jay's Treaty had been a particular problem. Concessions made to Great Britain by special envoy, Chief Justice John Jay, angered Congress and raised public ire. Yet, in an effort to avert further alliance with France, Washington signed the narrowly approved treaty. Other internal political conflicts plagued Washington's two terms as president. In the end, his loyalty and respect for those who had helped form the government was not sufficient to prevent those same individuals from polarizing his administration. Ideological battles between Alexander Hamilton, ever the Federalist, and Thomas Jefferson, ever the Republican, were particularly acute.

In his Farewell Address, Washington described the presidency as an "arduous trust" presented to an individual whose qualifications (at least in Washington's mind) were "inferior" to the office to which he was elected. He explained his retirement as a timely event, yet one that did not lessen his devotion to his country. Early in his address he stated, "I have the consolation to believe that, while choice and prudence invite me to quit the political scene, patriotism does not forbid it."

Central to Washington's gentle admonishments in his Farewell Address to those left to run the government was a warning not to form long-standing alliances with foreign governments. The Treaty of Alliance with France had included a perpetual pledge that stated, "The two Parties guarantee mutually from the present time and forever, against all other powers." Washington's wisdom would soon be realized. By 1797 diplomatic relations with France had broken down, replaced by hostility. In 1801 the Treaty of Alliance was terminated. Washington's persuasive argument would influence an isolationist philosophy in Congress for many decades to come.

Another warning Washington expressed in his Farewell Address was for the nation to avoid fragmenting into political parties, something which already had occurred by 1796. Washington considered political parties as pernicious, fearing they would ultimately lead to the dissolution of the republic because of the natural effort of one political party to dominate the others. However, his warnings did little to stifle the political maneuverings of the 1796 election.

In all, Washington's Farewell Address was an effort to impart a lasting parcel of advice to the country. Washington wrote,

> . . . if I may even flatter myself that they may be productive of some partial benefit, some occasional good; that they may now and then recur to moderate the fury of party spirit, to warn against the mischiefs of foreign intrigue, to guard against the impostures of pretended patriotism; this hope will be a full recompense for the solicitude for your welfare, by which they have been dictated.

Within three years Washington would die from a respiratory illness complicated by eighteenth century medical treatment.

NATIONAL ARCHIVES DOCUMENT

Friends and Fellow Citizens:

The name of American, which belongs to you in your national capacity, must always exalt the just pride of patriotism more than any appellation derived from local discriminations. With slight shades of difference, you have the same religion, manners, habits, and political principles. You have in a common cause fought and triumphed together; the independence and liberty you possess are the work of joint counsels, and joint efforts of common dangers, sufferings, and successes. . . .

. . . the Constitution which at any time exists, till changed by an explicit and authentic act of the whole people, is sacredly obligatory upon all. The very idea of the power and the right of the people to establish government presupposes the duty of every individual to obey the established government. . . .

The alternate domination of one faction over another, sharpened by the spirit of revenge, natural to party dissension, which in different ages and countries has perpetrated the most horrid enormities, is itself a frightful despotism. . . .

As a very important source of strength and security, cherish public credit. . . .

. . . a passionate attachment of one nation for another produces a variety of evils. . . .

I shall also carry with me the hope that my country will never cease to view them [his mistakes] with indulgence; and that, after forty five years of my life dedicated to its service with an upright zeal, the faults of incompetent abilities will be consigned to oblivion, as myself must soon be to the mansions of rest. . . . ✳

Below: This 1797 cartoon depicts the United States as a maiden being ill-treated by the French delegation. In the background are foreign leaders watching the event unfold.

PROPERTY PROTECTED, a la Françoise.

Critical Thinking

Classify Information

The Constitution of the Commonwealth of Massachusetts, adopted in 1780, defined the body politic as "formed by a voluntary association of individuals: it is a social compact, by which the whole people covenants with each citizen, and each citizen with the whole people, that all shall be governed by certain laws for the common good." How does Washington view the body politic?

Draw Conclusions

Why do you think Washington published his Farewell Address in the *Daily American Advertiser* as opposed to presenting it solely to Congress?

Point of View

Do you believe Washington advocated isolationism? Why or why not?

Research and Writing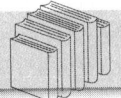

Historical Interpretation

The 1796 presidential election was shrouded in backdoor politics. Propelling the political events of 1796 was Article II, Section 1 of the United States Constitution which read in part, "The Person having the greatest Number of Votes shall be the President ... after the Choice of the President, the Person having the greatest Number of Votes of the Electors shall be the Vice President...." Though Washington had warned against the intrusion of political parties in government, the 1796 presidential election was shaped by them. Research the 1796 presidential election. Who was elected? How did political parties impact the election's outcome? What role did Hamilton play in the election? Do you think Washington's warnings were appropriate?

Relating Events

The French response to Jay's Treaty included an unwillingness to recognize American neutrality on the high seas. As a result, French warships seized almost 300 American ships bound for England. The breakdown of diplomatic relations between the United States and France precipitated the XYZ Affair. Research the provisions of Jay's Treaty. What prompted Washington to sign the treaty? Why did the treaty raise such a fury in the United States and in France? How did it lead to the XYZ Affair? How did the XYZ Affair affect American foreign and military policy?

Analysis

Access and read Washington's Farewell Address in its entirety. Analyze its significant points. Explain the rationale behind the concerns it expressed. Consider Washington's accomplishments as president. What do you think he desired to leave as his legacy?

1814 Treaty of Ghent

"We have met the enemy and they are ours."

–COMMODORE OLIVER H. PERRY
(UPON THE SURRENDER OF BRITISH WARSHIPS DURING THE BATTLE OF LAKE ERIE)

HISTORICAL BACKGROUND

AMERICA's entrance into the nineteenth century was filled with turmoil and the indicators of impending war. At the heart of international agitation were trade disputes that, once again, provoked European rivalries. By 1800 American merchants were realizing healthy profits from lucrative trade agreements with England, France, and Spain. Because of a vast trade in wheat, cotton, sugar, leather hides, and many other commodities, American merchant ships dominated the trade routes of the high seas. However, in the 1790s and early 1800s, merchant marines faced risks beyond those presented by the rough waters of the Atlantic.

In 1803 France and Great Britain were involved in a long and entangling war that would continue until the downfall of Napoleon Bonaparte in 1815. Yet, business was good for American merchants in 1803. The conflict provided new opportunities for American merchants to fill trade voids left by the frequently warring Europeans. However, by 1805 Britain had little tolerance for the neutrality claimed by American merchant ships. In 1806 the British government issued a series of *Orders in Council* meant to curb trade with or for France. Britain decreed that all ships headed for continental ports first must receive permission, or "papers," in order to proceed. Failure to do so raised the possibility of the ship's seizure by the British. France, under the leadership of Napoleon Bonaparte, retaliated, stating that ships of any country that complied with the British Orders in Council would be under threat of seizure by the French navy. It was a no-win situation for the Americans. To make matters worse, once the British boarded an American merchant ship, they not only seized the cargo but also frequently pressed American seamen into British naval service. It

became an intolerable situation that prompted a resurgence of American patriotism.

In 1807 President Jefferson asked Congress to impose an embargo against both France and England. He believed the embargo would force them to recognize American neutrality, since trade with the United States was critical to the economy of each side. It was an ill-fated strategy. Soon American merchants, farmers, financiers, and shopkeepers were immersed in widespread economic depression. Jefferson, strife-worn and weary, decided not to seek a third term as president. With the 1808 presidential election, the burden of international disputes passed to fellow Virginian, James Madison.

From the outset of his presidency, Madison was entangled in conflict both at home and abroad. Continued seizures of American merchant ships by both the French and British, impressments of Americans into the Royal Navy, failed trade policies, and Britain's unwillingness to acknowledge American neutrality pushed Congress to the brink of war. Also central to a declaration of war was the ongoing conflict with Native Americans. Finding British-made rifles at the Battle of Tippecanoe convinced many Americans that Britain was instigating Native American aggression against the United States while using Canada as the command center for their conniving.

Congress approved a declaration of war against Great Britain on June 18, 1812. It was a war against Native American resistance as much as against British policies of impressment and the seizure of American ships. The goal was to strike the British in Canada, where Madison reasoned they were most vulnerable. However, two years of fighting found American and British forces stalemated along the Canadian border. In the end, both countries grew weary of the political, financial, military, and social burdens of the War of 1812. The Treaty of Ghent was signed on Christmas Eve, 1814. News of the treaty, however, traveled at a typical early nineteenth-century pace. Meanwhile, at the battlefront the war continued, culminating in a belated American victory at the Battle of New Orleans on January 8, 1815.

The War of 1812 ushered the United States into a new era of politics, social change, and technological advancements. The country would soon move from an agrarian society to an industrialized nation.

NATIONAL ARCHIVES DOCUMENT

Treaty of Peace and Amity between His Britannic Majesty and the United States of America.

ARTICLE THE FIRST.
There shall be a firm and universal Peace between His Britannic Majesty and the United States, and between their respective Countries, Territories, Cities, Towns, and People of every degree without exception of places or persons. All hostilities both by sea and land shall cease as soon as this Treaty shall have been ratified by both parties as hereinafter mentioned. All territory, places, and possessions whatsoever taken by either party from the other during the war, or which may be taken after the signing of this Treaty, excepting only the Islands hereinafter mentioned, shall be restored without delay and without causing any destruction or carrying away any of the Artillery or other public property originally captured in the said forts or places, and which shall remain therein upon the Exchange of the Ratifications of this Treaty, or any Slaves or other private property; And all Archives, Records, Deeds, and Papers, either of a public nature or belonging to private persons, which in the course of the war may have fallen into the hands of the Officers of either party, shall be, as far as may be practicable, forthwith restored and delivered to the proper authorities and persons to whom they respectively belong. . . .

ARTICLE THE SECOND.
Immediately after the ratifications of this Treaty by both parties as hereinafter mentioned, orders shall be sent to the Armies, Squadrons, Officers, Subjects, and Citizens of the two Powers to cease from all hostilities: and to prevent all causes of complaint which might arise on account of the prizes which may be taken at sea after the said Ratifications of this Treaty . . .

ARTICLE THE THIRD.
All Prisoners of war taken on either side as well by land as by sea shall be restored as soon as practicable. . . .

ARTICLE THE NINTH.
The United States of America engage to put an end immediately after the Ratification of the present Treaty to hostilities with all the Tribes or Nations of Indians with whom they may be at war at the time of such Ratification, and forthwith to restore to such Tribes or Nations respectively all the possessions, rights, and privileges which they may have enjoyed or been entitled to in one thousand eight hundred and eleven previous to such hostilities. . . . ✳

Below: British forces entered Washington, D.C., on August 24, 1814, setting fire to the Capitol and presidential mansion.

Critical Thinking

Draw Conclusions

Why do you think many Federalists, individuals who were merchants and bankers, opposed war with Great Britain?

Point of View

British delegates in the Belgian city of Ghent at first demanded, among other things, control of the Great Lakes as well as a buffer zone of Indian land between Canada and the United States. The final treaty did not include Britain's initial demands nor did it address the American issues that precipitated the war, including impressments and neutral rights. Why do you think both the United States and England placed these issues aside in the name of peace?

Analyze Cause and Effect

What impact do you think England's twelve-year war with France had on its willingness to draft the Treaty of Ghent?

Research and Writing

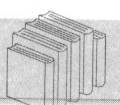

Relating Events

In the fall of 1814, anti-war Federalists convened in Hartford, Connecticut. While some Federalists called for secession from the United States, others adopted a more conservative stance. The delegates to the Hartford Convention recommended amendments to the Constitution which included, among other things, the following:

- Congress shall not have power to lay any embargo on the ships or vessels of the citizens of the United States, in the ports or harbors thereof, for more than sixty days.
- Congress shall not make or declare war, or authorize acts of hostility against any foreign nation, without the concurrence of two-thirds of both Houses.
- The same person shall not be elected President of the United States a second time; nor shall the President be elected from the same State two terms in succession [which, of course was a direct reference to Thomas Jefferson and James Madison, both from Virginia].

Research the Hartford Convention. Explain each of its proposed amendments. Why did the convention come to an abrupt halt? How was the Hartford Convention an example of sectionalism? What impact did the Hartford Convention have on the nation and the Federalist Party?

Historical Interpretation

The War of 1812 presented a series of military challenges for Americans, both at sea and on land. Of particular embarrassment to Madison's administration was the burning of Washington, D.C. Research the military events that led Madison to flee Washington, D.C., on the night of August 24, 1814. Contrast the American defeat that led to the occupation of Washington, D.C., with the defeat of the British at New Orleans just two weeks after the signing of the Treaty of Ghent. What was the military impact of each? What was the psychological impact? Ultimately, what were the political consequences of the War of 1812?

Link to the Past

On May 8, 1995, President Clinton signed an executive order establishing a trade embargo against Iran. The embargo branded Iran as a terrorist country. Research the 1995 embargo of Iran. How long did it last? What was its effect? What criticisms did President Clinton incur in regard to the embargo? How was nuclear capability a factor in the embargo? What changes have occurred since 1995 in the status of the embargo? Considering this embargo and the embargo preceding the War of 1812, how effective do you feel embargoes are as instruments of foreign policy?

1823 The Monroe Doctrine

"The best form of government is that which is most likely to prevent the greatest sum of evil."

–JAMES MONROE

Marcus 877 341 7556
(11/8/13)

HISTORICAL BACKGROUND

IN 1817 James Monroe, the last of the Virginia Dynasty, became president of the United States. He served as president until 1825. John Quincy Adams, the son of President John Adams and future president himself, served as Secretary of State in Monroe's administration. During his eight years in the State Department, Adams exerted a dominant influence over American foreign policy. Adams believed that the United States was destined to dominate North America. To that end, he looked to capitalize on the economic potential of the dissolving Spanish empire in South America. He also looked toward the expansion of the United States through the annexation of Florida and Spanish-held lands in the west. However, due to its vast land holdings north of America's boundaries and its potent Royal Navy, Adams also was keenly aware of the ever-present military and economic threat posed by Great Britain.

Adams proved to be a master of diplomacy. In 1818 he struck an agreement with Britain establishing the 49th parallel as the boundary between the United States and Canada, and with it British recognition of U.S. territorial claims, including all land gained via the Louisiana Purchase in 1803. In the meantime, however, trouble was brewing in Florida.

During the early 1800s Florida was held by the Spanish. The territory had become a haven for runaway slaves from the United States. It also was the home of the Seminole Indians. Over the years white settlements had encroached on Seminole land. In response to the threat posed by whites, the Seminole began raiding these settlements. Seeing an opportunity to acquire Florida, in 1817 President Monroe ordered General Andrew Jackson, hero of the War of 1812 and future president of the United States, to subdue the Seminoles. It was a welcomed order for Jackson, who not only disliked the Spanish

but also possessed a personal compulsion to banish all Native Americans to west of the Mississippi River. Jackson's army entered Florida wielding unrelenting force that resulted in the destruction of Seminole villages, the hanging of Seminole chiefs, and the conquest of Spanish villages.

Though the French and Spanish governments protested Jackson's aggressive military actions in Florida, Secretary Adams justified Jackson's exploits by claiming that Spain had been remiss in its governance of the territory. He coupled his chastisement with a threat that the United States would take further military action, if necessary, to secure the region. With little to gain by war with the United States, Spain signed the Adams-Onís Treaty on February 22, 1819. It was a triumph for John Quincy Adams. Spain ceded Florida to the United States and also relinquished all territories north of the 42nd parallel, paving the way for U.S. expansion into Oregon and the Pacific Northwest. In return the United States recognized Spain's claim to Texas and agreed to pay American merchants' claims against Spain of about $5 million for losses incurred during the Napoleonic Wars.

Other international concerns required careful diplomacy by Adams. In 1821 Russia claimed all land in the Pacific Northwest above the 51st parallel. Adams, perceiving a threat to U.S. interest in Oregon, informed Russia that North America was no longer open for colonization. By 1822 the United States recognized the newly independent countries of Argentina, Chile, Peru, Columbia, and Mexico, all former colonies of Spain. Inevitably, both Britain and the United States coveted harmonious South American trade agreements. To convolute issues further, in 1823 French troops marched into Spain in an effort to return Spain's King Ferdinand VI to the throne. Concerns were raised in the United States and Britain that this attempt to restore the Spanish monarchy would be accompanied by an attempt to restore Spain's colonies in the Americas.

In his 1823 annual message to Congress, President Monroe enunciated the foreign policy views held by Adams. The resulting "Monroe Doctrine" offered no basis for implementation and had no sense of political emergency. However, it became the philosophical cornerstone for U.S. foreign policy in the Western Hemisphere for the rest of the nineteenth century and beyond. In essence, its intent was to define the diplomatic parameters required to promote beneficial trade agreements for the United States with Latin America. To that end, it established

four points that had their roots in Washington's 1796 Farewell Address.

- That North and South America were no longer open to further colonization;

- That the political systems in Europe were counter to that established in the United States so that "to extend their system to any portion of this hemisphere [was] dangerous to our peace and safety";

- That the United States would refrain from interference in existing European colonies;

- That the United States would refrain from interference in the issues and wars of European countries.

National Archives Document

. . . At the proposal of the Russian Imperial Government, made through the minister of the Emperor residing here, a full power and instructions have been transmitted to the minister of the United States at St. Petersburg to arrange by amicable negotiation the respective rights and interests of the two nations on the northwest coast of this continent . . .

It was stated at the commencement of the last session that a great effort was then making in Spain and Portugal to improve the condition of the people of those countries, and that it appeared to be conducted with extraordinary moderation. It need scarcely be remarked that the results have been so far very different from what was then anticipated . . . In the wars of the European powers in matters relating to themselves we have never taken any part, nor does it comport with our policy to do so. It is only when our rights are invaded or seriously menaced that we resent injuries or make preparation for our defense. . . . The political system of the allied powers is essentially different in this respect from that of America. . . . But with the Governments who have declared their independence and maintain it, and whose independence we have, on great consideration and on just principles, acknowledged, we could not view any interposition for the purpose of oppressing them, or controlling in any other manner their destiny, by any European power in any other light than as the manifestation of an unfriendly disposition toward the United States. . . .

. . . Our policy in regard to Europe, which was adopted at an early stage of the wars which have so long agitated that quarter of the globe, nevertheless remains the same, which is, not to interfere in the internal concerns of any of its powers; to consider the government de facto as the legitimate government for us . . . ✳

Below: Map of the United States, 1810.

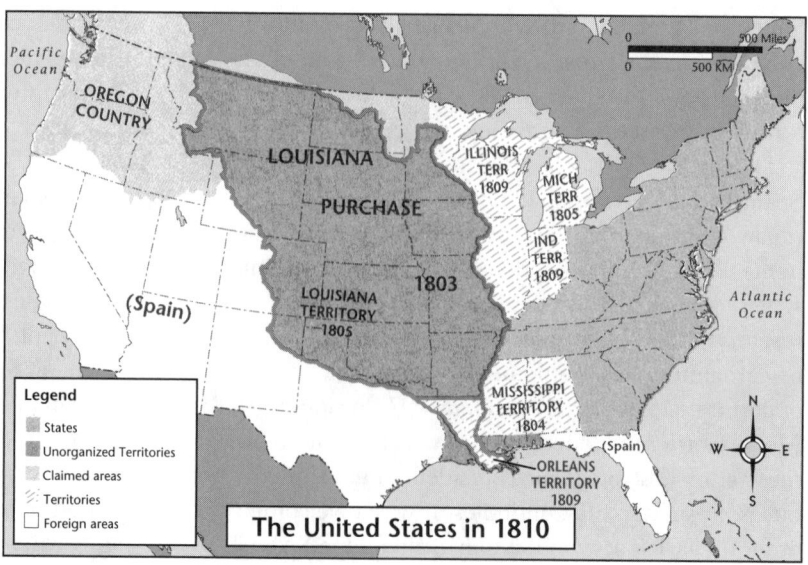

The United States in 1810

Critical Thinking

Analyze Cause and Effect

In what way did the Monroe Doctrine attempt to benefit U.S. trade relations with Latin America?

Determine Point of View

At the time of the Monroe Doctrine, Spain's remaining colonies lay off the coast of Florida. The lucrative trade and political advantage of acquiring these islands did not elude John Quincy Adams. However, in a letter to President Monroe, Thomas Jefferson advised the following:

> I candidly confess, that I have ever looked on Cuba as the most interesting addition which could ever be made to our system of States. The control which, with Florida Point, this island would give us over the Gulf of Mexico, and the countries and isthmus bordering on it, as well as all those whose waters flow into it, would fill up the measure of our political well-being. Yet, as I am sensible that this can never be obtained, even with her own consent, but by war; and its independence, which is our second interest, (and especially its independence of England,) can be secured without it, I have no hesitation in abandoning my first wish to future chances, and accepting its independence, with peace and the friendship of England, rather than its association, at the expense of war and her enmity.

Summarize Jefferson's point of view in regard to expansion into Cuba.

Draw Conclusions

How had the United States become a stakeholder in international affairs by 1823?

Research and Writing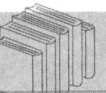

Analysis

The Adams-Onís Treaty foreshadowed white expansion onto the tribal lands of the Seminole Indians. Research the history and culture of the Seminole. What impact did the foreign policy of the Monroe Administration have on the Seminole Indians? What happened to the Seminole as whites rushed to settle Florida following the Adams-Onís Treaty? Who was Osceola and what did he attempt? What future struggles did the Seminole face? Where are the Seminole found today? In what ways have they preserved their culture and traditions?

Relating Events

In 1821 Russia claimed land in the Pacific Northwest. At the time Russia was part of what was termed the *Holy Alliance*, a coalition established between Russia, Prussia, and Austria. Along with control of Alaska, Czar Alexander I of Russia also claimed dominion over all Pacific Northwest lands north of the 51st parallel. On November 7, 1823, Adams wrote in his personal notes,

> I remarked that the communications recently received from the Russian Minister, Baron Tuyl, afforded, as I thought, a very suitable and convenient opportunity for us to take our stand against the Holy Alliance, and at the same time to decline the overture of Great Britain. It would be more candid, as well as more dignified, to avow our principles explicitly to Russia and France, than to come in as a cock-boat in the wake of the British man-of-war.

Research the encounter between Czar Alexander I and the Monroe Administration. What did Adams mean when he said he didn't want America "to come in as a cock-boat in the wake of the British man-of-war?" How did the British factor into this event? How effective was the Holy Alliance? What efforts did Adams take to reverse Russia's claim? What were the provisions of the 1824 treaty with Russia?

Link to the Past

Read the Monroe Doctrine in its entirety. Compare and contrast the tenets of the Monroe Doctrine with the foreign policy of the current administration. How does the United States today view its relationship with other nations? What role does the President advocate for the United States in the affairs of foreign governments? Focus on one recent event. How did current foreign policy impact diplomatic management of that event? Did American actions support or contradict the tenets of the Monroe Doctrine?

1848 Treaty of Guadalupe Hidalgo

"America is a poem in our eyes; its ample geography dazzles the imagination, and it will not wait long for meters."

–FROM THE POET BY RALPH WALDO EMERSON

HISTORICAL BACKGROUND

THE United States was at war again. This time its foe was not across the Atlantic Ocean, but instead its neighbor, Mexico. In office sat President James K. Polk, an expansionist who coveted the westward lands of California and New Mexico. The annexation of Texas was already underway when Polk took office. On March 1, 1845, outgoing President John Tyler signed a resolution to admit Texas as a state. On December 29, 1845, President Polk formally admitted Texas as the twenty-eighth state in the Union. Mexico, however, did not concur with the actions of the United States government. In fact, just two days after Polk took office, the Mexican ambassador returned home in protest over the Texas annexation. To fortify the American stance, Polk ordered General Zachary Taylor to position his troops between the Nueces River and the Rio Grande, in territory long disputed between Mexico and Texas. Polk believed that war was inevitable, but he wanted Mexico to fire the first shot. His provocation worked. On May 9, 1845, General Taylor sent word that his troops had been attacked. Polk decried that American blood had been shed on "American" soil. It was war.

The seeds of war had been planted many years earlier, however. The Red River had been established as the U.S. border in 1819 as part of the Adams-Onís Treaty, in which the United States recognized Spain's claim to Texas. After gaining independence from Spain, Mexico at first welcomed American settlers in Texas as a way to stabilize the border. However, by 1835 Americans in Texas outnumbered Mexicans in the region by ten to one. Tensions rose between Mexican authorities and the American settlers, tensions partially ignited by whether or not slavery could exist in Texas.

In 1834 dictator Antonio Lopez de Santa Anna gained control of Mexico's government. Resistance in both Mexico and Texas to Santa Anna's oppressive policies was immediate. By March 1836 Texans declared their independence from Mexico. In response, Santa Anna attacked a garrison of Texans who were fortified in an old mission called the Alamo. Santa Anna declared the Alamo a "glorious" victory. The call for revenge among Texans, however, was immediate. Hundreds of volunteer Texas fighters waged an assault on Santa Anna's forces near the San Jacinto River, all but destroying the Mexican army. Over the next year, American forces grew to over 100,000. For almost two years battles were fought from the Rio Grande, to California, to "the halls of Montezuma" in Mexico City.

On February 2, 1848, American envoy Nicholas P. Trist signed the Treaty of Guadalupe Hidalgo. It called for the United States to pay $15 million to Mexico as well as assume payment of $3.5 million in American citizens' claims against the government of Mexico. In return Mexico gave up all claims to Texas and agreed to the Rio Grande as its border with the United States. Moreover, Mexico ceded California and New Mexico to the United States. Privately Polk hoped to annex all of Mexico. Yet he knew such a contentious scheme meant possibly losing significant gains of land already slated to be annexed if the treaty became bogged down by disputes in Congress. To some, Polk appeared an insatiable expansionist who paved the way for westward growth. For others, the cost of the war did not justify the spoils.

American loses per thousand were the highest of any war (110 out of every 1,000 American combatants died). Military and naval expenditures totaled $98 million. The loss of land for Mexico was extensive, a full 55 percent of its territory. In the end, the Treaty of Guadalupe Hidalgo fulfilled a foreign policy formulated on the American quest for Manifest Destiny.

National Archives Document

The United States of America and the United Mexican States animated by a sincere desire to put an end to the calamities of the war which unhappily exists between the two Republics. . . .

ARTICLE I
There shall be firm and universal peace between the United States of America and the Mexican Republic, and between their respective countries, territories, cities, towns, and people, without exception of places or persons. . . .

ARTICLE V
The boundary line between the two Republics shall commence in the Gulf of Mexico, three leagues from land, opposite the mouth of the Rio Grande, otherwise called Rio Bravo del Norte . . . it is agreed that the said limit shall consist of a straight line drawn from the middle of the Rio Gila, where it unites with the Colorado, to a point on the coast of the Pacific Ocean. . . . The boundary line established by this article shall be religiously respected by each of the two republics. . . .

ARTICLE VIII
Mexicans now established in territories previously belonging to Mexico, and which remain for the future within the limits of the United States, as defined by the present treaty, shall be free to continue where they now reside, or to remove at any time to the Mexican Republic. . . .

ARTICLE XII
Immediately after the treaty shall have been duly ratified by the Government of the Mexican Republic, the sum of three millions of dollars shall be paid to the said Government by that of the United States, at the city of Mexico, in the gold or silver coin of Mexico. The remaining twelve millions of dollars shall be paid at the same place, and in the same coin, in annual installments of three millions of dollars each, together with interest on the same at the rate of six per centum per annum. . . .

ARTICLE XIII
The United States engage, moreover, to assume and pay to the claimants all the amounts now due them, and those hereafter to become due, by reason of the claims already liquidated and decided against the Mexican Republic. . . .

N. P. TRIST
LUIS P. CUEVAS
BERNARDO COUTO
MIGL. ATRISTAIN ✳

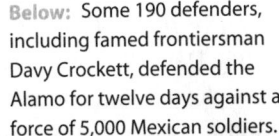

Below: Some 190 defenders, including famed frontiersman Davy Crockett, defended the Alamo for twelve days against a force of 5,000 Mexican soldiers.

Critical Thinking

Determine Point of View
Both Henry Clay and Daniel Webster, two leading politicians, denounced the Mexican War as an unwarranted act of aggression used as a ruse for an immoral land grab. How would you answer Clay's and Webster's accusations?

Draw Conclusions
How was Polk able to use the Monroe Doctrine to support his war plans?

Assess Significance
Though Daniel Webster disputed the war with Mexico, he recognized the trade potential and advantage of American ports on the Pacific Ocean. What role do you think economics played in the Mexican War?

Research and Writing

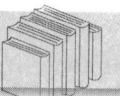

Biography
Research the life of Santa Anna, the self-proclaimed leader of Mexico. How did Santa Anna rise to power? Why was he exiled to Cuba? What bargain did he strike with President Polk? Why was he allowed to return to Mexico in 1846, only to take up arms once again against Americans? How did he become president of Mexico for a second time? What happened to Santa Anna after the defeat of his forces in the Mexican War?

Historical Interpretation
In 1846 David Wilmot, a representative from Pennsylvania, introduced a bill into Congress to prohibit slavery in any territory gained from Mexico as a result of the Mexican War. Known as the Wilmot Proviso, the failed bill exacerbated the sectional divisions within Congress and the nation. Though it was reintroduced into Congress several times, it continued to meet the same fate. Research the Wilmot Proviso. How did the Polk Administration respond to the proposed law? What were David Wilmot's beliefs regarding race and slavery? Why did the bill fail? Why was Polk accused of capitalizing on a mismanaged foreign policy as an excuse to provoke war with Mexico? In what way were the issues of slavery, expansion, political parties, and foreign policy interconnected?

Relating Events
In 1853 President Franklin Pierce appointed railroad promoter James Gadsden as Minister to Mexico. Soon Gadsden was negotiating with Mexican president Santa Anna for territory that would allow for a planned extension of a southern railroad route to the Pacific Ocean. At a cost of $10 million, the Gadsden Purchase involved a tract of approximately 19 million acres of Mexican land south of the U.S. - Mexican border (as established by the 1848 Treaty of Guadalupe Hidalgo). Research the events that prompted the Gadsden Purchase. Why was Santa Anna so willing to bargain land south of the Gila River? Why was the Gadsden Purchase Treaty unpopular in Mexico? How was the treaty viewed in the United States? Aside from the sale of land, what were the other provisions of the Gadsden Purchase Treaty?

1898 The De Lôme Letter

*"We must impose a harsh blockade [to] undermine
the peaceful population and decimate the Cuban army."*

—Breckenridge Memorandum, December 1897

Historical Background

ENRIQUE Dupuy de Lôme hadn't meant to spark an international incident. As Spain's minister to the United States, he was just expressing his assessment of Spanish involvement in Cuba, as well as his personal opinion of U.S. President William McKinley. It was a private letter intended for Don José Canelejas, the foreign minister of Spain. Yet, de Lôme's letter ignited a foreign relations bonfire for Spain, as well as inflame growing war sentiment in the United States. It would also bring a quick end to de Lôme's diplomatic career.

In his letter, de Lôme referred to President McKinley as "weak and a bidder for the admiration of the crowd besides being a would-be politician." Snatched from the mail by Cuban revolutionaries, de Lôme's letter was published in William Randolph Hearst's *New York Journal* on February 9, 1898, under the headline "The Worst Insult to the United States in Its History." The response to the letter was immediate. McKinley demanded an apology from the Spanish government. Politicians, such as assistant secretary of the navy and future president Theodore Roosevelt, clamored for war with Spain. And through it all, two competing newspapers, one owned by Hearst and the other by Joseph Pulitzer, reaped healthy profits, as readers sought sensationalized stories peddled by young New York newsboys.

Though de Lôme's letter ignited cries for war, the final break with Spain came six days later, on February 15, 1898, when the USS *Maine*, stationed in Spanish-controlled Havana Harbor, unexpectedly exploded. Some 266 sailors were lost as the battleship quickly sank in the harbor's waters. The pride of the American fleet, the *Maine* had sailed to Cuba the month before with de Lôme's knowledge, ostensibly as a sign of good will, although the actual intent was a show of U.S. strength. Despite the fact that an

investigation failed to prove that the Spanish had destroyed the ship, and though Spanish authorities had quickly rescued the surviving sailors, in the minds of Americans, Spain was the culprit. The *New York Journal* contributed to the country's war hysteria with headlines such as "The Destruction of the Warship Maine was the Work of an Enemy," and "Assistant Secretary Roosevelt was Convinced the Explosion of the War Ship was not an Accident," followed by "Naval Officers Think Maine was Destroyed by a Spanish Mine." For weeks the New York newspapers devoted page after page to the sinking of the *Maine*, as well as to the horrific conditions under which Spanish authorities forced the Cuban people to live. Two months later, on April 11, 1898, President McKinley stood before Congress to ask for "forcible intervention" by the United States into Cuba. On April 25, 1898, Congress declared war on Spain.

The Monroe Doctrine had guided American foreign policy throughout most of the nineteenth century. To that end, the United States had made offers to purchase Cuba, offers repeatedly declined by Spain. As an important center of trade and business, Cuba had remained under repressive Spanish domination during the 1800s. In the later half of the nineteenth century, however, American businesses had invested heavily in Cuba's profitable sugar industry. As a result, its sugar and cigar industries had become increasingly dependent on exports to the United States. The Wilson-Gorman Tariff in 1894 substantially raised duties on sugar, reducing sugar imports by half. The effect was devastating to the Cuban economy. Renewed uprisings against Spain and attacks on foreign-owned plantations did not escape the attention of Hearst and Pulitzer. Exploiting the rebellion in Cuba as a way of increasing their own profits, their newspapers' *yellow journalism* prompted an

American call for intervention in Cuba not only on humanitarian grounds, but also as a way to protect American businesses. De Lôme's letter and the sinking of the USS *Maine* provided the provocation for war.

The Spanish-American War lasted barely four months. Following the decimation of the Spanish fleet by a much stronger American navy, and the subsequent fall of Santiago, Spain called for peace negotiations. An armistice was signed between the United States and Spain on August 12, 1898. As a result of the peace agreement (Treaty of Paris), Spain relinquished sovereignty over Cuba. Additionally, the United States was allowed to acquire Puerto Rico, as well as the Philippines and Guam in the Pacific Ocean.

NATIONAL ARCHIVES DOCUMENT

Translation of letter written by Senor Don Enrique Dupuy de Lôme to Senor Don José Canelejas

My distinguished and dear friend:

. . . Besides the ingrained and inevitable bluntness with which is repeated all that the press and public opinion in Spain have said about Weyler, it once more shows what McKinley is, weak and a bidder for the admiration of the crowd besides being a would-be politician who tries to leave a door open behind himself while keeping on good terms with the jingoes of his party. . . .

I do not think sufficient attention has been paid to the part England is playing.

Nearly all the newspaper rabble that swarms in your hotels are Englishmen, and while writing for the Journal they are also correspondents of the most influential journals and reviews of London. It has been so ever since this thing began.

As I look at it, England's only object is that the Americans should amuse themselves with us and leave her alone, and if there should be a war, that would the better stave off the conflict which she dreads but which will never come about. . . .

So, Amblard is coming. I think he devotes himself too much to petty politics, and we have got to do something very big or we shall fail. . . .

Ever your attached friend and servant,

ENRIQUE DUPUY de LÔME. ✳

Below: A depiction of the USS *Maine* exploding.

Critical Thinking

Draw Conclusions
What conclusion can be drawn about de Lôme's feelings about Great Britain from his letter?

Assess Significance
On April 19, 1898, the Teller Amendment provided the justification and authorization to wage war against Spain. Included in the Amendment was the pledge "That the United States hereby disclaims any disposition or intention to exercise sovereignty, jurisdiction, or control over said Island except for the pacification thereof, and asserts its determination, when that is accomplished, to leave the government and control of the Island to its people." Why do you think the Teller Amendment was included as part of Congress's war resolution?

Determine Point of View
Public figures are used to being criticized. Why, then, do you think McKinley took such offense at comments made by de Lôme?

Research and Writing

Analysis
The term "yellow journalism" had its origins in a comic strip character clothed in yellow robes, called "The Yellow Kid." The creation of artist Richard Felton Outcault, the cartoon character appeared in rival New York newspapers owned by Pulitzer and Hearst. The cartoon characterization, found in the competing publications and drawn by competing cartoonists, came to represent the irresponsible, sensationalized, and fiercely competitive journalistic style of Pulitzer and Hearst.

Research tactics used by Pulitzer and Hearst to increase newspaper readership during the late 1800s. What role did yellow journalism play in provoking a war with Spain? What purpose did Hearst have in sending artist Frederic Remington and author Stephen Crane to Cuba? What conclusions can be drawn concerning the power of the media in shaping public opinion?

Link to the Past
The festering rebellion in Cuba prompted Spain to send 150,000 troops to the island in 1896. In order to contain potential insurgents, General Valeriano Weyler began relocating Cuban agricultural workers in relocation camps. General Weyler's strategy was to isolate individuals to minimize contact between rebel groups. The disease-ridden camps, however, became death camps for more than 200,000. General Weyler was branded a "butcher" by the American press.

In 1941, following the Japanese attack on Pearl Harbor, the American military set up relocation camps in several states including Arizona, California, Nevada, and as far east as Arkansas. Individuals of Japanese ancestry were removed from their homes and businesses and forced to live in these barbed-wire fenced, make-shift camps. Research the Japanese Internment Camps. What was the camps' purpose? What were conditions like in the camps? How did they affect the lives of Japanese-Americans? Why were detainees asked to take a Loyalty Oath? How did the United States government justify the camps? What prompted Roosevelt advisor, Milton S. Eisenhower, to write in *The President is Calling*, "How could such a tragedy have occurred in a democratic society that prides itself on individual rights and freedoms"?

Historical Interpretation
Theodore Roosevelt's Rough Riders fought the Battle of San Juan Hill in Cuba alongside the U.S. Tenth Cavalry, an African-American unit. The cavalry's bravery led to five Medals of Honor and 26 Certificates of Merit. Theodore Roosevelt's appreciation for their valiant efforts in combat prompted him to commend them as "…brave men worthy of respect. I don't think any Rough Rider will ever forget the tie that binds us to the Tenth cavalry." Research the Tenth Cavalry. What role did it play in the Battle of San Juan Hill?

1901 The Platt Amendment

*"Once the United States is in Cuba,
who will get her out?"*

–José Martí

Historical Background

THE lifelong hope of José Martí was for a free and independent Cuba. Prior to the Spanish-American War, Cuban revolutionary Martí believed that U.S. overtures to help liberate Cuba from Spain were, in truth, a prelude to America's imperialist plans for the island. Having lived in the United States, and aware of American business interests in Cuba, he was concerned that American intervention would quickly be followed by American domination. Martí was not alone in this belief. In fact, the Teller Amendment of 1898 was an attempt to placate those in Congress who opposed the potential annexation of Cuba.

On January 1, 1899, the United States established military control of Cuba. Years of Spanish domination and revolution had left Cuba a war-torn, devastated, and economically depleted island. In 1900 its population was 1.5 million, some 200,000 less than in 1895. Disease, poor sanitation, the lack of housing, and limited education were major problems. Cuba's infrastructure—its schools, roads, railroads, hospitals, and other public works projects—needed to be planned and built. Furthermore, there was the overriding question of Cuban sovereignty. In response, a transitional government was formed to address the immediate needs of the Cuban people.

From the start, President McKinley's administration recognized the political and economic difficulties of annexing Cuba. Not only would annexation be costly, but Cubans strongly opposed any U.S. plans for the annexation of their country. Moreover, entrenched racial prejudice among Americans drove strong opposition to the idea of annexing an island whose population was mostly of African-American and Hispanic descent. However, Cuba's location was strategically important for the United States. American businesses were heavily invested in Cuba as well. McKinley needed a plan that would satisfy both those who favored and those who opposed Cuban annexation. The resulting compromise, contrived by Secretary of War Elihu Root, was attached to the 1901 Army Appropriations Bill. Known as the Platt Amendment, after Senator Orville Platt of Connecticut, its sponsor, the amendment granted Cuba limited independence but also made it a protectorate of the United States.

The United States government insisted that the amendment be incorporated into Cuba's new constitution, making it clear that, should the amendment not be included, American trade and Cuban independence were both in doubt. Moreover, American military forces would remain in Cuba. With virtually no recourse available, Cuba ratified its constitution in 1901, with the Platt Amendment attached as an addendum. In 1903 the Platt Amendment became the basis for a permanent treaty between Cuba and the United States. Thirty-one years later, President Franklin D. Roosevelt signed a new treaty with Cuba which, in effect, repealed the Platt Amendment. However, under the 1934 treaty, the United States retained its lease agreement for a "coaling and naval" station, today known as the United States Naval Station at Guantanamo Bay, for an annual rental fee of $4,085.

NATIONAL ARCHIVES DOCUMENT

Whereas the Congress of the United States of America, by an Act approved March 2, 1901, provided as follows:

. . . the President is hereby authorized to "leave the government and control of the island of Cuba to its people" so soon as a government shall have been established in said island under a constitution which, either as a part thereof or in an ordinance appended thereto, shall define the future relations of the United States with Cuba, substantially as follows:

I. That the government of Cuba shall never enter into any treaty or other compact with any foreign power or powers which will impair or tend to impair the independence of Cuba, nor in any manner authorize or permit any foreign power or powers to obtain by colonization or for military or naval purposes. . . .

II. That said government shall not assume or contract any public debt. . . .

III. That the government of Cuba consents that the United States may exercise the right to intervene for the preservation of Cuban independence, the maintenance of a government adequate for the protection of life, property, and individual liberty, and for discharging the obligations with respect to Cuba. . . .

V. That the government of Cuba will execute, and as far as necessary extend, the plans already devised or other plans to be mutually agreed upon, for the sanitation of the cities of the island, to the end that a recurrence of epidemic and infectious diseases may be prevented, thereby assuring protection to the people and commerce of Cuba, as well as to the commerce of the southern ports of the United States and the people residing therein.

VII. That to enable the United States to maintain the independence of Cuba, and to protect the people thereof, as well as for its own defense, the government of Cuba will sell or lease to the United States lands necessary for coaling or naval stations at certain specified points to be agreed upon with the President of the United States.

VIII. That by way of further assurance the government of Cuba will embody the foregoing provisions in a permanent treaty with the United States. ✳

Below: Map of Cuba showing the location of Guantanamo Bay naval base.

Critical Thinking

Classify Information
Which provisions in the Platt Amendment benefited Cuba? Which provisions benefited the United States? Which were mutually beneficial?

Assess Significance
Of what significance was Article VIII of the Platt Amendment?

Analyze Cause and Effect
In what way did the Platt Amendment establish the United States as a protectorate of Cuba?

Research and Writing

Analysis
Research the territorial gains of the United States in the late 1800s. What did President McKinley mean when he stated in September 1899, "And so it has come to pass … in a few short months we have become a world power"?

Historical Interpretation
Puerto Rico had been acquired by the United States as part of the 1898 Treaty of Paris that ended the war with Spain. In 1900 the Foraker Act established Puerto Rico as an "unincorporated territory" of the United States. Puerto Rico's civilian government consisted of a governor (appointed by the President of the United States), a Supreme Court, and a House of Representatives. Moreover, all U.S. laws applied to the people of Puerto Rico, though citizenship would not be granted to Puerto Ricans until 1917. The Foraker Act prompted a series of lawsuits heard by the United States Supreme Court. Known as the "Insular Cases," the opinions rendered by the Court would define the rights of individuals living in American territories beyond the U.S. coastline. Research the Supreme Court cases of *De Lima v. Bidwell* (1901), *Downes v. Bidwell* (1901), and *Balzac v. Porto Rico* (1922). What were the issues in each case? How was each resolved? What was the impact of each decision?

Link to the Past
Guantanamo Bay is located in Oriente Province in the southeast corner of Cuba. The 1903 Lease Agreement between the United States and Cuba granted the United States

> the right to use and occupy the waters adjacent to said areas of land and water, and to improve and deepen the entrances thereto and the anchorages therein, and generally to do any and all things necessary to fit the premises for use as coaling or naval stations only, and for no other purpose.

Over the years, Guantanamo Bay served as a strategic base for the United States Navy. Following the September 11, 2001, terrorist attack on New York City, Guantanamo Bay became a detention center for suspected terrorists from several countries. On June 28, 2004, the United States Supreme Court ruled in *Rasul v. Bush* that "United States courts have jurisdiction to consider challenges to the legality of the detention of foreign nationals captured abroad in connection with hostilities and incarcerated at Guantanamo Bay." Research the status of Guantanamo Bay? Why is the 1903 Lease Agreement involved in questions concerning the detention of terrorists at the naval base? What is the effect of the *Rasul v. Bush* ruling?

1905 The Roosevelt Corollary to the Monroe Doctrine

"Speak softly and carry a big stick; you will go far."

—Proverb popularized by Theodore Roosevelt

Historical Background

I N 1898 Theodore Roosevelt advised a group of Massachusetts school children "...to do something worthwhile, that you are going to work hard and do the things you set out to do." It was, in essence, his personal credo. From western cowboy to President of the United States, Roosevelt lived his life with gusto, expecting only the best from himself and everyone around him. In an 1897 letter to John Hay, then ambassador to Great Britain, Roosevelt wrote,

> Is America a weakling, to shrink from the work of the great world powers? No! The young giant of the West stands on a continent and clasps the crest of an ocean in either hand. Our nation, glorious in youth and strength, looks into the future with eager eyes and rejoices as a strong man to run a race.

Roosevelt viewed the United States as he viewed himself: strong, vibrant, and unlimited in its potential. Thus, when he became president upon the assassination of McKinley, he brought to the White House the resolve to establish that the United States was the most powerful country in the world—that it would, as he often said, "walk softly, but carry a big stick." How better to prove America's might than to do what the French hadn't been able to—build a canal through Panama, a canal that would shave almost 8,000 miles from the lengthy crossing from the Atlantic to the Pacific Oceans.

From 1881 to 1887, at a cost of more than $300 million and a loss of almost 20,000 men, most of whom had succumbed to malaria and yellow fever, France had attempted to dig a six-mile-wide, sea-level canal through an isthmus connecting the Atlantic and Pacific Ocean, an area under Columbia's control at the time. Ultimately, French investors offered to sell their stake in the canal project to the United States. Secretary of State Hay offered Columbia $10 million and another $250,000

annual rent to purchase rights to build the canal across Panama. However, the Colombian Senate insisted on a payment of $25 million, a response Roosevelt found intolerable. Meanwhile, French engineer Philippe Bunau-Varilla, who was heavily invested in the French canal project, in concert with Panamanian investors, helped to organize a Panamanian revolt against Columbia, aided by the presence of the USS *Nashville* off shore. Within days, a pro-United States treaty was signed between Secretary Hay and the self-appointed Panamanian ambassador, Bunau-Varilla. The Hay-Bunau-Varilla Treaty provided for United States sovereignty over a planned ten-mile-wide Canal Zone for 100 years.

Two other international incidents in the early 1900s solidified Roosevelt's foreign policy regarding the western hemisphere. One was the default on debts owed by Venezuela to Great Britain and Germany, with a resulting naval blockade of Venezuela by the two nations. Concerned that the blockade would lead to war and the subsequent acquisition of Venezuelan land by Germany, Roosevelt interceded with his own threat of naval intervention. An international tribunal settled the debt repayment issue in 1904. Likewise, social unrest and the lack of payment of foreign debts provided Roosevelt with the opportunity to intervene in the foreign affairs of the Dominican Republic. The end result was a 1905 agreement between the two countries that, in effect, placed the United States as the de facto administrator of the Dominican Republic's finances until 1911.

To justify his actions toward the Dominican Republic and other countries in the western hemisphere, Roosevelt issued a corollary to the Monroe Doctrine in his December 1904 annual message to Congress. While the Monroe Doctrine had warned Europe to avoid intervention in the

Latin American countries, Roosevelt's corollary to it justified an increased military role in Central and South American affairs by the United States. As president, Roosevelt's "walk softly and carry a big stick" philosophy was enumerated when he explained to Congress that, ". . . in the Western Hemisphere the adherence of the United States to the Monroe Doctrine may force the United States, however reluctantly . . . to the exercise of an international police power. . . ."

NATIONAL ARCHIVES DOCUMENT

(Excerpted from Theodore Roosevelt's Annual Message to Congress, December 6, 1904)

. . . The steady aim of this Nation, as of all enlightened nations, should be to strive to bring ever nearer the day when there shall prevail throughout the world the peace of justice. . . . The goal to set before us as a nation, the goal which should be set before all mankind, is the attainment of the peace of justice, of the peace which comes when each nation is not merely safe-guarded in its own rights, but scrupulously recognizes and performs its duty toward others . . . The eternal vigilance which is the price of liberty must be exercised, sometimes to guard against outside foes; although of course far more often to guard against our own selfish or thoughtless shortcomings.

It is not true that the United States feels any land hunger or entertains any projects as regards the other nations of the Western Hemisphere save such as are for their welfare. All that this country desires is to see the neighboring countries stable, orderly, and prosperous. Any country whose people conduct themselves well can count upon our hearty friendship. If a nation shows that it knows how to act with reasonable efficiency and decency in social and political matters, if it keeps order and pays its obligations, it need fear no interference from the United States. . . .

. . . If every country washed by the Caribbean Sea would show the progress in stable and just civilization which with the aid of the Platt Amendment Cuba has shown since our troops left the island, and which so many of the republics in both Americas are constantly and brilliantly showing, all question of interference by this Nation with their affairs would be at an end. . . . ✳

Below: A political cartoon depicting President Theodore Roosevelt's "Big Stick" diplomacy. Roosevelt justified U.S. policing power of the Western Hemisphere as a necessary part of his Corollary to the Monroe Doctrine.

THE WORLD'S CONSTABLE.

Critical Thinking

Compare and Contrast

Compare the tenets of the Monroe Doctrine with the foreign policy expressed in Roosevelt's corollary to the Monroe Doctrine.

Assess Significance

In his 1904 annual address, Roosevelt postulated that "Chronic wrongdoing, or an impotence which results in a general loosening of the ties of civilized society, may in America, as elsewhere, ultimately require intervention by some civilized nation...." In regard to America, he noted that "the crime of lynching, is never more than sporadic...." What was the state of American racial and cultural prejudice in the 1900s?

Classify Information

How does Roosevelt's corollary to the Monroe Doctrine portray United States foreign policy as benevolent in intent and necessary as a deterrent to war?

Research and Writing
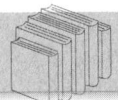

Historical Interpretation

Access and read the entire transcript of the Roosevelt Corollary to the Monroe Doctrine. Research the events in the Dominican Republic that led Roosevelt to issue this corollary. What monetary issues prompted intervention by the United States? How did the United States become a de facto administrator of the Dominican Republic? Why were concerns expressed in Congress, as well as by the Dominican people, over the possible annexation of the Dominican Republic by the United States? Do you think American intervention in the Dominican Republic improved that country's economic and political conditions? Why or why not?

Link to the Past

Building the Panama Canal was an extraordinary engineering feat initiated by backdoor diplomacy and accomplished through the toil of thousands of "gold" and "silver" workers, at a total cost of $350 million and the deaths of over 5,000 men. The result was a highly strategic waterway used for trade and military operations, and, by the provisions of the Hay-Bunau-Varilla Treaty, virtually owned by the United States government. By 1920 over 5,000 ships traversed the locks of the Panama Canal each year. In 1921 President Warren Harding paid Columbia $25 million, ostensibly to make amends for "misunderstandings" that led to Panamanian independence in November 1903.

On September 7, 1977, President Jimmy Carter signed the Panama Canal Treaty and Neutrality Treaty, repealing the 1903 Hay-Bunau-Varilla Treaty. Research the events leading to the Hay-Bunau-Varilla Treaty. Write a synopsis of the building of the Panama Canal. Why were workers termed "gold" and "silver"? Explain the strategic importance of the Panama Canal. Discuss the impact of the 1977 treaty.

Biography

Theodore Roosevelt led a colorful life which included, among other roles, a stint as a rancher following the deaths of his mother and wife, commissioner of the New York City Police Board, assistant secretary of the navy, and twenty-sixth president of the United States. Research Roosevelt's life. What did he feel were his greatest accomplishments? In 1907 he emphasized that "playgrounds should be provided for every child as much as schools. This means that they must be distributed over the cities in such a way as to be within walking distance of every boy and girl, as most children can not afford to pay carfare." What were some other ways Roosevelt addressed the social needs of the time? What was his legacy?

1917 The Zimmermann Telegram

*"There is such a thing as a nation being so right
that it does not need to convince others by force."*

–WOODROW WILSON

HISTORICAL BACKGROUND

IN contrast to Theodore Roosevelt's enthusiasm for naval might and war, President Woodrow Wilson was an idealist, entering office as a peacekeeper who firmly believed the application of moral principals could be used to mediate differences. His personal mandate was to promote democracy throughout the world, postulating that all people were capable of self-government if given the opportunity. Wilson believed that America should lead by example, apply itself as a role model of democracy, and couple that with the conviction that foreign governments should be able to deal with their own problems without American military involvement. From the onset of his presidency, however, those beliefs would be tested, beginning with ongoing rebellion in Mexico and the islands of the Caribbean.

In August 1914, war erupted in Europe, a war based on secret alliances and fueled by nationalism, international rivalries, and advances in weapons technology. The Great War, later termed World War I, began with the assassination of Austrian archduke Franz Ferdinand by Gavrilo Princip, a Serbian nationalist. The assassination precipitated a chain reaction of events, polarizing the two great alliance systems that existed in Europe: the Central Powers, led by Germany and Austria-Hungary, and the Allied Powers, led by Great Britain, Russia, and France. Wilson declared that the United States would be neutral in the conflict, though privately he was determined to aid Great Britain. American exports to the Allies increased significantly as the war continued into 1915. To stall any supplies headed to Germany, Great Britain declared the North Sea a war zone, littered the waters with mines, and announced it would seize ships carrying goods to enemy countries. Germany responded that the

waters surrounding Great Britain were a war zone too, and that it would sink any vessel supplying the Allies, even if it flew the flag of a neutral country.

Germany's means of enforcing this threat was a new weapon called a U-boat (short for "underwater boat"), or submarine, that was able to operate virtually undetected by the British navy. Germany had published warnings in American newspapers that it would sink the *Lusitania*, a British ocean liner suspected by the Germans of clandestinely transporting munitions, should it attempt to cross the Atlantic. Undeterred, the *Lusitania* set sail from New York on its return voyage to Great Britain. On May 7, 1915, a U-boat torpedoed the ship just off the British coast. It exploded and sank within minutes, carrying almost 2,000 passengers and crew to their deaths. Among them were 128 Americans. Former president Roosevelt declared the sinking an act of piracy. Americans were outraged. Wilson demanded and received assurances from the German government that in the future merchant vessels would not be sunk without warning as long as they did not try to escape.

In response to a dwindling military force, the 1916 National Defense Act expanded the military by authorizing a National Guard and increasing the size of the regular army from 90,000 to 223,000. The 1916 Naval Construction Act assigned up to $6 million for the building of new warships. Meanwhile, Europe was entrenched in a war whose devastation was compounded by the advancement of weapons technology and the use of chemical warfare. At the Battle of Somme in July 1916, for example, 20,000 British soldiers were killed and another 40,000 wounded in less that twenty-four hours. By November 1916 Allied forces had suffered 600,000 casualties at Somme.

The 1916 presidential election touted Wilson as the president who "kept us out of war." Due to his social reforms, and because many Americans were still divided on whether America should enter the conflict, Wilson won re-election by a narrow margin. In his 1917 Second Inaugural Address, Wilson stated,

> We stand firm in armed neutrality since it seems that in no other way we can demonstrate what it is we insist upon and cannot forget . . . We desire neither conquest nor advantage. We wish nothing that can be had only at the cost of another people . . . that governments derive all their just powers from the consent of the governed. . . .

Wilson, though publicly continuing to assert neutrality, privately recognized that America would eventually be drawn into the war. In February 1917, faced with a German declaration that all vessels in its established war zone were targets once again, Wilson broke off diplomatic relations with that nation. On February 23, the British delivered to President Wilson an intercepted telegram written by German Foreign Secretary Arthur Zimmermann to the German ambassador to Mexico. In it Zimmermann proposed an alliance with Mexico, should the United States abandon its neutrality. As an enticement, he offered the return of land Mexico lost in its war with the United States in the 1840s. News of the telegram was published in the American press. With anti-Mexican and anti-German sentiment strong among Americans, the Zimmermann Telegram forced the hand of Wilson's administration and pushed America even closer to war.

NATIONAL ARCHIVES DOCUMENT

(Decoded message text of the Zimmermann Telegram)
FROM 2nd from London # 5747.

Below: The Zimmermann Telegram.

"We intend to begin on the first of February unrestricted submarine warfare. We shall endeavor in spite of this to keep the United States of America neutral. In the event of this not succeeding, we make Mexico a proposal or alliance on the following basis: make war together, make peace together, generous financial support and an understanding on our part that Mexico is to reconquer the lost territory in Texas, New Mexico, and Arizona. The settlement in detail is left to you. You will inform the President of the above most secretly as soon as the outbreak of war with the United States of America is certain and add the suggestion that he should, on his own initiative, invite Japan to immediate adherence and at the same time mediate between Japan and ourselves. Please call the President's attention to the fact that the ruthless employment of our submarines now offers the prospect of compelling England in a few months to make peace."

Signed, ZIMMERMANN. ✳

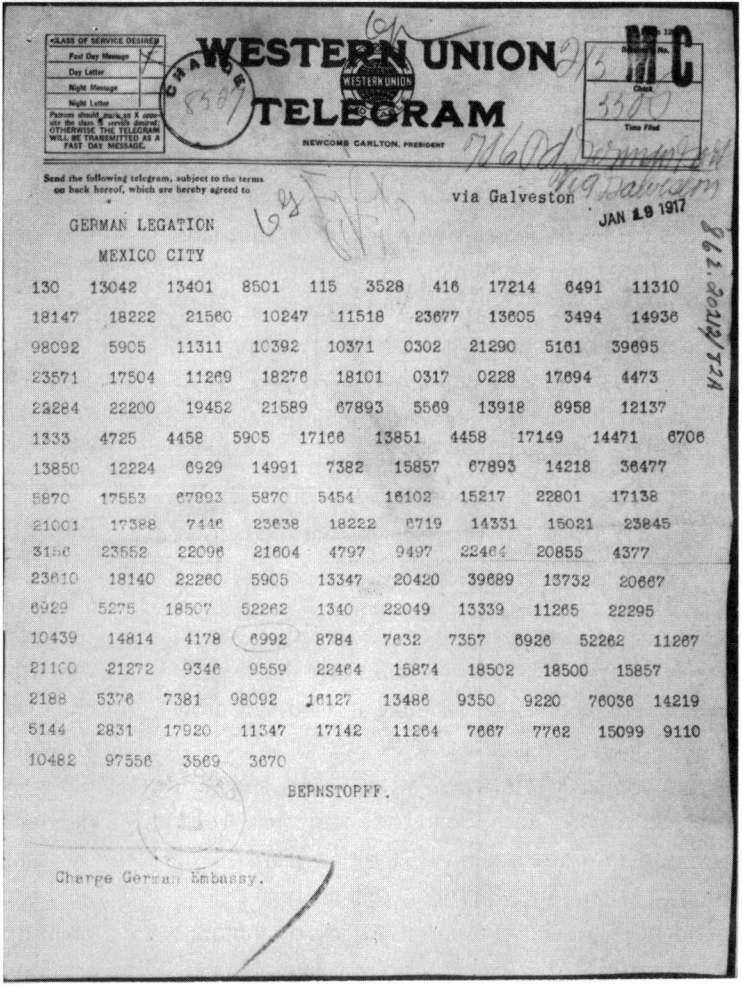

Critical Thinking

Determine Point of View

What do you think Wilson meant when he stated in his 1917 Inaugural Address, "We stand firm in armed neutrality since it seems that in no other way we can demonstrate what it is we insist upon and cannot forget"?

Make Predictions

Based on the Zimmermann Telegram, how did Germany view the outcome of the Great War? What collaborative plans did Germany have? Why did Germany expect a swift end to the war?

Draw Conclusions

America provided extended loans and supplied arms and other supplies to both Great Britain and Germany, though its exports to Great Britain far surpassed those to Germany. In your opinion, does the exportation of supplies to warring nations maintain or contradict a country's neutrality?

Research and Writing

Historical Interpretation

By 1910 more than 32 million individuals living in America were first- or second-generation immigrants. This represented approximately one-third of the total population of the United States. Millions of European immigrants entered the United States through Ellis Island, located in New York Harbor. Approximately 5,000 immigrants per day were processed at Ellis Island in the early 1900s. Research the history of Ellis Island. From where did most immigrants originate? What was Ellis Island like? Who was required to pass through the inspection process at Ellis Island? What was the process like? Why were only steerage passengers processed? What difficulties did immigrants face upon entering the United States? What political impact do you think immigrants had on America's desire to enter the Great War?

Relating Events

In 1913 General Victoriano Huerta overthrew President Francisco Madero and assumed control of the Mexican government. Soon after, Madero was killed. Woodrow Wilson refused to recognize Huerta as president of Mexico and, backed by an American naval presence near Veracruz, provided tacit support of another rebellion led by Venustiano Carranza. In 1915 the United States recognized Carranza as president of Mexico, a presidency filled with civil unrest. Attacks by another revolutionary leader, Pancho Villa, against Americans prompted President Wilson in early 1916 to dispatch an army of over 10,000 soldiers, commanded by General John Pershing, to capture him. Though in exile, Huerta, bolstered by the clandestine support of Germany, secretly planned a return to power in Mexico. Research Mexican history from the overthrow of President Porfirio Díaz in 1911 thorough the Zimmerman Telegram. What role did the United States government play in the politics of this time? Explain how events in Mexico provided the political climate for Germany's overtures enumerated in the Zimmerman Telegram.

Biography

The election of 1912 pitted New Jersey governor Woodrow Wilson, a Democrat, against Republican presidential incumbent William Howard Taft and former president Theodore Roosevelt, nominated by the progressive "Bull Moose" Party. Wilson entered office with an agenda centered on political and social reforms. Domestically, he reasoned that the federal government had a duty, through reform-minded legislation, to shield Americans from the impact of the industrial and social changes engulfing the country. In foreign relations, Wilson denounced former president Taft's "dollar diplomacy," declaring that the federal government's role did not include support of "special groups or interests" overseas. Research the life of Woodrow Wilson. How did he rise to the presidency? What influenced his political philosophy toward domestic and foreign affairs? With war raging in Europe, why did he caution Americans to be "impartial in thought"?

1917 Declaration of War Against Germany

"The world must be made safe for democracy."

—WOODROW WILSON

HISTORICAL BACKGROUND

SMOLDERING hostilities toward Germany as a result of the Zimmermann Telegram were exacerbated by the sinking of five American merchant vessels in March 1917. President Woodrow Wilson responded by issuing an executive order that allowed for the arming of U.S. merchant ships. The Germans had reasoned that the surest way to involve America in the Great War, as well as curtail supplies to Britain and France, was to have its U-boats target the American merchant marine. It worked. The ability of submarines to elude the U.S. Navy made Americans feel vulnerable to attack not only on the high seas but also at its shores. War fever ran high. The threat to exports, the safety of vessels at sea, and the possibility that the Allies might be defeated prompted Wilson to go before Congress on April 2, 1917, and ask for a declaration of war against Germany. A war resolution passed the Senate by a vote of 82 to 6 and the House of Representatives, 373 to 50.

With the war declaration behind it, Congress took up the burden of financing America's war effort. The social reforms instituted by Wilson's administration came to a halt as the country mobilized for war. American forces were woefully small. Planes—potent weapons that made their debut during the Great War—gas masks to counter the threat of a battlefield chemical attack, machine guns, uniforms, and just about every military supply essential to war was needed, and needed quickly. To pay for these needs Congress increased certain taxes, imposed an income tax on workers, and encouraged the purchase of government bonds, called Liberty Bonds. Americans were also encouraged to eat corn, oats, and garden-grown foods to save wheat, meat, and sugar "for the boys on the front." Wheatless Mondays and Wednesdays, meatless Tuesdays, and porkless Thursdays were promoted by the United States Food Administration. At sea, merchant vessels were protected from U-boat torpedo attacks by a new form of naval defense—the convoy, a system whereby naval destroyers sailed alongside a line of merchant vessels, placing the destroyers in harm's way as a means of protection for the merchant ships.

Conscription had been a controversial issue prior to America's involvement in the war. Yet, the nation needed soldiers. In May 1917, Congress passed the Selective Service Act authorizing the president to draft men into the military. Further legislation mandated that enlistees and draftees serve for the length of the war, with that service to end four months after peace was declared by the president. Soon, posters were seen everywhere of a stern-looking *Uncle Sam* admonishing "I Want You for U.S. Army," encouraging young men to seek out the nearest recruiting office. This effort prompted 24 million men to register for the draft, as required by law. The government inducted 2.8 million of these registrants into the army. Another 2 million Americans voluntarily served in the armed forces during the war.

The exodus of men from industrial jobs to military ones created an employment void filled by women, African-Americans, and ethnic minorities. In what has been termed the "Great Migration," over 400,000 African-Americans from the Deep South moved north to seek jobs in industry, sparking racial tensions in northern communities. Anti-German sentiment pervaded the country as well. In addition, the government actively pursued court action against individuals who defied the draft or impeded the war effort. According to the Espionage Act passed in 1917,

> whoever when the United States is at war, shall willfully cause or attempt to cause insubordination, disloyalty, mutiny, refusal of duty, in the military or naval forces of the United States, or shall willfully obstruct the recruiting or enlistment service of the United States, to the injury of the service or of the United States, shall be punished by a

fine of not more than $10,000 or imprisonment for not more than twenty years, or both . . . Whoever harbours or conceals any person who he knows, or has reasonable grounds to believe or suspect, has committed, or is about to commit, an offence under this title shall be punished by a fine of not more than $10,000 or by imprisonment for not more than two years, or both.

Clearly, the United States was determined to win the war in Europe at all costs. However, Americans at war soon learned of its unpredictability, of its never-ending horror, and of its cost in human life. The Great War was fought with new, highly destructive technology, with new rules of engagement, and, ultimately, with an effort among world leaders to find a way to end the possibility of future wars. With some 10 million killed and 20 million wounded, World War I was to be the "war to end all wars."

NATIONAL ARCHIVES DOCUMENT

Joint Address to Congress Leading to a Declaration of War Against Germany

ADDRESS:
GENTLEMEN OF THE CONGRESS:

On the third of February last I officially laid before you the extraordinary announcement of the Imperial German Government that on and after the first day of February it was its purpose to put aside all restraints of law or of humanity and use its submarines to sink every vessel that sought to approach either the ports of Great Britain and Ireland or the western coasts of Europe or any of the ports controlled by the enemies of Germany within the Mediterranean. . . . The new policy has swept every restriction aside. Vessels of every kind, whatever their flag, their character, their cargo, their destination, their errand, have been ruthlessly sent to the bottom: without warning and without thought of help or mercy for those on board, the vessels of friendly neutrals along with those of belligerents. . . .

When I addressed the Congress on the twenty-sixth of February last I thought that it would suffice to assert our neutral rights with arms, our right to use the seas against unlawful interference, our right to keep our people safe against unlawful violence. But armed neutrality, it now appears, is impracticable. Because submarines are in effect outlaws when used as the German submarines have been used against merchant shipping. . . .

With a profound sense of the solemn and even tragical character of the step I am taking and of the grave responsibilities which it involves, but in unhesitating obedience to what I deem my constitutional duty, I advise that the Congress declare the recent course of the Imperial German Government to be in fact nothing less than war against the government and people of the United States. . . .

We desire no conquest, no dominion. We seek no indemnities for ourselves, no material compensation for the sacrifices we shall freely make. We are but one of the champions of the rights of mankind. We shall be satisfied when those rights have been made as secure as the faith and the freedom of nations can make them. . . .

But the right is more precious than peace, and we shall fight for the things which we have always carried nearest our hearts,—for democracy. . . . ✳

Below: Posters like the one below encouraged Americans to buy war bonds to support American military involvement in World War I.

Critical Thinking

Analyze Cause and Effect
To what did President Wilson attribute the cause of America's entry into the war?

Draw Conclusions
Why do you think there was no great political fallout for Wilson in 1917, as the president who "kept us out of war" became the president leading the country into war?

Determine Point of View
What did Wilson view as the intent of America's entry into the war in Europe?

Research and Writing

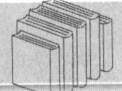

Historical Interpretation
Not everyone agreed with Congress's war resolution. Wisconsin Senator Robert La Follette openly opposed the war. Socialist Eugene V. Debs urged men to refuse to obey the federal conscription order. As a result of his outspoken, antimilitary beliefs, Debs was prosecuted under the Espionage Act and sentenced to jail. In Chicago, leaders of the Industrial Workers of the World were placed on trial and jailed for draft evasion and alleged antiwar activities. Research the actions taken to protest America's involvement in the Great War. Why did La Follette oppose the war? Why did Debs oppose the war? What actions were taken by the federal government to curtail antiwar activities? What actions were taken by the federal government to propagandize the war? How did Americans respond?

Relating Events
World War I saw the active enlistment of 13,000 women into the Marines and the Navy. Women also served in the Coast Guard and the Signal Corps. In all, 30,000 women served during the Great War to "free men to fight." Research the advent of active military service for women. What were the Army and Navy Nurse Corps? Where did women serve during World War I? In what capacity did they serve? What were their experiences? With what awards were they presented? What social barriers did they break?

Link to the Past
Congress passed the first draft bill in March 1863, as a temporary measure to provide troops for Union armies during the Civil War. Conscription was renewed in 1917. Research the history of the draft in the United States. What have been the arguments for conscription? What have been the arguments against it? How did personal wealth factor into the conscription process? When and why was the Selective Service started? How was the draft related to the adoption of the Twenty-sixth Amendment to the United States Constitution? When and why did the United States initiate an all-volunteer military? How has it changed the focus of the armed forces? How successful has it been in providing a viable military force?

1918 Woodrow Wilson's Fourteen Points

"I have loved but one flag and I can not share that devotion and give affection to the mongrel banner invented for a league."

–HENRY CABOT LODGE

HISTORICAL BACKGROUND

IN November 1917, Vladimir Lenin, head of the Bolshevik party, staged a successful coup against the provisional Russian government. Soon after, the Russian Soviet Congress elected Lenin to head the newly formed communist government. On March 3, 1918, the Central Powers and Russia's new government signed the Treaty of Brest-Litovsk. The Treaty of Brest-Litovsk signaled an end to the war between Russia and the Central Powers on the Eastern Front. President Woodrow Wilson viewed the subsequent realignment of nations in Eastern Europe with growing concern. To that end, Wilson, the scholar and the idealist, penned a plan for the peaceful settlement of differences between the Allied and the Central Powers. Known as Wilson's Fourteen Points, the plan captured the essence of Wilson's idealism—self-determination, democracy, and the right of a country to control its destiny.

Wilson delivered his peace proposal to a joint session of Congress on January 8, 1918, believing that his plan was the only one palatable to both the Allied and Central Powers. The Fourteen Points established the parameters for the withdrawal of forces from occupied lands. It established a new world order that called for freedom of the seas, renewed free trade, a reduction of arms, and an end to secret alliances. The keystone of Wilson's plan was Point 14, the establishment of a "general association of nations . . . for the purpose of affording mutual guarantees of political independence and territorial integrity. . . ." Wilson was resolute. He believed a League of Nations was the only way to ensure international stability and a lasting peace.

By May 1918 a million American soldiers were fighting alongside the French and British, and making a difference. Allied forces repelled German forces at Cantigny and Belleau Wood. The Second Battle of the Marne on July 15, 1918, became a turning point in the war when Allied forces repulsed another German advance. German forces stalled, then retreated along the Western Front into Belgium. American military victories at St. Mihiel and Meuse-Argonne drove the German army toward the German border. With German forces in retreat, an Allied victory seemed inevitable. In October 1918 the German government relayed to Wilson that it would be willing to accept an armistice based on his proposed Fourteen Points. Peace was at hand. On the eleventh hour of the eleventh day of the eleventh month, 1918, the shooting stopped. The Great War had come to an end.

The peace process convened at the Palace of Versailles, located south of Paris, on January 18, 1919. However, back in the United States, congressional elections had replaced a Democratic majority with Republican control in both the Senate and House of Representatives. Senator Henry Cabot Lodge, a Republican with an intense dislike of Wilson, became chair of the Senate Foreign Relations Committee. Wilson, however, failed to include influential Republicans in his peace delegation, leaving them in Washington, D.C, instead, to thwart his peace initiatives as he labored in Paris to create a charter for a League of Nations. He presented his League charter to the Versailles Peace Conference in February. By March, Henry Cabot Lodge, along with thirty-nine Republican senators, deemed the charter unacceptable. European leaders also expressed their reservations. Wilson, however, far from reticent on his ideological dream, pressed Georges Clemenceau of France, David Lloyd George of Great Britain, and Vittorio Orlando of Italy to embrace the concept of an international league dedicated to the peaceful resolution of differences.

The end result was the Treaty of Versailles. To Wilson's credit, it began with twenty-six articles dedicated to establishing a "Covenant of the League of Nations." Article 11 of the treaty stated, "Any war or threat of war, whether immediately affecting any of the Members of the League or not, is hereby declared a matter of concern to the whole League, and the League shall take any action that may be deemed wise and effectual to safeguard the peace of nations. . . ." Provisions in the treaty reorganized central Europe, creating new countries out of old. Other provisions of the treaty were not as unifying, however. Territory was stripped from Germany, creating a demilitarized zone between France and Germany for fifteen years. Control of Germany's coal-rich Saar region was given to the League of Nations. The treaty's "war guilt" clause forced Germany to accept responsibility for the Great War and, ultimately, assume $33 billion in reparations.

Germany and the Allies signed the Treaty of Versailles on June 28, 1919. However, to Wilson's great dismay, Congress refused to ratify the Treaty of Versailles, in particular because of congressional opposition to the League of Nations. On January 10, 1920, the League of Nations officially began operations, but without America's participation.

NATIONAL ARCHIVES DOCUMENT

It will be our wish and purpose that the processes of peace, when they are begun, shall be absolutely open and that they shall involve and permit henceforth no secret understandings of any kind. The day of conquest and aggrandizement is gone by. . . .

I. Open covenants of peace, openly arrived at, after which there shall be no private international understandings of any kind but diplomacy shall proceed always frankly and in the public view.

II. Absolute freedom of navigation upon the seas. . . .

V. A free, open-minded, and absolutely impartial adjustment of all colonial claims. . . .

VI. The evacuation of all Russian territory. . . .

VIII. All French territory should be freed and the invaded portions restored. . . .

XIV. A general association of nations must be formed under specific covenants for the purpose of affording mutual guarantees of political independence and territorial integrity to great and small states alike. . . .

For such arrangements and covenants we are willing to fight and to continue to fight until they are achieved; but only because we wish the right to prevail and desire a just and stable peace such as can be secured only by removing the chief provocations to war. . . . ✳

Below: While Woodrow Wilson was able to convince Europe of the value of a League of Nations as a means to prevent another world war, he was unsuccessful in gaining the support of the U.S. Congress.

PUNCH, OR THE LONDON CHARIVARI.—MARCH 26, 1919.

OVERWEIGHTED.

PRESIDENT WILSON. "HERE'S YOUR OLIVE BRANCH. NOW GET BUSY."
DOVE OF PEACE. "OF COURSE I WANT TO PLEASE EVERYBODY; BUT ISN'T THIS A BIT THICK?"

Critical Thinking

Assess Significance

Why did Wilson believe that Point 14 of his Fourteen Points peace plan would assure the success of the other thirteen points?

Draw Conclusions

Unable to ratify the Treaty of Versailles, on May 20, 1920, Congress passed a joint resolution declaring an end to the Great War. Wilson vetoed the resolution. Why do you think Wilson vetoed this resolution?

Make Predictions

French premier Clemenceau was intent on weakening Germany in retribution for the devastation caused to France by the Great War. In response to Wilson's Fourteen Points, Clemenceau responded, "God gave us the Ten Commandments and we broke them. Wilson gave us the Fourteen Points—we shall see." How did this statement foreshadow Clemenceau's degree of willingness to grant concessions to Germany during the peace process?

Research and Writing

Analysis

Access and read President Woodrow Wilson's Fourteen Points in their entirety. What justifications were given for entry into the war? Upon what principles did Wilson believe peace should rest? In what way did Wilson attempt to establish a lasting peace? Upon what foundation did a lasting peace rely? Which ideals are foremost in Wilson's Fourteen Points? How did the Fourteen Points attempt to establish national sovereignty for the nations at war?

Counterpoint

Congressional approval of the Treaty of Versailles stalled over the issue of a League of Nations. Though Wilson's concept of a League of Nations enjoyed popular support, partisan differences in Congress doomed the idea to defeat. "Reservationists," led by Senator Henry Cabot Lodge, wanted conditions attached to the Treaty of Versailles. "Irreconcilables," those who opposed the treaty on all grounds, joined forces with the "reservationists" in Congress to vote down United States approval of the Treaty of Versailles. What arguments were put forth by the "reservationists" and the "irreconcilables"? What amendments were attached to the Treaty of Versailles to make it more acceptable to Congress? Why did President Wilson oppose the amendments? Research Wilson's proposal for a League of Nations. Take on the role of the "reservationists" or the "irreconcilables." Write an essay countering Wilson's proposal.

Link to the Past

The 1917 Russian Revolution marked the beginning of several decades of communist domination in Eastern Europe. What was Russia's political and economic structure under communism? What precipitated Russian president Boris Yeltsin's November 1991 ban on the Communist Party of the Soviet Union? What were the political and economic results? How did the dissolution of the USSR impact American-Russian relations?

1941 Lend-Lease Act

*"We shall not fail or falter; we shall not weaken or tire. . . .
Give us the tools and we will finish the job."*

—WINSTON CHURCHILL

HISTORICAL BACKGROUND

IN 1928 the Kellogg-Briand Pact was signed. Among the fifteen signatories were Great Britain, the United States, Japan, Italy, and Germany. Although the treaty provided for "the renunciation of war as an instrument of national policy," the pact did not prevent Japan's subsequent aggression against China, Italy's conquest of Ethiopia, or Germany's military actions against Austria and Czechoslovakia. The League of Nations likewise proved impotent, as Japan and Germany simply withdrew from the League in 1933, followed by Italy in 1937. Though the United States viewed with trepidation the escalation of military power in Europe and the rise of two dictators, Mussolini in Italy and Hitler in Germany, a majority of Americans favored isolationism to involvement in foreign affairs, as reprehensible as world events might be.

In 1935 Congress passed the first in a series of neutrality acts, the intent being to insulate the United States from world conflict while providing tacit support for countries critical to the nation's defense. Amended in 1936, the first two neutrality acts established an arms embargo against "belligerents," banned travel on belligerent ships, and banned loans to nations at war. The 1937 Neutrality Act extended these bans and banned the arming of American merchant ships trading with belligerents. However, it allowed the sale of non-embargoed goods to warring nations, provided the goods were sold on a "cash and carry" basis and were transported on foreign vessels.

Although President Franklin Delano Roosevelt had pledged that he would keep American "boys" from the fray in Europe, he realized that the outbreak of war there, and American involvement in it, was virtually inevitable. German occupation of Czechoslovakia and Germany's September 1, 1939,

attack on Poland bolstered Roosevelt's resolve to undo the 1937 Neutrality Act. In addressing Congress on September 21, 1939, Roosevelt advised that, "I regret equally that I signed that act." In few words Roosevelt foreshadowed the coming years.

> I should like to be able to offer the hope that the shadow over the world might swiftly pass. I cannot. The facts compel my stating, with candor, that darker periods may lie ahead. The disaster is not of our making; no act of ours engendered the forces which assault the foundations of civilization. Yet we find ourselves affected to the core; our currents of commerce are changing, our minds are filled with new problems, our position in world affairs has already been altered.

In November, Congress passed yet another Neutrality Act "to preserve its neutrality in wars between foreign states and desiring also to avoid involvement therein. . . ." The provisions of the 1939 act included:

- The resumption of previously embargoed arms sales to belligerents, but only on a cash and carry basis;
- Continuation of sales of nonmilitary supplies on a cash and carry basis;
- Transport of arms and other supplies only on foreign vessels;
- Exclusion of United States vessels from war zones;
- Prohibition on United States citizens sailing on ships belonging to belligerent nations.

Hitler unleashed his *Blitzkrieg* in the spring of 1940. Denmark, Norway, Belgium, Luxembourg, and the Netherlands quickly fell to German forces. On June 22, 1940, France surrendered to Germany, signing the conditions of the surrender in the same railway car in which Germany had surrendered in 1918. Americans were stunned. Soon after, the Battle of Britain exhausted Great Britain's military resources. In an effort to bolster Great Britain's military reserves, the U.S. government exchanged fifty aging American destroyers for ninety-nine year leases on British bases in Newfoundland and the Caribbean.

However, although Britain was in great peril, the neutrality laws—in particular, the Johnson Act of 1934—prohibited loans to foreign governments. Roosevelt's answer was the lend-lease program. Introduced into Congress on January 10, 1941, the bill underwent two months of heated debate. Isolationists saw it as an entry into war; Roosevelt argued that the security of the United States depended on a strong British navy. Congress passed the Lend-Lease Act on March 11, 1941. It authorized the president to lend war equipment to countries critical to the defense of America on the condition that it would eventually be returned, or returned in kind. Britain and China were the first recipients of lend-lease, however Roosevelt approved it for the Soviet Union in October of the same year. The Lend-Lease Act thus functioned as a compromise between isolationists in Congress and those who sought to give aid to belligerent countries, in particular to Great Britain.

NATIONAL ARCHIVES DOCUMENT

SEC. 3. (a) Notwithstanding the provisions of any other law, the President may, from time to time, when he deems it in the interest of national defense, authorize the Secretary of War, the Secretary of the Navy, or the head of any other department or agency of the Government—

(2) To sell, transfer title to, exchange, lease, lend, or otherwise dispose of, to any such government any defense article. . . .

    (d) Nothing in this Act shall be construed to authorize or to permit the authorization of convoying vessels by naval vessels of the United States.

    (e) Nothing in this Act shall be construed to authorize or to permit the authorization of the entry of any American vessel into a combat area in violation of section 3 of the neutrality Act of 1939. . . .

SEC. 6. (a) There is hereby authorized to be appropriated from time to time, out of any money in the Treasury not otherwise appropriated, such amounts as may be necessary to carry out the provisions and accomplish the purposes of this Act. . . .

SEC. 8 The Secretaries of War and of the Navy are hereby authorized to purchase or otherwise acquire arms, ammunition, and implements of war produced within the jurisdiction of any country to which section 3 is applicable, whenever the President deems such purchase or acquisition to be necessary in the interests of the defense of the United States. . . .

SEC. 10. Nothing in this Act shall be construed to change existing law relating to the use of the land and naval forces of the United States, except insofar as such use relates to the manufacture, procurement, and repair of defense articles, the communication of information and other noncombatant purposes enumerated in this Act. . . .

Approved, March 11, 1941. ✳

Below: Isolationists in the United States felt America would remain untouched by the war raging in Europe.

"Ho hum! When he's finished pecking down that last tree he'll quite likely be tired."

Critical Thinking

Draw Conclusions

How did the Lend-Lease Act allow the United States to participate in World War II without committing troops or declaring war?

Assess Significance

How did Section 10 of the Lend-Lease Act strike a compromise between isolationists and the Roosevelt administration?

Compare and Contrast

How did the lend-lease program satisfy the Neutrality Act of 1939 and the Johnson Act and yet allow for the arming of nations seen as critical to the defense of the United States?

Research and Writing

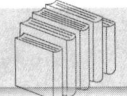

Point of View

In *Tomorrow in the Making*, Senator Gerald P. Nye of North Dakota wrote in 1939,

> When the World War came to an end, with its appalling waste of human life and of material resources as well, we were all resolved never to let it happen again.... Woodrow Wilson's charge to his countrymen to be "neutral in thought and deed" fell upon many unwilling ears.... If we will cease letting American corporations, assisted by our military establishment, arm all the world with instruments of warfare; if we will stop financing other people's wars; if we will make profit from any other war in which we may engage impossible, and destroy as far as possible the motive of profit in our mad armament races; if we will learn to be content with a national defense that guarantees protection against attack; if we will give to the people a voice in determining whether this country shall engage in foreign war; if we will do these things, we shall not write off all danger of war, but we shall very definitely assure a fuller measure of security to the finest democracy to be found upon this earth....

Isolationism had popular support in America during the 1930s. Research the role isolationists played in American foreign policy in the 1930s. What claims did isolationists make about American involvement in World War I? What did they view as deterrents against war? Why were isolationists agreeable to a policy of lend-lease? How did isolationists justify American isolationism at a time when the world seemed on the brink of another world war?

Historical Interpretation

The Nine-Power Treaty of 1922 acknowledged the sovereignty of China and attempted to establish international equity in trade. The Nine-Power Treaty was one of several treaties that emerged from a series of international naval conferences first held in 1908. With the outbreak of World War II in 1939, the work of the naval conferences was abandoned. Research the treaties produced by the international naval conferences. What were their provisions? How were the treaties adjusted over the years? Access and read the Kellogg-Briand Pact. How were the naval-conference treaties in stark contrast to the Kellogg-Briand Pact? How effective were the naval-conference treaties? What role did American foreign policy play in crafting the treaties?

Relating Events

In August 1941, Roosevelt and Winston Churchill, prime minister of Great Britain, met secretly to draft a joint statement of international principles. Termed the Atlantic Charter, and similar in text to Wilson's Fourteen Points, it called for freedom of the seas, a continuation of the Open Door policies, and the right of people to self-determination. Compare and contrast the Atlantic Charter with Wilson's Fourteen Points. What was the purpose of the Atlantic Charter? What did it accomplish? Why did it later receive the endorsement of the Soviet Union?

1941 Declaration of War Against Japan

"December 7, 1941,—a date which will live in infamy."

−Franklin Delano Roosevelt

Historical Background

WHILE events unfolded in Europe during the late 1930s, the United States carefully monitored the advance of a highly trained Japanese military force as it made its way into China. By 1939 the powerful Japanese army had conquered most of northeastern China, as well as controlled most of its important coastal seaports. Although still at war with China, by the summer of 1940 Japan had turned its attention to French Indochina, the Dutch East Indies, British Malaya, and Burma. These regions were rich in resources, such as oil and rubber, needed for Japan's war effort.

The Export Control Act of July 1940 allowed President Roosevelt to deny export of "any military equipment or munitions, or component parts thereof, or machinery, tools, or materials or supplies necessary for the manufacture [of armaments]. . . ." This included arms, ammunition, chemicals, rubber, fibers such as cotton and wood, aircraft parts, and machinery. Over the next months, Roosevelt utilized his embargo powers to curtail military supplies to Japan, including scrap iron and gasoline. From his "Europe-first" vantage point, it seemed critical to weaken Japan's efforts to wage war in order for the United States to focus on military events occurring across the Atlantic. To that end, the United States approved $25 million in military aid for China in 1940. In the spring of 1941, the United States granted another $145 million in lend-lease aid for China.

On September 27, 1940, Japan signed the Tripartite Pact with Germany and Italy. Then, on April 13, 1941, Japan signed a nonaggression pact with the Soviet Union. In June, Germany invaded Russia. With Russia battling Germany, Japan turned its sights south. For many years, the government of Japan had felt justified in its own manifest destiny—the colonization of South Asia. With the complicity of the German-supported Vichy government of France, Japan established a protectorate over French Indochina, as a part of its so-called Greater East Asia Co-Prosperity Sphere, a plan whereby Japan assumed control over a bloc of Asian countries. The Co-Prosperity Sphere afforded Japan access to abundant oil, rubber, and other products crucial to its military and political ambitions. In response to these acts of imperialism, Roosevelt imposed even harsher restrictions on Japan, including freezing Japanese assets in the United States and curtailing oil exports to Japan. Roosevelt also warned Japan that, according to the terms of the Atlantic Charter, the United States and Britain had agreed to "the enjoyment by all States, great or small, victor or vanquished, of access, on equal terms, to the trade and to the raw materials of the world which are needed for their economic prosperity."

Diplomatic relations between Japan and the United States continued to sour in the face of these events. On November 26, 1941, a Japanese naval force set sail for an assault on American forces some 5,000 miles away at Pearl Harbor in Hawaii. The attack was swift and sure. Shortly before 8 A.M. on December 7, 1941, Japanese aircraft launched a devastating assault on the unsuspecting American bases there. Over the course of two hours, gunfire, bombs, and torpedoes pounded American warships and aircraft. Sailors, some caught with no ammunition on board, watched in horror as enemy aircraft flew over at will, leaving a path of destruction in their wake. With the exception of American aircraft carriers that fortuitously had been out to sea, the attack left virtually all U.S. warships disabled or sunk, almost two hundred aircraft destroyed, over 2,000 servicemen and civilians killed, and another

1,178 wounded. Assaults on Pearl Harbor were followed by similar attacks on the Philippines, Guam, Midway, and the Malay Peninsula.

On December 8, 1941, Roosevelt called on Congress to declare war on Japan. The vote, save for that of Jeanette Rankin, a devoted pacifist who also had voted against war in 1917, was unanimous. Three days later Germany and Italy declared war on the United States. This time, nearly the entire world was at war.

NATIONAL ARCHIVES DOCUMENT

Joint Address to Congress
Leading to a Declaration of War Against Japan (1941)

Mr. Vice President, and Mr. Speaker, and Members of the Senate and House of Representatives:

Yesterday, December 7, 1941—a date which will live in infamy—the United States of America was suddenly and deliberately attacked by naval and air forces of the Empire of Japan.

The United States was at peace with that Nation and, at the solicitation of Japan, was still in conversation with its Government and its Emperor looking toward the maintenance of peace in the Pacific. Indeed, one hour after Japanese air squadrons had commenced bombing in the American Island of Oahu, the Japanese Ambassador to the United States and his colleague delivered to our Secretary of State a formal reply to a recent American message. And while this reply stated that it seemed useless to continue the existing diplomatic negotiations, it contained no threat or hint of war or of armed attack.

It will be recorded that the distance of Hawaii from Japan makes it obvious that the attack was deliberately planned many days or even weeks ago. During the intervening time the Japanese Government has deliberately sought to deceive the United States by false statements and expressions of hope for continued peace.

The attack yesterday on the Hawaiian Islands has caused severe damage to American naval and military forces. I regret to tell you that very many American lives have been lost. In addition American ships have been reported torpedoed on the high seas between San Francisco and Honolulu . . .

Hostilities exist. There is no blinking at the fact that our people, our territory, and our interests are in grave danger. . . .

I ask that the Congress declare that since the unprovoked and dastardly attack by Japan on Sunday, December 7, 1941, a state of war has existed between the United States and the Japanese Empire. ✳

Below: The attack on Pearl Harbor, December 7, 1941, killed over 2,000 civilians and servicemen and disabled or destroyed every U.S. warship in port.

Critical Thinking

Assess Significance

Upon learning of the attack on Pearl Harbor, isolationist Gerald P. Nye first expressed doubt, then incredulity, then resolve. While leaving a meeting of American Firsters, on December 7, 1941, Nye stated "'We have been maneuvered into this by the President, but the only thing now is to declare war and to jump into it with everything we have and bring it to a victorious conclusion.'" How important do you think the retreat of isolationists was to American foreign policy as it entered World War II?

Determine Point of View

Access and read Roosevelt's entire December 8, 1941 address to Congress. In what way does Roosevelt express the indignation of the people of the United States?

Draw Conclusions

Why do you think the Japanese risked an attack on Pearl Harbor? What did Japan hope to accomplish as a result of the coordinated attacks? Did they succeed?

Research and Writing

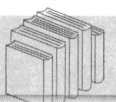

Analysis

Roosevelt repudiated Japan's military advances in Southeast Asia and China. Japan's War Minister, Hideki Tojo, responded that, if the United States would stop its stream of supplies to China, Japan would agree to occupy China for no longer than twenty-five years, a plan unacceptable to the United States. As a result of upheaval in the Japanese government, Tojo soon became premier. War plans were in the making, though outwardly Japan appeared willing to negotiate a settlement of differences concerning its military advances in Asia. On November 20, 1941, Japan presented its peace offer to Secretary of State Cordell Hull. Research this proposal. Why was it unacceptable to the United States? What was the response of Roosevelt's administration? In what way was the plan a ruse? How were Japan's plans for war against the United States miscalculated by the American military?

Relating Events

Two significant events signaled the oncoming attack against Pearl Harbor. One occurred within an hour of the attack when American radar detected what appeared to be a group of fifty planes headed toward Pearl Harbor. The radar pattern was assumed to be that of American planes originating from the mainland and was disregarded. The other occurred at 6:37 A.M. on the morning of December 7, when the USS *Ward* spotted what appeared to be the conning tower of a submarine. Though at 6:45 A.M. the *Ward* reported, "We have attacked, fired upon, and dropped depth charges on a submarine operating in defensive sea areas," the report was not immediately regarded as critical. The thinking was that the young and inexperienced crew was participating in a training drill or was mistaken in its understanding of its target. Command would soon learn differently. The attack on Pearl Harbor included the use of five Japanese Type A midget submarines. Research the planned role of midget submarines in Japan's attack on Pearl Harbor. Why was Pearl Harbor ill-prepared for Japan's attack? What role did the Atlantic Charter play in American foreign policy regarding Japan and the eventual attack on Pearl Harbor? What impact did the attack have on America's naval capabilities? How did the United States respond?

Counterpoint

Aircraft carriers played a significant role during World War II. Fortunately, U.S. aircraft carriers were not in port on the day of the attack on Pearl Harbor. To some, the absence of air craft carriers at Pearl Harbor indicated that Roosevelt had prior knowledge of the attack. However, this "conspiracy theory" has never been proven. Research the role of air craft carriers in World War II. What impact did the attack on Pearl Harbor have on U.S. naval capabilities? What other circumstances surrounding the attack would lead some to implicate Roosevelt in a conspiracy to use an attack on Pearl Harbor as a means to enter the war? What is your conclusion?

1944 General Eisenhower's Order of the Day

". . . it seems to me a pure miracle that we ever took the beach at all."

—ERNIE PYLE (STANDING ON OMAHA BEACH, JUNE 7, 1944)

HISTORICAL BACKGROUND

THE story of D-Day—June 6, 1944—is the story of an extraordinary military mission called *Operation Overlord*, a mission that succeeded against all odds. Initial plans for D-Day had been carefully discussed in Tehran, Iran, in November 1943. Here Roosevelt, Churchill, and Stalin agreed to launch a multinational, coordinated assault via the English Channel against German forces entrenched in France. It was a risky, win-at-all-cost mission that would test the military might and organizational skill of the Allied forces. Stalin also agreed at Tehran to join the Allies in war against Japan after Germany had been defeated. In addition, the three leaders agreed to create a new international peace-keeping organization once the guns of war were silenced.

Prior to meeting with Stalin, Roosevelt and Churchill had agreed to the Cairo Declaration, an agreement struck with Chiang Kai-shek that all lands taken by the Japanese government would be restored to China following the defeat of Japan. The U.S. and British pledge also provided "that in due course Korea shall become free and independent." Thus, the course of the war was charted, a course involving the exhaustive coordination of the naval, air, and ground forces of several Allied countries. What was left was to find someone who would be capable of commanding the critical first step in the war's endgame—the invasion of Western Europe and defeat of its Nazi occupiers. For that job, Roosevelt chose General Dwight D. Eisenhower.

By the end of 1943, Allied air power over France had begun to take a toll on German forces. Months of aerial warfare had resulted in the bombardment of railroad lines, bridges, roads, and airfields, pieces of the infrastructure Germany needed to continue its assault against Great Britain. In early 1944 General Eisenhower arrived in London at the headquarters of the Allied Expeditionary Force. Soon over a million troops were positioned along England's coastline. During "the Big Week," February 20–25, 1944, wave after wave of B-17 and B-24 bombers of the Eighth Air Force, along with their escort fighter planes, took off from England's shores to confront the German Luftwaffe, Germany's elite air force, deep inside Germany. Combined bombing expeditions by the United States and Britain's Royal Air Force (which included planes piloted by such groups as the Kosciusko Polish Squadron) targeted German aircraft plants in an effort to thwart Germany's air supremacy. The strategy worked. Flying some 3,300 sorties, Allied bombers destroyed almost all the industrial facilities targeted during the week's briefings. Allied forces also shot down 692 German aircraft in vicious and chaotic fighting. Yet, the toll for the Allied forces was high: 256 planes were lost, including 244 heavy bombers from flak and Nazi interceptor planes, with almost 2,600 Allied casualties.

Once the Allies had gained air supremacy, the next step was to "soften the beaches." German soldiers had mined the waters and beaches along the French coastline against an amphibious assault. Deep trenches lined with barbed wire had been dug to protect the almost insurmountable machine-gun nests and concrete emplacements strategically placed along the 100-foot bluff that lined the beach. From these high points, German guns could cover every inch of the beachhead.

On June 4, over 1,000 bombers from the Eighth Air Force pummeled the Boulogne area. Most Allied troops in England believed the intended target of the upcoming assault was to be the shortest line into occupied territory, the coast around Boulogne. To the surprise of even the German high command, the true target was 150 miles to the south. On the afternoon of June 5, the airmen of the Eighth Air Force were summoned to hear of the next day's plans: the bombing of Boulogne had been a ruse, the real target was Normandy. Against this backdrop, Eisenhower issued his Order of the Day. In the early morning of June 6, 1944, some 5,000 ships, 800 transport planes, 300 bombers, and 175,000 men crossed the English Channel to launch Operation Overlord.

NATIONAL ARCHIVES DOCUMENT

SUPREME HEADQUARTERS
ALLIED EXPEDITIONARY FORCE

Soldiers, Sailors, and Airmen of the Allied Expeditionary Force!

You are about to embark upon the Great Crusade, toward which we have striven these many months. The eyes of the world are upon you. The hope and prayers of liberty-loving people everywhere march with you. In company with our brave Allies and brothers-in-arms on other Fronts, you will bring about the destruction of the German war machine, the elimination of Nazi tyranny over the oppressed peoples of Europe, and security for ourselves in a free world.

Your task will not be an easy one. Your enemy is well trained, well equipped and battle-hardened. He will fight savagely.

But this is the year 1944! Much has happened since the Nazi triumphs of 1940–41. The United Nations have inflicted upon the Germans great defeats, in open battle, man-to-man. Our air offensive has seriously reduced their strength in the air and their capacity to wage war on the ground. Our Home Fronts have given us an overwhelming superiority in weapons and munitions of war, and placed at our disposal great reserves of trained fighting men. The tide has turned! The free men of the world are marching together to Victory!

I have full confidence in your courage, devotion to duty and skill in battle. We will accept nothing less than full Victory!

Good luck! And let us beseech the blessing of Almighty God upon this great and noble undertaking. ✳

Below: General Dwight D. Eisenhower, Supreme Commander of the Allied Expeditionary Force, speaks to paratroopers prior to the Normandy invasion.

Critical Thinking

Assess Significance

Eisenhower's Order of the Day was distributed to each member of the expeditionary force assigned to participate in D-Day the following morning. What do you think was Eisenhower's purpose in issuing the order as it was written?

Analyze Cause and Effect

What events had occurred that gave Eisenhower the confidence that Operation Overlord could be successful?

Draw Conclusions

Russell Douglas of La Valle, Wisconsin, was assigned to the 390th Bombardment Group, which was attached to the Eighth Air Force and stationed at Framlingham, England, in June 1944. A Bomb Sight and Turret Specialist, Douglas recalled that "everyone knew something big was going to happen, though we certainly weren't privileged to know the plans. The island was just crammed with service men, tanks, planes, and every piece of military hardware imaginable." He was correct in his observation for almost 3 million Allied troops stood ready in southern England. On June 4, Eisenhower had to make the decision to risk the operation's failure due to the inclement weather or delay the invasion for two weeks, possibly sacrificing the attack's element of surprise. Why, with elaborate preparations by the Germans already in place along the French coastline, was surprise critical to the success of D-Day?

Research and Writing

Analysis

For months the Germans had been securing the French coastline against an Allied assault that all believed was sure to come. Ernie Pyle, reporting for Scripps-Howard from Omaha Beach, wrote the following account:

> …Our men simply could not get past the beach. They were pinned down right on the water's edge by an inhuman wall of fire from the bluff. Our first waves were on that beach for hours, instead of a few minutes, before they could begin working inland…. You can still see the foxholes they dug at the very edge of the water, in the sand…. The first crack in the beach defenses was finally accomplished by terrific and wonderful naval gunfire, which knocked out the big emplacements. They tell epic stories of destroyers that ran right up into shallow water and had it out point-blank with the big guns in those concrete emplacements….

Research the obstacles, from weather to logistics to German preparations, facing the Allied forces as they embarked on D-Day. Where did most fighting occur? What was the cost in lives and loss of equipment? Explain Ernie Pyle's quote on page 109. How did the Allied forces overcome the almost insurmountable obstacles facing them on D-Day?

Link to the Past

The Tehran Conference, held from November 28–December 1, 1943, resulted in an accord among the Three Powers: Great Britain, the United States, and the Soviet Union, to defeat Germany through a coordinated military plan to be "launched" in May 1944. The accord also recognized the sovereignty of Iran. Research the Tehran Conference. What agreements were reached by the Three Powers? Why was the conference held in Tehran, Iran? What was Iran's strategic significance? What events led to the erosion of diplomatic relations between the United States and Iran? What is the current status of American foreign policy toward Iran?

Biography

Following World War II, Dwight D. Eisenhower took command of the North Atlantic Treaty Organization (NATO) forces. In 1952 Eisenhower was elected as the thirty-fourth president of the United States. Research the life of Dwight D. Eisenhower. Why was Eisenhower popular with voters? What foreign policies and events dominated his two presidential terms?

"Nuts!"

—RESPONSE OF GENERAL ANTHONY McAULIFFE AT BASTOGNE
(WHEN INFORMED OF THE GERMAN DEMAND FOR HIS SURRENDER)

HISTORICAL BACKGROUND

By the winter of 1944, Paris had been liberated and Allied forces were advancing toward Germany. However, a shortage of supplies, intensified fighting, and harsh winter weather halted the Allied advance. Following considerable planning, on the morning of December 16, 1944, over 200,000 German soldiers attacked Allied troops along a thinly defended front in Luxemburg and Belgium. The German offensive eventually created a "bulge" in the Allied lines that extended some eighty miles wide and fifty miles deep. Known as the Battle of the Bulge, the grueling fighting stalled at Bastogne where Allied troops, low on supplies and penned in, became desperate for relief. For six days the besieged soldiers at Bastogne repelled an all-out German assault. Finally, on December 26, Allied aircraft attacked the German lines, turning the tide of the battle.

The Battle of the Bulge was the largest land battle in which American forces participated. Lasting until January 28, 1945, it involved a fighting force of 500,000 American and 55,000 British soldiers against a force of 600,000 Germans. The Battle of the Bulge was the last large-scale German offensive of World War II. Soon after, in February 1945, the Big Three—the leaders of the United States, Great Britain, and Soviet Union—met at Yalta in the Crimea to plan for a postwar Europe. Based on the Yalta Declaration of Liberated Europe, Germany would be temporarily partitioned into four separate zones, three of which would be occupied by Great Britain, the United States, and the Soviets, and the fourth, at its discretion, by France. The three leaders—Churchill, Roosevelt, and Stalin—also agreed to "[assist] the peoples liberated from the domination of Nazi Germany and the peoples of the former Axis satellite states of Europe to solve by democratic means their pressing political and economic problems." For

Stalin, however, the establishment of independent, democratic governments out of the political rubble of World War II was to be a bogus promise.

With Berlin on the brink of collapse, and the Red Army poised to capture the city, on April 30 Hitler retreated into his bunker in Berlin, named the zealous Nazi, Admiral Karl Doenitz, to succeed him as president of the Reich, and sealed his fate by committing suicide. On May 2, 1945, the Red Army claimed Berlin. By May 4, German forces in Italy, Holland, Denmark, and in the northwest section of Germany had laid down their arms. Subsequently, on May 6, Doenitz directed General Alfred Jodl, chief of staff of the German Army, to negotiate an armistice agreement with General Eisenhower. On May 7, 1945, Jodl signed the Act of Military Surrender at the headquarters of the Allied Expeditionary Force in Rheims, France. On May 8, elation filled the streets of the Allied countries as the people of Europe and the United States celebrated V-E (Victory in Europe) Day. With Roosevelt's death on April 12, 1945, the reigns of the war had passed to Vice President Harry S. Truman. In his V-E Day radio broadcast, President Truman paid tribute to a steadfast Roosevelt and then reminded Americans that full victory was yet to be achieved.

This is a solemn but a glorious hour. I only wish that Franklin D. Roosevelt had lived to witness this day. . . . We must work to finish the war. Our victory is but half-won. The West is free, but the East is still in bondage to the treacherous tyranny of the Japanese. When the last Japanese division has surrendered unconditionally, then only will our fighting be done. We must seek to bind up the wounds of a suffering world—to build an abiding peace, a peace rooted in justice and in law. We can build such a peace only by hard, toilsome, painstaking work—by understanding and working with our allies in peace as we have in war. . . .

NATIONAL ARCHIVES DOCUMENT

Only this text in English is authoritative

ACT OF MILITARY SURRENDER

We the undersigned, acting by authority of the German High Command, hereby surrender unconditionally to the Supreme Commander, Allied Expeditionary Forces and simultaneously to the Soviet High Command all forces on land, sea and in the air who are at this date under German control.

The German High Command will at once issue orders to all German military, naval and air authorities and to all forces under German control to cease active operations at 2301 hours Central European time on 8 May and to remain in the positions occupied at that time. No ship, vessel, or aircraft is to be scuttled, or any damage done to their hull, machinery or equipment.

The German High Command will at once issue to the appropriate commander, and ensure the carrying out of any further orders issued by the Supreme Commander, Allied Expeditionary Force and by the Soviet High Command.

This act of military surrender is without prejudice to, and will be superseded by any general instrument of surrender imposed by, or on behalf of the United Nations and applicable to GERMANY and the German armed forces as a whole.

In the event of the German High Command or any of the forces under their control failing to act in accordance with this Act of Surrender, the Supreme Commander, Allied Expeditionary Force and the Soviet High Command will take such punitive or other action as they deem appropriate.

Below: The Battle of the Bulge was Germany's last large-scale offensive of World War II, and the deadliest battle for U.S. forces.

Signed at RHEIMS at 0241 on the 7th day of May, 1945. France
On behalf of the German High Command.

JODL

IN THE PRESENCE OF

On behalf of the Supreme Commander,
Allied Expeditionary Force.
W. B. SMITH

On behalf of the Soviet High Command
SOUSLOPAROV

F SEVEZ
Major General, French Army
(Witness) ✳

Critical Thinking

Analyze Cause and Effect

Why was Roosevelt willing to make political and territorial concessions to Stalin in return for his commitment to assist the Allies in war against Japan?

Draw Conclusions

Why do you think General Eisenhower insisted that Germany surrender "simultaneously" to both the Allied Expeditionary Force and to the Soviet High Command?

Assess Significance

Why did President Truman issue a precautionary note in his V-E Day address to the nation?

Research and Writing

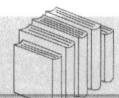

Relating Events

Since the beginning of the war—for four long years—the Germans had occupied Paris, the French capital. As Allied forces moved eastward through France, Dietrich von Choltitz, commanding general of the German forces, had been ordered by Hitler to burn the main bridges and buildings of Paris in advance of an Allied occupation of the city. Von Choltitz ignored the order, reasoning that it was a futile and an unnecessarily ruthless plan that would result in no military gain for Germany. Instead Choltitz ordered the city evacuated. On August 25 he signed an order surrendering the city to French resistance forces. Research the liberation of Paris. Who were the Free French? What part did Allied forces play in its liberation? What was Roosevelt's response to the liberation of Paris? Who was Charles de Gaulle? What role did he play in Germany's surrender to the Allied forces?

Analysis

Following the Yalta Conference, Roosevelt and Churchill were criticized for acquiescing to Stalin's territorial demands in Eastern Europe. Much has been made of Roosevelt's ill health during negotiations with Stalin as the reason the President lost his resolve to maintain Poland's sovereignty and for the establishment of free and independent governments in Eastern Europe. Other historians believe that Roosevelt realized the Soviets had already established dominion over Eastern Europe by virtue of the presence of the Red Army in Eastern European nations. Thus, it has been argued that Roosevelt had few options but to bow to Stalin's demands, with the hope that Stalin would keep his promise to join the Allies in an offensive against Japan. Research the concessions made to Stalin at the Yalta Conference. How did they affect the political map of Eastern Europe? What prompted Roosevelt to later decree, "We can't do business with Stalin. He has broken every one of the promises he made at Yalta."

Historical Interpretation

Churchill felt the fall of Berlin should be the prize of the Western Allies and pressed Roosevelt to direct General Eisenhower to craft plans for an Allied assault aimed at capturing Berlin ahead of the Red Army. Eisenhower at first contemplated then dismissed such a plan when General Omar Bradley estimated that it would cost 100,000 American lives to capture Berlin. Research the Battle of Berlin. Why did Eisenhower feel that Berlin was not a political prize worth the lives of thousands of American soldiers? On May 2, 1945, Berlin fell to the Red Army. What was the cost of the Battle of Berlin? What did the Soviets gain from the battle? Why do you think the Soviets insisted that Germany sign a second Act of Military Surrender in Berlin on May 8, 1945?

1945 United Nations Charter

"We must do that which we think we cannot."

—ELEANOR ROOSEVELT

HISTORICAL BACKGROUND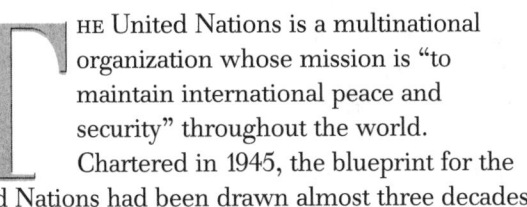

THE United Nations is a multinational organization whose mission is "to maintain international peace and security" throughout the world. Chartered in 1945, the blueprint for the United Nations had been drawn almost three decades earlier when President Woodrow Wilson proposed a League of Nations to settle international disputes.

In its short, twenty-seven year history, the League of Nations had produced some remarkable diplomatic results, including the arbitration of post-World War I differences and the extension of aid for World War I refugees. Additionally, in 1935 the League of Nations had managed a plebiscite in Saarland, the disputed Saar territory whose coal mines had been awarded to the French following World War I. When 90 percent of the people living in Saarland voted to return the territory to Germany, the League of Nations oversaw the transfer of power (though the region again was in dispute following World War II). At times the League of Nations flexed its might, such as its expulsion of the USSR following the Soviet invasion of Finland in 1939. However, throughout its tenure, the League of Nations was beset by its general inability to halt global military aggression, with its ultimate collapse foreshadowed by the 1938 Munich Pact.

On January 2, 1942, delegates from twenty-six nations met in Washington, D.C., to endorse the Atlantic Charter by signing a Declaration of the United Nations. With the accord, each nation agreed "not to make a separate armistice or peace with the enemies. . . ." in effect establishing a multilateral agreement uniting all signatories for the benefit of each nation. In October, at the Moscow Conference, the United States, Great Britain, the Soviet Union, and China agreed to "the necessity of establishing at the earliest practicable date a general international organization, based on the principle of the sovereign equality of all peace-loving states, and open to membership by all such states, large and small, for the maintenance of international peace and security." Soon after, representatives from the Allied countries founded such international organizations as the United Nations Relief and Rehabilitation Administration, and the United Nations Educational, Scientific, and Cultural Organization, and the International Monetary Fund and World Bank.

At the Dumbarton Oaks Conference (August–October 1944) United States, British, Soviet, and Chinese representatives (the Big Four) established the framework for an international peacekeeping organization. Recommended was a General Assembly of all member nations, as well as a Security Council whose membership would include the Big Four plus other temporary members chosen by the General Assembly. At the Yalta Conference in February 1945, Roosevelt, Churchill, and Stalin agreed to the basic structure of a proposed "world organization," including its membership, the composition of the Security Council, and the veto power of its permanent members. The founding conference for the United Nations was held in San Francisco beginning in April 1945. Here representatives from fifty nations, inclusive of all countries that had signed the 1942 Declaration of United Nations, as well as those that had declared war on Germany and Japan, met to draft a charter for an international organization that would help secure world peace. The United Nations Charter was completed and signed on June 16, 1945.

In stark contrast to America's failure to join the League of Nations, on July 28, 1945, the U.S. Senate approved the United Nations Charter by a vote of 89–2. On October 24, 1945, twenty-nine nations ratified the United Nations Charter, thereby establishing the international organization. The United Nations General Assembly met for the first time in London on January 10, 1946.

NATIONAL ARCHIVES DOCUMENT

WE THE PEOPLES OF THE UNITED NATIONS DETERMINED to save succeeding generations from the scourge of war, which twice in our lifetime has brought untold sorrow to mankind, and to reaffirm faith in fundamental human rights, in the dignity and worth of the human person, in the equal rights of men and women and of nations large and small, and to establish conditions under which justice and respect for the obligations arising from treaties and other sources of international law can be maintained, and to promote social progress and better standards of life in larger freedom, AND FOR THESE ENDS to practice tolerance and live together in peace with one another as good neighbours, and to unite our strength to maintain international peace and security, and to ensure, by the acceptance of principles and the institution of methods, that armed force shall not be used, save in the common interest, and to employ international machinery for the promotion of the economic and social advancement of all peoples, HAVE RESOLVED TO COMBINE OUR EFFORTS TO ACCOMPLISH THESE AIMS Accordingly, our respective Governments, through representatives assembled in the city of San Francisco, who have exhibited their full powers found to be in good and due form, have agreed to the present Charter of the United Nations and do hereby establish an international organization to be known as the United Nations. ✳

Below: The United Nations General Assembly.

Critical Thinking

Classify Information
Classify the political, social, and military aims of the United Nations as specified in the preamble to the United Nations Charter.

Assess Significance
Membership in the United Nations has grown from twenty-six nations in 1945 to almost two hundred today. Along with its international security role, it also is involved in humanitarian efforts through such agencies as the International Children's Emergency Fund (UNICEF), the Educational, Scientific, and Cultural Organization (UNESCO), and the World Health Organization (WHO). In what way are humanitarian efforts intertwined with international security?

Draw Conclusions
Funding for the United Nations began with an $8.5 million gift of land from John D. Rockefeller, Jr. The 18 acres of real estate along the East River in New York City was subsequently converted to international territory. Why was it important for the buildings of the United Nations to be built on international territory rather than on land of any member country? What implications does its status as international territory have for its own security?

Research and Writing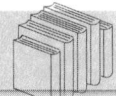

Analysis
Access and read the entire United Nations Charter. What is the mission of the United Nations? How is it structured? How does it function? What are its powers?

Biography
As the United States delegate to the United Nations, Eleanor Roosevelt chaired the committee that drafted the 1948 Declaration of Human Rights. In addressing the committee, she posed the following:

> Where, after all, do universal human rights begin? In small places, close to home—so close and so small that they cannot be seen on any map of the world. Yet they are the world of the individual person: The neighbourhood he lives in; the school or college he attends; the factory, farm or office where he works. Such are the places where every man, woman and child seeks equal justice, equal opportunity, equal dignity without discrimination. Unless these rights have meaning there, they have little meaning anywhere. Without concerted citizen action to uphold them close to home, we shall look in vain for progress in the larger world.

Research the life of Eleanor Roosevelt. How did her commitment to human rights, as indicated by this remark, reflect her life's work? What was her contribution to the United Nations? What was her human rights legacy in general?

Link to the Past
Initially comprised of the Allied nations of World War II, the United Nations was conceptualized as an international organization that would operate with relative unanimity toward securing peace throughout the world. With the onset of the Cold War, the tenuous nature of international unanimity tested the tenets of the United Nations Charter. In 1950, for example, the Soviet Union boycotted the Security Council over the United Nations' refusal to seat the People's Republic of China as a member. The absence of the Soviet Union, however, allowed the Security Council to create a military force to repel the attack on South Korea by communist North Korea, and with it the establishment of the United Nations Security Force (UNSF).

Research the use of the UNSF as an international peacekeeping force. Where and under what circumstances has it been used? How effective has it been? What is its current role in the world?

" . . . that from this solemn occasion a better world shall emerge."

–General Douglas MacArthur

Historical Background

WITH Allied forces in pursuit of a retreating German military, and Germany on the edge of capitulation, the early months of 1945 found American ground, air, and naval forces engaged in vicious fighting against the Japanese far across the Pacific Ocean. Beginning on February 19, 1945, some 110,000 American Marines invaded Iwo Jima, a small volcanic island approximately 700 miles from Tokyo, with the intent of securing the island as an air strip for American fighter planes and bombers. They encountered approximately 22,000 Japanese defenders who fought from underground rooms connected by sixteen miles of tunnels dug deep into the upper elevations of the island. Though the Marines could not see the Japanese, each American landing on Iwo Jima was within the sights of a Japanese gun. Nearly 7,000 Marines were killed during the month-long battle.

While savage fighting raged on Iwo Jima, American B-29 Superfortresses, under the command of General Curtis LeMay, engaged in carpet-bombing missions aimed at large urban areas in Japan. In a radical tactical move, LeMay ordered the guns of each B-29 bomber replaced with incendiary bombs filled with jellied gasoline (napalm). Plummeting from low altitudes, the incendiaries instantly ignited their wooden targets. On the nights of March 9 and 10 alone, 334 B-29 bombers firebombed Tokyo, destroying a quarter of the city and killing 84,000 people. By July, B-29 firebombs had killed approximately 500,000 Japanese civilians and military personnel and had destroyed large sections of Japan's major urban centers.

On April 1, 1945, United States armed forces began an assault against Okinawa. Just 350 miles from Tokyo, Okinawa was viewed as an essential staging point for an invasion of Japan. For over three months, some 300,000 battle-worn troops fought against the well-fortified Japanese. At sea, naval vessels withstood a barrage of hundreds of Kamikaze attacks from the air. When resistance finally collapsed, an estimated 140,000 Japanese defenders had died, while American casualties ranked the greatest for any Pacific engagement: 77,000 casualties including 19,000 dead.

On July 25, President Truman, Stalin, and Clement Attlee, the newly elected prime minister of Great Britain, met at Potsdam, Germany. The resulting Potsdam Declaration, endorsed by Great Britain, the United States, and China, and based in part on the 1943 Cairo Declaration, demanded for "Japan to proclaim now the unconditional surrender of all Japanese armed forces…the alternative [being Japan's] prompt and utter destruction." Two days later, when informed that Japan has rejected the terms of the Potsdam Declaration, Truman authorized a plan to drop America's secret weapon, the atomic bomb, on Japan. On August 6, 1945, the *Enola Gay*, carrying an atomic bomb dubbed Little Boy, opened its bomb-bay doors over Hiroshima. The ensuing fireball killed 80,000 people immediately and incinerated the city. Another 60,000 would later die from burns and radiation poisoning. Two days later (and 3 months after Germany had surrendered) the Soviet Union declared war on Japan. On August 9, with no evidence of a forthcoming surrender, a second atomic bomb, code-named Fat Man, was dropped on the seaport city of Nagasaki, killing 40,000 people. Five days later, on August 14, Japan agreed to surrender to the Allied forces.

On September 2, 1945, aboard the USS *Missouri*, General Douglas MacArthur accepted Japan's surrender. He first directed Japan's Foreign Minister Mamoru Shigemitsu, followed by General

Yoshijiro Umezu, to sign the two Instruments of Surrender. General MacArthur, as Supreme Commander of the Allied Powers signed next. In short order, representatives from the United States, China, the United Kingdom, the Soviet Union, Australia, Canada, France, the Netherlands, and New Zealand affixed their signatures to the documents. Lasting under thirty minutes, the surrender ceremony ended with a military salute by the officers of the *Missouri* as the Japanese representatives debarked from the battleship.

Japan's surrender signaled the end to a horrific world war that cost some 50 million military and civilian deaths worldwide. In the United States, some 300,000 gold military stars placed on a background of bright red cloth, and proudly displayed in the windows of homes across the country, had their been replaced by black stars. Yet, the United States had remained untouched by the ruin that pervaded Europe and Asia. Its industries intact, its cities safe, the United States could move forward toward an era of prosperity.

NATIONAL ARCHIVES DOCUMENT

INSTRUMENT OF SURRENDER

We, acting by command of and in behalf of the Emperor of Japan, the Japanese Government and the Japanese Imperial General Headquarters, hereby accept the provisions set forth in the declaration issued by the heads of the Governments of the United States, China, and Great Britain on 26 July 1945 at Potsdam, and subsequently adhered to by the Union of Soviet Socialist Republics, which four powers are hereafter referred to as the Allied Powers.

We hereby proclaim the unconditional surrender to the Allied Powers of the Japanese Imperial General Headquarters and of all Japanese armed forces and all armed forces under the Japanese control wherever situated. . . .

Below: Surrender of Japan aboard the USS *Missouri*.

We hereby command the Japanese Imperial Government and the Japanese Imperial General Headquarters at once to liberate all allied prisoners of war and civilian internees now under Japanese control and to provide for their protection, care, maintenance and immediate transportation to places as directed.

The authority of the Emperor and the Japanese Government to rule the state shall be subject to the Supreme Commander for the Allied Powers who will take such steps as he deems proper to effectuate these terms of surrender. . . . ✳

Critical Thinking

Make Predictions

As part of the Potsdam Declaration, China, the United States, and Great Britain had decreed that "the full application of our military power, backed by our resolve, will mean the inevitable and complete destruction of the Japanese armed forces and just as inevitably the utter devastation of the Japanese homeland...." With the loss of Iwo Jima and Okinawa, the destruction of its navy, and significant portions of its urban centers destroyed, Japan poised for an invasion of its mainland islands. What do you think would have been the outcome of a ground, naval, and air assault against Japan?

Draw Conclusions

Even with Little Boy's destruction of Hiroshima, the Japanese military continued to stubbornly refuse conditions of surrender. Why didn't Japan capitulate following the attack on Hiroshima?

Determine Point of View

Approximately 37% of all U.S. prisoners held by Japan died in prisoner-of-war camps, where U.S. and Allied prisoners of war were subjected to a long list of atrocities including slave labor, medical experiments, and inhumane punishments. Japan's government had issued an order to execute some 100,000 Allied prisoners held in Japan at the onset of an invasion of its mainland. Moreover, it was estimated that an invasion of Japan might cost up to 250,000 Allied casualties. How do you think these projections entered into Truman's decision to use atomic warfare against Japan?

Research and Writing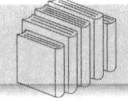

Relating Events

In 1945 the Aztec Eagles of the 201st Squadron of the Mexican Expeditionary Air Force attached to the United States Fifth Air Force, 58th Fighter Group, piloted P-47 Thunderbolt fighter planes in 59 combat missions against Japanese forces in Luzon and Formosa. Research the history of this decorated squadron. What was Mexico's role in World War II? Who were the Aztec Eagles? What was their contribution to World War II?

Historical Interpretation

The development of the atomic bomb was achieved by a group of physicists led by Dr. J. Robert Oppenheimer. Termed the Manhattan Project, the secret work of Oppenheimer and his colleagues occurred at a specially built laboratory located at Los Alamos, New Mexico. Research the Manhattan Project. Who else was involved in the project? What was the cost of development? In what way did Truman use the atomic bomb as a trump card at the Potsdam Conference?

Link to the Past

On July 16, 1945, scientists from the Manhattan Project exploded its first atomic bomb, igniting a force equal to approximately 20,000 tons of TNT, thus successfully completing the Trinity Test in the New Mexico desert and shepherding in the Atomic Age. Following the Trinity Test Oppenheimer reflected,

> We knew the world would not be the same. A few people laughed, a few people cried, most people were silent. I remember the line from the Hindu scripture, the Bhagavad-Gita. Vishnu is trying to persuade the Prince that he should do his duty and to impress him takes on his multi-armed form and says, 'Now, I am become Death, the destroyer of worlds.' I suppose we all thought that one way or another.

Research the ethical issues scientists at Los Alamos wrestled with when contemplating the nuclear arms race that was sure to occur. Which countries currently pose a nuclear threat to the world? What is the status of nuclear disarmament? How has nuclear capability impacted American foreign relations?

1947　The Truman Doctrine

"It must be the policy of the United States to support free peoples."

—President Harry S. Truman

Historical Background

THE end of World War II signaled a new era in United States foreign policy. Among those setting America's world course was George F. Kennan. A career diplomat, Kennan would influence American foreign policy decisions for over forty years. During World War II Kennan served as a United States diplomat to the Soviet Union. Distrustful of Stalin, and wary of an ever-increasing communist presence in Eastern Europe, in February 1946 Kennan sent the State Department an ominous 8,000-word telegram in which he advised a policy of "containment." Kennan cautioned that the U.S.S.R. had expansionist ambitions accompanied by a strong desire to spread its military power and political influence beyond its borders. He further warned that the intent of the Soviet Union was to disrupt United States "authority" in the world as a means to secure Soviet domination.

A year later Kennan penned an article in *Foreign Affairs* under the pseudonym X, titled "The Sources of Soviet Conduct." In it he advised that,

> . . . Soviet pressure against the free institutions of the western world is something that can be contained by the adroit and vigilant application of counter-force at a series of constantly shifting geographical and political points. . . . [The United States] must continue to regard the Soviet Union as a rival, not a partner, in the political arena. It must continue to expect that Soviet policies will reflect no abstract love of peace and stability, no real faith in the possibility of a permanent happy coexistence of the Socialist and capitalist worlds, but rather a cautious, persistent pressure toward the disruption and, weakening of all rival influence and rival power., corresponding to the shifts and maneuvers of Soviet policy. . . .

Kennan reasoned that American political and geographical containment of the Soviet Union, would result in "either the break-up or the gradual mellowing of Soviet power."

Kennan's opinions came on the heels of postwar Soviet expansion into Eastern Europe. Estonia, Latvia, and Lithuania had been annexed by the Soviet Union, and puppet governments established in Poland, Romania, and Bulgaria. Moreover, the Soviet Union had delayed its withdrawal from Iran following World War II, supporting dissident forces while attempting to gain oil concessions from the Iranian government. With the political map in flux, and the coveted Mediterranean and Middle East regions in political disarray, it was feared that Soviet influence would saturate first the Mediterranean region, followed by a movement into the Middle East and Western Europe. Containment appeared not only politically and economically feasible, but essential to the preservation of post-World War II democracy.

Following World War II, a series of political events in Greece had resulted in civil war. Though the Greek government had maintained British backing in its battle against a procommunist insurgency, in February 1947 Great Britain informed the United States that it could not longer afford to provide military assistance and would soon withdraw its troops from Greece. A firm believer in the policy of containment, Secretary of State Dean Acheson articulated that should Greece fall to communism, Turkey, the Middle East, and Africa would be venerable to Soviet domination, and that even the governments of Italy and France might eventually be threatened. Convinced, President Truman called on Congress to provide "financial and economic assistance" to Greece in order to "restore internal order and security. . . ."

Truman's request for $400 million to both Greece and Turkey, essentially for military aid, established the Truman Doctrine, a policy whereby the United States financially strengthened countries threatened with "subjugation by armed minorities or by outside pressure." The Truman Doctrine fundamentally paved the way for American intervention in the foreign affairs of countries seen as vital to America's political and economic interests, and precipitously ushered in the impending Cold War.

NATIONAL ARCHIVES DOCUMENT

Mr. President, Mr. Speaker, Members of the Congress of the United States:

The United States has received from the Greek Government an urgent appeal for financial and economic assistance. Preliminary reports from the American Economic Mission now in Greece and reports from the American Ambassador in Greece corroborate the statement of the Greek Government that assistance is imperative if Greece is to survive as a free nation. . . .

The very existence of the Greek state is today threatened by the terrorist activities of several thousand armed men, led by Communists, who defy the government's authority at a number of points, particularly along the northern boundaries. A Commission appointed by the United Nations security Council is at present investigating disturbed conditions in northern Greece and alleged border violations along the frontier between Greece on the one hand and Albania, Bulgaria, and Yugoslavia on the other. . . .

The United States must supply that assistance. . . .

We have considered how the United Nations might assist in this crisis. But the situation is an urgent one requiring immediate action and the United Nations and its related organizations are not in a position to extend help of the kind that is required. . . .

Greece's neighbor, Turkey, also deserves our attention.

The future of Turkey as an independent and economically sound state is clearly no less important to the freedom-loving peoples of the world than the future of Greece. . . .

One of the primary objectives of the foreign policy of the United States is the creation of conditions in which we and other nations will be able to work out a way of life free from coercion. . . .

Should we fail to aid Greece and Turkey in this fateful hour, the effect will be far reaching to the West as well as to the East. . . .

The free peoples of the world look to us for support in maintaining their freedoms. . . . ✳

Below: According to the Domino Theory, allowing Communism to exist in one country would precipitate the fall of other governments to Communism.

Critical Thinking

Draw Conclusions

According to the Truman Doctrine, what should be the goal of American foreign policy?

Compare and Contrast

Compare the policy of containment with isolationism. Why did the United States abandon isolationism following World War II? Would isolationism have been a more effective foreign policy as a deterrent to the spread of communism?

Determine Point of View

The policy of containment had its disbelievers, among them Senator Robert Taft who branded the policy as unwise. Taft's continued criticism of Truman's containment policies compelled presidential advisor Averell Harriman to assert that "Taft would execute the foreign policy of Stalin." In truth, Taft's scorn of Stalin reached back to the Yalta Conference, yet he believed the inclination of the United States to assert its political will on other countries would only result in a Soviet counter-assertion, in effect polarizing the world between two global powers. Do you agree or disagree with Taft's assessment of the effect of the policy of containment? Why or why not?

Research and Writing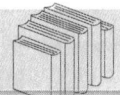

Historical Interpretation

In 1950 President Truman, prompted by what would become known as the "domino theory," approved military aid to the French battling the Viet Minh in Indochina, as a means to stop the spread of communism in the region. Aid to the French continued into Eisenhower's presidency. The term "domino theory" was coined as a result of a 1954 news conference where, when queried about the "the strategic importance of Indochina to the free world," Eisenhower replied,

> …you have broader considerations that might follow what you would call the 'falling domino' principle. You have a row of dominoes set up, you knock over the first one, and what will happen to the last one is the certainty that it will go over very quickly. So you could have a beginning of a disintegration that would have the most profound influences.…

Research the political reasons for American involvement in Indochina. What events prompted both Truman and Eisenhower to extend aid to the French in the early 1950s?

Analysis

Access and read Truman's entire March 12, 1947, address to Congress. What rationalization does Truman offer to justify his request for funding for Greece and Turkey? In what way was Kennan's policy of containment a keystone of the Truman Doctrine?

Relating Events

In Truman's 1949 Inaugural Address, the president outlined four points of action he believed would lead to greater world wide prosperity. He stated that, "On the basis of these four major courses of action we hope to help create the conditions that will lead eventually to personal freedom and happiness for all mankind." Access and read Truman's 1949 Inaugural Address in its entirety. What were the main points made by Truman in his address? How did his four-point plan relate to the policy of containment? In what ways did Truman implement his four-point plan?

1948 The Marshall Plan

"If man does find the solution for world peace it will be the most revolutionary reversal . . . we have ever known."

–GEORGE MARSHALL

HISTORICAL BACKGROUND

WHILE the conclusion of World War II found America's cities and countryside intact, Europe lay in ruins. With many of its cities bombed and a large extent of its railroads, bridges, and industries destroyed, homelessness, unemployment, and illness caused havoc on the politically restless and often destitute people of Europe. A severe drought in 1947, followed by a harsh winter, destroyed cropland, adding to the misery and death of many Europeans. Meanwhile, the United States monitored communist influences in France and Italy with escalating apprehension.

In 1947 Secretary of State George Marshall presented a plan for the economic reconstruction of Europe in an address to Harvard graduates. Marshall had served as the Army Chief of Staff during World War II and had orchestrated Allied victories both in Germany and in Japan. As political and military events unfolded in Europe, Marshall became increasingly concerned that the economic despair enveloping fledgling democracies in Western Europe would spawn Soviet subversion throughout the region. Though nearly $20 billion in loans had been extended to individual countries, great challenges remained before Europe would be economically viable, and time was of the essence. Moreover, with little money for goods, Europeans could ill afford to purchase America's huge volume of available exports, which created a potential threat to American prosperity. In response, Marshall's masterful relief plan, first presented in his Harvard address, proposed that massive amounts of relief be offered to qualifying European countries. Under Marshall's proposed plan, countries would be able to purchase the goods needed to rebuild their economies and infrastructures, and to establish new

industries. In Marshall's words, the success of the plan depended on providing "a cure rather than a mere palliative." Equally appealing, the plan would be short-lived, lasting only four years, in order to relieve American taxpayers from the long-term burden of rebuilding Europe.

Following Marshall's address at Harvard, Truman called upon Congress to pass a European aid package based on the framework of Marshall's plan. In February 1948 Communists took over the government of Czechoslovakia. The fall of another country in Eastern Europe to communism assured swift passage of the 1948 Economic Cooperation Act. Between 1948 and 1952, almost $12 million in grants were provided to such war-torn European nations as Austria, France, Denmark, Germany, and Italy. Though aid was also offered to the Soviet Union, it was quickly rejected by Stalin as an imperialist ploy by the United States. By 1951, with industries in Europe churning out goods beyond prewar levels, the brilliance of Marshall's work was evident. As the innovator of a plan that revitalized European industry and agriculture, thus preventing almost certain mass famine and political unrest, George Marshall received the Nobel Peace Prize in 1953.

In an effort to strengthen Germany, in the spring of 1948 the United States, Great Britain, and a reluctant France merged their zones of occupation, while the Soviets retained control of the eastern zone. Though Berlin rested within the Soviet zone, it too had been divided, with the Soviets in control of East Berlin. Leary of the reunification of Germany and derisive of the Marshal Plan, in June 1948 the Soviets established a blockade of goods entering West Berlin by truck and train from the west. In response, Truman ordered an around-the-clock airlift of well over five tons of food, medical supplies, and other goods into West Berlin every day (unofficially code-named Operation Vittles). Flying in close formation, relief planes landed every three minutes, bringing supplies to the 2.5 million inhabitants of West Berlin. To press his point, in July Truman ordered long-range B-29 bombers to fly in and out of West Berlin every day as a warning to the Soviets not to interfere with the airlifts. By May 1949 the Soviet Union reopened transportation lines to West Berlin, though the airlift continued until September. The Berlin Airlift, along with the Marshall Plan, proved that humanitarian relief could prevail against political aggression.

NATIONAL ARCHIVES DOCUMENT

I need not tell you gentlemen that the world situation is very serious. . . . [T]he rehabilitation of the economic structure of Europe quite evidently will require a much longer time and greater effort than had been foreseen. . . .

The truth of the matter is that Europe's requirements for the next 3 or 4 years of foreign food and other essential products—principally from America—are so much greater than her present ability to pay that she must have substantial additional help, or face economic, social, and political deterioration of a very grave character. . . .

Aside from the demoralizing effect on the world at large and the possibilities of disturbances arising as a result of the desperation of the people concerned, the consequences to the economy of the United States should be apparent to all. It is logical that the United States should do whatever it is able to do to assist in the return of normal economic health in the world, without which there can be no political stability and no assured peace. Our policy is directed not against any country or doctrine but against hunger, poverty, desperation, and chaos. Its purpose should be the revival of working economy in the world so as to permit the emergence of political and social conditions in which free institutions can exist. . . .

An essential part of any successful action on the part of the United States is an understanding on the part of the people of America of the character of the problem and the remedies to be applied. Political passion and prejudice should have no part. With foresight, and a willingness on the part of our people to face up to the vast responsibilities which history has clearly placed upon our country, the difficulties I have outlined can and will be overcome. ✳

Below: The cartoon depicts efforts by Stalin to block the shipment of goods to war-torn Europe. Stalin rejected the Marshall Plan as an imperialist ploy.

Critical Thinking

Determine Point of View

In his address at Harvard, Marshall noted that,

> …It would be neither fitting nor efficacious for this Government to undertake to draw up unilaterally a program designed to place Europe on its feet economically. This is the business of the Europeans. The initiative, I think, must come from Europe. The role of this country should consist of friendly aid in the drafting of a European program so far as it may be practical for us to do so. The program should be a joint one, agreed to by a number, if not all European nations.

In what way did this statement clarify the role of the United States and that of the countries of Europe?

Compare and Contrast

How does the Cold War compare to World War II? How does it contrast?

Assess Significance

How significant was the Soviet Union's rejection of the Marshall Plan?

Research and Writing

Link with the Past

In an attempt to stop the exodus of hundreds of thousands of residents fleeing from communist East Berlin to democratic West Berlin, in 1961 the East German government built a concrete and barbed wire wall dividing East and West Berlin. Escapees to West Berlin risked death from sharpshooters strategically placed in guard towers overlooking the wall. Communication between family and friends virtually came to a halt for twenty-eight years. Then, on November 9, 1989, the Berlin Wall was opened, much to the joy of East and West Berliners. Research the political events that led to the building of the Berlin Wall. Chronicle the Berlin Wall from the time it was constructed until it was torn down. What precipitated the destruction of the Berlin Wall? What is the status of Berlin today?

Relating Events

On April 4, 1949, twelve nations signed the North Atlantic Treaty, with fourteen additional nations eventually becoming members of the North Atlantic Treaty Organization (NATO). Building on the strength of the United Nations, the signatories agreed, "that an armed attack against one or more of them in Europe or North America shall be considered an attack against them all…." In 1950, NATO created a military force to insure the security of member nations. In 1955 NATO's counterpart, the Warsaw Treaty Organization, was formed under the tenets of the Warsaw Pact. Research the history of NATO and the Warsaw Treaty Organization. How did these two organizations embody the polarization of the Cold War?

Analysis

Access and read the entire Marshall Plan. How did Marshall justify the plan? What was his premise for the plan? What did he hope to accomplish?

1948　United States Recognition of Israel

> *"Unless both sides win, no agreement can be permanent."*
>
> —President Jimmy Carter

Historical Background

WORLD War I signaled the end of the extensive Turkish Ottoman Empire that had dominated the Middle East for 400 years. In 1917 the British government, having succeeded in invading the Middle East, which had long been ruled by Germany's Ottoman allies, issued the Balfour Declaration. In a letter to Lord Rothschild, head of the Zionist Federation in Great Britain, British Foreign Secretary Arthur James Balfour communicated the following:

> . . . His Majesty's Government views with favour the establishment in Palestine of a national home for the Jewish people, and will use our best endeavors to facilitate the achievement of this object, it being clearly understood that nothing shall be done which may prejudice the civil and religious rights of existing non-Jewish communities in Palestine, or the rights and political status enjoyed by Jews in any other country.

In June 1919 the League of Nations adopted the Mandates System. Accordingly, Article 22 of the League on Nations Covenant stipulated that,

> To those colonies and territories which as a consequence of the late war have ceased to be under the sovereignty of the States which formerly governed them and which are inhabited by peoples not yet able to stand by themselves under the strenuous conditions of the modern world . . . should be entrusted to advanced nations who by reason of their resources, their experience or their geographical position can best undertake this responsibility, and who are willing to accept it, and that this tutelage should be exercised by them as Mandatories on behalf of the League. . . .

Palestine, one of several former Ottoman Arab territories, was placed under Great Britain's administration through the Mandates System. In 1921, Winston Churchill, who at the time was Colonial Secretary, split Palestine to create a new Arab emirate called Transjordan. In 1922 the League of Nations issued the Palestine Mandate establishing a Jewish homeland based on the 1917 Balfour Declaration. It read in part,

> Whereas the Principal Allied Powers have also agreed that the Mandatory should be responsible for putting into effect the declaration originally made on November 2nd, 1917, by the Government of His Britannic Majesty, and adopted by the said Powers, in favor of the establishment in Palestine of a national home for the Jewish people. . . . Whereas recognition has thereby been given to the historical connection of the Jewish people with Palestine and to the grounds for reconstituting their national home in that country; and . . . Whereas the Principal Allied Powers have selected His Britannic Majesty as the Mandatory for Palestine. . . . The Mandatory shall be responsible for placing the country under such political, administrative and economic conditions as will secure the establishment of the Jewish national home. . . .

From 1919 to 1947 European Jews escaped persecution by emigrating to Palestine. Though British policy was to limit immigration, over 100,000 Jews immigrated to Palestine during the 1920s, with some 256,000 more immigrating during the 1930s. There, much to the resentment of the Palestinians, they purchased land and established Jewish enclaves. By 1948 the British had allotted approximately 2 percent of cultivatable land to Jews with another approximately 46 percent set aside for Arabs. Throughout the years, Palestinians demanded independence and resisted Jewish immigration. Ultimately, Great Britain asked the United Nations to resolve the problem.

To address the issue, the United Nations created a Special Committee on Palestine (UNSCOP). The committee proposed that Palestine be partitioned into two independent states: one Palestinian Arab and a second Jewish.

On November 29, 1947, the United Nations General Assembly approved the partition plan, which essentially divided the British mandate in half, though Jewish settlements at the time constituted far less land. Soon after, war raged between Arabs and Jews. The 1948 war was the first in a series of conflicts between Israel and its Arab neighbors. Over the course of the 1948 war, more than 500,000 Arab residents either fled or were expelled from Palestine. At midnight, on May 14, 1948, the Provisional Government of the Jewish homeland proclaimed its independence as Israel. Later that same day, President Truman recognized the government in a short press release.

NATIONAL ARCHIVES DOCUMENT

Press Release Announcing U.S. Recognition of Israel 1948

This Government has been informed that a Jewish state has been proclaimed in Palestine, and recognition has been requested by the provisional Government thereof.

The United States recognizes the provision government as the de facto authority of the new State of Israel. ✳

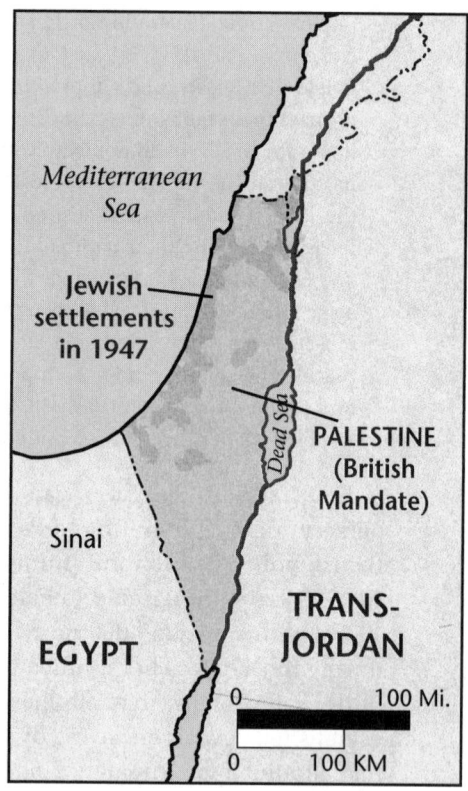

Left: Map of Israel and disputed territory.

Critical Thinking

Assess Significance

Jews had already established settlements in what they considered to be their Holy Land several years before the Balfour Declaration. Historians have postulated that the Balfour Declaration was issued in order to secure Jewish support during World War I. It also has been suggested that Great Britain planned to use the newly established Jewish homeland as a way to maintain British lines of trade with India and East Africa, trade lines that had been shut down under Turkish rule. How significant was the 1917 Balfour Declaration? How significant was Truman's recognition of the State of Israel?

Compare and Contrast

Compare and contrast the 1917 Balfour Declaration with the 1922 Palestine Mandate.

Draw Conclusions

Truman publicly recognized the government of Israel through his press release without first notifying United States delegates to the United Nations or advisors within his administration. Why do you think Truman approached Israel's recognition in this manner?

Research and Writing

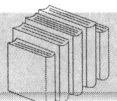

Counterpoint

Zionism is a political and ideological belief that the Jewish people have a right to a national homeland. Since the 1948 recognition of a State of Israel by the United States, Zionism has been defined as the right of the people of Israel to develop and defend their homeland. Palestinians counter that their lands have been unjustly annexed by Israel.

The clash between Jews and Arabs has been marked by bloody vengeance, with a seemingly irreconcilable hatred pervading the volatile region. Peace often has appeared unattainable. Through it all, much to the ire of Arabs throughout the world, the United States has supported the right of Israel to exist, and to that end has provided military assistance to the country. Research the 1949 Armistice. How was the land repartitioned? What impact did the 1949 Armistice have on future Israeli-Arab conflicts? What ideologies drive these disputes? What is the current policy of the United State in regard to the disputes in the region? What possible solutions have been presented to stabilize the region?

Relating Events

On June 5, 1967, Israel launched a preemptive strike against Egypt, Syria, and Jordan, known as the Six-Day War. Israel justified its strike as a defense against troops and warplanes amassed on its border. The war resulted in a large loss of land for the Arab countries, including the Sinai Peninsula and Gaza Strip for Egypt, the West Bank and Jerusalem for Jordan, and the Golan Heights for Syria. In 1978 President Carter succeeded in brokering an accord between Egypt and Israel. Known as the Camp David Accords, the unprecedented agreement between the two countries provided for the withdrawal of Israel from the Sinai Peninsula, as well as plans to negotiate Palestinian autonomy in the West Bank and Gaza Strip.

Research the Six-Day War. How did this war affect American foreign policy? Why were Egyptian President Anwar Sadat and Israeli Prime Minister Menachem Begin chosen as joint recipients of the Nobel Peace Prize in 1978? Why did President Carter feel compelled to become involved in the affairs of foreign rivals? What were the results of the Camp David Accords?

Link to the Past

The West Bank has been a hotbed of conflict as Jewish settlements meet strong resistance from Palestinians. In July 2004 the United Nations International Court of Justice ruled that a security fence being built across the West Bank must be dismantled. At the time of the decision, the planned 447-mile barrier already had been partially constructed in a zigzag manner as it stretched around the limit of Jewish settlements into the West Bank. Research the history behind the West Bank. What lands constituted Occupied Palestinian Territory? What role has the Palestine Liberation Organization played in the West Bank conflict? What was Israel's response to the demand that Jewish settlers leave the West Bank territory?

1953 The Restoration of South Korea

"There is no substitute for victory."

—General Douglas MacArthur

Historical Background

IN 1904 and 1905, Japanese forces invaded Korea, forced its ruler to sign the Japan-Korea Protection Treaty, and proceeded to take over governance of Korea. Soon after, in 1910, Japan dethroned the Korean king and demanded that Korea sign the Japan-Korea Annexation Treaty. The changeover from an insular country whose borders had been closed to foreigners (thus being termed the Hermit Kingdom) to a country ruled by Japan was tantamount to a cultural cleansing for Korea. Once annexed, Japanese religion and culture were imposed on Korea. Koreans no longer were able to use the Korean language in schools or businesses. Similarly, people were forced to adopt Japanese names. On March 1, 1919, Korean citizens took to the streets of Seoul to demand independence. The independence movement was brutally crushed by the Japanese. Some 7,500 Koreans were killed and another 16,000 wounded. Over 47,000 Koreans were arrested. During World War II, Japan harnessed Korea's natural resources and its people to wage war against the Allies. It occupied Korea until Japan's surrender to the Allies at the close of the war.

Full restoration of Korean independence did not occur in 1945, however. Instead, Korea was divided along the 38th Parallel, effectively cutting the country in half. Soviet forces occupied Korea north of this line, with a United States counteroccupation in the south. In an effort to reunite Korea and return sovereignty to its people, in 1947 the United Nations called for an election throughout the entire country. However, when Soviets refused to allow a UN delegation north of the 38th Parallel, Korea's "national" election occurred only in the American zone. In August 1948 the United States, eager to be rid of the political situation, relinquished power to a dubiously elected South Korean government. The U.S. Army packed up and began withdrawing its troops. By June 1949 only 500 American military advisors remained in South Korea, leaving a weak South Korean army to defend it.

By September 1949, two governments ruled Korea: the communist Democratic People's Republic of Korea, under the thumb of the Soviet Union in the north, and the Republic of Korea, with Syngman Rhee as president of an equally repressive government in the south. Each government claimed sovereignty over the entire peninsula and coveted the reunification of Korea under its leadership. In December, however, the United Nations General Assembly declared the Republic of Korea to be Korea's "lawful government." Meanwhile, Mao Zedong was concluding a long and successful revolt to establish a communist government in neighboring China. In October 1949, the Chinese Communists proclaimed the People's Republic of China. Moreover, the Soviet Union was rapidly establishing a well-armed and powerful military in North Korea.

As these events were taking place, however, the United States was preoccupied elsewhere. The Marshall Plan, an overriding concern about Soviet expansion in Europe, and the knowledge the Soviets now possessed nuclear capabilities, combined to focus American attention on Europe. By early 1950 the United States appeared to have summarily abandoned Korea to its own destiny. In a speech before Washington's National Press Club, Secretary of State Dean Acheson declared that the United States was prepared to use military might to defend the government of Japan and the Philippines as part of America's Asian security perimeter. Korea, however, was considered of "lesser" interest.

Then, in a surprise move, on June 25, 1950, North Korea's communist forces plunged south of the 38th Parallel. Fully equipped with Soviet weaponry, the North Koreans quickly overwhelmed the outmatched South Korean forces. The United Nations Security Council soon after passed a resolution condemning the invasion. On June 27, 1950, a second United Nations resolution called for member nations "to provide such assistance to the Republic of Korea as may be necessary . . . to restore international peace. . . . " On June 30, 1950, Truman authorized American military intervention in South Korea. Ultimately, almost 2 million American troops would serve in the Korean War. Three years later, on July 17, 1953, Army Lt. Gen. William K. Harrison, Jr., senior delegate, United Nations Command Delegation and North Korean Gen. Nam Il, senior delegate, Delegation of the Korean People's Army and the Chinese People's Volunteers signed a military armistice agreement at Panmunjom.

NATIONAL ARCHIVES DOCUMENT

Armistice Agreement for the Restoration of the South Korean State 1953

Article I

Military Demarcation Line and Demilitarized Zone

1. A military demarcation line shall be fixed and both sides shall withdraw two (2) kilometers from this line so as to establish a demilitarized zone between the opposing forces. A demilitarized zone shall be established as a buffer zone to prevent the occurrence of incidents which might lead to a resumption of hostilities. . . .

Article II

Concrete Arrangements for Cease-Fire and Armistice

A. General
12. The Commanders of the opposing sides shall order and enforce a complete cessation of all hostilities in Korea by all armed forces under their control, including all units and personnel of the ground, naval, and air forces, effective twelve (12) hours after this armistice agreement is signed . . .

43. Neutral nations Inspection Teams shall be stationed at the following ports of entry.

Below: Battle of Inchon.

Territory under the military contrail of the United Nations Command

INCHON . . . . (37 28'N, 126 38'E)

TAEGU . . . . (35 52'N, 128 36'E)

PUSAN . . . . (35 45'N, 129 02'E)

KANGNUNG . . . . (37 45'N, 128 54'E)

KUNSAN . . . . (35 59'E, 126 43'E)

Territory under the military control of the Korean People's Army and the Chinese People's Volunteers

SINUJU . . . . (40 06'N, 124 24'E)

CHONGJIN . . . . (41 46'N, 129 49'E)

HUNGNAM . . . . (39 50'N, 127 37'E)

MANPO . . . . (41 46'N, 126 18'E)

SINANJU . . . . (39 36'N, 125 36'E) ✳

Critical Thinking

Assess Significance

On June 25, 1950, the United Nations called for the cessation of hostilities in Korea, the "forthwith" withdrawal of North Korean troops to the 38th Parallel, and the commitment of "assistance to Republic of Korea as may be necessary to repel the armed attack and to restore international peace and security in the region." The Soviet delegation was not present at the United Nations at the time this resolution was passed, having boycotted the UN for its refusal to accept delegates from the People's Republic of China. As a member of the United Nations Security Council, a "no" vote by the Soviets would have blocked UN aid to the South. How significant is it that the Soviet Union did not have a vote in deciding the UN's response?

Make Predictions

The arbitrary division of Korea along the 38th Parallel gave rise to economic difficulties. Rice needed by the North was available in the southern part of the peninsula. Industry and hydroelectric power needed by the South was predominately found in the North. In what way might such economic factors have foreshadowed the coming of the Korean War?

Draw Conclusions

What set of factors combined to give the appearance that South Korea was vulnerable to an attack from the North in the spring of 1950?

Research and Writing

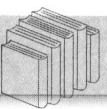

Biography

Bill Mauldin (1921–2003) was a cartoonist who chronicled the events of the time through his wry and often poignant drawings. His fame began with World War II, where the realities of a soldier's life were depicted through two unshaven and weary GIs named "Willie" and "Joe." Mauldin's drawings were published in the Army newspaper *Stars and Stripes*, where inevitably Willie and Joe's attitudes toward military leaders earned him an upbraiding from General George S. Patton. In 1945 Mauldin won the first of two Pulitzer Prizes for his series "Up Front with Mauldin," the youngest individual ever to receive the prestigious award. Following the 1952 publication *Bill Mauldin in Korea*, Mauldin's drawings focused on civil and human rights. Research the life and drawings of Bill Mauldin. Why did Eisenhower consider Mauldin's cartoons a morale builder? Research Mauldin's cartoons and writings. What was the political impact of his work?

Relating Events

On April 14, 1950, the United States National Security Council endorsed NSC-68. Concerned with the possibility of global communism as well as Soviet atomic capabilities, NSC-68 established that,

Soviet efforts are now directed toward the domination of the Eurasian land mass. The United States, as the principal center of power in the non-Soviet world and the bulwark of opposition to Soviet expansion, is the principal enemy whose integrity and vitality must be subverted or destroyed by one means or another if the Kremlin is to achieve its fundamental design.

Research NSC-68. What were its political and military implications? What role did it have in the commitment of American troops in South Korea? How did it define American foreign policy during the Cold War era?

Historical Interpretation

The Korean War, often called the "forgotten war," resulted in over 100,000 American casualties and some 54,000 deaths. Though the United States carried the largest burden, troops from other countries sustained almost 17,000 casualties while fighting against the North Koreans. South Korea suffered almost 1.4 million casualties. Research the Korean War. What was America's involvement in the war? What was the involvement of the United Nations? What was the impact of the war on the Korean people? Why was a cease-fire as opposed to a peace treaty drafted and signed? What implications did the agreement have for the future?

"We're eyeball to eyeball and I think the other fellow just blinked."

—Secretary of State Dean Rusk

Historical Background

By 1962 the nuclear arms race was in full swing. In response to the failed Bay of Pigs invasion, and leery of a possible takeover by the United States, Cuban leader Fidel Castro requested military assistance from the Soviet Union. Subsequently, the U.S.S.R. shipped some three dozen nuclear missiles, capable of hitting American cities, to Cuba. In addition, the Soviets sent a contingent of military commanders with authority to launch the weapons, 42,000 troops, and a supply of antiaircraft missiles to the island. Suspicious of an increased movement of goods to Cuba, the United States began a photographic surveillance of each Cuba-bound Soviet vessel. On September 13, 1962, President John F. Kennedy sent a message to Soviet Premier Nikita Khrushchev. In part it stated,

> If at any time the Communist buildup in Cuba were to endanger or interfere with our security in any way . . . or if Cuba should ever . . . become an offensive military base of significant capacity for the Soviet Union, then this country will do whatever must be done to protect its own security and that of its allies.

Ignoring the warning, the Soviets secretly continued to install intermediate-range ballistic missiles in Cuba. Though Khrushchev assured Kennedy that no nuclear weapons were being installed on the island, aerial photos obtained by a U-2 reconnaissance flight on October 16 clearly showed that Khrushchev had lied. Kennedy immediately convened the Executive Committee of the National Security Council (Ex Comm). It would be the first of many anxious gatherings of Ex Comm in the coming days. Tense meetings followed as Kennedy and his advisors, among them his brother, Attorney General Robert Kennedy, debated how best to proceed. While some of the president's advisors recommended a surprise air strike, ultimately he decided on a naval blockade, terming it a "quarantine" to avoid the action being considered an act of war. On October 22, Kennedy felt it appropriate to apprise the nation of the grave situation via a television and radio address. For thirteen days the world watched and waited as the United States and the Soviet Union teetered on the brink of nuclear war.

On October 24, five Soviet freighters carrying munitions stopped short of American warships marking the quarantine line near Cuba. The next day the freighters reversed course, while other Russian ships allowed Navy search teams to board them. On October 26, in a long and patronizing communication to Kennedy, Khrushchev charged, "for our part, will declare that our ships, bound for Cuba, will not carry any kind of armaments. You would declare that the United States will not invade Cuba. . . ." The following day Khrushchev boldly charged,

> You have placed destructive missile weapons, which you call offensive, in Turkey, literally next to us. How then can recognition of our equal military capacities be reconciled with such unequal relations between our great states? This is irreconcilable.

Ultimately, Kennedy agreed to dismantle obsolete American missiles in Turkey and Italy in return for the Soviets' nuclear disarmament of Cuba. On November 20, he announced that the standoff had ended. "I have been informed by Chairman Khrushchev that all of the IL-28 bombers in Cuba will be withdrawn in thirty days. . . . I have this afternoon instructed the Secretary of Dense to lift our naval quarantine." The world breathed a collective sigh of relief. For the time being, at least, a peaceful solution had averted nuclear war.

Radio and Television Report to the American People on the Soviet Arms Buildup in Cuba

President John F. Kennedy
The White House
October 22, 1962

Good evening my fellow citizens:

This Government, as promised, has maintained the closest surveillance of the Soviet Military buildup on the island of Cuba. Within the past week, unmistakable evidence has established the fact that a series of offensive missile sites is now in preparation on that imprisoned island. The purpose of these bases can be none other than to provide a nuclear strike capability against the Western Hemisphere. . . .

The characteristics of these new missile sites indicate two distinct types of installations. Several of them include medium range ballistic missiles capable of carrying a nuclear warhead for a distance of more than 1,000 nautical miles. Each of these missiles, in short, is capable of striking Washington, D.C., the Panama Canal, Cape Canaveral, Mexico City, or any other city in the southeastern part of the United States, in Central America, or in the Caribbean area. . . .

To halt this offensive buildup, a strict quarantine on all offensive military equipment under shipment to Cuba is being initiated. All ships of any kind bound for Cuba from whatever nation or port will, if found to contain cargoes of offensive weapons, be turned back. . . .

I call upon Chairman Khrushchev to halt and eliminate this clandestine, reckless and provocative threat to world peace and to stable relations between our two nations. . . .

My fellow citizens: let no one doubt that this is a difficult and dangerous effort on which we have set out. No one can see precisely what course it will take or what costs or casualties will be incurred. Many months of sacrifice and self-discipline lie ahead-months in which our patience and our will will be tested-months in which many threats and denunciations will keep us aware of our dangers. But the greatest danger of all would be to do nothing. . . .

NATIONAL ARCHIVES DOCUMENT

Left: A U-2 spy plane photo showed the installation of medium-range nuclear weapons, capable of striking major American cities within minutes, being installed in Cuba. The photo sparked the Cuban Missile Crisis.

Critical Thinking

Analyze Cause and Effect

On October 27, an American U-2 reconnaissance plane was shot down over Cuban air space by a Soviet surface-to-air missile. The pilot, Major Rudolf Anderson, Jr., was killed. In a memo to Secretary of State Dean Rusk, Robert Kennedy reported on a conversation he had with Soviet Ambassador Dobrynin.

> I explained to him that in the last two hours we had found that our planes flying over Cuba had been fired upon and that one of our U-2's had been shot down and the pilot killed. I said these men were flying unarmed planes.... I told him that this was an extremely serious turn in events. We would have to make certain decisions within the next 12 or possibly 24 hours. There was a very little time left. If the Cubans were shooting at our planes, then we were going to shoot back.... He raised the point that the argument the Cubans were making was that we were violating Cuban air space. I replied that if we had not been violating Cuban air space then we would still be believing what he and Khrushchev had said—that there were no long-range missiles in Cuba.

What impact do you think this event might have had on the negotiating process?

Draw Conclusions

Toward the end of the Cuban Missile Crisis, a U-2 plane mistakenly flew over Russia, only to be chased out of Russian air space by Soviet MIGs. Secretary of Defense Robert McNamara pledged to go to war with the Soviets over the incident. In reply, President Kennedy explained that there's always some individual who "doesn't get the message," and instead chose to avoid the event. How important was Kennedy's reaction at this time in history?

Assess Significance

Following the Cuban Missile Crisis, Kennedy and Khrushchev agreed to install a telephone "hot line" between the two nations as a way to avert a future nuclear war precipitated by the misunderstanding of intentions. How significant was this agreement? Explain your assessment.

Research and Writing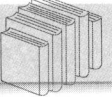

Relating Events

Following World War II, Cuba's government faced difficult challenges, including widespread food shortages, spiraling inflation, and social unrest. In March 1952 Fulgencio Batista staged a military coup against the government. By the end of the month, Batista's new government was formally recognized by President Eisenhower. Research the history of the Batista regime. How did the balance of power and wealth shift during his rule? How and why did Castro come to power? How did the political, social, and economic structure of Cuba change under Castro? What prompted the United States to impose a trade embargo on Cuba?

Historical Interpretation

On April 10, 1961, presidential aide Arthur Schlesinger, Jr., in a memo to President Kennedy wrote,

> The United States is emerging again as a great, mature and liberal nation, coolly and intelligently dedicated to the job of stopping Communism, strengthening the free and neutral nations and working for peace. It is this reawakening world faith in America which is at stake in the Cuban operation....

Schlesinger continued in his memo to recommend ways to offset political fallout, should a planned invasion of Cuba fail. One week later, the United States supported some 1,300 Cuban exiles in just such attempt to overthrow Castro's government. Research the Bay of Pigs invasion. How and why was it organized? What role did the Central Intelligence Agency (CIA) play in the operation? What happened? What was the Soviet response to the Bay of Pigs? Why was the invasion considered a foreign policy fiasco, as well as a huge embarrassment to Kennedy?

Link to the Past

What is the current United States foreign policy in regard to Cuba? What is the basis for the policy?

1963 Test Ban Treaty

"A journey of a thousand miles begins with one step."

–John F. Kennedy, quoting a Chinese proverb

Historical Background

The destructive capability of the atomic bombs dropped on Japan during the closing days of World War II paled in comparison to the detonation of "Mike," a hydrogen bomb that vaporized the Enewetak Atoll in the Marshall Islands, some 3,000 miles west of Hawaii. The explosion represented the most powerful annihilation device of its time. Dropped on November 1, 1952, it unleashed a 10.4-megaton explosive force, 693 times greater than the atomic bomb that destroyed Hiroshima. The ensuing fireball reached outward and upward for three miles, turning the water around the island into churning steam. Gone forever was the atoll, and with it the island home of the Enewetakese, who had been evacuated 120 miles to another atoll for the test. In its place was a 1.2-mile-wide crater.

Within a year, the Soviet Union detonated its own thermonuclear weapon. Between 1953 and 1958, more than 200 atmospheric tests of nuclear weapons were conducted by the United States, the Soviet Union, and the United Kingdom. People around the world expressed concern for the cumulative environmental effects of continued nuclear testing. In 1954 Prime Minister Nehru of India proposed a worldwide halt to such explosions. In 1955 the Russell-Einstein Manifesto, in calling for "abolition of thermo-nuclear weapons," explained that,

It is stated on very good authority that a bomb can now be manufactured which will be 2,500 times as powerful as that which destroyed Hiroshima. Such a bomb, if exploded near the ground or under water, sends radio-active particles into the upper air. They sink gradually and reach the surface of the earth in the form of a deadly dust or rain. It was this dust which infected the Japanese fishermen and their catch of fish. No one knows how widely such lethal radio-active particles might be diffused, but the best authorities are unanimous in saying that a war with H-bombs might possibly put an end to the human race.

President Eisenhower agreed, asserting in 1956 that, "humanity has now achieved, for the first time in its history, the power to end its history." In 1958, more than 9,000 scientists signed a petition urging the United Nations to intervene to stop the testing of nuclear bombs.

In May 1955, the United Nations Disarmament Commission began meeting to discuss the possibility of a nuclear test ban treaty. They continued to meet over the course of eight years. From 1958 to 1961 the United States, Great Britain, and the Soviet Union participated in an unverifiable moratorium on nuclear testing.

With the Cold War in full swing, however, in 1961 the United States and the Soviet Union resumed testing, conducting some 200 nuclear tests both in the ground and in the atmosphere. By 1962 four countries—the United States, the USSR, Great Britain, and France—had conducted nuclear tests. In addition, China and Israel appeared on the verge of gaining nuclear capability. The need to curtail the threat of nuclear weapons was obvious to President Kennedy. Against this backdrop, the 1962 Cuban Missile Crisis provided the wake-up call that motivated world leaders to acknowledge the urgent need to address the growing nuclear threat.

In the summer of 1963, the long work of the United Nations Disarmament Commission culminated in an international treaty banning nuclear weapons. Signed by the United States, the Soviet Union, and Great Britain, it banned nuclear testing in the atmosphere, under water, and in space. It did not, however, prohibit underground testing. Nor did it affect the future proliferation of nuclear weapons. Yet, the international treaty proved to be a solid first step in world acknowledgment of the need to control the effects of nuclear testing. In the years that followed, 108 other countries signed on to the treaty. Notably absent, however, were the signatures of France and China.

NATIONAL ARCHIVES DOCUMENT

TREATY

banning nuclear weapon tests in the atmosphere, in outer space and under water

The Governments of the United States of America, the United Kingdom of Great Britain and Northern Ireland, and the Union of Soviet Socialist Republics, hereinafter referred to as the "Original Parties,"

Proclaiming as their principal aim the speediest possible achievement of an agreement on general and complete disarmament under strict international control in accordance with the objectives of the United Nations which would put an end to the armaments race and eliminate the incentive to the production and testing of all kinds of weapons, including nuclear weapons,

Seeking to achieve the discontinuance of all test explosions of nuclear weapons for all time, determined to continue negotiations to this end, and desiring to put an end to the contamination of mans environment by radioactive substances,

Have agreed as follows:

Article I

1. Each of the Parties to this Treaty undertakes to prohibit, to prevent, and not to carry out any nuclear weapon test explosion, or any other nuclear explosion, at any place under its jurisdiction or control:

   (a) in the atmosphere; beyond its limits, including outer space; or under water, including territorial waters or seas; or

   (b) in any other environment if such explosion causes radioactive debris to be present outside the territorial limits of the State under whose jurisdiction or control such explosion is conducted. . . . ✳

Left: November 1952 "Mike" test—hydrogen bomb.

Critical Thinking

Draw Conclusions

The United States Senate ratified the Test Ban Treaty on September 24, 1963, by a vote of 80 to 19. Why do you think the vote was not unanimous?

Assess Significance

Of what significance was it that both China and France refused to sign the 1963 Test Ban Treaty?

Analyze Cause and Effect

In 1954 the United States launched the USS *Nautilus*, the first nuclear-powered submarine. The sub immediately broke speed and distance records. By 1962 the United States Navy operated 26 nuclear-powered submarines, with 30 more under construction. In 1960 the U.S. Navy armed its fleet of nuclear-powered subs with Polaris missiles. The missiles, with ranges varying from 1,400 to 2,800 miles, each packed a nuclear warhead. It was the beginning of a nuclear arms race at sea. Why did the advent of nuclear power at sea pose a new international threat?

Research and Writing

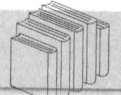

Relating Events

In the 1950s and 1960s, school children across the United States participated in "duck and cover" drills in which children would spring from their seats, squeeze themselves under their desks, and cover their heads with their arms. Anxious families dug fallout shelters in their backyards, stocking them with water, food, and other provisions as safe havens in case of a nuclear attack. Familiar yellow-and-black air raid shelter signs were displayed on public buildings, providing a false sense of protection for a society focused the ever-present threat of nuclear war. Young children were cautioned not to eat snow for fear that radioactive fallout from Soviet atomic bombs tests dotted every snowflake. Research the efforts by Americans to safeguard themselves against radioactive fallout as well as against a nuclear attack. How did fear of a nuclear attack reach into the homes and daily lives of Americans? What did the federal government do to safeguard citizens?

Analysis

In a 1963 address at American University, President Kennedy called for an enlightened approach to the banning of nuclear weapons. He stated,

> I speak of peace because of the new face of war. Total war makes no sense in an age when ... a single nuclear weapon contains almost 10 times the explosive force delivered by all the Allied air forces in the Second World War.... The one major area of these negotiations where the end is in sight is in a treaty to outlaw nuclear tests.... Chairman Khrushchev, Prime Minister Macmillan, and I have agreed that high-level discussions will shortly begin in Moscow looking toward early agreement on a comprehensive test ban treaty. Our hopes must be tempered with the caution of history, but with our hopes go the hopes of all mankind.

Access and read the 1963 Test Ban Treaty in its entirety. Access and read Kennedy's June 10, 1963, address at American University. Did the Test Ban Treaty meet Kennedy's vision for peace?

Link to the Past

The 1963 Test Ban Treaty did not stop the testing of nuclear weapons. In the 1960s the United States conducted more nuclear tests than it had in the 1950s, though each test was conducted underground. Under Kennedy, the United States continued to build its nuclear arsenal. Yet, in 1968 the United States and the Soviet Union were among 43 countries adding their signatures to the Treaty on the Non-Proliferation of Nuclear Weapons. In 1996, some 71 countries signed the Comprehensive Nuclear Test Ban Treaty. This treaty prohibited nuclear explosions in all environments. What other treaties dealing with the reduction of a nuclear threat have been signed since 1963? Which countries currently have nuclear capability? How do nuclear arms continue to threaten world peace?

1964 Tonkin Gulf Resolution

"Intend to open fire if necessary self defense."

—CAPTAIN JOHN J. HERRICK

HISTORICAL BACKGROUND

THE Vietnam War was a long and costly battle, beginning in 1961 and ending with the fall of Saigon in 1975. It was both a ground war fought in the thick brush and rice paddies of South Vietnam, Cambodia, and Laos, and a pounding air war as well that crossed into North Vietnam. It began as an extension of the Truman Doctrine, with a focus on the geographical containment of communism, was propelled onward by the "domino theory," and ended with some 300,000 American casualties, including over 58,000 dead.

The road to America's involvement in Vietnam began with aid provided to France in its failed effort to re-establish control over French Indochina following World War II. After its defeat at the Battle of Dien Bien Phu in 1954, France agreed to peace terms struck at the Geneva Conference. As a result of these accords, Vietnam was temporary divided into two zones, with plans for reunification once a national election was held. However, the election never occurred. Instead, a communist government headed by Ho Chi Minh was established in the North, while an American-backed and dubiously elected government headed by Ngo Dinh Diem ruled the South.

Concerned with a communist takeover of South Vietnam and the spread of communism throughout the region, the United States began sending military advisors to that country. In addition, in 1962 the Central Intelligence Agency (CIA) began using South Vietnamese commandos, trained and assisted by U.S. Navy SEALs, to conduct clandestine missions against targets in the coastal waters of North Vietnam. On January 24, 1964, covert operations against North Vietnam were transferred to the newly formed Special Operations Group (SOG) under the command of General Paul D. Harkins. Operating under the code name 34 Alpha, SOG conducted missions against bridges, railways, and coastal installations in North Vietnam. The operations were supported by U.S. Navy swift boats (fast patrol craft), U.S. SEALs, and Marine reconnaissance teams. Also supporting the missions was intelligence gained by "Desoto patrols," the code name given to patrols by U.S. destroyers equipped with specially designed eavesdropping equipment.

Although Desoto missions typically operated more than 20 miles offshore, by 1964 U.S. destroyers were given authority to approach within four miles of the North Vietnamese coastline. The intelligence gained through Desoto missions proved valuable to SOG missions. On July 30, 1964, four patrol boats embarked on a clandestine mission against three targets located in the Gulf of Tonkin. As a result, several buildings, a gun emplacement, and a communications tower were destroyed. During the course of the mission, gunfire tore through the bow of one boat, wounding four South Vietnamese. Though all four patrol boats safely returned to their base in Da Nang, the covert nature of the operation had been compromised. Within days, the North Vietnamese lodged a complaint with the International Control Commission, the group established to oversee the provisions of the Geneva Accords. North Vietnam also increased its naval presence in the Gulf of Tonkin waters, moving its Swatows (Russian-built torpedo boats) southward.

On July 28, 1964, the destroyer USS *Maddox* left Taiwan for the Gulf of Tonkin to engage in intelligence-gathering operations. On August 2, Captain John J. Herrick of the *Maddox* communicated to his superiors that he anticipated "serious reaction [to] my movements in near future." When what appeared to be three North Vietnamese patrol boats failed to identify themselves, the *Maddox* fired three shots across the bow of the lead boat. What followed was twenty-nine minutes of intense naval engagement between the *Maddox* and North Vietnamese Swatows.

Upon hearing of the naval confrontation in the Gulf of Tonkin, Secretary of Defense Robert McNamara responded, "We cannot sit still as a nation and let them attack us on the high seas and get away with it." Though the details of additional naval engagements were unclear, in an August 5 address to Congress, President Lyndon Johnson reported that

Last night I announced to the American people that the North Vietnamese regime had conducted further deliberate attacks against U.S. naval vessels operating in international waters, and I had therefore directed air action against gunboats and supporting facilities used in these hostile operations.

On August 7 Congress passed the Gulf of Tonkin Resolution. It proved to be America's entrée to a full-scale war in Vietnam.

NATIONAL ARCHIVES DOCUMENT

Eighty-eighth Congress of the United States of America

AT THE SECOND SESSION

Whereas naval units of the Communist regime in Vietnam, in violation of the principles of the Charter of the United Nations and of international law, have deliberately and repeatedly attacked United Stated naval vessels lawfully present in international waters. . . .

Whereas these attackers are part of deliberate and systematic campaign of aggression that the Communist regime in North Vietnam has been waging against its neighbors. . . .

Whereas the United States is assisting the peoples of southeast Asia to protest their freedom and has no territorial, military or political ambitions in that area. . . .

Resolved . . . That the Congress approves and supports the determination of the President, as Commander in Chief, to take all necessary measures to repel any armed attack against the forces of the United States and to prevent further aggression. . . .

This resolution shall expire when the President shall determine that the peace and security of the area is reasonably assured. . . . ✳

Below: Vietnam War map.

Critical Thinking

Classify Information

Was the Gulf of Tonkin Resolution a conditional or unconditional mandate to Johnson, as commander in chief?

Draw Conclusions

By the end of 1965, some 184,000 American troops were in Vietnam. In August 1966, Johnson authorized an increase to 429,000 troops. By 1968, troop strength had grown to over 500,000, including several Army and Marine units that had been ordered back to Vietnam for a second tour of duty. Other soldiers volunteered for a second tour in Vietnam. Many Vietnam vets have expressed sentiments similar to Dan Hillcoat, who, when asked about his tour in Vietnam responded, "It was strictly a war fought for the benefit of individuals who wanted political gains. Thousands of lives were lost, and for nothing, absolutely nothing. But, I would do it over again in a heartbeat to help my brothers come home." Why do you think some soldiers volunteered for a second tour of duty? What do you think Hillcoat meant?

Assess Significance

The Vietnam Veterans Memorial sits as part of the National Mall in Washington, D.C. The open, V-shaped black granite memorial wall rises from the ground to a height of slightly over ten feet at its apex and then stretches back to the ground to finish the V, one wing pointing to the Washington Monument, the other toward the Lincoln Memorial. Along the wall are etched the names of over 58,000 service personnel who died in the Vietnam War—the first to die as visitors meet the wall and the last to die at its end. In 2004 an additional marker was added to honor those who died later as a result of their service in Vietnam. In what way does the memorial honor those who died, as well as pay homage to all who served in the Vietnam War?

Research and Writing

Counterpoint

Research the controversy surrounding reports from the USS *Maddox* and USS *Turner Joy* in the Gulf of Tonkin on August 2–4, 1964. Access and read in their entirety Johnson's August 5 address to Congress and the August 7 Gulf of Tonkin Resolution. Write an essay in which you either support or oppose the Gulf of Tonkin Resolution.

Relating Events

The Pentagon Papers, commissioned by Secretary of Defense Robert McNamara, is a 7,000-page series of top-secret reports chronicling U.S. involvement in Vietnam. In 1971 Daniel Ellsberg, who worked on the Pentagon Papers, leaked them to both *The New York Times* and the *Washington Post*. The Pentagon Papers damaged the credibility of the Vietnam War and caused a national stir. President Nixon sought to halt the publication of the Pentagon Papers, first through pressure exerted by the Executive Branch and then through court action. In *New York Times Co. v. United States* (1971), the U.S. Supreme Court ruled "the Government's case against the *Washington Post* should have been dismissed and that the injunction against the *New York Times* should have been vacated." Research the Pentagon Papers. What incriminating evidence regarding Vietnam did they expose? Why did Nixon want to halt their publication? What was the impact of the decision in *New York Times Co. v. United States*?

Link to the Past

In November 1973, Congress passed the War Powers Resolution. Research the circumstances surrounding the passage of the War Powers Resolution. What were the provisions of the legislation? Why was it passed? When since 1973 has it been implemented? How effective has the War Powers Resolution been in restricting the power of the president to wage war?

Expansion

"Other nations have tried to check . . . the fulfillment of our manifest destiny to overspread the continent."

—JOHN LOUIS O'SULLIVAN (1813–1895)

Prologue

A look to the west began from the moment the first colonists stepped on America's shores. Western lands were filled with intrigue and danger. They held the thrill of discovery, an opportunity to explore and conquer the unknown. Americans moved west in search of fortune and homestead, and with it the promise of a better life. Along their journey they were awestruck by the land's beauty and abundance in resources and wildlife. They also experienced great hardships in life and fortunes lost. The expansion that occurred over the course of one century transformed a nation and forever changed the way of life of Native Americans. Westward expansion is the story of triumph and defeat, of unimaginable gain and incalculable loss. Land to the west was an enticement. To some it was also an inevitability. In 1845 John L. O'Sullivan provided westward expansion with a higher purpose. "In its magnificent domain of space and time, the nation of many nations is destined to manifest to mankind the excellence of divine principles." America, said O'Sullivan, was "the great nation of futurity." In this fourth unit, you will read of how the country expanded, of the people who made it happen, and of the obstacles overcome along the way.

1787 Northwest Ordinance

"Religion, morality, and knowledge being necessary to good government . . . schools and the means of education shall forever be encouraged."

—Article 3 of the Northwest Ordinance

Historical Background

THE 1783 Treaty of Paris not only signaled the end of the American Revolution, it also opened up a vast expanse of land to the west. The United States now reached from the shores of the Atlantic, beyond the Appalachian Mountains, to the bank of the Mississippi River. Land ceded by the British equaled approximately 260,000 square miles, about the size of present-day Texas and California combined. Following the American Revolution, many states re-extended their borders west of the Appalachian Mountains, with states such as North Carolina, Georgia, and South Carolina claiming land all the way to the Mississippi River.

Virginia's colonial land grant was from "sea to sea." However, over the years its borders had shrunk due to disputes over British land claims by rival European nations. At independence, Virginia claimed land west to the Mississippi River and north to Lake Superior. By far the new nation's largest state, Virginia's enormity did not sit well with states like Rhode Island and Delaware, which had no land claims in the west. In fact, one such "landless" state, Maryland, refused to ratify the Articles of Confederation until states with large western claims agreed to relinquish their lands to the national government. As a result, the new nation's first constitution was not ratified until 1781, when the Revolutionary War was all but over. To completely resolve the issue, the Northwest Ordinance read in part, "There shall be formed in the said territory, not less than three nor more than five States; and the boundaries of the States, as soon as Virginia shall alter her act of cession, and consent to the same . . ."

The Northwest Ordinance of 1787 was the last of three important legislative actions taken by Congress to develop a method of establishing new states in the west. By 1779 the Continental Congress had decided to treat the western lands not as colonies but as future states, replete with the rights of states already established. Once peace was won, the task of managing the vast new lands in the west lay before the Confederation Congress. As they had done so often before, the states turned to Thomas Jefferson, this time to establish a workable plan for the territory termed the "Old Northwest." It was a ripe opportunity for Jefferson to create a federal course of action representative of his most cherished belief—that of self-governance.

In the Ordinance of 1784, Jefferson established that land "already purchased or shall be purchased of the Indian inhabitants, and offered for sale by Congress, shall be divided into distinct states. . . ." Jefferson's plan allowed for creation of a temporary government within settled lands, as well as established the parameters for future statehood. Ever conscious of the debt incurred by the Revolutionary War, he set as paramount a system by which newly developed areas would shoulder a proportionate share of the national debt. Congress embraced Jefferson's proposal with two exceptions. It deleted the section that prohibited slavery or "involuntary servitude" in the new areas after 1800. It also rejected his proposed scholarly names for the new states—among others, Cherronesus, Assenisippia, Metropotamia, Sylvania, and possibly Pelisipia.

Jefferson followed the Ordinance of 1784 with a system for structuring the new lands, as well as a means for generating revenue from them. Both ideas were embodied in the Ordinance of 1785. Jefferson recognized that one of the difficulties with land ownership was disputes over boundaries. In the past, land claims had been marked with rocks, trees, rivers, and the like. Rocks, of course, could be moved and trees could be cut. Moreover, Jefferson understood that prudent land speculators would buy only the best land available, passing over irregular plots and pockets of unwanted wasteland. Therefore, he proposed the orderly creation of rectangular plots, the basic unit of which would be the township. Each township would be a six mile-by-six mile square totaling 36 square miles. Each one-mile square would constitute a "section" of 640 acres. Offered for sale at $1 per acre, each section would generate $640 in revenue for the government. Over time, however, the proposed section of land proved too large for a family farm and too costly for most people to afford.

The Ordinance of 1787, or the Northwest Ordinance, was based on the 1784 law. It provided that the territory north of the Ohio River eventually would be divided into no less than three, but no more than five territories (eventually becoming Indiana, Illinois, Ohio, Michigan, and Wisconsin). Each territory would become a new state when its number of free inhabitants reached 60,000, and other conditions were met. Civil liberties were guaranteed in these territories, education was encouraged, and most significantly, slavery was forever banned in all of them.

NATIONAL ARCHIVES DOCUMENT

An Ordinance for the government of the Territory of the United States northwest of the River Ohio.

Section 1. Be it ordained by the United States in Congress assembled, That the said territory, for the purposes of temporary government, be one district, subject, however, to be divided into two districts, as future circumstances may, in the opinion of Congress, make it expedient. . . .

Sec. 9. So soon as there shall be five thousand free male inhabitants of full age in the district, upon giving proof thereof to the governor, they shall receive authority, with time and place, to elect a representative from their counties or townships to represent them in the general assembly: Provided, That, for every five hundred free male inhabitants, there shall be one representative. . . .

Sec. 11. The general assembly or legislature shall consist of the governor, legislative council, and a house of representatives. . . .

Art. 6. There shall be neither slavery nor involuntary servitude in the said territory, otherwise than in the punishment of crimes whereof the party shall have been duly convicted: Provided, always, That any person escaping into the same, from whom labor or service is lawfully claimed in any one of the original States, such fugitive may be lawfully reclaimed and conveyed to the person claiming his or her labor or service as aforesaid. . . . ✳

Below: Virginia in 1783 and 1787.

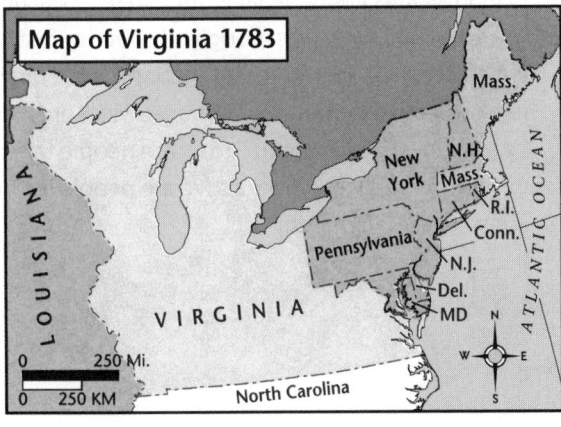

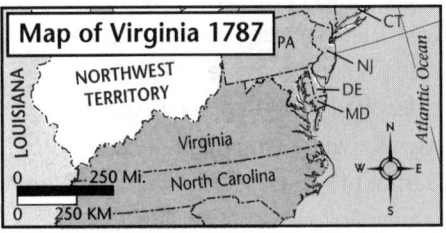

Critical Thinking

Assess Significance

Although lands ceded by the British to the United States were inhabited by many Indian nations, no provision to strike agreements with them was included in the Treaty of Paris. Both the British and the Americans were certainly aware of the inevitability of conflict between Native Americans and whites once the land opened to westward expansion. Why was it assumed that the British were free to cede land without the consent of Native Americans?

Classify Information

Jefferson's Ordinance of 1785, in essence, took land that belonged to the United States government, and thus to the people of the United States (although a concept certainly disputed by Native Americans), and planned to sell it to Americans. What distinction was Jefferson making between public and private ownership?

Make Predictions

How would the prohibition of slavery in the Northwest Territory impact North-South relations in the near future?

Research and Writing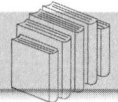

Analysis

Access and read Section 14 of the Northwest Ordinance. What rights were granted to individuals living in the Northwest Territory? What familiarity do the rights granted though Section 14 have with the Bill of Rights proposed by Congress in 1789? What rights are granted by Section 14 that are not included in the Bill of Rights? What policies are encouraged rather than legislated? What reference is made to Native Americans in Article 3? How did Article 6 protect individuals against slavery but not protect those who had been enslaved?

Relating Events

In 1768 the British and Iroquois Indians signed the Treaty of Fort Stanwix. With this agreement, the Iroquois ceded the rights to lands lying east and south of the Ohio River. The Shawnee and other native tribes, however, refused to move from the lower Ohio Valley. Violent clashes resulted when Virginia surveyors began mapping the area for white settlement. In 1774 Lord Dunmore, governor of Virginia, sent some 1,000 Virginia militia into the area. Following the Battle of Point Pleasant, Cornstalk, leader of the Shawnee, signed the Treaty of Camp Charlotte. With this treaty, the Shawnee relinquished their lands south of the Ohio River. In 1784 the United States reaffirmed its claim to the Ohio Valley when the Iroquois and the United States signed the second Treaty of Fort Stanwix, also known as the 1784 Treaty with the Six Nations. Research Lord Dunmore's War. Why were the Shawnee willing to sign the Treaty of Camp Charlotte? What led the Shawnee to fight for the British during the American Revolution? Why was the 1784 Treaty with the Six Nations disputed by other tribes of the Ohio Valley? What led to the 1795 Treaty of Greenville? What were its provisions?

Link to the Past

Townships, as a unit of local government, can be found in many states today. What is your state's local unit of government? How was it originally determined? How is it structured? How does it function? Is it a direct or representative democracy? What services are provided by your local government? How are people taxed to pay for the services? How active are people in your area's local government?

1803 Lewis and Clark Expedition

"The object of your mission is to explore . . ."

–Letter from President Jefferson to Meriwether Lewis,
June 20, 1803

Historical Background

IMAGINE being given the mission to leave from St. Louis, Missouri, traverse the plains of America's heartland, and cross over the high Rocky Mountains as you follow the Columbia River to reach the "Western Ocean" more than 3,000 miles later. You will walk, paddle, and ride horses as you move your gear and your group from campsite to campsite. Eventually you will need to find shelter during the treacherous, snow-filled, subzero winter. Throughout the journey, you will encounter several different native peoples, some friendly, others not. A caveat to your mission is that you have no maps and no prior knowledge of the rivers or lands you will cross. In addition, your provisions should last about two weeks. After that, you are on your own to find food. You must carry your supplies and, when need be, your canoes across the land. You will be joined by up to fifty skilled, trail-blazing men from the United States and Canada, including your co-leader's slave, a man by the name of York. You will call yourself the "Corps of Discovery," because you have been charged with discovering new animals, plants, and routes others will take after you. You must keep a detailed account of all that you see as you travel, remembering to gather specimens of each discovery along the way. You will have no quick means of communicating with those back home, no way of getting help if struck by tragedy, and no option to turn back, save your own safety, when travel becomes difficult. One more point of interest—when you get to where you are going, you must turn around and come back to where you started.

Sound exciting? It did to Meriwether Lewis and William Clark in 1803. The cross-country adventure was of Jefferson's imaginings. He first proposed the remarkable expedition in a secret message to Congress on January 18, 1803. In it he underplayed the complexity and danger of the plan.

In total, Jefferson requested $2,500 from Congress for the grand expedition. To avoid debate, he explained that the mission would be of extraordinary value in accomplishing trade agreements with the Indians and serve "[to extend] the external commerce of the United States." The secrecy was necessary because most of the land he proposed to cross was at the time still claimed by France (Louisiana), with other land claimed by Great Britain and Spain (Oregon Country). Yet, with the mission Jefferson hoped to learn more about the vast land between the Mississippi River and Pacific Ocean, map it, and eventually open it to American settlement. It was to be an expedition extraordinaire, and Jefferson didn't want to miss the opportunity to plan, propose, and execute it. The bonus came in April when France offered to sell all of Louisiana to the United States. With that agreement, Jefferson could freely send his trusted secretary and able mountaineer, Meriwether Lewis, and Lewis's choice for co-leader, army-trained William Clark, on the adventure of their lives.

Jefferson's June 20, 1803, letter to Meriwether Lewis showed how painstakingly he considered every precaution critical to the mission's success, from recognition of its undertaking by France, Spain, and the "Minister of England" to procedural instructions on what should occur if Lewis suffered accidental death. Prior to the onset of the expedition, Jefferson provided Lewis with his personal library of scientific books. Lewis spent considerable time learning about meteorology, geography, paleontology, and the intricacies of surveying equipment and other scientific instruments necessary for the observations he was charged with making. Additionally, he gathered over 2,300 pounds of supplies and equipment including books, clothing, camping gear, navigational equipment, rifles and muskets, a 55-foot keelboat, 2 pirogues (open boats), 35 oars, and 2 horses. Lewis, Clark, and their able assistants carried these items and more over land and water with the destination of the "Western Ocean" firmly in mind. They weathered harsh winters, hot summers, insects, wild animals, raging rivers, high waterfalls, and sensitive negotiations for assistance and shelter with native tribes. In the end, the assemblage registered only one death in traveling almost 8,000 miles over twenty-eight months. They returned as heroes to a citizenry that had given them up for dead. And, they changed forever the lives of the Native Americans they encountered, as the West became coveted by whites hoping to capture the beauty and spirit of freedom described by Lewis and Clark.

National Archives Document

Jefferson's Secret Message to Congress
Regarding the Lewis & Clark Expedition

Confidential

Gentlemen of the Senate, and of the House of Representatives:

As the continuance of the act for establishing trading houses with the Indian tribes will be under the consideration of the Legislature at its present session, I think it my duty to communicate the views which have guided me in the execution of that act, in order that you may decide on the policy of continuing it, in the present or any other form, or discontinue it altogether, if that shall, on the whole, seem most for the public good.

The Indian tribes residing within the limits of the United States, have, for a considerable time, been growing more and more uneasy at the constant diminution of the territory they occupy . . . In order peaceably to counteract this policy of theirs, and to provide an extension of territory which the rapid increase of our numbers will call for, two measures are deemed expedient. First: to encourage them to abandon hunting, to apply to the raising stock, to agriculture and domestic manufacture, and thereby prove to themselves that less land and labor will maintain them in this, better than in their former mode of living. . . .

It is, however, understood, that the country on that river is inhabited by numerous tribes, who furnish great supplies of furs and peltry to the trade of another nation, carried on in a high latitude, through an infinite number of portages and lakes, shut up by ice through a long season. . . .

TH. Jefferson
Jan. 18. 1803. ✳

Below: Lewis and Clark traveled some 8,000 miles by horse, on foot, and in canoe as they explored America's northwest.

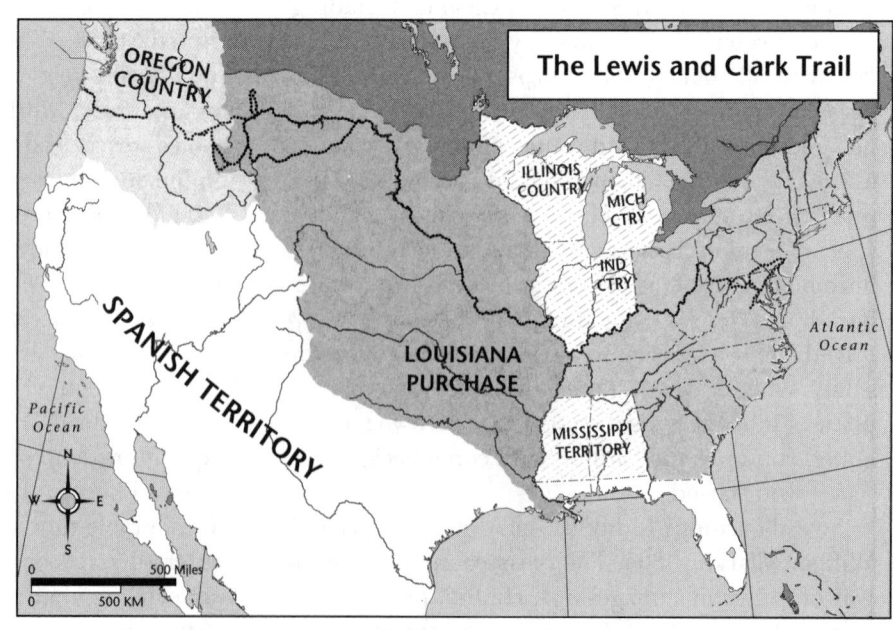

The Lewis and Clark Trail

Critical Thinking

Analyze Cause and Effect

What plan did Jefferson have to counter the ire already felt by Native Americans over the loss of tribal lands to white settlement? What do you think of Jefferson's plan?

Assess Significance

Why did Jefferson first discuss his expedition with Congress? What gave Congress the power to authorize such a mission?

Draw Conclusions

Along the expedition Lewis and Clark were befriended by Native Americans. They wintered among 4,000 Mandan in present-day North Dakota and received guidance and provisions from the Nez Perce, Sioux, and other tribes. Although Lewis informed each tribe that the United States claimed their land, hostilities with Native Americans were rare. Only two hostile deaths among the Blackfoot were chronicled. Why didn't Lewis and Clark encounter more resistance to their travels across native lands?

Research and Writing

Biography

Meriwether Lewis and William Clark served in the military during the American Revolution. Both were men of great talents. Though Lewis was officially in charge of the mission, as great friends, the men shared equal command. Personal accounts by men who served in the expedition report that Lewis and Clark never quarreled, instead discussing each leg of the journey until an agreement was reached about the best plan. Research these two intriguing explorers. What were the men's backgrounds? What talents did they bring to the mission? What roles did they play in the expedition? What happened to them after their famous journey?

Historical Interpretation

While wintering at Fort Mandan, Meriwether Lewis asked fur trader Toussaint Charbonneau to serve as an interpreter. Charbonneau brought along his young Shoshone Indian bride, Sacagawea, for the mission. Unfortunately he couldn't swim, prompting Lewis to describe him as "perhaps the most timid waterman in the world." Sacagawea, on the other hand, was considered by all as calm and resourceful. She is undeniably credited as critical to the mission's success. Research the contribution of Sacagawea to the expedition. In what ways did this audacious young woman ensure the success of the mission? What trials did she face along the mission? What happened to her?

Relating Events

Read Jefferson's secret message to Congress regarding the Lewis and Clark expedition in its entirety. Highlight the points of the mission as defined by Jefferson. Then read Jefferson's June 20, 1803, letter to Meriwether Lewis. Highlight the goals of the mission. Research the Lewis and Clark expedition. Study the chronicles of Lewis and the maps created by Clark. Did the expedition accomplish Jefferson's goals? How did what they learned benefit society?

1803　The Louisiana Purchase

> *"To lose our country by a scrupulous adherence*
> *to written law would be to lose the law itself."*
>
> —THOMAS JEFFERSON

HISTORICAL BACKGROUND

THE Louisiana Territory was a vast expanse of land stretching westward from the Mississippi River across the Great Plains to the Rocky Mountains. Though its northern border was undefined, to the south the border diagonally cut from present-day New Mexico to the city of New Orleans. To Thomas Jefferson and others, the area seemed a natural addition for the westward expansion of the United States. The land was rich in lucrative furs, would provide seemingly unlimited farmland for landless easterners seeking an agrarian way of life, and could serve as a buffer zone against foreign incursions. Moreover, the Mississippi River had become a vital transportation route for farmers who had settled along its tributaries. Farm goods traveled down river to New Orleans, where they were shipped to markets along the East Coast. All things considered, with the potential to double the size of the United States, the Louisiana Territory was an ideal piece of real estate.

The rich Mississippi River Valley was first claimed by the French in the late 1600s. Defeated in the French and Indian War in 1763, France ceded its claims east of the Mississippi River to Britain, while the Louisiana Territory and the important river port of New Orleans were forfeited to Spain. According to the provisions of the Treaty of San Lorenzo (Pinckney's Treaty) in 1795, Spain guaranteed western settlers the "right of deposit" to unload their goods in New Orleans for export. However, commercial enterprise on the lower Mississippi changed dramatically in 1801, when Spain secretly ceded New Orleans and the entire Louisiana Territory back to France. In 1802, the French closed the port of New Orleans to American commerce. More alarming was news that Napoleon Bonaparte had plans to re-establish a French empire in America, west of the Mississippi River.

Western farmers, who depended on the Mississippi River for sale of their products, called for military action to rid New Orleans of the French. Jefferson also recognized the threat the French presence posed to the future westward expansion of the United States. He proceeded with preparations against the French, resigned to the prospect of having to "marry ourselves to the British fleet and nation" if military action were needed. But before risking conflict with the French, he prudently decided first to attempt a diplomatic solution to the situation. He dispatched James Monroe and Robert Livingston to France with instructions to offer up to $10 million for New Orleans and West Florida. To Monroe and Livingston's amazement, instead of having to barter for New Orleans, they were confronted with Napoleon's offer to sell not only New Orleans, but the entire Louisiana Territory as well, some 828,000 square miles, for just $5 million more. At the astounding price of approximately 3 cents per acre, Monroe quickly sealed the deal.

Though elated with the transaction, the purchase of the Louisiana Territory presented Jefferson with a dilemma. Jefferson had long supported a strict interpretation of the Constitution, and nowhere in it was there a provision allowing for the acquisition of land. However, the Constitution did give the President the right to make treaties. Though Jefferson would have preferred to amend the Constitution to allow for land purchases, expedience dictated otherwise. Aware of the unique opportunity, as well as the economic and political benefits of extending America's borders beyond the Mississippi, he advanced a treaty with France to Congress. On December 20, 1803, Congress approved the Louisiana Purchase Treaty. It was a triumph for Jefferson. The United States doubled in size and New Orleans was once again open for American commerce. Moreover, in the spirit of adventure, acquisition of knowledge, and the fervent hope of westward expansion, the Louisiana Purchase opened the door for Lewis and Clark to embark on their great expedition.

The Louisiana Purchase was concluded through signatures on three documents. The treaty itself provided for the cession of Louisiana Territory to the United States, though its boundaries were somewhat obscure. In addition, a convention, or formal agreement, spelled out the purchase price for the land—60 million francs, or $11, 250,000. In a second convention, the United States agreed to assume debts lodged against the French government by Americans. This would cost the United States another 20 million francs, or $3,750,000. The deal was a boon for the United States. For Native Americans, however, it was the harbinger of a coming storm. The impact of the Louisiana Purchase would not only change their way of life, it would challenge their very survival.

NATIONAL ARCHIVES DOCUMENT

TREATY BETWEEN THE UNITED STATES OF AMERICA AND THE FRENCH REPUBLIC

The President of the United States of America and the First Consul of the French Republic in the name of the French People desiring to remove all Source of misunderstanding . . .

Article I
. . . His Catholic Majesty promises and engages on his part to cede to the French Republic six months after the full and entire execution of the conditions and Stipulations herein relative to his Royal Highness the Duke of Parma, the Colony or Province of Louisiana with the Same extent that it now has in the hand of Spain, & that it had when France possessed it; and Such as it Should be after the Treaties subsequently entered into between Spain and other States.

And whereas in pursuance of the Treaty and particularly of the third article the French Republic has an incontestible [sic] title to the domain and to the possession of the said Territory—The First Consul of the French Republic desiring to give to the United States a strong proof of his friendship doth hereby cede to the United States in the name of the French Republic for ever and in full Sovereignty the said territory with all its rights and appurtenances as fully and in the Same manner as they have been acquired by the French Republic in virtue of the above mentioned Treaty concluded with his Catholic Majesty. . . .

A CONVENTION BETWEEN THE UNITED STATES OF AMERICA AND THE FRENCH REPUBLIC

Art: 1
The Government of the United States engages to pay to the French government in the manner Specified in the following article the sum of Sixty millions of francs independant [sic] of the Sum which Shall be fixed by another Convention for the payment of the debts due by France to citizens of the United States. . . .

CONVENTION BETWEEN THE UNITED STATES OF AMERICA AND THE FRENCH REPUBLIC

Art: 1
The debts due by France to citizens of the United States contracted before the 8th Vendémiaire ninth year of the French Republic (30th September 1800) Shall be paid according to the following regulations with interest at Six per Cent; to commence from the period when the accounts and vouchers were presented to the French Government. . . . ❋

Critical Thinking

Draw Conclusions

Monroe accepted Napoleon's offer to sell the Louisiana Territory without first consulting President Jefferson. Why do you think he took the liberty to commit the American government to the deal presented by Napoleon?

Determine Point of View

Reread Jefferson's quote on page 150. To what was Jefferson referring? Do you agree or disagree with him? Why?

Make Predictions

In what ways do you think the U.S. purchase of the Louisiana Territory impacted the native peoples west of the Mississippi River?

Research and Writing

Relating Events

The 1763 Treaty of Paris ended the Seven Years' War (1756–1763) fought between France and Great Britain. The French and Indian War (1754–1763), so named because Native Americans fought alongside the French against the British, was the colonial part of the conflict. The French and Indian War began as a dispute over settlement in the Ohio River Valley, with Britain and France in disagreement over who "owned" the area rich in furs and fertile soils. The war began in May 1754, when George Washington, commanding some 160 men, attacked a small group of French soldiers, killing ten of them, including their commander. Research the French and Indian War. How did the conflict escalate to involve the great powers of Europe? Why was Spain awarded the Louisiana Territory? What role did this war play in westward expansion?

Analysis

Napoleon Bonaparte's offer to sell the Louisiana Territory was prompted by his need of money to renew war with Britain. Also, Napoleon had just suffered a humiliating defeat on the Caribbean island of Santo Domingo (now Haiti and the Dominican Republic), where thousands of French troops had died in an attempt to quash a slave rebellion against French rule. Research the revolt in Santo Domingo. Who was Toussaint Louverture? Why were the French involved on Santo Domingo? What impact did events there have on Napoleon's plans to create a new French empire in America?

Historical Interpretation

Though France had played a critical role in America's independence, diplomatic relations certainly had soured by the early 1800s. When pondering French control of New Orleans, Jefferson observed, "There is on the globe one single spot, the possessor of which is our natural and habitual enemy. It is New Orleans." Research the later half of the eighteenth century. What events sparked distrust between France and the United States? Why did Jefferson call France "our natural and habitual enemy"? Why was Jefferson far more concerned with French claims to land west of the Mississippi River than he had been when Spain claimed the same area? Why was the purchase of the Louisiana Territory given such great importance?

1862 The Homestead Act

*"Other nations have tried to check . . . the fulfillment
of our manifest destiny to overspread the continent."*

–JOHN LOUIS O'SULLIVAN

HISTORICAL BACKGROUND

THE sound of "Westward Ho" echoed across the plains of America during the mid 1800s. With an eye to the west and a thirst for open land, young families packed their most precious belongings into wagons of all sizes, hitched up the horses or oxen, and said their goodbyes to loved ones they most likely would never see again. It was the equivalent of an immigrant's voyage across the great Atlantic—a similar dream for a new life filled with hope, but overshadowed with uncertainty. For those who trekked the long westward wagon trails, the voyage was often beleaguered with peril and disease, and for many, with the birth and death of children.

It was America's Manifest Destiny, land open for settlement as far as the eye could see. The term *manifest destiny* was first coined in July 1845 by John Louis O'Sullivan, who was editor of the *United States Magazine and Democratic Review* at the time. Sullivan postulated that America's greatness and expansion west was providential, destined to include Texas and California and all that lay between. Little concern was voiced for the thousands of Native Americans who were moved off the land to make room for the multitude of white settlers. Land was for the taking, and take it they would. For some nineteenth-century farmers, homesteading was part of a national duty to cultivate "empty" lands. For most, it was simply an opportunity built on self-reliance and luck.

Americans trekked westward by the tens of thousands. Between 1841 and 1849 alone, some 350,000 migrants braved the 2,400-mile Oregon Trail. Each packed some 200 pounds of flour, 150 pounds of bacon, chipped beef, sugar, coffee, tools, kettles, rifles and shot, perhaps some limes to ward off scurvy and possibly some laudanum given in vain attempts to cure the dysentery that plagued the westward emigrants. Though traveling in large groups, the birth of a child, illness, or a broken wagon wheel meant being left behind. The rest of the wagon train snaked on, the goal always to keep moving in order to cross the Continental Divide before the winter snows fell. Amelia Steward Knight, who gave birth to her eighth child while traveling along the Oregon Trail, on June 1, 1853, wrote the following in her diary:

> It has been raining all day and we have been traveling in it so as to be able to keep ahead of the large droves [of other wagons]. The men and boys are all soaking wet and look sad and comfortless. (The little ones and myself are shut up in the wagons from the rain. Still it will find its way in and many things are wet; and take us all together we are a poor looking set, and all this for Oregon. I am thinking while I write, "Oh, Oregon, you must be a wonderful country." Came 18 miles today). . . .

While in the throes of the Civil War, President Abraham Lincoln signed the Homestead Act of 1862. The law turned over a vast expanse of land, some 270 million acres, once occupied by Native Americans and now considered public domain, to private citizens. The law's provisions were simple enough. A homesteader need only be at least twenty-one years of age (male or female, including former slaves) and pay an $18 filing fee to claim up to 160 acres of land. A homesteader was required to build a small house and farm the land for five years, all part of the "proving up" process required to meet the stipulations of the law. If an individual had the capital, he or she could purchase the land outright for $1.25 an acre after six months and forego "proving up."

The concept of free land whose ownership could not be questioned was enticing to thousands of individuals who laid claim to their acres and went about the business of building a home, quite often of sod cut from the prairie soil. However, as idyllic as it sounded, for the majority of the homesteaders, life was difficult at best. Though the land was "free," up to $1,000 was required for tools, animals, fencing, seed, and the many other items needed for a working homestead. Homesteaders braved the elements, including dreaded prairie fires, and struggled to adjust to ever-changing crop prices. They dealt with swarms of grasshoppers that devastated every plant in their path and could destroy a season's crop in just a few days. Yet, despite all, many homesteaders persevered. Homesteading was viewed as central to America's Manifest Destiny, and in fact, the Homestead Act would remain in effect for over one hundred years, until its repeal in 1972.

NATIONAL ARCHIVES DOCUMENT

CHAP. LXXV. — *An Act to secure Homesteads to actual Settlers on the Public Domain*.

Be it enacted by the Senate and House of Representatives of the United States of America in Congress assembled, That any person who is the head of a family, or who has arrived at the age of twenty-one years, and is a citizen of the United States, or who shall have filed his declaration of intention to become such, as required by the naturalization laws of the United States, and who has never borne arms against the United States Government or given aid and comfort to its enemies, shall, from and after the first January, eighteen hundred and sixty-three . . . be entitled to enter one quarter section or a less quantity of unappropriated public lands . . . be subject to preemption at one dollar and twenty-five cents, or less, per acre; or eighty acres or less of such unappropriated lands, at two dollars and fifty cents per acre . . . Provided, That any person owning and residing on land may, under the provisions of this act, enter other land lying contiguous to his or her said land, which shall not, with the land so already owned and occupied, exceed in the aggregate one hundred and sixty acres. . . . ✳

Below: Sod house homesteaders.

Critical Thinking

Draw Conclusions

One of the stipulations for a homesteader to gain a "patent" to the land was that the individual had "never borne arms against the Government of the United States or given aid and comfort to its enemies." Why do you think this stipulation was placed in the Homestead Act?

Compare and Contrast

In 1841, Congress passed the Preemption Act. It allowed settlers to stake a 160-acre claim on land that had not yet be surveyed by the federal government and later purchase it before it was offered for public sale. Interest in preemption faded following passage of the 1862 Homestead Act, and the Preemption Act was repealed by Congress in 1891. Why would settlers prefer the provisions of the Homestead Act to those of the Preemption Act?

Analyze Cause and Effect

Homesteading caused exactly what many southern representatives in Congress had feared before the Civil War—the growth of states in the West. Kansas became a state in 1861, Nevada in 1864, and Nebraska in 1867. Why would southerners be concerned, before 1862, about areas in the West petitioning Congress for statehood?

Research and Writing

Relating Events

As Native Americans were moved off their lands, cattle ranching took the place of buffalo roaming the open plains. By the end of the Civil War, some five million longhorn cattle grazed just the Texas grassland alone. In 1867 Joseph G. McCoy convinced railroad executives to run a railroad line from Kansas to what had become the meat-packing center of the United States—Chicago, Illinois. Cattle and cowboys multiplied as railroad lines stretched deep into America's plains states, with cattle towns in tow. Life on the open range changed dramatically, however, with Joseph Glidden's invention of barbed wire. Research the life of the cowboy and the growth and eventual demise of cow towns. Who were America's cowboys? How did cowboys lend to the allure of the "wild west"? What prompted range wars? How did cattle help to define westward expansion in the nineteenth century?

Analysis

For pioneering women, adversity was a constant. Women worked alongside their husbands to clear the land, farm the tough prairie sod, and, in many cases, brave the subzero temperatures and fierce blizzards that, at times, lasted for days as they fought to survive on the windswept plains. Though they led more egalitarian lives than their eastern counterparts—with states such as Wyoming leading the effort to grant women the right to vote—women settling west of the Mississippi River often faced traditional legal and social barriers. Research the role women played in the westward movement. How did they live? What rights did they have? What barriers did they face? Access and read the entire Homestead Act of 1862. In what way did the Homestead Act recognize the reality that women settling on America's vast prairie could quickly become widows solely dependent on their own resources for survival?

Biography

John Charles Frémont was an adventurer, teacher, soldier, explorer, and politician. In 1842 Frémont set off on a series of explorations that crossed the Rocky Mountains. Congress published 10,000 copies of Frémont's annotated maps and journal notes detailing available water and food, the terrain, and information about the Indian tribes encountered along what became the well-traveled Oregon Trail. Research the life of John Charles Frémont. How did he fulfill the roles of adventurer, teacher, soldier, and explorer? How did he inspire westward expansion? What were his ties to the California gold rush? Write a biography of Frémont's life of politics and adventure.

1862 The Pacific Railway Act

*"The astonishing rapidity with which this railroad has been built
has become the subject of general wonder throughout the country."*

–NEW YORK TRIBUNE, 1868

HISTORICAL BACKGROUND

IN 1832 an editorial in a Michigan newspaper, *The Emigrant*, suggested the possibility of railroads linking America's eastern and western shores. It was an innovative idea that ignited discussions on the unlimited possibilities of the vast western frontier. The potential benefits of a transcontinental railroad seemed as endless as the frontier itself. Upon returning from a business trip to far-off China in the early 1840s, Asa Whitney put pen to paper to set in motion a plan for a railroad line linking the Pacific coast with Lake Michigan. His idea went before Congress in 1845. Whitney suggested building a Pacific railroad at cost of about $60 million. He asked that Congress sell him a sixty-mile-wide strip of land for 10 cents per acre along a stretch of land totaling some 2,030 miles. Being an enterprising businessman, Whitney then planned to sell tracts of land along the proposed railroad corridor for 88 cents per acre. This, he reasoned, would be sufficient to finance the construction of a railway line linking the Great Lakes to the Pacific Ocean. Though unsuccessful, Whitney continued to promote the idea of a transcontinental railway line.

In 1844 Samuel F. B. Morse tapped a series of dots and dashes on a new contraption called a telegraph, sending the first inter-city message along telegraph lines strung between Washington, D.C., and Baltimore, Maryland. The telegraph was an instant success. By 1854, some 23,000 miles of telegraph wire were in use. Telegraph lines followed the routes taken by the railroads, linking America's growing cities. America was certainly a nation on the move, and time was of the essence.

By 1850, America was in the throws of a western land-grab. Moreover, the Gold Rush attracted thousands of eager prospectors to California hoping to strike it rich in mining. Railroads, as a major facilitator of expansion, symbolized a nation determined to tame the western frontier. In 1853 Congress appropriated money to "ascertain the most practicable and economical route for a railroad from the Mississippi River to the Pacific Ocean." Between 1853 and 1855, five routes were surveyed—the Northern, Mormon, Buffalo, Thirty-fifth Parallel, and Southern routes. However, with sectionalism gripping a contentious Congress, that body was in no mood to decide if the route should be more southerly or take a more northern path. However, there was no doubt as to the efficacy of railroad lines spanning the continent. In speaking for a Select Committee charged with ascertaining the feasibility of a transcontinental railroad, Representative James Denver from California began his report to Congress with the following statement.

> The necessity that exists for constructing lines of railroad and telegraphic communication between the Atlantic and Pacific coasts of this continent is no longer a question for argument; it is conceded by every one. In order to maintain our present position on the Pacific, we must have some more speedy and direct means of intercourse than is at present afforded by the route through the possessions of a foreign power. . . . A railroad across the continent would open up a vast extent of country to settlement. . . .

In 1861, the South seceded from the Union, giving urgency to the construction of a transcontinental railroad. The needs of the military required an efficient transportation system. Furthermore, a transcontinental railroad would make a strong political statement about the resources and strength of the federal government. On June 28, 1861, a group of wealthy businessmen formed the Central Pacific Railroad Company of California. Subsequently, they sought Congressional approval of a rail line spanning the continent from the Missouri River to the Pacific Ocean. Congress responded with the Railway Act of 1862. The act authorized the Central Pacific to build a railroad eastward from the Pacific Ocean. It also established the Union Pacific Railroad Company, giving it authority to build westward, with Omaha, Nebraska, negotiated as the eastern starting point. Money was lent to both companies: $16,000 a mile in level country, $32,000 a mile as land rose to meet the Rocky Mountains, and $48,000 a mile for mountainous terrain.

After six years of blasting stone and laying track, Leland Stanford, one of the organizers of the Central Pacific, and governor of California, drove a final, golden spike into the ground at Promontory Summit in Utah. It was the beginning of a network of rail and telegraph lines that ultimately would transform the western United States.

Railroads were one of the major contributors to westward expansion. In effect, the railroads symbolized the transition from an untamed frontier to progression of white settlement.

NATIONAL ARCHIVES DOCUMENT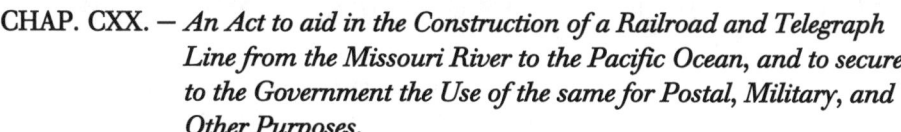

CHAP. CXX. — *An Act to aid in the Construction of a Railroad and Telegraph Line from the Missouri River to the Pacific Ocean, and to secure to the Government the Use of the same for Postal, Military, and Other Purposes.*

SEC. 2. And [be] it further enacted, That the right of way through the public lands be . . . granted to said company for the construction of said railroad and telegraph line; and the right . . . is hereby given to said company to take from the public lands adjacent to the line of said road, earth, stone, timber, and other materials for the construction thereof; said right of way is granted to said railroad to the extent of two hundred feet in width on each side of said railroad where it may pass over the public lands, including all necessary grounds for stations, buildings, workshops, and depots, machine shops, switches, side tracks, turntables, and, water stations. The United States shall extinguish as rapidly as may be the Indian titles to all lands falling under the operation of this. . . .

SEC. 3. And be . . . granted to the said company, for the purpose of aiding in the construction, of said railroad and telegraph line, and to secure the safe and speedy transportation of the mails, troops, munitions of war, and public stores thereon, every alternate section of public land, designated by odd numbers, to the amount of five alternate sections per mile on each side of said railroad, on the line thereof, and within the limits of ten miles on each side of said railroad, . . . not sold, reserved, or otherwise disposed of by the United States, and to which a preemption or homestead claim may not have attached. . . . That all mineral lands shall be excepted from the operation of this act; but where the same shall contain timber, the timber thereon is hereby granted to said company. And all such lands, so granted by this section, which shall not be sold or disposed of by said company within three years after the entire road shall have been completed, shall be subject to settlement and preemption, like other lands, at a price not exceeding one dollar and twenty-five cents per acre, to be paid to said company. ✳

Below: In 1852 Congress granted the Hannibal & St. Joseph Railroad 600,000 acres of land to build a railroad from Hannibal, Missouri westward to St. Joseph. Like other railroads, the Hannibal & St. Joseph sold land to would-be settlers along its rail line.

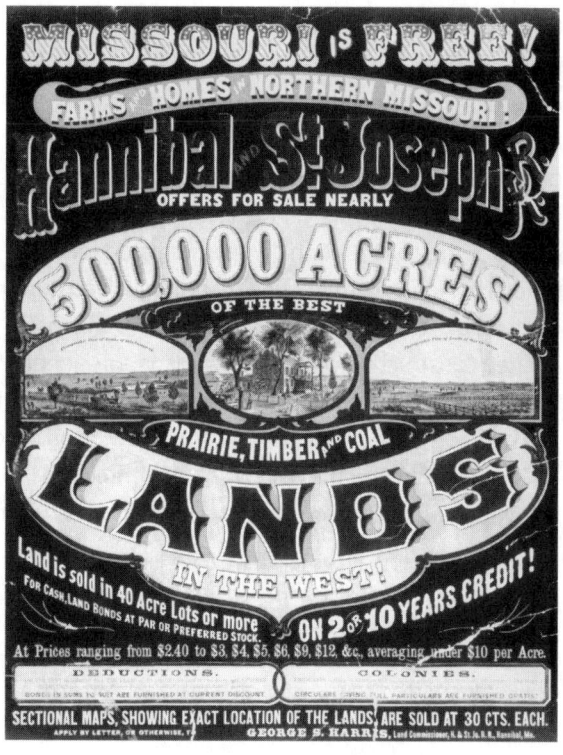

Critical Thinking

Draw Conclusions

The federal government granted 6,400 acres of public land to the railroads for each mile of track completed. Between 1851 and 1871 some 200 million acres of land located along rail lines, once set aside for homesteaders, were given to railroads in the form of land grants. The railroads turned around and sold the land to prospective settlers. Why was it advantageous for settlers to live near railroad lines?

Make Predictions

How did the Railway Act of 1862 impact the lives of Native Americans?

Assess Significance

The Union Pacific built 1,086 miles of track to the Central Pacific's 689 miles. What benefit did a railroad have to gain by laying more miles of track than its competitor?

Research and Writing

Relating Events

Research the workforce that built the transcontinental railroad. From where did the workers originate? What types of jobs did they perform? How were the camps organized? What discriminatory practices permeated the use of immigrant labor? What happened to the workforce once the railroad had been built?

Counterpoint

Both the Union Pacific and Central Pacific railroad companies contracted directly with construction companies for materials and laborers. With little concern for the obvious conflict of interest, the same directors who sat on the railroad boards often sat on the governing boards of the construction companies created for building the railroad, setting the stage for profiteering on a grand scale. One congressional investigation, in particular, focused on Crédit Mobilier of America, the construction company created for the Union Pacific. The profiteering scandal involved dummy companies, manipulation of stock prices, and grossly inflated construction costs. Sidney Dillon, president of the Union Pacific Railway Company, writing in the April 1891 edition of *The North American Review*, in an article titled "The West and the Railroads," presented the following rationalization for the accumulation of wealth.

> No one asserts that railways have been laid from philanthropic motives; and therefore, since among the promoters, contractors, and capitalists who have done the work we find men who have acquired large fortunes, western railroad construction and management in general

> …Now, a railway is simply a manifestation of capital put to work … A citizen, simply as a citizen, commits an impertinence when he questions the right of any corporation to capitalize its properties at any sum whatever.

Research the Crédit Mobilier of America and the dealings of Charles Crocker and Company. What types of profits were realized from building the transcontinental railroad? Why were they questioned? Write an essay in agreement with or in rebuttal of Dillon's assertions.

Historical Interpretation

Great herds of buffalo once grazed the prairies of America's heartland. Buffalo supplied Native Americans with food, clothing, shelter, bedding, ropes, and religious items. It was a revered animal upon which Native Americans were dependent for their survival. In speaking before Congress, Secretary of Interior Columbus Delano in 1874 stated,

> The buffalo are disappearing rapidly, but not faster than I desire. I regard the destruction of such game as Indians subsist upon as facilitating the policy of the Government, of destroying their hunting habits, coercing them on reservations, and compelling them to begin to adopt the habits of civilization.

Research the near extermination of the buffalo. How did it happen? When did it occur? What was its purpose? What role did buffalo have in the ecological health of the Great Plains? How did elimination of the buffalo impact Native Americans?

1868 Purchase of Alaska

*"To offend so powerful a friend as Russia
for the trifle of $7,000,000 would be unwise."*

–MARK TWAIN

HISTORICAL BACKGROUND

ON October 18, 1867, the Russian flag was lowered over the city of Sitka, Alaska. In its place waved the stars and stripes of the American flag. Secretary of State William H. Seward orchestrated the purchase of Alaska in 1867. For years a thriving fur trade had made Alaska a profitable land for ownership and occupation. However, by 1860 over-harvesting made Alaska look more like a frozen wasteland than a territory worth braving for profit. Even after the purchase, the U. S. government took a lax attitude toward it, first administering it through the War Department, followed by the Treasury Department. To Seward, "Alakshah," as he called it, seemed like a natural expansion of America's greatness. Alaska, with its abundance in fish and seemingly unlimited expanse of land, presented wide-open commercial possibilities. To acquire it was an irresistible opportunity.

The United States, however, was preoccupied with Reconstruction. Foreign markets were an afterthought, as bitterly debated postwar domestic issues consumed Congress. Moreover, the United States still held to the foreign policies outlined in the 1823 Monroe Doctrine. Foreign governments had been warned at that time to steer clear of any colonial aspirations in the Western Hemisphere. In this context, any impulse to expand America's own colonial empire in the 1860s was seen, for the most part, as simply unwarranted. Thus, when Seward signed a treaty with Denmark to purchase the Virgin Islands for $7.5 million, Congress said no. When a proposal came before Congress for exclusive rights to build a canal through Columbia, Congress said no. An 1870 treaty providing for the annexation of the Dominican Republic met a similar fate in Congress. However, Seward achieved success with the purchase of far-off Alaska.

Some called it "Seward's folly." Others termed it "Seward's icebox." The *New York Tribune* coined the term "Walrussia." However, in 1867 Seward enlisted the help of Charles Sumner, chairman of the Senate Foreign Relations Committee, to convince Congress to purchase a land that was twice the size of Texas. At $7.2 million, the expanse cost a mere 2 cents per acre. The offer to sell came in 1866 from Russia, which had held the territory since 1741. Over the years both British and American settlements dotted Alaska's southern border, raising eventual territorial quarrels. Short on funds, and not wishing to see an expansion of colonial claims by Great Britain, Russia directed Baron Edouard de Stoeckl, Russia's minister to the United States, to negotiate sale of Alaska to the United States. Seward quickly offered $5 million for the frozen land. Stoeckl, aware of Seward's passion for expansion and cognizant of the need for Congress to approve the deal before it recessed, countered with a price of $7.2 million in gold. The deal was struck. However, Congress didn't fully approve the treaty or release the monies until 1868.

In addition to the purchase of Alaska, Seward convinced Congress to annex the uninhabited Midway Islands, located about halfway between California and the Asian continent. These tiny islands had been claimed for the United States in 1859 by Captain N.C. Brooks, who found it only right to name the atolls "Middlebrooks." Seward reasoned that the islands could serve as a base for the United States in the Pacific. Pleased with his success, in May 1867 Seward penned the following poem:

> Abroad our empire shall no limits know,
> But like the sea in boundless circles flow.

Although white settlement had expanded as far west as the continent would allow, additional opportunities awaited American ingenuity overseas. The expansion of railroad and telegraph lines, the growth of cities, exportation of such industrial products as steel and motors, and western statehood hurried America into a new era. In the meantime, the purchase of Alaska opened another uncharted frontier, with challenges and discoveries beyond the imagination. However, statehood would wait until 1959, when Alaska entered the Union as the forty-ninth state.

NATIONAL ARCHIVES DOCUMENT

March 30, 1867

Treaty concerning the Cession of the Russian Possessions in North America by his Majesty the Emperor of all the Russias to the United States of America; Concluded March 30, 1867; Ratified by the United States May 28, 1867; Exchanged June 20, 1867; Proclaimed by the United States June 20, 1867. . . .

ARTICLE I.

His Majesty the Emperor of all the Russias agrees to cede to the United States, by this convention, immediately upon the exchange of the ratifications thereof, all the territory and dominion now possessed by his said Majesty on the continent of America. . . .

ARTICLE III.

The inhabitants of the ceded territory, according to their choice, reserving their natural allegiance, may return to Russia within three years; but if they should prefer to remain in the ceded territory, they, with the exception of uncivilized native tribes, shall be admitted to the enjoyment of all the rights, advantages, and immunities of citizens of the United States, and shall be maintained and protected in the free enjoyment of their liberty, property, and religion. The uncivilized tribes will be subject to such laws and regulations as the United States may, from time to time, adopt in regard to aboriginal tribes of that country. . . .

ARTICLE V.

Immediately after the exchange of the ratifications of this convention, any fortifications or military posts which may be in the ceded territory shall be delivered to the agent of the United States, and any Russian troops which may be in the territory shall be withdrawn as soon as may be reasonably and conveniently practicable. . . .

Below: Check for the purchase of Alaska.

ARTICLE VI.

In consideration of the cession aforesaid, the United States agree to pay at the treasury in Washington, within ten months after the exchange of the ratifications of this convention . . . seven million two hundred thousand dollars in gold. . . . ✻

Critical Thinking

Analyze Cause and Effect

In January 1868 writer Mark Twain chided Congress for holding up payment to purchase Alaska. Twain wrote:

> If the Senate should refuse to pay for it [Alaska], they would do a very absurd thing. To offend so powerful a friend as Russia for the trifle of $7,000,000 would be unwise. Russia, by her simple attitude of friendship, and without lifting a hand, is able to save us from wars with European powers that would eat up the price of Walrussia in four days.

Why did Twain consider $7 million a trifle? What was he suggesting?

Assess Significance

One of the first natural resources exploited following the purchase of Alaska was salmon. In 1881, canneries packed 9,000 cases of salmon. By 1888, the number grew to 714,000 cases. By 1917, half of the world's canned salmon was packed by canneries that dotted the northwest coastline. What other markets developed as a result of the purchase of Alaska?

Compare and Contrast

How does the purchase of Alaska compare with the Louisiana Purchase? How does it contrast? Was the purchase of either a "folly"?

Research and Writing

Relating Events

Beginning with the discovery of gold at Sutter's Mill in California in 1848, mining, and the elusive hope of striking it rich, became a driving force in western expansion during the second half of the nineteenth century. Thousands of would-be miners, consumed with "gold fever," poured into the West seeking to stake a claim on ground that would make them rich beyond their dreams. In 1898 gold was discovered on the Klondike River, far north in the Yukon. The ensuing Klondike Stampede brought some 60,000 adventures to Alaska. Research the impact of mining on westward expansion. How did the discovery of gold and silver spur the growth of cities? Where did the discoveries take place? How long did they last? What were their social and economic impacts?

Biography

William H. Seward was born in New York in 1801. He began his political career as New York state senator. Research the life of William Seward. What were his political achievements? How did his strong abolitionist and expansionist beliefs influence his political decisions? What influence did he exert as secretary of state?

Link to the Past

In 1968 oil was discovered in Prudhoe Bay. Soon after, several oil companies joined to form the Alyeska consortium. This group proposed, designed, and subsequently built an 800-mile pipeline linking the oil found in Prudhoe Bay with the ice-free port at Valdez. Since the pipeline's completion, billions of barrels of oil have been pumped through and loaded into tankers for transport to domestic and foreign ports. Constructed between 1975 and 1977, the pipeline was a colossal undertaking, crossing rivers, streams, and mountains. Over half of it had to be built above ground due to the Alaskan permafrost. At the time of its construction, environmentalists worried that construction and possible oil spills would harm Alaska's pristine environment. Research the history of oil exploration in Alaska. What have been the economic benefits? What efforts were taken to protect the environment? What problems have been encountered? Why do some Americans feel the economic benefits gained by tapping into Alaska's oil fields justify the environmental risks? Draw your own conclusion concerning this environmental/economic debate. Construct a well-documented essay to explain your conclusion.

1898 Annexation of the Hawaiian Islands

"We need Hawaii . . . It is manifest destiny."

–PRESIDENT WILLIAM McKINLEY

HISTORICAL BACKGROUND

MARK Twain once described Hawaii as "the loveliest fleet of islands that lies anchored in any ocean." Historians believe that British explorer James Cook became the first European to sight the Hawaiian Islands in 1778. In 1792 Captain George Vancouver introduced livestock to the Hawaiians. American involvement in the Hawaiian Islands began in 1820, when Christian missionaries from New England arrived. They busied themselves with building schools, translating the Bible into Hawaiian, and creating a written Hawaiian alphabet. By mid-century, frame houses and horse-drawn carriages were found among the established settlements. In the 1830s an American company introduced sugarcane farming to the Hawaiians. Soon missionaries and American investors began purchasing land to establish sugar plantations. To address labor shortfalls, plantation owners brought thousands of immigrants from mainland China, Japan, and other Pacific islands to work the sugar fields of Hawaii. In 1842, the United States officially recognized Hawaii's sovereignty as an independent nation. By that time, however, Americans were exerting substantial influence on the economic structure of the island.

In 1875 the Hawaiian monarch signed a trade agreement with the United States. It allowed for Hawaiian sugar to enter the United States without tariffs. Sugar exports soared, as did the profits of sugar plantation owners. Twelve years later, a new agreement allowed the United States to establish a naval base at Pearl Harbor. The purpose of the American military presence there was twofold. First, defending the islands' sugar industry from foreign interference seemed paramount. Second, Hawaii was seen as an important staging point for American military operations in the Pacific. By 1887 Americans dominated both the economic as well as the political winds of Hawaii, a control secured by Hawaii's new pro-American constitution and government.

In 1890, Congress passed the McKinley Tariff. This law eliminated Hawaii's favored position in the sugar trade, and put sugar from all foreign countries on a duty-free list. More importantly, it granted sugar growers in the United States a two-cent-per-pound subsidy. The American sugar growers in Hawaii felt this put them at a competitive disadvantage with U.S. growers. The only solution they saw was for Hawaii to become a part of the United States.

In 1891 Queen Liliuokalani became Hawaii's monarch. She soon instituted measures that significantly eroded the power held by American sugar growers. In 1893 she recommended a new constitution to restore political power to native Hawaiians. An alarmed group of American planters, led by Sanford B. Dole, appealed to John L. Stevens, the U.S. minister to Hawaii. Stevens responded by calling on U.S. Marines from nearby warships to assist in a coup orchestrated by American sugar growers. Queen Liliuokalani was deposed and the monarchy was ended. Stevens gleefully reported to Washington, "The Hawaiian pear is now fully ripe, and this is the golden hour for the United States to pluck it." On July 4, 1894, the Republic of Hawaii was established, with Stanford B. Dole as its president.

The new government sent a delegation to Washington with a treaty that provided for Hawaii's annexation. Though signed by President Benjamin Harrison, the Senate failed to ratify it. Incoming U.S. president Grover Cleveland called the American interference in Hawaii "disgraceful," and promptly withdrew the annexation treaty from consideration by Congress. He also recommended that Queen Liliuokalani be restored to the throne. The planter-controlled government refused.

Annexationists, empowered by political clout and the wealth of the Hawaiian sugar industry, and bolstered by an annexation provision in the constitution governing the Republic of Hawaii, continued to lobby Congress. In 1896 William McKinley was elected president. McKinley, an ardent expansionist, asked the Senate to approve the annexation treaty; however, it failed to garner the required two-thirds majority vote required by the Constitution for ratification. Undeterred, McKinley next supported a joint resolution of the House and Senate in 1898 to allow annexation of Hawaii. When a House filibuster threatened to defeat the resolution, McKinley countered with a threat of his own—to use his war powers to militarily seize the islands instead. Congress approved the annexation of Hawaii in July 1898. The islands officially became a U.S. territory in 1900. Statehood followed in 1959 when Hawaii entered the Union as the fiftieth state.

National Archives Document

Fifty-fifth Congress of the United States of America; At the Second Session, . . .

Whereas, the Government of the Republic of Hawaii having, in due form, signified its consent, in the manner provided by its constitution, to cede absolutely and without reserve to the United States of America, all rights of sovereignty of whatsoever kind in and over the Hawaiian Islands and their dependencies, and also to cede and transfer to the United States, the absolute fee and ownership of all public, Government, or Crown lands, public buildings or edifices, ports, harbors, military equipment, and all other public property of every kind and description belonging to the Government of the Hawaiian Islands, together with every right and appurtenance thereunto appertaining: Therefore,

Resolved by the Senate and House of Representatives of the United States of America in Congress assembled, That said cession is accepted, ratified, and confirmed, and that the said Hawaiian Islands and their dependencies be, and they are hereby, annexed as a part of the territory of the United States. . . .

The existing treaties of the Hawaiian Islands with foreign nations shall forthwith cease and determine, being replaced by such treaties as may exist, or as may be hereafter concluded, between the United States and such foreign nations. . . . ✳

Below: Queen Liliuokalani

Critical Thinking

Analyze Cause and Effect
What impact did the American sugar industry in Hawaii have on the annexation of Hawaii?

Compare and Contrast
How do the territorial acquisitions of Alaska and Hawaii differ? How are they alike?

Determine Point of View
When presented with the treaty to annex Hawaii, members of Congress argued that protecting it would take extensive naval power. They also believed that acquiring Hawaii as a territory of the United States was tantamount to unconstitutional colonialism. Reread McKinley's quote on page 162. How did he justify annexing Hawaii? With whom do you agree? Why?

Research and Writing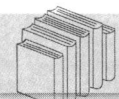

Analysis
A paragraph near the bottom of the joint resolution that provided for the annexation of Hawaii reads:

> There shall be no further immigration of Chinese into the Hawaiian Islands, except upon such conditions as are now or may hereafter be allowed by the laws of the United States; and no Chinese, by reason of anything herein contained, shall be allowed to enter the United States from the Hawaiian Islands.

During the 1800s, thousands of laborers from China, Korea, the Philippines, and other countries arrived at the beckoning of plantation owners to work the Hawaiian sugar fields. Research the history of sugar plantations in Hawaii. What role did immigration play in its commercial development? What prompted the inclusion of this paragraph in the joint resolution? Who would benefit from this provision? What was at stake?

Relating Events
In 1878 Samoa signed a treaty granting the United States special trading rights, as well as authority to establish a military base on Pago Pago. Samoa signed similar treaties the following year with Great Britain and Germany. Tensions rose as the three countries vied for trading rights in the region, with warfare between them in the offing. To avert military confrontation, in 1899 the United States, Great Britain, and Germany signed the Anglo-German Treaty. Without consulting the Samoans, and much to their discontent, the three countries agreed to divide the islands. The United States and Germany split ownership of Samoa, while Great Britain agreed to withdraw from the area in return for control of other Pacific islands. Research American and European imperialism in the Pacific region during the second half of the nineteenth century. What countries and islands were involved? What was at stake? What was gained? What was lost? Was William Seward's long-held goal for commercial domination "on the Pacific and its islands and continents" realized?

Analysis
In 1898 Queen Liliuokalani wrote a letter of protest to the United States House of Representatives. In part, she said:

> I, Liliuokalani of Hawaii, named heir apparent on the 10th day of April, 1877, and proclaimed Queen of the Hawaiian Islands on the 29th day of January, 1891, do hereby earnestly and respectfully protest against the assertion of ownership by the United States of America of the so-called Hawaiian Crown Islands amounting to about one million acres and which are my property, and I especially protest against such assertion of ownership as a taking of property without due process of law and without just or other compensation.
>
> Therefore …I call upon the President and the National Legislature and the People of the United States to do justice in this matter and to restore to me this property.…

Access and read the entire *1898 Joint Resolution To Provide for Annexing the Hawaiian Islands to the United States*. Research the coup that deposed Queen Liliuokalani. In a well-documented essay, support or reject Queen Liliuokalani's assertion found in her 1898 letter to Congress.

Inventions

"Concern for man himself and his fate must always form the chief interest for all technical endeavors . . ."

–ALBERT EINSTEIN (1879–1955)

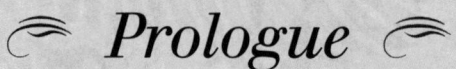

Prologue

The popular author Tom Clancy once wrote, "Man is a creature of hope and invention, both of which belie the idea that things cannot be changed." Ingenuity, the genius behind invention, can be defined by the simple phrase, "just imagine." When Ben Franklin grew weary of taking his glasses off and on, he invented bifocals. When Thomas Jefferson wanted to dazzle his guests with unusual cuisine, he invented the macaroni machine. For traveling, he invented his own portable copy press for all the important writing he had to do. "The fact is," commented Jefferson, "that one new idea leads to another, that to a third, and so on through a course of time until someone, with whom no one of these ideas was original, combines all together, and produces what is justly called a new invention." "All progress, all success, springs from thinking," said Thomas Edison, the prolific inventor who "could never pick up a thing without wishing to improve it." In this fifth unit, you will have the opportunity to see how necessity, combined with ingenuity, not only built America, but gave it the tools for unimaginable destruction.

1794 Patent for the Cotton Gin

*"If a machine could be invented which would
clean the cotton with expedition . . ."*

–ELI WHITNEY

HISTORICAL BACKGROUND

IN 1792 Eli Whitney sailed from New York to Georgia. His final destination was to be South Carolina, where a sought-after position as a schoolmaster awaited him. He never made it. Instead, a stopover at Mulberry Grove, the Georgia home of General Nathaniel Greene's widow, forever changed his life. There Whitney learned of the need for a machine to clean the seeds from raw cotton. He quickly put his creative genius in motion. Ten days later he wrote his father, "I made a little model, for which I was offered, if I would give up the right and title to it, a Hundred Guineas." Whitney had visions of a self-made fortune. Little did he know that his invention, which he named the Cotton Gin, would shackle generations of enslaved African-Americans to a Southern economy based on a single commodity. In the end, it would shape the entire political and economic landscape of the Deep South.

The population of the United States in 1790 was 3.9 million people. Of those, 700,000 were slaves tied to a southern plantation system built on a "free" labor source. The remaining population was split fairly equally between the North and the South. Population growth, however, favored Northern urban centers. Meanwhile, in the South, the economy was at a lull. The once-thriving rice and tobacco markets were on the decline. For a while, southern farmers attempted to grow wheat, but soon found the cool-weather crop unsuitable. What was needed was a crop that preferred heat and moisture. The answer to the South's agrarian dilemma was cotton.

Cotton requires 200–210 frostless days to mature. It thrives with an abundance of moisture early in its growing season. Southern farmers discovered that cotton flourished anywhere south of mid-state Virginia. Moreover, though cotton could be grown in small patches, it also was well suited for large field production. It seemed the perfect answer for southern plantation owners—a reliable crop that promised a ready profit. The slaves upon which plantation owners had made their wealth growing rice and tobacco could now be utilized for cotton production. Plus, cotton had a promising market. It had long been considered a luxury product, imported from India or Egypt. Cotton cloth was far preferred to the wool still worn in the late 1700s. It was easier to clean, cooler, and by far more comfortable.

For years, long-staple cotton (long-fibered) had been grown on the islands off the coasts of Georgia and South Carolina. A second, short-staple variety grew well on inland soils. The problem, however, was that short-staple cotton was cursed with seeds that refused to separate easily from the fibers. Yet once separated, short-staple cotton proved far superior to its long-staple cousin for making cloth.

Past attempts at sending the cotton bolls through a type of "gin" (short for "engine"), had resulted in seed parts scattered throughout the raw cotton, rendering it virtually unusable. Whitney's cotton gin, however, solved that problem. It was a simple machine into which one individual could feed the cotton and then turn the crank to process it. Whitney's gin used wire teeth set on a cylinder. The teeth tore at the cotton fibers as the cotton was rolled through the machine. While the seeds dropped to a waiting box, other wire brushes pulled the cotton fibers off the teeth. Whereas in the past it had taken from sunup to sundown for an individual to clean the seeds from one pound of cotton by hand, with Whitney's invention, that person could clean fifty pounds in a single day.

In 1800 cotton represented about 7 percent of all U.S. exports. By 1840 cotton exports had soared to comprise almost 52 percent of the export market. However, though Whitney's invention reduced the labor needed for processing the fluffy white cotton bolls, it exponentially increased the demand for slaves. By the outbreak of the Civil War, one in three southerners was an African-American slave. An auction price of a field slave averaged $600 in 1800. By 1860, with cotton production thirty times that of 1790, the auction price of a field slave had tripled. The South's economy had become dependent on profits made from marketing farm commodities, in particular cotton, and on slave hands, with no indication of change in the offing.

NATIONAL ARCHIVES DOCUMENT

". . . I made one before I came away which required the labor of one man to turn it and with which one man will clean ten times as much cotton as he can in any other way before known and also cleanse it much better than in the usual mode. This machine may be turned by water or with a horse, with the greatest ease, and one man and a horse will do more than fifty men with the old machines. It makes the labor fifty times less, without throwing any class of People out of business. . . ."

—Eli Whitney

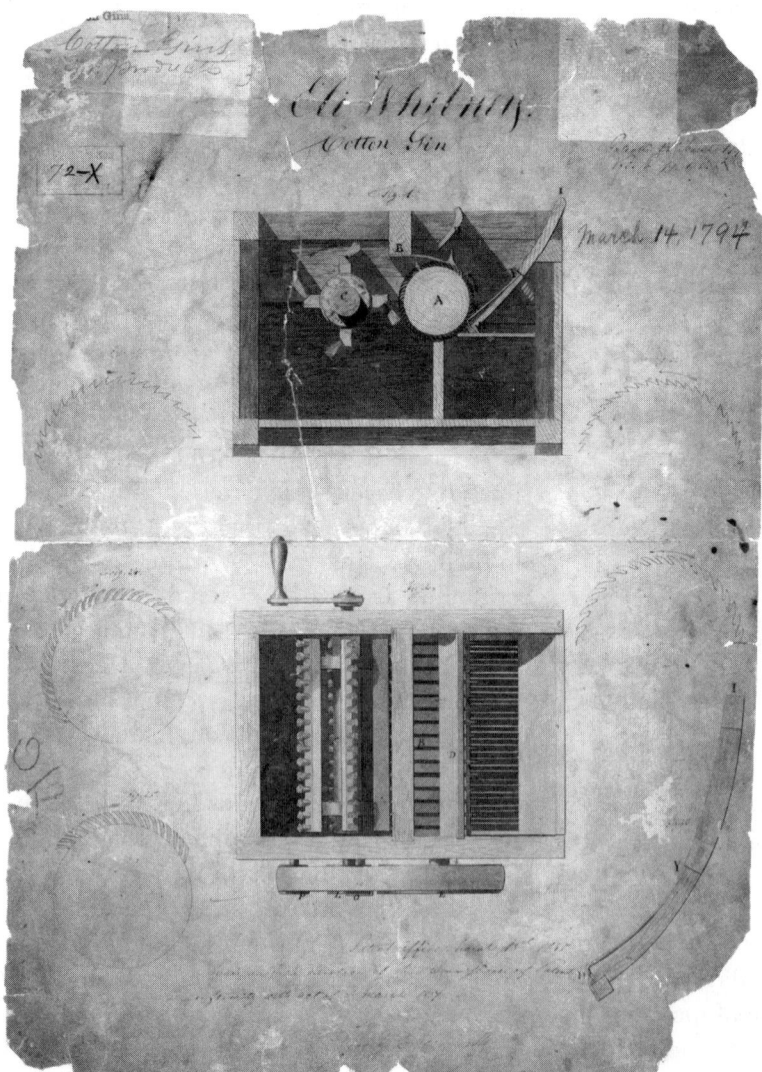

Left: Eli Whitney's patent application for the cotton gin included a description of how the machine worked. While reducing the amount of labor needed to clean cotton, the machine made growing cotton more profitable, thereafter increasing the demand for land and slave labor.

Critical Thinking

Draw Conclusions

By the mid 1800s, cotton had become the predominant commodity of the South. What are the economic benefits of focusing on one commodity? What are the risks?

Assess Significance

Great Britain became an important market for American cotton. In 1780 less than 7 million pounds of cotton had been exported to Britain. In 1787 the amount jumped to a whopping 22 million. By 1837, however, exports soared, with approximately 407 million pounds of cotton marketed to the United Kingdom. What factors led to the growth of this foreign market? In what way did foreign markets contribute to the growth of the cotton industry?

Determine Point of View

Would you consider the cotton gin to have benefited the South or to have harmed it?

Research and Writing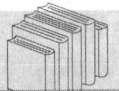

Analysis

Research the growth of the southern economy during the first half of the nineteenth century. What were the commodities of the Upper South? Why did cotton become the prime commodity of the Deep South? In what way did both regions become dependent on slave labor? How did the South's dependence on agrarianism help to fuel the social and political divisions that culminated in Civil War?

Relating Events

In 1793 Samuel Slater built a factory in Pawtucket, Rhode Island, for the company of Almy and Brown. Inside, a spinning mill equipped with 100 spindles was attended by a labor force of women and children. Their job was to spin long-staple cotton into cotton thread. Slater preferred the cleaner long-staple cotton. Though business was good, it was by no means flourishing. That all changed with the introduction of the cotton gin, which dramatically reduced the price of short-staple cotton. The demand for cotton cloth would be a boon to the development of the factory system. Research the growth of the textile industry in America during the early- to mid-nineteenth century. What was Slater's contribution? What was the Lowell System? How did the growth of the cotton economy in the South spur the growth of industry in the North? In what way did the invention of the cotton gin impact the economic landscapes of both the North and the South?

Biography

Eli Whitney obtained a patent for his cotton gin in 1794. He wrote to his father that,

> I returned to the Northward for the purpose of having a machine made on a large scale and obtaining a Patent for the invention [sic]. I went to Philadelphia …made myself acquainted with the steps necessary to obtain a Patent, took several of the steps and the Secretary of State Mr. Jefferson agreed to send the Pattent [sic] to me as soon it could be made out—so that I apprehended no difficulty in obtaining the Patent….

Though he asked his father to keep his new invention a "secret," news of his successful cotton gin soon filtered out from Mulberry Grove. Almost immediately Whitney's machine was copied, and though he had hoped for a quick fortune, he instead found himself penniless. Research the life of Eli Whitney. How did Whitney plan to market his cotton gin? Why didn't Whitney's patent protect his invention? What were the financial repercussions for Whitney? Why was his contribution in doubt? What were some of Whitney's other inventions? How did Whitney finally make his fortune?

1880 Patent for the Light Bulb

*"Genius is one percent inspiration
and ninety-nine percent perspiration."*

–THOMAS EDISON

HISTORICAL BACKGROUND

LIFE in the later half of the nineteenth century must have felt a bit like a whirlwind, for invention had certainly captured the American spirit. By 1870 telegraph wire spanned not only the nation, but connected America with Europe as well. With a code of tapped-out dots and dashes, ideas and information were transmitted across miles. In 1876 Alexander Graham Bell filed for a patent for electromagnetic voice communication, more commonly known as the telephone. Communication was no longer limited to a series of tappings; people could now speak directly to one another. By the time Bell's patent expired in 1893, over 250,000 telephones were in operation. Out West, John Deere's plow and Cyrus McCormick's reaper revolutionized the ability of farmers to plow the tough prairie soils and harvest prairie wheat. A network of railroads crisscrossed the nation from coast to coast. Refrigerated railroad cars brought meat from Chicago to butcher shops in the East. Household chores were eased with the invention of the home washing machine in 1858 and the "sweeping machine" in 1869. Yet, the invention that perhaps most revolutionized American life was Thomas Edison's light bulb, for upon that invention rested even more amazing inventions yet to come.

Each innovation required a patent to protect it from unscrupulous copiers waiting to make a dollar off someone else's "inspiration" and "perspiration." The power of the federal government to grant patents is secured through Article I, Section 8, Clause 8 of the United States Constitution. The Patent Act of 1790 authorized the government to issue patents for "any art, manufacture, engine, machine or device." During its first decade of existence the U.S. Patent Office registered 276

inventions. One hundred years later, during the 1890s, 234,956 patents were registered. Among the most prolific patent seekers was Thomas Edison. Considered the quintessential inventor, Edison received more than 1,000 patents over his lifetime. These included patents for the phonograph, vitascope (or motion picture), picture projector, telephone transmitter, storage battery, and dictating machine. Many of these patents came as the result of his research team housed at his "invention factory" in rural Menlo Park, New Jersey. Here Edison assembled the best mechanics, craftsmen, mathematicians, and scientists who could augment his inventive genius. Provided with the finest equipment money could buy and a large library, Edison and his team set out to create the unimaginable.

Though Edison's inventions were many, it is the light bulb for which he is by far most famous. Based on his successful 1877 invention of the tinfoil phonograph, financiers J.P Morgan, the wealthy Vanderbilt family, and others advanced Edison $30,000 to support his claim that he could invent a light bulb. It was not an easy task. Edison and his team failed hundreds of times before their tenacity bore fruit. In October 1879 they finally found a way to keep a lamp glowing for nearly fifteen hours, giving off a light with the brightness of thirty candles. The secret to success was switching from a filament made of platinum to one made of carbon. Though seemingly unusable because of its propensity to burn quickly, Edison discovered that the filament would not burn out if surrounded by a vacuum. He then baked cardboard in an oven until it was charred (carbonized). The cardboard was attached to a wire filament, to which was added an electric current. The filament glowed. The electric light was born.

In 1882 J.P Morgan assisted Edison further with the financing of The Edison Electric Illuminating Company. Soon the company was providing electric current to customers in New York City. Edison's genius invention had one major flaw, however—its direct current lighting system was limited to a radius of about two miles. A different type of current would be needed for longer distances, a current that began with a greater voltage and then gradually reduced in steps by transformers along its route. George Westinghouse lent his innovative talents to solve this problem. The result was the invention of the alternating current system in 1886. Once again, a single invention would alter American society in unforeseeable ways. No longer would factories need to locate near waterfalls, rivers, or other sources of energy or fuel. Electricity could be brought from long distances to light homes and power industry. As the country entered the twentieth century, America was on the brink of a technology revolution, a revolution first energized by the invention of the electric light bulb.

NATIONAL ARCHIVES DOCUMENT

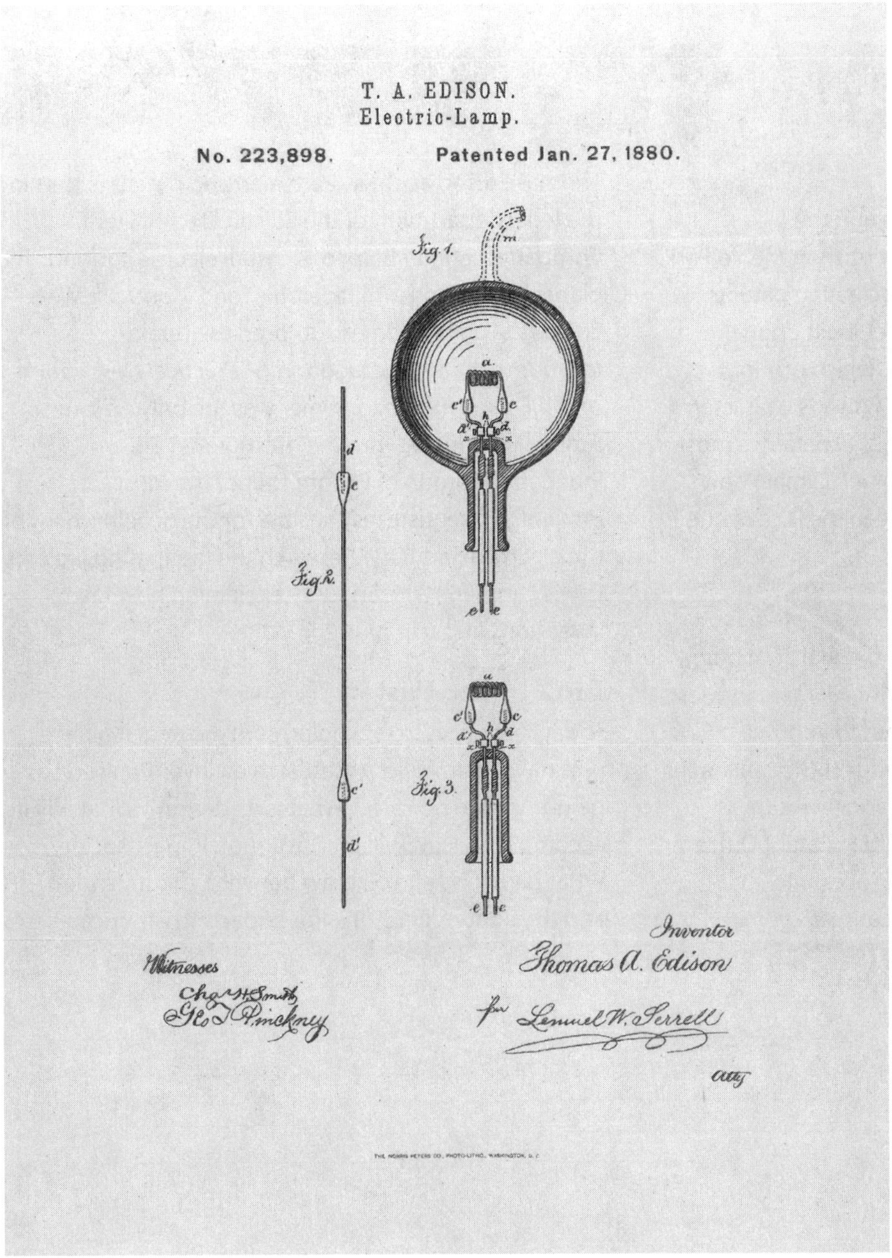

Left: Edison applied for a patent for his electric light bulb in 1879. He received it the following year. His first light worked for almost fifteen hours, giving off light equal to thirty candles.

T. A. EDISON.
Electric-Lamp.

No. 223,898.   Patented Jan. 27, 1880.

Critical Thinking

Draw Conclusions

Over the years inventions have taken many forms. From the cotton gin to the light bulb, to the television, to satellite communications, inventions have impacted and changed society. Identify ten inventions. Which of these inventions do you feel most significantly impacted American life? Why?

Assess Significance

Thomas Edison was one of the last independent inventors of his time. Soon after, companies, beginning with the General Electric Laboratory in 1901, started funding their own electric research. Science became industry-based, with companies directing problem solving. The result was a wave of innovation. Why was it so difficult for independent inventors to compete with industry-based science labs? Is one preferable to the other?

Determine Point of View

Thomas Edison once said, "To invent, you need a good imagination and a pile of junk." Is this enough? What is your opinion?

Research and Writing

Analysis

Research the life of Thomas Edison and the collaborative efforts of Edison's scientists at Menlo Park. Describe some of Edison's most fascinating patents. Which were most significant? Which built upon the success of others? In your opinion, which brought Edison his greatest success? Of all Edison's character traits and experiences, which trait or experience most significantly drove his creative genius? Explain how this factor inspired him to continue in the face of one failure after another.

Biography

One of the problems with Edison's original light bulb was the short life span of the glowing filament inside the glass bulb. Lewis Latimer set out to improve Edison's light bulb. He created a longer lasting filament, making light bulbs less expensive and far more practical for home use. In 1882 the U.S. Patent Office granted Latimer a patent for the "Process of Manufacturing Carbons." In 1890 Latimer was hired by Thomas Edison as chief draftsman and patent expert in the legal department of the Edison Electric Light Company. Latimer helped to install electric lighting plants in New York, Philadelphia, and Montreal. With Edison's urging, Latimer authored the book *Incandescent Electric Lighting: A Practical Description of the Edison System*. Latimer was the only African-American inducted into the prestigious "Edison Pioneers," a group of twenty-four of the most influential scientists responsible for the development of the electrical industry. Research the fascinating life of Lewis Latimer. Write an essay explaining how his inventions impacted American life.

Link to the Past

Today, advances in technology are moving at a pace unparalleled in history. Research an invention seen as being "on the horizon." What is its design? What will it accomplish? How will this invention impact society? What parallels can you draw between this invention and the light bulb in 1879 for impacting American life?

1928 Boulder Canyon Project Act

". . . the greatest engineering work of its character ever attempted by the hand of man."

–HERBERT HOOVER

HISTORICAL BACKGROUND

THE vision achieved by the Boulder Canyon Project arose long before funds for it were approved by Congress. People had been attempting to tame the Colorado River for many years, a feat finally accomplished by the project begun in 1928. Though originally planned for Boulder Canyon, the dam was actually built at Black Canyon. Here, the rocky walls of the canyon were more dense, making it a better place for the massive dam. However, in keeping with the spirit of its origin, the federal undertaking continued to be referred to as the Boulder Canyon Project, and subsequently as Boulder Dam.

The Boulder Canyon Project had its beginnings some 70 years earlier when, in 1859, the California legislature granted Oliver Wozencraft title to 10 million acres of Colorado Desert. The Colorado Desert is a huge two thousand square mile western extension of the Sonoran Desert. Wozencraft hoped to cut a channel from the Colorado River to the Colorado Desert to provide water to the parched area. The federal government, however, did not share Wozencraft's vision, and the project was scuttled. In hindsight, the government's skepticism seems reasonable. The Colorado Desert receives little or no summer precipitation. Daytime temperatures can reach 125°F. Surely, in 1859 the idea of growing crops in this region appeared to be sheer lunacy.

Decades later, Charles Rockwood, a surveyor and engineer, had better luck than Wozencraft. He convinced an investor named George Chaffey of the lucrative potential of diverting a stream of water from the Colorado River to irrigate the Colorado Desert area. Chaffey underwrote the project to the tune of $150,000. To give the project a more positive image, the Colorado Desert was renamed the Imperial Valley. Digging for the canal commenced, and on May 14, 1901, the first water flowed from the Colorado River to its new destination. Land was sold in the Imperial Valley. Some 7,000 people settled there. The projected boon in land sales and agriculture was realized beyond expectation. However, disaster struck in 1904 when a four-mile stretch of the canal became clogged with silt carried into it from the river. Water in the canal stopped flowing. Irrigation came to a halt, and crops withered for lack of water.

The answer to the problem seemed easy enough—simply build another canal. Rockwood dove right into the project only to have his plans undone once again by Mother Nature. In March 1905 churning waters from a spring flood broke through the new canal. In November 1905 more floodwaters raged into the area, covering some 150 square miles with sixty feet of water and wiping out carefully tended crops. Of even greater concern was the soil erosion occurring along the canal in parts of southwest Arizona and southeast California. Something needed to be done, and quickly. Federal intervention returned the river back to its original flow by February 1907. The Colorado River struck back, however, in 1910. This time it took one million dollars to build a set of levees to check the river's flow. In 1916 flooding on the Gila River resulted in four feet of water in Yuma, Arizona. To federal authorities, the river clearly needed further taming.

In 1920 representatives from seven states affected by the Colorado River met to discuss the most efficient means to distribute its water. Headed by future Secretary of Commerce Herbert Hoover, the resulting agreement, known as the

Hoover Compromise, eventually led to the Colorado River Compact, signed on November 24, 1922. Soon after, efforts began to gain approval for the construction of the Boulder Dam. Disputes arose between the states over concerns that a thirsty California would divert water naturally intended for Arizona. Finally, after years of political wrangling, the Boulder Canyon Project Act was signed into law on December 21, 1928, by President Coolidge. It became effective in June 1929, following the ratification of the Colorado River Compact by six states. Arizona, the dissenting seventh state, finally consented to the agreement in 1944.

National Archives Document

AN ACT To provide for the construction of works for the protection and development of the Colorado River Basin, for the approval of the Colorado River compact, and for other purposes.

Be it enacted by the Senate and House of Representatives of the United States of America in Congress assembled, That for the purpose of controlling the floods, improving navigation and regulating the flow of the Colorado River, providing for storage and for the delivery of the stored waters thereof for reclamation of public lands and other beneficial uses exclusively within the United States, and for the generation of electrical energy as a means of making the project herein authorized a self-supporting and financially solvent undertaking, the Secretary of the Interior, subject to the terms of the Colorado River compact hereinafter mentioned, is hereby authorized to construct, operate, and maintain a dam and incidental works in the main stream of the Colorado River at Black Canyon or Boulder Canyon. . . .

SEC. 3. There is hereby authorized to be appropriated from time to time, out of any money in the Treasury not otherwise appropriated, such sums of money as may be necessary to carry out the purposes of this Act, not exceeding in the aggregate $165,000,000. . . .

SEC. 20 Nothing in this Act shall be construed as a denial or recognition of any rights, if any, in Mexico to the use of the waters of the Colorado River system. . . . ✳

Below: Boulder Dam, now known as Hoover Dam.

Critical Thinking

Make Predictions

Part of the Boulder Dam project was to harness the river's energy to create hydroelectric power. This was accomplished in 1935 with the installation of generators by General Electric and Westinghouse Electric. What would be the impact of electrical power on the Colorado River Basin?

Assess Significance

Stipulations in the contracts between the federal government and the major companies hired to construct the dam included language prohibiting "Mongolian" labor. Moreover, African-Americans were forced to live outside the housing provided in Boulder City for the project's almost five thousand workers. Instead, black workers often had to travel to Las Vegas for lodging, some thirty-five miles away. Why didn't the federal government intervene to rectify both the discriminatory language in the contract and the daily discrimination shown to black workers?

Analyze Cause and Effect

How did western expansion eventually lead to the Boulder Canyon Project Act?

Research and Writing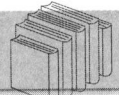

Relating Events

At the dedication ceremony to commence the Boulder Dam project on September 17, 1930, President Herbert Hoover was represented by Secretary of the Interior Ray L. Wilbur. In his dedication speech, Wilbur referred to Boulder Dam as Hoover Dam. President Hoover was not very popular in 1930, so the renaming of the dam did not sit well with many people. However, Hoover felt the huge project would project an image that his administration was sensitive to the needs of the people. With the potential to employ thousands of people, and with thousands of dollars to be distributed in construction contracts, Hoover believed the dam would assist his re-election plans. Hoover, however, lost the election to Franklin D. Roosevelt. The new Secretary of the Interior, Harold Ickes, declared on May 8, 1933, that the name should revert to its original—Boulder Dam. In 1947, Herbert Hoover was appointed to a special commission by President Harry Truman. On April 30, 1947, Congress passed a resolution again renaming the dam Hoover Dam. Today it continues to be known as Hoover Dam, though reference is also made to Boulder Dam. Research the administration of Herbert Hoover. What economic and domestic issues at the time impacted his re-election bid? Why did many people reject the idea of renaming Boulder Dam? What prompted Ickes to rename the dam? What reasoning was used to rename it Hoover Dam again in 1947? In what way did politics become intertwined with the naming of this major federal construction project?

Analysis

Hoover Dam and Lake Mead are located on the Arizona-Nevada state line. The Colorado River basin covers over 252,000 square miles. It includes parts of Nevada, Arizona, California, Utah, New Mexico, Wyoming, Colorado, as well as some 2,000 square miles in Mexico. In total, about 15,000,000 acre-feet of water flow annually down the Colorado River. Research the construction of Boulder Dam. What is the geography of this area? Where does the Colorado River originate? Where does it flow? How was the site for the dam chosen? How was it accomplished? How did construction of the dam impact the region's ecology and economy?

Link to the Past

Concerns about water scarcity were at the heart of the dispute that prevented Arizona from signing the Colorado River Compact in 1922. The issue continued to fester until it finally was resolved in 1964 by the U.S. Supreme Court. In *Arizona v. California*, the Court interpreted the 1928 Boulder Canyon Act as investing authority over water dispersion in the Lower Colorado Basin with the U.S. Department of the Interior. Additionally, Native American water rights guaranteed by the 1964 decision now must be considered in any new agreements concerning water distribution. Research current issues regarding projected water needs for the Colorado River basin. In what way did the Boulder Canyon Project play a role in the issues presenting themselves today?

1933 Tennessee Valley Authority Act

". . . a corporation clothed with the power of Government but possessed of the flexibility and initiative of a private enterprise."

—FRANKLIN D. ROOSEVELT,
MESSAGE TO CONGRESS, APRIL 10, 1933

HISTORICAL BACKGROUND

IN 1933 poverty gripped the United States. The United States was mired in the Great Depression. Almost half of the nation's 24,000 banks had failed. Millions of people were either out of work or working at jobs that left them barely able to buy food and pay their mortgage or rent. In his 1933 Inaugural Address, President Franklin Roosevelt addressed the nation's need for improvement and employment by proposing that government act as the employer of thousands of workers.

Our greatest primary task is to put people to work. This is no unsolvable problem if we face it wisely and courageously. It can be accomplished in part by direct recruiting by the Government itself, treating the task as we would treat the emergency of a war, but at the same time, through this employment, accomplishing greatly needed projects to stimulate and reorganize the use of our natural resources.

On May 18, 1933, Roosevelt signed the Tennessee Valley Authority Act. The law formed a government corporation—the Tennessee Valley Authority or TVA—responsible for the comprehensive development of the Tennessee River basin, an expanse of 41,000 square miles that extended into seven states. The TVA was charged not only to improve the navigability of the Tennessee River, but also to resolve problems created by persistent and devastating flooding, land erosion, a severely depressed local economy, and the out-migration of a workforce needed to revitalize the area. In all, the TVA was given bold authority to do what was needed to improve "the economic and social well-being of the people living in said river basin." The immediate answer was to build a series of dams to control the river's flow. Within a year over nine thousand people were employed by the TVA.

Between 1933 and 1944 an amazing sixteen dams were built on the Tennessee River and its tributaries.

The work of the TVA helped to raise the standard of living for 3.5 million people. Economic conditions in the Tennessee River basin were severely depressed. Most families survived on subsistence farming, many as tenant farmers. Almost all were without electricity or running water in their homes. Public education was extremely limited, as were public health facilities. Most farmers plowed by hand. Life was hard, with few tangible rewards. People survived from year to year with what they could raise on the farmed-out land. Though generations of families had lived in the region, by 1933 the youth of the Tennessee River basin looked to cities as an escape from its abject poverty. The TVA's projects were intended to employ thousands of people from the region, curtail its population loss, and bring the benefits of electricity to the economically disadvantaged region.

The TVA's success attests to the genius and resolve of all involved in the colossal project—from the politicians who contrived the legislation, to the bureaucrats who administered it, to the engineers and workers involved in dam construction and installation of miles of power lines. The TVA succeeded in jumpstarting an entire region. Crop yields increased, forests were replanted, houses were built, and most of all, electricity reached the lives of thousands of people who previously had lived by the lantern. Electricity also attracted industries to the region, providing desperately needed jobs. Though some may have rued the loss of a backwoods life, for the thousands of people living in the Tennessee River basin, the TVA firmly planted them in a modernized twentieth century.

National Archives Document

Be it enacted by the Senate and House of Representatives of the United States of America in Congress assembled, That for the purpose of maintaining and operating the properties now owned by the United States in the vicinity of Muscle Shoals, Alabama, in the interest of the national defense and for agriculture and industrial development, and to improve navigation in the Tennessee River and to control the destructive flood waters in the Tennessee River and Mississippi River Basins, there is hereby created a body corporate by the name of the "Tennessee Valley Authority" (hereinafter referred to as the "Corporation"). . . .

Sec. 4. Except as otherwise specifically provided in this Act, the Corporation—

(h) Shall have power in the name of the United States of America to exercise the right of eminent domain . . . the title to such real estate shall be taken in the name of the United States of America, and thereupon all such real estate shall be entrusted to the Corporation as the agent of the United States to accomplish the purposes of this Act. . . .

(i) Shall have power to acquire real estate for the construction of dams, reservoirs, transmission lines, power houses, and other structures, and navigation projects at any point along the Tennessee River, or any of its tributaries, and in the event that the owner or owners of such property shall fail and refuse to sell to the Corporation at a price deemed fair and reasonable by the board, then the Corporation may proceed to exercise the right of eminent domain, and to condemn all property that it deems necessary for carrying out the purposes of this Act. . . .

(j) Shall have power to construct dams, reservoirs, power houses, power structures, transmission lines, navigation projects, and incidental works in the Tennessee River and its tributaries, and to unite the various power installations into one or more systems by transmission lines. . . . ✳

Below: The TVA brought electricity to thousands of rural families living in the Tennessee River basin.

Critical Thinking

Compare and Contrast

In what way are the Boulder Canyon Project and the work of the TVA similar? How do they differ?

Assess Significance

Building Norris Dam required flooding a 239-square-mile area. First, however, approximately 3,500 families, who had lived in Clinch River basin for generations, needed to relocate. Not everyone was willing to move. The acquisition of this property was accomplished though the TVA's authority to exercise its right of *eminent domain*. Land was purchased or condemned in order to gain title to the property. How important was the TVA's ability to exert eminent domain? Did the end justify the means?

Analyze Cause and Effect

A long-time champion of the Tennessee Valley Authority was Senator George W. Norris of Nebraska. Prior to its creation in 1933, Norris introduced six bills that allowed the federal government to retain control over Muscle Shoals, a thirty-mile-long stretch of the Tennessee River that was impossible to navigate due to its 140-foot drop. Muscle Shoals had been acquired by the federal government in 1916 as a good site for a dam. Electricity generated by the dam was to be used to produce explosives for World War I. However, by the time the facilities were built, the war had ended. Though Henry Ford had offered to purchase the project, Norris led the battle in Congress to retain federal control over the site. Why do you think Norris and other members of Congress were unwilling to sell the dam to private interests?

Research and Writing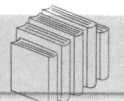

Analysis

The federal government created the Rural Electric Administration (REA) in 1935 to bring cheap power to the Tennessee Valley. Opposition arose from local electric companies, who saw the REA as unfair competition. Some members of Congress felt the workings of the REA resembled socialism. Yet by 1939, the REA's efforts resulted in the formation of over 400 rural electric cooperatives. Research the electrification of the Tennessee Valley. Explain the reasoning behind opposition to the REA. How did the REA operate? What was the EHFA? How did electricity impact the lives of farmers throughout the region?

Counterpoint

Despite its accomplishments, the TVA has not escaped criticism, led principally by environmental groups. Of most concern has been the TVA's nuclear power program, its purchase of pollution credits from Wisconsin Power and Light in 1992, and the building of the Tellico Dam and Reservoir on the Little Tennessee River. Each highlights environmental concerns never anticipated by the 1933 legislation. For example, efforts to halt construction of the Tellico Dam began when a tiny, previously unknown perch, called the Snail Darter, was discovered in the waters of the proposed dam.

Research the impact of environmental issues on the Tennessee Valley Authority. Which environmental issues are most significant? What has been the impact of the Endangered Species Act on TVA projects? What conclusions can be drawn?

Link to the Past

The dams built along the Tennessee River were the engineering wonders of the time, drawing tourists even during the years of the Depression. The construction of locks allowed for ships to traverse the series of dams, opening a 650-mile commercial channel along the Tennessee River. By the 1950s the TVA had become the nation's largest supplier of electricity. Senator George W. Norris, considered the father of the TVA, once said, "I have been everlastingly proud of the great contributions of the TVA...." Research the accomplishments of the TVA since its inception in 1933. What role does it currently serve in the region?

"We're cooking!"

–RECORDED IN THE MANHATTAN PROJECT NOTEBOOK
FOLLOWING THE FIRST SUCCESSFUL NUCLEAR CHAIN REACTION EXPERIMENT

HISTORICAL BACKGROUND

IN 1931 renowned physicist Albert Einstein said in a speech at the California Institute of Technology,

Concern for man himself and his fate must always form the chief interest for all technical endeavors, . . . in order that the creations of our mind shall be a blessing and not a curse for mankind. Never forget this in the midst of your diagrams and equations.

Einstein was a pacifist at heart. He believed scientists have a responsibility to consider the social ramifications of their work. Therefore, when fellow physicists Leo Szilard, Eugene Wigner, and Edward Teller asked him to write a letter requesting that President Roosevelt initiate a nuclear research program, he reluctantly agreed. Einstein was gravely concerned that Nazi Germany might gain an atomic bomb before the United States. His letter to the President stated, "A single bomb of this type, carried by boat and exploded in a port, might very well destroy the whole port together with some of the surrounding territory."

The letter convinced Roosevelt of the need to understand and harness atomic energy. He subsequently established an Advisory Committee on Uranium. Soon after, on June 28, 1941, the Office of Scientific Research and Development was organized. Then, one day before Japan's attack on Pearl Harbor, on December 6, 1941, Roosevelt authorized the Manhattan Engineering District, more commonly known as the Manhattan Project. The United States no longer was jogging, but instead sprinting toward the development of a nuclear bomb. In 1948, some three years after the fateful use of atomic weapons against Japan, Einstein warned of the magnitude of nuclear arms proliferation. He concluded,

In this time of fateful decisions, we must, above all, impress this fact upon our fellow-citizens; whenever the belief in the omnipotence of physical force dominates the political life of a nation, this force takes on a life of its own and becomes even stronger than the very men who intended to use it as a tool. . . .

The Manhattan Project was top secret. It involved the greatest scientific minds of the time, including Robert Oppenheimer and Nobel prize-winning physicist Enrico Fermi. Many of the scientists working on the Manhattan Project were émigrés from Germany, Hungary, and other Eastern European countries, individuals who had first-hand knowledge and fear of the power of Nazi Germany. They firmly believed their complicated experiments were pitted against comparable investigations by Nazi scientists. In fact, German scientists had already demonstrated in 1938 that uranium atoms could be split when bombarded with neutrons. The discovery of nuclear fission set the scientific community on edge. Fermi, Nobel laureate physicist Arthur Holly Compton, Szilard, and others were soon hard at work attempting to discover how to utilize uranium to create a nuclear chain reaction.

The *Eureka!* occurred on December 2, 1942, in a squash court under the West Stands of Stagg Field at the University of Chicago. Here, under Fermi's direction, a "pile," or nuclear reactor, was constructed using graphite, uranium bricks, and wooden timbers. The carefully assembled pile included 22,000 uranium slugs, 380 tons of graphite, 40 tons of uranium oxide, and 6 tons of uranium metal. Cadmium rods were inserted into the pile as a way to control the nuclear reaction. Fifty scientists watched over a three-man "suicide squad" that stood nearby to douse the reactor, should a catastrophic mishap occur. Fortunately for the "suicide squad," instead of failure there was a 28-minute success—the first ever self-sustaining nuclear chain reaction. Fermi carefully logged each aspect of the event in his Manhattan Project notebook. Though the power liberated by the reaction would barely light a lamp, the exuberant group of scientists immediately popped open a bottle of wine for a toast to their success. Exuberance soon turned to quiet, however, as the enormity of what had just happened settled on the scientists.

Though Einstein was not privy to the experiments taking place at the secret lab in Chicago, his early work had led directly to the understanding of nuclear energy. Its use for weapons, however, would haunt him. In retrospect Einstein said, "The release of atom power has changed everything except our way of thinking . . . the solution to this problem lies in the heart of mankind. If only I had known, I should have become a watchmaker."

National Archives Document

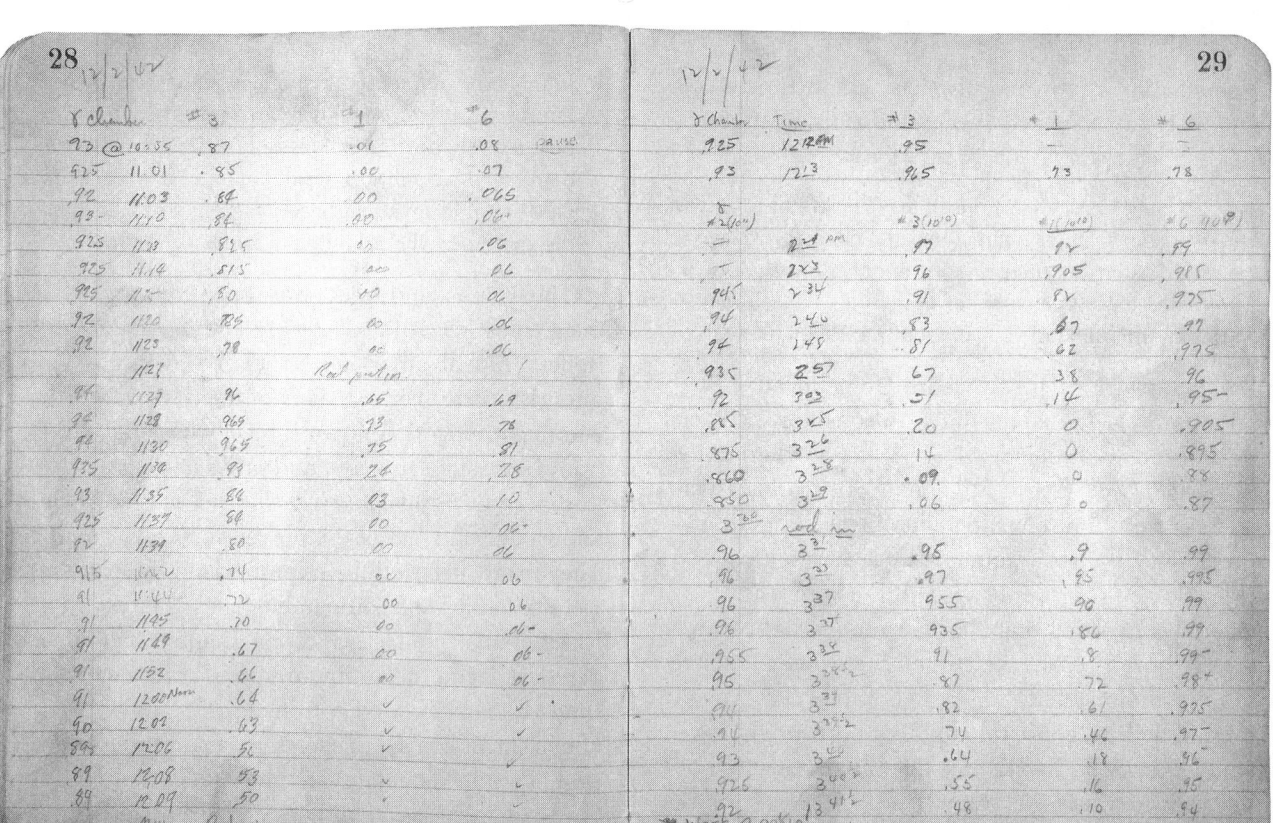

Above: The progress of the first nuclear chain reaction was recorded on these notebook pages on December 2, 1942.

Left: Enrico Fermi

Critical Thinking

Draw Conclusions

What risks were taken with the experiment conducted below the stands at Stagg Field?

Assess Significance

The only woman scientist working on the Manhattan Project was Leona Woods. Why were so few women scientists involved?

Make Predictions

Work on the Manhattan Project was considered top secret. How difficult do you think it was to maintain the secrecy of this project?

Research and Writing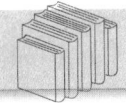

Biography

Enrico Fermi was born in Rome in 1901. By 1922 he held a doctorate in physics from the University of Pisa. By 1938, when Fermi immigrated to the United States, he was well established as the foremost expert on neutrons. Other scientists, such as Leo Szilard, Eugene Wigner, and Edward Teller immigrated to the United States from Hungary. Each had a primary role in the American nuclear research program. Research the main scientists involved in the Manhattan Project. Why did they leave their native countries to conduct research in the United States? Choose one scientist. Chronicle his life's achievements.

Historical Perspective

Even while the Manhattan Project moved toward the creation of an atomic weapon, there was a general consensus among the physicists that dropping an atomic bomb on Japan was a cataclysmic idea. Leo Szilard had a letter in hand to deliver to President Roosevelt, via Mrs. Roosevelt, urging consideration to not use the atomic bomb to achieve military advantage. However, anxiety turned to shock as Szilard learned of Roosevelt's death. Subsequently, he circulated a petition, eventually signed by sixty-eight scientists at the Chicago lab, urging President Truman not to drop the atomic bomb on Japan. Following Japan's surrender, Szilard and other prominent scientists lobbied for defeat of the May-Johnson bill. This bill would have granted a dominant role in nuclear research to the military. It also would have prohibited the sharing of scientific information specific to nuclear research with foreign countries. The sharing of such information was deemed critical by the physicists at the time. Albert Einstein, who was not included in the Manhattan Project because the U.S. Army had denied him a security clearance, echoed Szilard's concern. In 1946 Einstein became chairman of the Emergency Committee of Atomic Scientists, a group whose mission was to help establish policy on the development of atomic energy. In an essay, explain why so many scientists involved in making an atomic weapon would lobby against its military use.

Link to the Past

Though the Manhattan Project focused on "atoms for war," there was an acute awareness among the scientists involved that atomic energy could be applied for peaceful means as well. Industrial and medical uses, as well as the harnessing of nuclear energy to create electricity, were all viewed by Fermi, Szilard, and many other Manhattan Project scientists as having the potential to impact society in positive ways. What are the current uses of nuclear energy? Reread Einstein's quote on page 179. Have the advances in nuclear energy been true to Einstein's charge that "creations of our mind shall be a blessing and not a curse for mankind"?

1956 National Interstate and Defense Highways Act

". . . the whole interstate system must be authorized as one project."

—PRESIDENT EISENHOWER,
1956 STATE OF THE UNION ADDRESS

HISTORICAL BACKGROUND

IN 1919 future president Dwight D. Eisenhower sat in an army vehicle as it rumbled across the United States as a part of the first transcontinental motor convoy. At that time Eisenhower was a lieutenant colonel engaged in a military exercise to test the feasibility of moving an entire army across the United States. A contingent of 24 officers and 258 enlisted men manned eighty-one "motorized" army vehicles across 3,251 miles. From July 7 to September 6, they traversed roads described as "average to non-existent." It took sixty-two days to reach San Francisco from Washington, D.C.

Today, sixty-two days to cross the United States is more appropriate of a very leisurely vacation than a mission to traverse the nation as quickly as possible. However, in 1919 the trip was anything but leisurely. Over half the roads traveled were dirt roads, wheel paths, or mountain trails. Vehicles sank in quicksand or mud, overturned, or ran over embankments. Moreover, bridges needed to be built or rebuilt to withstand the loads passing over them. Over 230 accidents marked the route. Yet the military deemed the adventure a success. For Eisenhower, however, the experience underscored the importance of having a dependable system of roads. Later, during World War II, he witnessed the advantages gained, first by Hitler's army and then by the Americans, as military vehicles moved rapidly across the autobahns of Germany. Eisenhower, by then Supreme Commander of the Allies' war in Europe, commented that "The old convoy had started me thinking about good, two-lane highways, but Germany had made me see the wisdom of broader ribbons across the land."

Others shared Eisenhower's vision. Prior to World War II, President Roosevelt had proposed an interstate network of six toll roads. His aim was to put people to work by building America's highways. To accomplish this, in 1938 Congress passed the Federal-Aid Highway Act. With Europe on the verge of war, however, attention was diverted from the immediate needs of America to the alarming events across the Atlantic Ocean. It wasn't long, though, before renewed concerns for a reliable system of roads across the United States emerged.

In 1944 Congress funded a proposal to construct 40,000 miles of roads, creating a national system of interstate highways. Almost ten years later, when Eisenhower became the country's president, only 6,500 of those miles had been built. In Eisenhower's 1954 State of the Union Address, he drew attention to America's meager road system.

> To protect the vital interest of every citizen in a safe and adequate highway system, the Federal Government is continuing its central role in the Federal Aid Highway Program. So that maximum progress can be made to overcome present inadequacies in the Interstate Highway System, we must continue the Federal gasoline tax at two cents per gallon. This will require cancellation of the 1/2 cent decrease which otherwise will become effective April 1st, and will maintain revenues so that an expanded highway program can be undertaken.

Though legislation was in place, political wrangling in Congress continued to stall the design and construction of America's interstate roadways. At the heart of the debate was the apportionment of funding between the federal government and the states. Undaunted, in 1955 Eisenhower told Congress, "A modern, efficient highway system is essential to meet the needs of our growing population, our expanding economy, and our national security." In 1956, with growing impatience, he again requested funding: "In my message of February 22, 1955, I urged that measures be taken to complete the vital 40,000 mile interstate system over a period of 10 years at an estimated Federal cost of approximately 25 billion dollars. No program was adopted." He pressed on with the need for federal oversight of essential construction. "Only in this way can industry efficiently gear itself to the job ahead. Only in this way can the required planning and engineering be accomplished without the confusion and waste unavoidable in a piecemeal approach."

Congress finally responded to the president's insistence with passage in 1956 of the National Interstate and Defense Highways Act. It expanded the interstate highway network to 41,000 miles, with 25 billion dollars budgeted to pay for construction costs. Subsequently, legislation in 1958 expanded federal funding as a means to hasten construction and increase employment. By the end of the decade, America had become a nation on the move. A house in the suburbs, Sunday afternoon drives in the country, drive-in restaurants, and drive-in movies had become central components of the American culture, as well as a measures of an individual's success.

NATIONAL ARCHIVES DOCUMENT

TITLE I—FEDERAL-AID HIGHWAY ACT OF 1956

To amend and supplement the Federal-Aid Road Act approved July 11, 1916, to authorize appropriations for continuing the construction of highways; to amend the Internal Revenue Code of 1954 to provide additional revenue from the taxes on motor fuel, tires, and trucks and buses; and for other purposes. . . .

For the purpose of carrying out the provisions of the Federal-Aid Road Act approved July 11, 1916 (39 Stat. 355), and all Acts amendatory thereof and supplementary thereto, there is hereby authorized to be appropriated for the fiscal year ending June 30, 1957, $125,000,000 in addition to any sums heretofore authorized for such fiscal year; the sum of $850,000,000 for the fiscal year ending June 30, 1958; and the sum of $875,000,000 for the fiscal year ending June 30, 1959. The sums herein authorized for each fiscal year shall be available for expenditure as follows:

(A) 45 per centum for projects on the Federal-aid primary highway system.

(B) 30 per centum for projects on the Federal-aid secondary highway system.

(C) 25 per centum for projects on extensions of these systems within urban areas.

It is hereby declared to be essential to the national interest to provide for the early completion of the "National System of Interstate Highways," as authorized and designated in accordance with section 7 of the Federal-Aid Highway Act of 1944 (58 Stat. 838). It is the intent of the Congress that the Interstate System be completed as nearly as practicable over a thirteen-year period and that the entire System in all the States be brought to simultaneous completion. Because of its primary importance to the national defense, the name of such system is hereby changed to the "National System of Interstate and Defense Highways." . . . ❋

Below: The American dream in the 1950s included a new car for traveling America's expanding highways.

Critical Thinking

Draw Conclusions

President Eisenhower made reference to roads being essential for "national security" in both his 1955 and 1956 State of the Union addresses. In what way can a system of interstate highways augment national security?

Compare and Contrast

Today there are over 160,000 miles of interstate highways. Though interstate highways represent only four percent of the nation's highways, they carry more than forty percent of the nation's traffic.

What comparisons and contrasts can be made between the growth of railroads during the latter half of the nineteenth century with the growth of the nation's highways during the latter half of the twentieth century?

Make Predictions

Today great demands are being placed on the roads that cut through and around America's cities. How can government possibly meet the transportation needs created by urban development? How will it be funded?

Research and Writing

Link to the Past

In criticizing the Federal-Aid Highway Act of 1958, Eisenhower complained, "Congress has constructively endeavored to encourage the States to regulate advertising along the Interstate System . . . Certain exceptions which might permit advertising to go unchecked in some areas should be removed." In 1995 President Clinton expressed the same apprehension when Congress allowed states oversight on where highway advertising takes place. Research the laws in your state governing advertising along your state's highways. What restrictions are in place? Do you feel the laws are reasonable? Write an essay detailing the advantages and disadvantages of highway billboard advertising.

Historical Perspective

President Eisenhower signed H.R. 9821, the Federal-Aid Highway Act of 1958, with "serious misgivings." First, he objected to a change in the cost-share funding formula which resulted in placing a larger financial burden for the construction of interstate roads on the federal government. He also objected to a provision in the legislation that allowed the federal government to advance money to the states to help pay for their share in building "additional primary, secondary, and urban highway construction authorized by this legislation." Today, financing of America's highways far exceeds the two-cents-per-gallon federal tax originally levied on gasoline. Federal cost-share programs are critical to the road building efforts of individual states, so much so that highway funding has been tied to state compliance with federal legislation. In 1974, for example, the federal government mandated that speed limits be set at 55 mph on all interstate highways as an energy-saving measure. A 1995 federal law required states to adjust their illegal blood alcohol level to meet federal standards for drivers under 21 or face the loss of federal highway funds. Research how America's national highways are funded. What taxes are levied? How are they distributed? Do you think the federal government is justified in using cost-share revenue as a means for forcing states to take action in areas that typically are the sole domain of state law? Why or why not?

Analysis

Inventions come in many forms, but they all begin with a concept. In 1940 Dick and Mac McDonald opened a restaurant in San Bernardino, California. In 1948 they added the concept of assembly-line hamburger construction. It was an immediate success. Ray Kroc approached the McDonald brothers in 1954 with an idea to duplicate their system. Kroc opened his first *McDonald's* restaurant in Des Plaines, Illinois. The word "motel" also got its beginnings in the mid-1950s as hotels for motorists—motels—opened along America's highways. What other "inventions" have occurred as the result of America's ever expanding highway system? What have been the social and economic ramifications of the inventions? How have they changed American life?

1960 Establishment of the Peace Corps

"Ask not what your country can do for you—
ask what you can do for your country."

—President John Kennedy,
1961 Inaugural Address

Historical Background

Sometimes ideas for inventions are carefully contrived, planned detail by detail over time until something tangible emerges. Other times great inventions seem to burst out of nowhere. A simple discussion leads to a grand idea that appears to have been the obvious. The Peace Corps was such an invention. Though volunteer service in foreign countries had been a part of mission work for years, the idea of non-sectarian volunteer work had received only limited discussion in Congress. Almost two decades after the inception of the Peace Corps, President Jimmy Carter reaffirmed its worth.

> The spirit of the Peace Corps springs from the deepest wells in our culture, from the reasoned and strongly felt impulses of our people to share with their neighbors their caring and their labor.

The Peace Corps was given life late one October night in 1960, when John F. Kennedy extemporaneously addressed students at the University of Michigan. Kennedy was a senator and presidential candidate at the time. He stood on the steps of the Michigan Union late into the night before a crowd of some 10,000 students. Kennedy spoke of the intrinsic value of service to others. He challenged his listeners to devote a short time in their lives to help people in Latin America, Asia, or Africa. They would be on a mission of peace, he said, lending a hand to those in need. The essence of an idea was born. Two weeks later, in a speech at San Francisco, California, Kennedy dubbed the idea the *Peace Corps*. The idea spread like wildfire. Within a few weeks, several hundred students pledged to serve in the Peace Corps. A petition drive gathered 1,000 signatures in favor of the idea. Letters enthusiastically supporting the concept of an international peace mission flowed into Democratic headquarters. The Peace Corps was an idea whose time had come, an invention inspired by the desire to help others—to volunteer in the name of peace.

Though the collegiate response had been overwhelmingly positive, not everyone was as supportive. With war in Vietnam threatening, critics claimed that an organization such as the proposed Peace Corps would be nothing more than a home for draft dodgers—young men offering to serve others as a means to shirk their military responsibility. Others doubted if volunteers, in particular college students, could have the resolve and the knowledge to serve in Third World countries. However, Kennedy captured the heart of his idea in his 1961 Inaugural Address.

> To those peoples in the huts and villages across the globe struggling to break the bonds of mass misery, we pledge our best efforts to help them help themselves, for whatever period is required—not because the Communists may be doing it, not because we seek their votes, but because it is right. If a free society cannot help the many who are poor, it cannot save the few who are rich.

On March 2, 1961, President Kennedy signed Executive Order 10924. The directive officially established the Peace Corps within the framework of the federal government. The first order of business for newly appointed director Sargent Shriver was to establish goals for the organization. These became simply

> to help the people of interested countries and areas in meeting their needs for trained workers, to help promote a better understanding of Americans on the part of the peoples served, and to help promote a better understanding of other peoples on the part of Americans.

Congress approved legislation establishing the Peace Corps on September 22, 1961. By 1963 some 7,000 volunteers agreed to dedicate two years of their lives to serve in one of forty-four countries. Over half the volunteers worked in education, with others serving in the areas of community development, health care, public works, and agriculture. In July 1971 President Nixon merged the Peace Corps with other volunteer agencies, placing them all under the umbrella agency ACTION. In 1979, however, President Jimmy Carter gave the Peace Corps greater autonomy when he signed an executive order establishing it as an independent agency within ACTION. Legislation passed by Congress in 1981 restored the Peace Corps as an independent federal agency. The Peace Corps today remains a legacy to President Kennedy, as well as to an idea born at an impromptu college gathering some forty years ago.

National Archives Document

Executive Order 10924

ESTABLISHMENT AND ADMINISTRATION OF THE PEACE CORPS IN THE DEPARTMENT OF STATE

By virtue of the authority vested in me by the Mutual Security Act of 1954, 68 Stat. 832, as amended (22 U.S.C. 1750 et seq.), and as President of the United States, it is hereby ordered as follows:

SECTION 1. Establishment of the Peace Corps. The Secretary of State shall establish an agency in the Department of State which shall be known as the Peace Corps. The Peace Corps shall be headed by a Director.

SEC. 2. Functions of the Peace Corps. (a) The Peace Corps shall be responsible for the training and service abroad of men and women of the United States in new programs of assistance to nations and areas of the world, and in conjunction with or in support of existing economic assistance programs of the United States and of the United Nations and other international organizations.

(b) The Secretary of State shall delegate, or cause to be delegated, to the Director of the Peace Corps such of the functions under the Mutual Security Act of 1954, as amended, vested in the President and delegated to the Secretary, or vested in the Secretary, as the Secretary shall deem necessary for the accomplishment of the purposes of the Peace Corps.

SEC. 3. Financing of the Peace Corps. The Secretary of State shall provide for the financing of the Peace Corps with funds available to the Secretary for the performance of functions under the Mutual Security Act of 1954, as amended.

SEC. 4. Relation to Executive Order No. 10893. This order shall not be deemed to supersede or derogate from any provision of Executive Order No. 10893 of November 8, 1960, as amended, and any delegation made by or pursuant to this order shall, unless otherwise specifically provided therein, be deemed to be in addition to any delegation made by or pursuant to that order.

JOHN F. KENNEDY
THE WHITE HOUSE,
March 1, 1961. ✳

Below: During the 1960s, Peace Corp rallies took place on college campuses across America.

Critical Thinking

Draw Conclusions

President Bill Clinton once said,

> The Peace Corps is a remarkable tradition that emphasizes that our country is about more than power and wealth. It is also about the power of our values and the power of a helping hand, the ethic of service, and the understanding that we have an obligation not only to our own people, but to people around the world to help them make the most of their own lives.

Do you agree or disagree with this description and assessment? Explain your position.

Make Predictions

Following the September 11, 2001, terrorist attacks, President George W. Bush proposed to double the size of the Peace Corps within five years. To that end, Congress increased its funding. What role do you foresee for the Peace Corps? What value might it have in shaping America's image in the world?

Determine Point of View

The cornerstone of the Peace Corps is the spirit of volunteerism. Today many high schools require community service as a requirement for graduation. More and more colleges also are using community service as one of the factors they weigh in making admission decisions. Community service can involve Earth Day activities, helping at day care centers or nursing homes, community clean-ups, and many other types of volunteer work. Do you feel community service should be a requisite for a high school diploma? Why or why not?

Research and Writing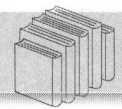

Link to the Past

Over 170,000 volunteers have served in the Peace Corps since its inception in 1961. Each year almost 7,000 individuals, most of whom are college graduates, serve in 136 countries throughout the world. They work in small villages and communities training volunteers to fight AIDS and other diseases, assisting in agricultural efforts, helping to protect the environment, and addressing other complex social and economic problems. Research the current role of the Peace Corps in the world community. Who are its volunteers? What is their mission? In which countries do they work? What role do they play? How do they spread peace?

Counterpoint

Controversy quickly surrounded the early months of the Peace Corps. In October 1961 Peace Corps volunteer Marjorie Michelmore wrote on the back of a postcard,

> With all the training we had, we really were not prepared for the squalor and absolutely primitive living conditions rampant both in the city and in the bush. We had no idea what "underdeveloped" meant. It really is a revelation and after we got over the initial horrified shock, a very rewarding experience. Everyone except us lives in the streets, cooks in the streets, sells in the streets, and even goes to the bathroom in the streets.

Michelmore, an honors graduate from Smith College, had had seven weeks of training at Harvard University before leaving for teacher training at University College at Ibadan in Nigeria. Her misplaced postcard was found by students who resented the characterization of their country as primitive. They immediately accused the Peace Corps volunteers of being spies for the United States government. Though the issue was finally resolved, it didn't stop others over the years from branding the work of the Peace Corps as having less than altruistic purposes. Research the work done by Peace Corps volunteers throughout the world. Why would some see the work of Peace Corps volunteers as politically motivated? Is it possible to divorce the work of volunteers from world politics? Explain your position.

Relating Events

Past Peace Corps volunteers can be found among university professors, members of Congress, film directors, writers, and myriad other professions. Research the lives of three Peace Corps volunteers. Where did they volunteer? What were their experiences? How did their time as a Peace Corps volunteer impact their lives?

1962 John Glenn's Official Communication

"This is Friendship 7. A real fireball outside."

–JOHN GLENN

HISTORICAL BACKGROUND

ON October 4, 1957, the Soviet Union launched the world's first artificial satellite into space. The unexpected event stunned the United States. The Russians named their satellite *Sputnik*, meaning "fellow traveler on earth." Though only the size of a basketball and a mere 183 pounds, its successful launch caused political fireworks. How could another nation, especially a communist country, be more advanced than the United States, Americans asked. Did the Soviets now have the capability of spying on Americans from space? Could their space rockets be used as missiles to launch nuclear bombs into the United States? In the midst of America's preoccupation with communism on its doorstep, Russia's success in space embarrassed government leaders, unnerved Americans, and made them feel bested by the nation's greatest political rival.

Fear soon turned to indignation, however. At a press conference five days later, the first question posed to President Eisenhower came as a challenge.

> Mr. President, Russia has launched an earth satellite. They also claim to have had a successful firing of an intercontinental ballistics missile, none of which this country has done. I ask you, sir, what are we going to do about it?

The answer was clear. The United States was not about to sit still and watch a communist country rule space. The ramifications of that were far too grave to consider. First, however, American scientists needed to accomplish what an earlier project named Vanguard had intended to do— launch a satellite into space. This was accomplished on January 31, 1958, when *Explorer I*, a grapefruit-sized satellite much smaller than *Sputnik*, was launched into orbit. Then, determined to win the race for space, Congress moved forward with passage of the National Aeronautics and Space Act.

The purpose of this 1958 legislation was to "provide for research into problems of flight within and outside the earth's atmosphere, and for other purposes." The legislation created the National Aeronautics and Space Administration, or NASA, whose mission was to "plan, direct, and conduct aeronautical and space activities."

NASA immediately went to work on plans for human space flight, highlighted by its first project, Project Mercury, so named on October 7, 1958. Project Mercury ran from 1959 to 1963. Several goals were established for the program. The top three goals were to "place a manned spacecraft in orbital flight around the earth, investigate man's performance capabilities and his ability to function in the environment of space, and recover the man and the spacecraft safely."

Though Russian cosmonaut Yuri Gagarin had accomplished the very first orbital flight on April 12, 1961, John Glenn became the first American astronaut to orbit Earth. It was a great triumph for America. Riding in *Friendship 7*, Glenn was launched into space on February 20, 1962. He flew at a speed of 17,544 mph, some 99 to 162 miles above Earth, for almost five hours. In all, Glenn made three orbits before landing in the Atlantic Ocean near the Bahamas. His flight was not without its perils. Though several minor problems had delayed the mission, Glenn lifted off with little hint of the problems that plagued the latter half of the flight. Toward the end of his first orbit, he noticed that the automatic controls seemed to be malfunctioning. He switched to manual control to correct a slight drift to the right taken by the space capsule—first problem solved.

Glenn's most pressing problem, however, would occur during re-entry. Indicators showed that the heatshield and compressed landing bag were loose, both potentially fatal defects. The heatshield was designed to dissipate heat generated by friction during re-entry. Only a retrorocket package strapped to the heatshield could possibly keep the shield in place long enough to get the capsule through re-entry. Glenn reported seeing bits of the retro-package fly past his window during re-entry, yet the shield held long enough to protect the capsule. Fortunately, the compressed landing bag performed correctly. Glenn splashed into the ocean. A waiting naval vessel stood ready to retrieve Glenn as he emerged from the bobbing space capsule. America finally had its own "first," and with it a new frontier to conquer. Astonishing new inventions in its future would help it do just that.

NATIONAL ARCHIVES DOCUMENT

Elapsed time from launch in hours, minutes, and seconds	Duration in seconds of each communication	Communicator CC = capsule P = pilot CT = communications technician	Communication
04 37 18	2.4	P	This is Friendship 7, going to manual control.
04 37 21	1.3	CC	Ah, Roger, Friendship 7.
04 37 23	2.7	P	This is banging in and out here; I'll just control it manually.
04 39 01	22.1	CC	We are recommending that the retropackage not, I say again, not be jettisoned. This means that you will have to override the 05g switch which is expected to occur at 04 43 53. This is approximately 4-1/2 minutes from now. This also means that you will have to retract the scope manually. Do you understand?
04 39 25	9.7	P	Ah, Roger, understand. I will have to make a manual 05g entry when it occurs, and bring the scope in, ah, manually. Is that affirm?
04 39 35	2.5	CC	That is affirmative, Friendship 7.
04 47 59	2.8	P	My condition is good, but that was a real fireball, boy.
04 48 05	3.2	P	I had great chunks of that retropack breaking off all the way through.
04 48 08	2.1	CC	Very good; it did break off, is that correct?
04 48 17	0.3	P	Roger.

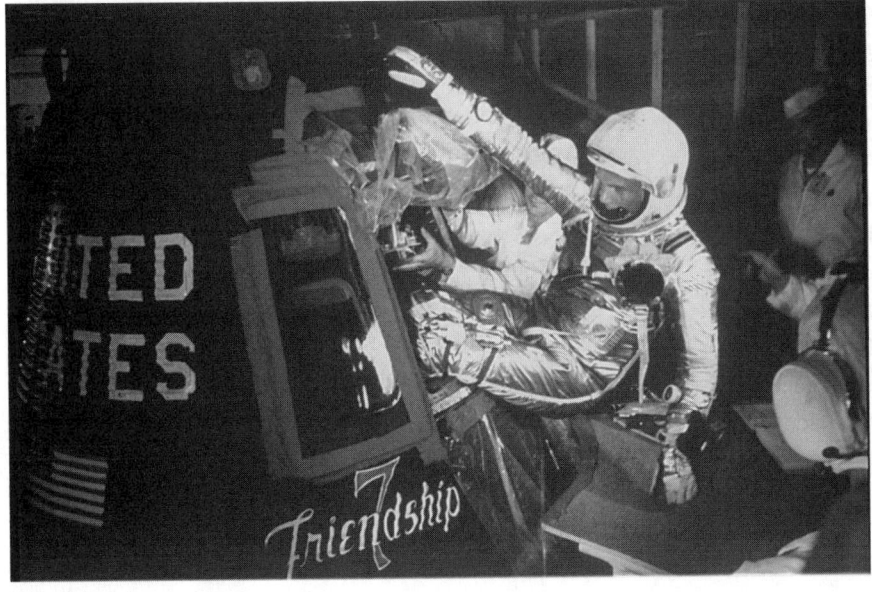

Left: On Feb. 20, 1962, astronaut John Glenn climbed into the *Friendship 7* capsule in preparation for America's first manned flight into space. Once inside, Glenn had little room to move. Glenn orbited Earth three times during his historic five-hour flight in space.

Critical Thinking

Draw Conclusions

In 1958 Congress enacted the National Defense Education Act (NDEA). This law funded college scholarships and loans, provided for teacher training, and expanded public school math and science curriculums. At its core, the NDEA encouraged secondary schools to direct students toward an advanced education in college or at a technical school. Students who took advantage of available funding, however, had to first swear allegiance to the United States, as well as sign an affidavit that they had no intention of overthrowing the U.S. government. In what way did this legislation interweave Cold War politics with mainstream education?

Assess Significance

Why was it critically important for the Mercury Project to be successful?

Determine Point of View

On September 12, 1962, at Rice University Stadium in Houston, Texas, President John F. Kennedy said the following:

> We set sail on this new sea because there is new knowledge to be gained, and new rights to be won, and they must be won and used for the progress of all people. For space science, like nuclear science and all technology, has no conscience of its own.

> Whether it will become a force for good or ill depends on man, and only if the United States occupies a position of preeminence can we help decide whether this new ocean will be a sea of peace or a new, terrifying theater of war.

What did Kennedy mean?

Research and Writing

Relating Events

In 1952 the International Council of Scientific Unions established July 1, 1957–December 31, 1958 as the International Geophysical Year (IGY) because scientists knew solar activity would be especially high during that time. In October 1954 the same council passed a resolution calling for the construction and launch of satellites during the IGY as a means to map Earth's surface. In 1955 the United States announced plans to launch a satellite capable of orbiting Earth. And though Eisenhower publicly congratulated Russian scientists following the successful *Sputnik* launch, behind closed doors he demanded to know how the United States had fallen behind. Fury rose again just one month later when Russia launched *Sputnik II*, this time carrying a much heavier payload, in addition to Laika, the first dog to enter space. Research the history of the space race. Write an essay explaining the flurry of scientific activity that occurred between America's scientific wake-up call in 1957 and John Glenn's space mission.

Analysis

For many years NASA did not consider women as astronaut candidates. This all changed in 1983 when Sally Ride became the first American woman in space. The Soviet Union, however, had sent the first woman into space, Valentina Tereshkova, twenty years earlier. Research women in space. Who have they been? What barriers did they need to overcome? What have been their accomplishments? What women are currently involved in NASA's space program?

Link to the Past

Forty years after the launch of *Sputnik*, the international science community was hard at work planning for an ongoing community in space. In 1998 construction of the International Space Station began with the launch of the Russian-built, but U.S.-owned, Zarya Control Module from the Baikonur Cosmodrome in Kazakhstan. In turn, the United States contributed the U.S.-built Unity Connecting Module, carried into space by the Space Shuttle *Endeavor* on December 4, 1998. Research the International Space Station. What is its current status? Which countries are involved? What difficulties has it experienced? What are its achievements? What promise does it hold for the future?

Civil Rights

"And so even though we face the difficulties of today and tomorrow, I still have a dream."

–MARTIN LUTHER KING JR. (1929–1968)

Prologue

How could it have happened? How could huge tracts of land be confiscated from people who had lived on it for centuries? How could generations of people be enslaved in the land of the free? How could people be denied a seat on a bus, or in a restaurant, or in a classroom solely because of the color of their skin? How could justice be denied to any group of people in a country whose citizens recite "with liberty and justice for all"? And yet, it all happened. And when it did, others rose up with courage to speak out against it. While some upheld laws designed to discriminate, or turned a blind eye to prejudice, others stood firm to ensure that civil rights guaranteed by the U.S. Constitution were denied to no one. "Injustice anywhere is a threat to justice everywhere." This wise observation by Martin Luther King, Jr. tells the story of civil rights in America. It is a story of righteous indignation. It also is the story of valor and perseverance as people sought to undo the wrongs of the past and ensure equality for all. In this sixth unit, you will traverse America's civil rights journey.

1798 Alien and Sedition Acts

"To repel . . . insinuations so derogatory to the honor and aggressions so dangerous to the . . . independence of the nation is an indispensable duty."

–JOHN ADAMS

HISTORICAL BACKGROUND

JOHN Adams was an ardent Federalist. His confidence in the power of a national government ran deep. Adams, Alexander Hamilton, and other Federalists were men of wealth and property who felt it was not only improper, but potentially dangerous to criticize those elected to office. Fiscally, they had aligned themselves with Great Britain, in particular because of tariff revenue gained from British imports. The aim of the Federalists was to establish a country with a stable government, where commerce flourished and men of property had the greater voice.

Thomas Jefferson, James Madison, and other Democratic Republicans (popularly known as "Republicans," they were ironically the forerunner of today's Democratic Party) differed both philosophically and politically with the Federalists. Socially, the Republicans represented farmers and craftsmen. They generally perceived the French Revolution, which was occurring at the time, as more the embodiment of democratic ideals than of mob rule. The Federalists, on the other hand, viewed the French Revolution with contempt. For the Federalists, the overthrow of the French monarchy, the confiscation of property, and the hundreds of people being led to the guillotine (including the former king and queen) represented not a democratic rebellion, but instead a country steeped in chaos. The arrival in 1793 of the new minister of the French Republic, Edmund Genet, and his subsequent actions to stir trouble in the states, galvanized Federalists' disdain for the French. Moreover, provisions in Jay's Treaty with the British resulted in a complete break in diplomatic relations between the United States and France.

It was in this political climate that the 1796 presidential election was held. Adams, elected president, and Jefferson, elected vice-president, placed the executive branch at political odds. The XYZ Affair (in which three French representatives demanded $10 million before initiating discussion to resolve disputes between America and France) enraged Americans and exacerbated the political malaise already affecting the workings of the federal government. When one French representative threatened the United States with "the power and violence of France," the die was cast. Federalists called for war against France. Republicans, on the other hand, rallied against Federalist "war fever." Though neither country had declared war, a "quasi-war" with France began. Between 1798 and 1800, the American navy captured more than 80 French ships. Congress did its part by suspending commerce with France. Fear of a French invasion gripped the Federalists. Jefferson's continued support of the French eventually led to irreconcilable political differences with Adams. To make matters worse, the Federalists pushed through a series of laws, the intent of which was to squelch criticism of Adams and of Congress, as well as to curtail French influence in America.

In June 1798, the Naturalization Act became the first of the "Alien and Sedition Acts." It increased the period of time from five to fourteen years that immigrants needed to wait before they could become naturalized citizens. The Aliens Friends Act (June 1798) granted the president the power to deport any alien he believed threatened the security of America. The act allowed deportation to occur without a stated reason or a trial. The Alien Enemies Act (July 1798) provided that all alien males could be arrested and deported once war was declared. Had Congress declared war against France, the law would have had the potential of expelling some 25,000 French citizens living in America. The Sedition Act (July 1798) was perhaps the most insidious of the hated acts. This law placed grave restraints on First

Amendment rights. It also provided stiff punishments for anyone who violated it.

The wrath of the Sedition Act was swift and sure, targeting Republican newspapers and just about any other act of defiance of the government. The political fallout, though, was certainly not what the Federalists had anticipated. Republicans remained united against the Alien and Sedition Acts. Disagreements between Adams and Hamilton over the conflict with France resulted in a messy 1800 presidential campaign filled with innuendoes and back-door politics. Moreover, taxes imposed on the people to finance the conflict with France had infuriated the common man. In the end, Jefferson gained the presidency, with Aaron Burr holding the reins as vice-president. Jefferson pardoned all those still imprisoned as a result of the Sedition Act soon after becoming president.

National Archives Document

Naturalization Act

Be it enacted . . .

That no alien shall be admitted to become a citizen of the United States, or of any state, unless . . . he shall have declared his intention to become a citizen of the United States, five years, at least, before his admission, . . .

Alien Friends Act

That it shall be lawful for the President of the United States . . . to order all such aliens as he shall judge dangerous to the peace and safety of the United States . . . to depart out of the territory of the United States. . . .

Alien Enemies Act

That whenever there shall be a declared war between the United States and any foreign nation or government . . . and the President of the United States shall make public proclamation of the event, all natives, citizens, denizens, or subjects of the hostile nation or government . . . shall be liable to be apprehended, restrained, secured and removed, as alien enemies.

Sedition Act

That if any persons shall unlawfully combine or conspire together, with intent to oppose any measure or measures of the government of the United States . . . shall be punished by a fine not exceeding five thousand dollars, and by imprisonment during a term not less than six months nor exceeding five years. . . .

And be it further enacted, That if any person shall write, print, utter or publish, or shall cause or procure to be written, printed, uttered or published, . . . any false, scandalous and malicious writing or writings against the government of the United States, or either house of the Congress of the United States, or the President of the United States, with intent to defame the said government, . . . for opposing or resisting any law of the United States, or any act of the President of the United States, . . . or to resist, oppose, or defeat any such law or act . . . then such person, being thereof convicted before any court of the United States having jurisdiction thereof, shall be punished by a fine not exceeding two thousand dollars, and by imprisonment not exceeding two years. ❋

Critical Thinking

Assess Significance

What type of broad discretionary powers does *An Act Concerning Aliens* give the president?

Draw Conclusions

In what way could the Naturalization Act ultimately limit voting?

Determine Point of View

After both had retired from public life and office, Thomas Jefferson wrote the following to John Adams.

> I have thus stated my opinion on a point on which we differ, not with a view to controversy, for we are both too old to change opinions which are the result of a long life of inquiry and reflection; but on the suggestion of a former letter of yours, that we ought not to die before we have explained ourselves to each other. We acted in perfect harmony thro' a long and perilous contest for our liberty and independance [sic]. A constitution has been acquired which, tho neither of us think perfect, yet both consider as competent to render our fellow-citizens the happiest and the securest on whom the sun has ever shone. If we do not think exactly alike as to it's imperfections, it matters little to our country which, after devoting to it long lives of disinterested labor, we have delivered over to our successors in life, who will be able to take care of it, and of themselves.

Jefferson and Adams both died on July 4, 1826, fifty years after the signing of the Declaration of Independence. What conclusion do you think both Jefferson and Adams had reached concerning the events occurring during their years of public service?

Research and Writing

Counterpoint

The sedition law provoked debate over the intent of the First Amendment. James Madison argued that the act assaulted "the right of freely examining public characters and measures, and of free communication among the people." The Federalists, however, argued that due to the looming foreign threat and contentious political climate, the law was "wise and necessary." At the heart of the debate was whether the government should have the power to punish individuals for expressing their views on actions taken by that government. Access and read *An Act in Addition to the Act, Entitled "An Act for the Punishment of Certain Crimes Against the United States."* What were its provisions? What restrictions did it place on the tenets of the First Amendment? With whom would you agree—the Republicans or the Federalists? Why?

Relating Events

Two documents were written in opposition to the Alien and Sedition Acts. The Kentucky Resolution, written by Vice-President Thomas Jefferson, declared that "said alien and sedition laws, are … palpable violations of the said constitution." The counterpart of the Kentucky Resolution was the Virginia Resolution, written by James Madison. Madison wrote, "the General Assembly doth particularly protest against the palpable and alarming infractions of the Constitution, … the first of which exercises a power no where delegated to the federal government, and … subverts the general principles of free government." Access and read these resolutions. What were the main points of each resolution? Then access and read the Sedition Act of 1918. What comparisons can be drawn between the actions of the federal government in 1798 and 1918? Would the Kentucky and Virginia Resolutions apply to actions of the federal government in 1918?

Link to the Past

In the case of *United States v. Cooper* (1800), Thomas Cooper was indicted for "being a person of wicked and turbulent disposition, designing and intending to defame the President … and to bring him into contempt and disrepute, and excite against him the hatred of the good people of the United States." Research *United States v. Cooper* (1800) and other actions considered seditious by Adams's administration. Then research the cases of *New York Times v. Sullivan* (1964) and *Texas v. Johnson* (1989). How do these two cases compare to the "seditious" actions of the late 1790s? What was the outcome of each case?

1830 "On Indian Removal"

> *"We are stripped of every attribute of freedom. . . . We have neither land nor home, nor resting place that can be called our own."*
>
> –Cherokee Chief John Ross, 1836

Historical Background

ETWEEN 1790 and 1830, thousands of whites trekked across the Appalachian Mountains to settle lands to the west. The population of Georgia alone grew sixfold. Native Americans had long feared the consequences of white land acquisition. Prejudice, intolerance for Native American cultures, and sheer greed combined to effectively remove Native American peoples from lands that had been home to their ancestors for centuries. Treaties, such as the 1825 Treaty of Indian Springs, which removed the Creek Indians from Georgia, were treaties of convenience written and imposed on the proud people who once lived freely on land now coveted by whites. In 1827 the Georgia legislature passed a resolution stating "that the Indians are tenants at [Georgia's] will." The legislation paved the way for federal legislation that would forever change Native American life.

In 1830 Congress passed the Indian Removal Act. The title of the act, along with its first provision, immediately identified its intent.

> That it shall and may be lawful for the President of the United States to cause so much of any territory belonging to the United States, west of the river Mississippi, not included in any state or organized territory, and to which the Indian title has been extinguished, as he may judge necessary, to be divided into a suitable number of districts, for the reception of such tribes or nations of Indians as may choose to exchange the lands where they now reside, and remove there.

The Indian Removal Act of 1830 established the federal government as protectorate over Indian tribes. It established acreage termed Indian Territory in present-day Oklahoma. It set aside $500,000 for improvements, such as houses and businesses, on lands occupied by relocated Native

Americans. It also guaranteed land in Indian Territory in equal exchange for what was surrendered in the East. Tools and provisions would be provided during the first year of resettlement. The act also stipulated that federal troops would protect "against all interruption and disturbance."

Thus, with the Indian Removal Act of 1830, the fate of the Cherokee was destined by Congress. In fighting the loss of their lands, the Cherokee sought recourse in the only place possible—federal court. Two court cases challenged the right of the federal government to establish dominion over the Cherokee. Their rulings seem to conflict. In *Cherokee Nation v. Georgia* (1831) the Supreme Court set forth an ambiguous ruling, allowing only that the Cherokee were a "domestic dependent nation. They occupy a territory to which we assert a title independent of their will, which must take effect in point of possession when their right of possession ceases." Yet, in *Worchester v. Georgia* (1832) the Supreme Court ruled that "The Cherokee Nation, then, is a distinct community, occupying its own territory . . . in which the laws of Georgia can have no force, and which the citizens of Georgia have no right to enter but with the assent of the Cherokees." The Supreme Court in its *Worchester v. Georgia* ruling seemed to have recognized the independence of the Cherokee nation. Yet President Andrew Jackson simply chose to ignore the Court's ruling. Instead he proceeded with plans for a lottery to distribute former Cherokee lands.

The Cherokee had won an illusory and short-lived victory in court. Thousands of Cherokee were forcibly removed from their Georgia lands. Some 25 percent died before reaching Indian Territory. Other Native Americans, such as the Seminole in

Florida and the Sauk and Fox in Illinois resisted relocation, prompting bloody wars. By the time Jackson left office, over 45,000 Indians had been relocated west of the Mississippi River, relinquishing over 100 million acres of land to the United States. In return, they received about 38 million acres of western land and about $68 million in payments for improvements and for subsidies.

NATIONAL ARCHIVES DOCUMENT

Andrew Jackson's Annual Message

It gives me pleasure to announce to Congress that the benevolent policy of the Government, steadily pursued for nearly thirty years, in relation to the removal of the Indians beyond the white settlements is approaching to a happy consummation. . . .

The consequences of a speedy removal will be important to the United States, to individual States, and to the Indians themselves. . . . It will relieve the whole State of Mississippi and the western part of Alabama of Indian occupancy, and enable those States to advance rapidly in population, wealth, and power. It will separate the Indians from immediate contact with settlements of whites; free them from the power of the States; enable them to pursue happiness in their own way and under their own rude institutions; will retard the progress of decay, which is lessening their numbers, and perhaps cause them gradually, under the protection of the Government and through the influence of good counsels, to cast off their savage habits and become an interesting, civilized, and Christian community.

. . . Can it be cruel in this Government when, by events which it can not control, the Indian is made discontented in his ancient home to purchase his lands, to give him a new and extensive territory, to pay the expense of his removal, and support him a year in his new abode? How many thousands of our own people would gladly embrace the opportunity of removing to the West on such conditions! If the offers made to the Indians were extended to them, they would be hailed with gratitude and joy.

And is it supposed that the wandering savage has a stronger attachment to his home than the settled, civilized Christian? Is it more afflicting to him to leave the graves of his fathers than it is to our brothers and children? Rightly considered, the policy of the General Government toward the red man is not only liberal, but generous. He is unwilling to submit to the laws of the States and mingle with their population. To save him from this alternative, or perhaps utter annihilation, the General Government kindly offers him a new home, and proposes to pay the whole expense of his removal and settlement. ❋

Below: As a result of the Indian Removal Act of 1830, Native Americans were forcibly removed from their lands.

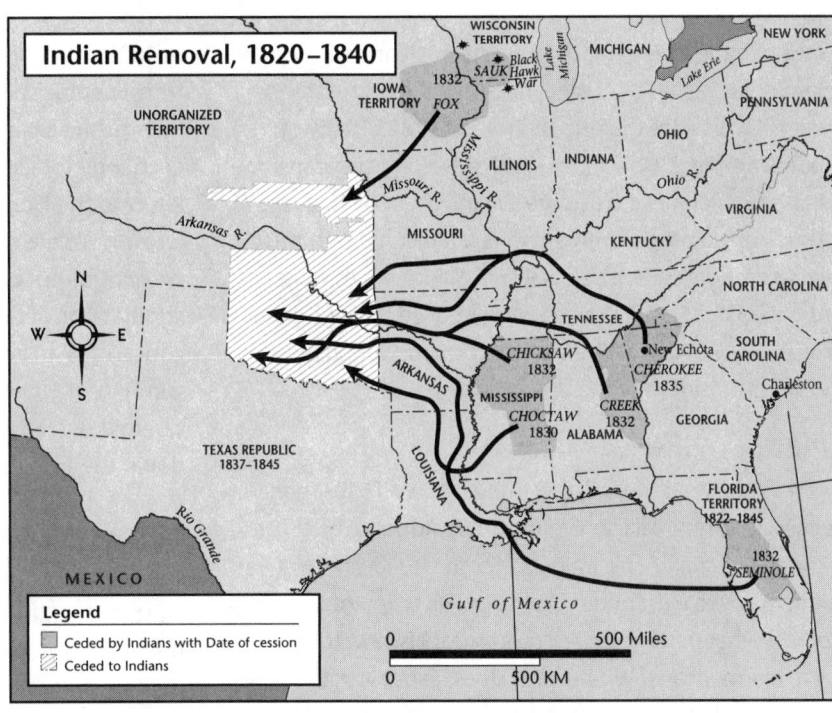

Indian Removal, 1820–1840

Critical Thinking

Draw Conclusions

Reread the excerpts from President Jackson's Annual Message. How would you characterize his words to Congress?

Determine Point of View

Do you think the face value of the Indian Removal Act was a fair deal for Native Americans? Why or why not?

Assess Significance

In 1832 Chief Black Hawk led a band of Sauk and Fox Indians in an effort to reclaim lands lost to white settlers in northern Illinois. As the result of a highly questionable treaty signed in 1805, Sauk and Fox leaders ceded nearly 50 million acres to the United States in exchange for $1,000 per year, plus the freedom to live on the land for as long as the U.S. government owned it.

With white population booming to near 150,000, in 1828 the federal government told the Sauk and Fox peoples to begin relocating west of the Mississippi River. In 1831 whites took over Black Hawk's village and plowed under sacred burial grounds. In 1832 Black Hawk and a band of Sauk and Fox returned. Soon the Illinois militia and federal troops were called out to hunt down Black Hawk and his followers. A four-month war ensued. Black Hawk was pursued into Wisconsin, where he was finally captured. After a year in prison, Black Hawk returned to his people, now in Iowa, a broken man. Chief Black Hawk once said, "How smooth must be the language of the whites, when they can make right look like wrong, and wrong like right." What did Black Hawk mean by this statement? Refer to Jackson's address to formulate your answer.

Research and Writing

Analysis

Research the Creek War of 1813 and 1814 and the First Seminole War in 1817. What happened in each of these wars? What were the provisions of the 1825 Treaty of Indian Springs? How did prejudice, westward expansion, an insatiable quest to acquire all lands held by Native Americans, and government deceit affect native tribes living east of the Mississippi River? Which tribes were removed by treaty? Which were removed through other means? What was Jackson's involvement during his years as president of the United States?

Point of View

Access and read the Indian Removal Act of 1830. Then access and read Jackson's entire 1830 Address to Congress. Analyze his rationale for the removal of Native Americans to west of the Mississippi River, point by point. What parts of his address reveal his view toward Native Americans? What words does he use to rationalize and support the Indian Removal Act of 1830? In what way does he promote the removal of Native Americans as paternal, understandable, and acceptable?

Relating Events

In 1835 a faction of the Cherokee signed the Treaty of New Echota. The treaty stipulated that the Cherokee relinquish all lands east of the Mississippi River in exchange for land in the Indian Territory. In an 1836 letter to the House of Representatives, Chief John Ross wrote, "We are constrained solemnly to declare, that we cannot but contemplate the enforcement of the stipulations of this instrument on us, against our consent, as an act of injustice and oppression." In the summer of 1838 the U.S. Army rounded up some 3,000 Cherokee, loaded them onto boats, and sent them down the Tennessee, Ohio, Mississippi, and Arkansas rivers to Indian Territory. Then, in the winter of 1838–1839, under the watchful eye of the U.S. Army, some 14,000 Cherokees were marched 1,200 miles to west of the Mississippi River. Some 4,000 died along the way from exposure, disease, and exhaustion. The journey was memorialized by the Cherokee as the "trail where they cried," giving rise to the name Trail of Tears. Research the specifics of the Treaty of New Echota. Who signed it? Why did it factionalize the Cherokee? Beyond the Trail of Tears, what were the repercussions of the treaty?

1857 Scott v. Sandford

"I believe this government cannot endure permanently half slave and half free."

—ABRAHAM LINCOLN

HISTORICAL BACKGROUND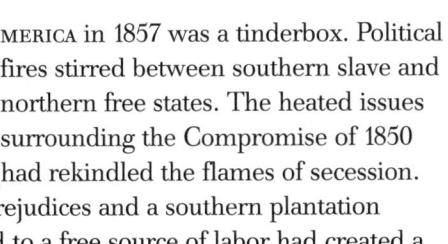

AMERICA in 1857 was a tinderbox. Political fires stirred between southern slave and northern free states. The heated issues surrounding the Compromise of 1850 had rekindled the flames of secession. Long-held prejudices and a southern plantation economy tied to a free source of labor had created a social climate that was steeped in injustice and bigotry. Anti-black sentiments in northern cities created settings that certainly were not the safe havens sought by African-Americans. Even more problematic was the fact that, within the federal government, racial bigotry ran deep. Seven of the nine justices sitting on the U.S. Supreme Court at the time had been appointed by proslavery presidents. In his March 1857 Inaugural Address, President James Buchanan dismissed the question of slavery as an issue solely within the purview of the states. The concern was not about inhumanity imposed on a race of people, but rather of the well-being of white slaveholders.

> All agree that under the Constitution slavery in the States is beyond the reach of any human power except that of the respective States themselves wherein it exists. . . . But this question of domestic slavery is of far graver importance than any mere political question, because, should the agitation continue it may eventually endanger the personal safety of a large portion of our countrymen where the institution exists. In that event no form of government . . . can compensate for the loss of peace and domestic security around the family altar. Let every Union-loving man, therefore, exert his best influence to suppress this agitation.

In regards to restricting slavery in the western territories, an extremely sensitive and critical issue of the time, Buchanan stated that it was "happily, a matter of but little practical importance. Besides, it is a judicial question, which legitimately belongs to the Supreme Court of the United States, before whom it is now pending, and will, it is understood, be speedily and finally settled."

Buchanan could emphatically make this statement because he was privileged to an upcoming Supreme Court decision that he believed would settle the issue of slavery in the country once and for all. The case was *Scott v. Sandford*, commonly known as the Dred Scott Decision. Instead, the judgment would further propel the country toward civil war. Rendering the decision for the Court was Chief Justice Roger Taney. As Attorney General, in 1831 Taney had declared that discrimination against blacks by local and state officials was certainly justified since blacks already were a "separate and degraded people." It was in this environment that Dred Scott awaited the decision about whether he would remain a slave or be a free man.

Dred Scott was born into slavery in Virginia. In 1832 he was living in Missouri when he was sold to Dr. John Emerson. Scott later followed Emerson to the free state of Illinois, and then, in 1836, to the Wisconsin Territory. There he married Harriet Robinson, a slave whose ownership then transferred to Emerson. Subsequent moves brought Scott and Harriet to Louisiana and then back to St. Louis, Missouri. Following Emerson's death, Scott sought freedom through the courts, contending that his stay in Illinois and in Wisconsin, both places where slavery was prohibited, allowed for his release from bondage. In 1850 the St. Louis Circuit Court ruled that Scott and his family were free. However, two years later, the Missouri Supreme Court reversed the lower court ruling. Scott appealed his case to the U.S. Circuit Court for Missouri. The federal court upheld the ruling of the Missouri Supreme Court. The only recourse for Scott was to appeal to the United States Supreme Court.

The resulting decision had enormous ramifications. On March 6, 1857, Chief Justice Taney held that since

Scott was a slave, he was not a citizen. Thus, as a noncitizen, he could not expect protection from the courts or the federal government. Additionally, Scott's four-year residence in free territory did not grant him freedom. Moreover, Taney continued, Congress had no constitutional authority to ban slavery from a federal territory. The decision went to the heart of the social and political dichotomy that had engulfed the nation. Though southern Democrats were thrilled with the decision, northern Republicans accused the Taney Court of conspiring with the southern "slave power." Regardless of alleged motive, the match for the tinderbox had been struck, and it appeared little could be done to put out the flames.

NATIONAL ARCHIVES DOCUMENT

. . . There are two leading questions presented by the record:

1. Had the Circuit Court of the United States jurisdiction to hear and determine the case between these parties? And

2. If it had jurisdiction, is the judgment it has given erroneous or not? . . .

The question is simply this: Can a negro, whose ancestors were imported into this country, and sold as slaves, become a member of the political community formed and brought into existence by the Constitution of the United States, and as such become entitled to all the rights, and privileges, and immunities, guarantied by that instrument to the citizen? One of which rights is the privilege of suing in a court of the United States in the cases specified in the Constitution. . . .

The words "people of the United States" and "citizens" are synonymous terms, and mean the same thing. They both describe the political body who, according to our republican institutions, form the sovereignty, and who hold the power and conduct the Government through their representatives. They are what we familiarly call the "sovereign people," and every citizen is one of this people and a constituent member of this sovereignty. The question before us is, whether the class of persons described in the plea in abatement compose a portion of this people, and are constituent members of this sovereignty? We think they are not, and that they are not included, and were not intended to be included, under the word "citizens" in the Constitution, and can therefore claim none of the rights and privileges which that instrument provides for and secures to citizens of the United States. . . .

Below: Dred Scott

And upon a full and careful consideration of the subject, the court is of opinion, that, upon the facts stated in the plea in abatement, Dred Scott was not a citizen of Missouri within the meaning of the Constitution of the United States, and not entitled as such to sue in its courts; and, consequently, that the Circuit Court had no jurisdiction of the case, and that the judgment on the plea in abatement is erroneous. . . .

Upon these considerations, it is the opinion of the court that the act of Congress which prohibited a citizen from holding and owning property of this kind in the territory of the United States north of the line therein mentioned, is not warranted by the Constitution, and is therefore void; and that neither Dred Scott himself, nor any of his family, were made free by being carried into this territory; even if they had been carried there by the owner, with the intention of becoming a permanent resident. ✳

Critical Thinking

Analyze Cause and Effect

What impact did the *Scott v. Sandford* decision have on the 1820 Missouri Compromise?

Draw Conclusions

Part of Justice Taney's decision in *Scott v. Sandford* included the following.

> The language of the Declaration of Independence is equally conclusive:
>
> It then proceeds to say: 'We hold these truths to be self-evident: that all men are created equal....'
>
> The general words above quoted would seem to embrace the whole human family, and if they were used in a similar instrument at this day would be so understood. But it is too clear for dispute, that the enslaved African race were not intended to be included, and formed no part of the people who framed and adopted this declaration; for if the language, as understood in that day, would embrace them, the conduct of the distinguished men who framed the Declaration of Independence would have been utterly and flagrantly inconsistent with the principles they asserted; and instead of the sympathy of mankind, to which they so confidently appealed, they would have deserved and received universal rebuke and reprobation.

Why do you think Taney referred to the men who wrote and adopted the Declaration of Independence in his opinion?

Make Predictions

Why did northerners believe the only way to rectify the Court's decision in *Scott v. Sandford* was through the ballot box?

Research and Writing

Analysis

Not long after publication of both the majority and dissenting opinions in the *Scott v. Sandford* case, newspapers weighed in on the decision. On March 12, the *Chicago Tribune* expressed outrage.

> We must confess we are shocked at the violence and servility of the Judicial Revolution caused by the decision of the Supreme Court of the United States. We scarcely know how to express our detestation of its inhuman dicta or fathom the wicked consequences which may flow from it ... To say or suppose, that a Free People can respect or will obey a decision so fraught with disastrous consequences to the People and their Liberties, is to dream of impossibilities.

The *Daily Union* (Washington, D.C.), however, had a vastly different perspective.

> We cherish a most ardent and confident expectation that this decision will meet a proper reception from the great mass of our intelligent countrymen; that it will be regarded with soberness and not with passion; and that it will thereby exert a mighty influence in diffusing sound opinions and restoring harmony and fraternal concord throughout the country ... It would be fortunate, indeed, if the opinion of that court on this important subject could receive the candid and respectful acquiescence which it merits.

Research reaction to the *Scott v. Sandford* decision. How did the ruling rouse the political emotions of the country?

Counterpoint

Access the *Scott v. Sandford* decision. Read the dissenting opinions of Justice John Mclean and Justice Benjamin Curtis. What was the basis of each dissenting argument?

Biography

Roger Taney was Chief Justice of the United States for twenty-eight years. Research his life and service on the country's high court. What were his beliefs in regard to states' rights? Did his beliefs affect his rulings? How much political power did the court wield during Taney's tenure as Chief Justice?

1863 Emancipation Proclamation

*"As I would not be a slave, so I would not be a master.
This expresses my idea of democracy."*

−ABRAHAM LINCOLN

HISTORICAL BACKGROUND

IN May 1860 the Republican Party nominated Abraham Lincoln for president. At the heart of the presidential campaign was the issue of slavery. Though Republicans opposed slavery's spread into the western territories, they accepted its presence where it already existed as a foregone social and political conclusion. Lincoln received virtually no votes in many southern states, yet he ultimately garnered almost 40 percent of the total popular vote. Three other candidates, Stephen Douglas, John Breckinridge, and John Bell split the remaining sixty percent, thus tipping the 1860 election to Lincoln.

Southern states had threatened to secede from the Union if Lincoln became president. In his March 4 Inaugural Address, he beseeched all citizens to respect the integrity of the Constitution rather than incite the emotions of secession. However, he also issued a firm warning to southerners.

> In *your* hands, my dissatisfied fellow-countrymen, and not in *mine*, is the momentous issue of civil war. The Government will not assail *you*. You can have no conflict without being yourselves the aggressors. *You* have no oath registered in heaven to destroy the Government, while I shall have the most solemn one to "preserve, protect, and defend it."

Warnings aside, the die had already been cast. By March, seven states had already seceded from the Union. Four more states would soon follow their lead. Lincoln was by no means a supporter of slavery, yet he led the country into war ardently believing that military action was required to preserve the Union. For Lincoln and many other Americans, individual states simply had no constitutional authority to secede. Slavery was a secondary issue, one that rightfully belonged to the authority of the states. Moreover, Lincoln believed the Constitution did not grant the president authority to free the slaves. Though Lincoln viewed slavery as morally abhorrent, he did not perceive it as an issue that should result in the dissolution of the Union. In fact, he had enumerated his position on slavery on many occasions. For example, in an 1858 speech in Chicago, Lincoln stated,

> I have always hated slavery, I think as much as any Abolitionist. . . . I have always hated it. . . . I always believed that everybody was against it, and that it was in course of ultimate extinction. I have said a hundred times, and I have now no inclination to take it back, that I believe there is no right, and ought to be no inclination in the people of the free States to enter into the slave States, and interfere with the question of slavery at all.

When the Civil War began, few expected the anguish of the war to prolong itself month after month, and then into years. Both northern and southern commanders believed their forces were far superior and their cause far more just, giving both sides confidence in a swift and victorious end to the conflict. Yet, as the war escalated, the issue of a state's right to determine its social and economic fate dulled. In its place stood the moral ideal of a nation built upon the pillar of equality. Plus, at the head of the Union was Lincoln, a pragmatist. Lincoln well understood that some form of emancipation proclamation, whether southern states viewed it as binding or not, would fragment the slave system. Slaves who viewed themselves as free would flee southern plantations, leaving the South with a diminished labor force. Moreover, the North had not fared well in battles up to that point. It was hoped that emancipation would help galvanize the North on the side of a noble cause—liberty. Finally, a moral high road would potentially ward off European intervention on the side of the South.

On January 1, 1863, Lincoln issued the Emancipation Proclamation. Two political images at the time define its reception. A Northern image showed a pensive Lincoln thoughtfully drafting a document. A Southern image, on the other hand, created the picture of a disheveled man using the Bible as a footstool. A caricature of a devil was depicted as holding the pen's inkwell from which Lincoln wrote. Very quickly, the Emancipation Proclamation became a fire bolt that provoked the passions of soldiers and citizens across the country.

NATIONAL ARCHIVES DOCUMENT

By the President of the United States of America:

A Proclamation.

. . . That on the first day of January, in the year of our Lord one thousand eight hundred and sixty-three, all persons held as slaves within any State or designated part of a State, the people whereof shall then be in rebellion against the United States, shall be then, thenceforward, and forever free; and the Executive Government of the United States, including the military and naval authority thereof, will recognize and maintain the freedom of such persons, and will do no act or acts to repress such persons, or any of them, in any efforts they may make for their actual freedom.

. . . And by virtue of the power, and for the purpose aforesaid, I do order and declare that all persons held as slaves within said designated States, and parts of States, are, and henceforward shall be free. . . .

. . . And I further declare and make known, that such persons of suitable condition, will be received into the armed service of the United States to garrison forts, positions, stations, and other places, and to man vessels of all sorts in said service.

And upon this act, sincerely believed to be an act of justice, warranted by the Constitution. . . . ✳

Below: Reading the Emancipation Proclamation, an 1864 engraving by J.W. Watts.

EMANCIPATION PROCLAMATION.

Critical Thinking

Analyze Cause and Effect

The Emancipation Proclamation not only declared slaves living in the Confederate states as free, it also allowed for their entry into the Union Army and Navy. The reaction in the South to the Emancipation Proclamation was swift. Confederate leaders responded with the threat that any slave caught in a Union uniform would be executed. Since states that had seceded from the Union no longer viewed Lincoln as president, why then did Southern leaders view the Emancipation Proclamation with such alarm?

Draw Conclusions

Abraham Lincoln is often referred to as the Great Emancipator. Yet, Lincoln's early stance was that slavery would eventually run its course, become less viable, and ultimately fail as a social institution. Though he didn't personally believe in slavery, politically he took the middle ground. Why then is Lincoln revered as the "Great Emancipator"?

Determine Point of View

Reread the opening quote on page 202. What did Lincoln mean?

Research and Writing

Analysis

Read the entire Emancipation Proclamation. Then read Lincoln's First Inaugural Address. Compare and contrast Lincoln's position on slavery found in the two documents.

Counterpoint

Lincoln viewed the Emancipation Proclamation as a military necessity prompted by states engaged in rebellion. His ability to issue such an order, he reasoned, was granted to him through his constitutional powers as commander-in-chief. In contrast to the liberty granted by the Emancipation Proclamation, two years earlier Lincoln suspended the writ of habeas corpus by executive order of April 27, 1861. This right, guaranteed by Article 1, Section 9 of the U. S. Constitution, requires that an individual may not be held in jail without charges being lodged against the individual, "unless when in cases of rebellion or invasion the public safety may require it." Lincoln's actions raised the ire of Supreme Court Chief Justice Roger Taney. In *Ex Parte Merryman* (1861), Justice Taney wrote the following:

> As the case comes before me, therefore, I understand that the president not only claims the right to suspend the writ of habeas corpus himself, at his discretion, but to

delegate that discretionary power to a military officer, and to leave it to him to determine whether he will or will not obey judicial process that may be served upon him.…I had supposed it to be one of those points of constitutional law upon which there was no difference of opinion, and that it was admitted on all hands, that the privilege of the writ could not be suspended, except by act of congress.

Research the case of *Ex Parte Merryman*. What was the issue? What were the specifics of the case? What other rights were restricted during the Civil War? Were the actions of the federal government hypocritical to the principle of liberty inherent in the Emancipation Proclamation? Were they justified? Write an essay in support or dissent of the restrictions placed on civil liberties during the Civil War.

Relating Events

Strong reaction to the Emancipation Proclamation occurred in both the North and the South. Research the response among slaves and among slave states to Lincoln's order. Research how the North responded. How did influential leaders such as Jefferson Davis and Frederick Douglass respond? Write an essay chronicling events precipitated by the Emancipation Proclamation. How effective was the Emancipation Proclamation in achieving its purpose?

"This is your golden opportunity."

–FREDERICK DOUGLASS

HISTORICAL BACKGROUND

ON April 10, 1861, Confederate forces opened fire on Fort Sumter in Charleston Harbor, South Carolina. It would prove to be the first volley of the American Civil War. In response, President Lincoln issued an order for 75,000 state militiamen to answer the call for federal service. Among those who enthusiastically responded to the President's call to arms were freed African-Americans, only to be summarily turned away. The barrier to military service by African-Americans was found in the Militia Act of 1792. This law stipulated

> That each and every free able-bodied white male citizen of the respective States, resident therein, who is or shall be of age of eighteen years, and under the age of forty-five years (except as is herein after excepted) shall severally and respectively be enrolled in the militia. . . . That every citizen, so enrolled and notified, shall, within six months thereafter, provide himself with a good musket or firelock.

Though Lincoln considered allowing blacks to enlist in the army, his first and foremost concern was that such a move would provoke border states to join the Confederacy. Lincoln's reasoning had merit, for Kentucky, Arkansas, Virginia, North Carolina, Missouri, and Tennessee refused to comply with Lincoln's order to take up arms against fellow Southerners. In fact, all but Kentucky and Missouri used the call to justify seceding from the Union and joining the Confederacy. The opportunity for blacks to join the military, however, was on the horizon.

In August 1861 Congress passed the Confiscation Act. This law allowed for any property used in insurrection against the government to be confiscated as contraband. According to the law's provisions, slaves, considered to be the property of slaveholders, were to be set free. Within a year the number of escaped and seized slaves in confiscation camps had escalated. Moreover, by mid 1862, white enlistments had declined, yet the need for Union soldiers was increasing. In response, on July 17, 1862, Congress passed the Second Confiscation Act. This law provided that "every person who shall hereafter commit the crime of treason against the United States, and shall be adjudged guilty thereof, shall suffer death, and all his slaves, if any, shall be declared and made free." Subsequently, Congress passed the Militia Act of 1862 stipulating that "the President be, and he is hereby, authorized to receive into the service of the United States, for the purpose of constructing intrenchments [sic], or performing camp service or any other labor, or any military or naval service for which they may be found competent, persons of African descent." The law also provided that family members would be granted their freedom once a male relative enlisted into military service. Additionally, the law stipulated payment of $10 per month for service, $3 less than their white counterparts.

The recruitment of African-Americans increased following Lincoln's Emancipation Proclamation. The first official black regiments were filled by volunteers from South Carolina, Tennessee, and Massachusetts. In response to the burgeoning number of black volunteers, in May 1863 Congress established the Bureau of Colored Troops under General Order 143. Nearly 200,000 African-Americans served in the army and navy during the Civil War, comprising some ten percent of the entire Union Army. Sixteen African-Americans received the Medal of Honor. Almost 40,000 blacks died as the result of service in the Union forces. African-Americans served in the infantry, as guards, scouts, spies, pilots, carpenters, chaplains, and in many other capacities. Eighty African-Americans became commissioned officers. Discrimination, however, permeated the Union ranks. Blacks lived in segregated housing, were generally commanded by white officers, and until June 1964, were paid less than white soldiers. Moreover, being taken as prisoner by Confederate forces promised excessively harsh treatment or death. Yet, African-American soldiers and sailors rose above the barriers of discrimination and the horror of battle to serve with distinction in a war that placed into question the very survival of the nation.

NATIONAL ARCHIVES DOCUMENT

GENERAL ORDERS,
No. 143
WAR DEPARTMENT,
ADJUTANT GENERAL'S OFFICE,
Washington, May 22, 1863.

I—A Bureau is established in the Adjutant General's Office for the record of all matters relating to the organization of Colored Troops. . . .

IV—No persons shall be allowed to recruit for colored troops except specially authorized by the War Department. . . .

VI—Colored troops maybe accepted by companies, to be afterward consolidated in battalions and regiments by the Adjutant General. The regiments will be numbered seriatim, in the order in which they are raised, the numbers to be determined by the Adjutant General. They will be designated: "—— Regiment of U. S. Colored Troops."

VIII—The non-commissioned officers of colored troops may be selected and appointed from the best men of their number in the usual mode of appointing non-commissioned officers. Meritorious commissioned officers will be entitled to promotion to higher rank if they prove themselves equal to it. . .

BY ORDER OF THE SECRETARY OF WAR:
E. D. TOWNSEND,
Assistant Adjutant General ✳

Above: Nearly 200,000 African-Americans served in the army and navy during the Civil War. The first official African-American regiments were filled with volunteers from South Carolina, Tennessee, and Massachusetts following Lincoln's Emancipation Proclamation.

Critical Thinking

Analyze Cause and Effect

Abolitionists such as Frederick Douglass encouraged blacks to join the Union Army and Navy as a means to eventually gain full citizenship. In what way do you think this affected the enlistment of blacks? Why?

Draw Conclusions

Though when approached by Confederate officers in 1864 to press slaves into the Confederate forces, Confederate President Jefferson Davis refused. One year later, Davis signed General Order 14. It stipulated,

> In order to provide additional forces to repel invasion, maintain the rightful possession of the Confederate States, secure their independence, and preserve their institutions, the President be, and he is hereby, authorized to ask for and accept from the owners of slaves, the services of such number of able-bodied negro men as he may deem expedient, for and during the war, to perform military service in whatever capacity he may direct.

Why do you think Davis decided to sign legislation allowing for the enlistment of slaves into the Confederate army?

Assess Significance

In March 1863 Congress passed the Enrollment Act. It required military service, with the exception for those who could pay $300 commutation fee. An individual also could find someone else to take his place. The law was greeted with riots in New York City, leading to the deaths of almost 1,000 people, many of whom were black. Some 250,000 Northerners were drafted by lottery under the Enrollment Act, yet only about 46,000 served. Why do you think conscription was rejected on such a large scale by northern whites?

Research and Writing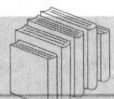

Analysis

African-Americans served with honor in several engagements during the Civil War. Though black soldiers faced many discriminatory hurdles, they soon proved their valor, beginning with a battle at Island Mount in Missouri in October 1862. In a February 1863 report, Colonel T. W. Higgins, Union commander of the First South Carolina Volunteers, wrote, "It would have been madness to attempt with the bravest white troops what I have successfully accomplished with the black ones." Research five battles fought by African-American units during the Civil War. Who comprised the unit? Who was in command? Where was the battle fought? What was the result?

Relating Events

The Civil War dramatically changed the roles played by women. Research the role of women in the Civil War. How did they assist both the Union and Confederate armies? What roles did African-American women in particular play in the Civil War? In what way did the Civil War redefine the roles traditionally held by women?

Historical Interpretation

The term *Buffalo Soldier* was given by the Cheyenne and Comanche to African-American cavalry soldiers serving in the West. They constituted almost twenty percent of all soldiers assigned to the western frontier during the late 1800s. As members of the 9th Cavalry stationed in Texas and the 10th Cavalry stationed in Kansas and the Indian Territory, Buffalo Soldiers were given some of the most difficult missions to be carried out on some of the most inhospitable terrain of the country. Several Buffalo Soldiers were awarded Medals of Honor for their military service. Research the Buffalo Soldiers. When did they serve? How were they formed? What were their missions? What hardships did they endure? What discrimination did they face? How did they distinguish themselves?

1863 Gettysburg Address

". . . that government of the people by the people for the people, shall not perish from the earth."

—ABRAHAM LINCOLN

HISTORICAL BACKGROUND

IT had been a long and arduous battle. Nearly one-third of the Army of Northern Virginia had been lost, including 3,903 killed and 24,000 other soldiers wounded or missing. The Union Army hadn't fared much better. More than one-quarter of those who had fought were lost from their units. A total of 3,155 Union soldiers had been killed and some 20,000 wounded or missing. The battle was Gettysburg. The time was the first three days of July, 1863. In all, over 51,000 men were killed, wounded, captured, or missing, marking Gettysburg as the bloodiest battle of the Civil War.

Though Gettysburg was not the final battle of the Civil War, it was symbolic of the great tragedy that had engulfed the country. Estranged families had become a microcosm of the political division that had swept the nation. Brothers, fathers, uncles, and cousins, individuals whose relationships had been severed over an ideology, were brought together as enemies in combat among the smoke and horror of the battlefield. Colonel Joshua Chamberlain, who led the 20th Maine Infantry, described a flashpoint in the battle at Little Round Top at Gettysburg.

The roar of all this tumult reached us on the left and heightened the intensity of our resolve. Meanwhile the flanking column worked around to our left and joined those before us in a fierce assault, which lasted with increasing fury for an intense hour. The two lines met and broke and intermingled in the shock. The crush of musketry gave way to cuts and thrusts, grapplings and wrestlings. The edge of conflict swayed to and fro, with wild pools and eddies. At times I saw around me more of the enemy than of my own men; gaps opening, swallowing, closing again with sharp, convulsive energy; squads of stalwart men who had cut their way through us, disappearing as if translated all around me, strange, mingled roars—shouts of defiance, rally and desperation.

The final fighting at Gettysburg occurred on July 3, when 15,000 determined Confederates from the divisions of Longstreet, Pickett, and Pettigrew, emerged from the woods for a final assault west of Cemetery Ridge. Musket fire, canister, and grapeshot honed in on the doomed soldiers. Fewer than half of them made it back to the Confederate lines. A man of great honor, Confederate General Robert E. Lee blamed the pivotal military disaster on himself. As he moved among his shattered forces, he was heard to say, "Don't be discouraged. It was all my fault this time."

On July 4, Lee's bedraggled army retreated south, their dismal situation made all the worse by a driving rainstorm. Of great consternation to President Abraham Lincoln was the fact that the commanding Union general at Gettysburg, General Meade, chose to rest his troops rather than pursue Lee as his shattered army straggled across the Potomac River. Lincoln wrote to Meade,

My dear general, I do not believe you appreciate the magnitude of the misfortune involved in Lee's escape. He was within your easy grasp, and to have closed upon him would, in connection with our other late successes, have ended the war. As it is, the war will be prolonged indefinitely.

Lincoln's words would prove prophetic. The carnage and immense misery of the Civil War continued for almost two more years.

On November 19, 1863, President Lincoln traveled by train to Gettysburg to dedicate the Soldiers National Cemetery. The purpose was to honor all soldiers, Union and Confederate, who had perished at Gettysburg a short four months earlier. Lincoln stood and spoke for a scant three minutes to a hushed crowd. His humbling words would memorialize the hallowed ground where so many men had died.

The Civil War had a devastating impact on American families. In all, over 630,000 Americans died fighting in battles on land they called home. The magnitude of the war weighed heavily on Lincoln. In 1864 Lincoln was re-elected president. In his Second Inaugural Address, he expressed the heart-felt sentiment found in the Gettysburg Address through a simple message: "With malice toward none; with charity for all...."

NATIONAL ARCHIVES DOCUMENT

Four score and seven years ago our fathers brought forth, upon this continent, a new nation, conceived in liberty, and dedicated to the proposition that "all men are created equal."

Now we are engaged in a great civil war, testing whether that nation, or any nation so conceived, and so dedicated, can long endure. We are met on a great battle field of that war. We have come to dedicate a portion of it, as a final resting place for those who died here, that the nation might live. This we may, in all propriety do. But, in a larger sense, we can not dedicate—we can not consecrate—we can not hallow, this ground—The brave men, living and dead, who struggled here, have hallowed it, far above our poor power to add or detract. The world will little note, nor long remember what we say here; while it can never forget what they did here.

It is rather for us, the living, we here be dedicated to the great task remaining before us—that, from these honored dead we take increased devotion to that cause for which they here, gave the last full measure of devotion—that we here highly resolve these dead shall not have died in vain; that the nation, shall have a new birth of freedom, and that government of the people by the people for the people, shall not perish from the earth. ✳

Below: Lincoln's Gettysburg Address lasted only three minutes, but his eloquence paid honor to all who had perished at Gettysburg.

Critical Thinking

Analyze Cause and Effect

Although the Battle of Gettysburg would not alone determine the outcome of the Civil War, the defeat of the Confederate forces at Gettysburg marked the first great victory for the North. A second critical victory came on July 4, the day of Lee's retreat, when the entire Confederate army at Vicksburg, Mississippi, surrendered to Union forces commanded by General Ulysses S. Grant. What do you think was the psychological effect of the Union victories on both the North and the South? Do you agree with Lincoln's assessment in his letter to General Meade?

Draw Conclusions

When General Lee asked Confederate President Jefferson Davis to relieve him of command following the defeat at Gettysburg, Davis replied, "To ask me to substitute you by some one in my judgment more fit to command, or who would possess more of the confidence of the army, or of the reflecting men of the country, is to demand an impossibility." What impact do you think the resignation of General Lee would have had on Confederate soldiers?

Determine Point of View

"We have come to dedicate a portion of it, as a final resting place for those who died here, that the nation might live." What do you think Lincoln meant when he spoke these words?

Research and Writing

Relating Events

Research a major battle that followed Gettysburg. Where was it held? Who was victorious? What was the cost? What military strategies were used? What impact did the battle have on the course of the war?

Analysis

With Confederate forces woefully diminished, hungry, and exhausted, Lee finally agreed to Grant's conditions of surrender. Lee was worn out from being pursued and tired of seeing his men die in battles steeped in futility and carnage. Thus, when Grant sent the following note to Lee, surrender became a repugnant consideration.

> General R. E. Lee, Commanding C.S.A.:
> 5 P.M., April 7th, 1865.
>
> The results of the last week must convince you of the hopelessness of further resistance on the part of the Army of Northern Virginia in this struggle. I feel that it is so, and regard it as my duty to shift from myself the responsibility of any further effusion of blood by asking of you the surrender of that portion of the Confederate States army known as the Army of Northern Virginia.
>
> U.S. Grant, Lieutenant-General

> April 7th, 1865.
>
> General: I have received your note of this date. Though not entertaining the opinion you express of the hopelessness of further resistance on the part of the Army of Northern Virginia, I reciprocate your desire to avoid useless effusion of blood, and therefore, before considering your proposition, ask the terms you will offer on condition of its surrender.
>
> R. E. Lee, General.

Research the final battles that led to Lee's surrender of the Army of Northern Virginia. What led General Lee to comment that "After four years of arduous service marked by unsurpassed courage and fortitude, the Army of Northern Virginia has been compelled to yield to overwhelming numbers and resources"?

Biography

Both Robert E. Lee and Ulysses S. Grant were opposing generals in several ways. Research the background of these two men. In what ways were they alike? How were they different? Who do you think was the better war strategist? Who was the better leader? Explain your assessments. What happened to each man following the end of the Civil War?

1865 Thirteenth Amendment

"Neither slavery nor involuntary servitude . . .
shall exist within the United States."

–Thirteenth Amendment

Historical Background

On April 8, 1864, the United States Senate passed the Thirteenth Amendment to the Constitution by a vote of 38–6. The House of Representatives—"the people's house"—followed suit on January 31, 1865, voting 119–56. By the end of the year enough states had ratified the amendment to make it the law of the land. It was momentous legislation that solidified the intent of the Emancipation Proclamation. Slavery as an institution had finally found its end. It required a Civil War and the life of President Lincoln to accomplish, but it was done. Slavery had been a part of the American culture for more than two centuries. It had been referred to as the "peculiar institution," a misnomer that hardly described its inhumanity.

Thomas Jefferson identified the malevolence of slavery when he said, "The whole commerce between master and slave is a perpetual exercise of the most unremitting despotism on the one part, and degrading submission on the other." By 1860 almost four million African-Americans were enslaved, representing approximately one-third of the South's population. In South Carolina and Mississippi, slaves outnumbered free individuals. Though the Thirteenth Amendment set slaves free, they simply had nowhere to go. As abolitionist Frederick Douglass reflected, former slaves "had neither money, property, nor friends. He was free from the old plantation, but he had nothing but the dusty road under his feet. . . . He was turned loose naked, hungry, and destitute to the open sky."

In 1865 a plan was introduced into Congress to grant each newly freed slave forty acres of land confiscated during the Civil War. Such land was certainly available. The Confiscation Act of 1862 and subsequent legislation allowed the federal government to confiscate "abandoned" lands or assume ownership of those properties for which taxes had not been paid. Even the estate of Confederate General Robert E. Lee had been confiscated. However, the rumor that freed slaves would receive "forty acres and a mule," proved too much to sustain the plan. As one former Confederate general stated, freed slaves had "nothing but freedom."

On March 3, 1865, Congress established the Bureau of Refugees, Freedmen, and Abandoned Lands—popularly known as the "Freedmen's Bureau"—with the mission to provide "such issues of provisions, clothing, and fuel [as needed] for the immediate and temporary shelter and supply of destitute and suffering refugees and freedmen and their wives and children." Established before the official end of the Civil War, the office within the Department of War was to remain in existence for one year, though Congress subsequently extended this timeline. The job of the Bureau was to assume control of confiscated lands, negotiate labor contracts between former slaves and planters, provide medical care, and set up schools. It was a daunting task. Although the Freedmen's Bureau attempted to distribute 850,000 acres of confiscated land, President Andrew Johnson instead returned the land to pardoned Confederates. Yet the Bureau did attain success with the establishment of over 1,000 schools, the funding of teacher-training institutes, and the establishment of black colleges. But with inadequate funds to assist its mission, the work of the Bureau ended in 1872.

The Thirteenth Amendment freed African-Americans from slavery. Yet it could not guarantee their freedom in a society steeped in racial bigotry. In response to the emancipation of slaves, southern states passed a series of laws, termed Black Codes, which restricted the freedom of African-Americans. Vagrancy laws allowed authorities to arrest those deemed idle, fine them, and contract their labor if the fine could not be paid. Other laws apprenticed minors under the age of 18 to a "master or mistress," with the understanding that the, "apprentice shall be bound by indenture, in case of males until they are twenty-one years old, and in case of females until they are eighteen years old." Black Codes tied former slaves to toil on the land, limiting their jobs to those involving agriculture or domestic work. They effectively regulated the lives of African-Americans, preventing them from raising their own crops or entering towns without permission. Black Codes, however, were quickly erased from jurisprudence when federal officials suspended them in 1866.

Many former slaves were left to rent a 20-to-50 acre plot of land from their former master. The harvested crop would then be shared as rent for the land. Sharecropping was riddled with inequity. Sharecroppers often found themselves so far in debt to the landowner that the conditions imposed mimicked former circumstances of slavery. In the end, though the Thirteenth Amendment freed the slaves, it would take several decades and additional legislation by Congress to ensure the civil rights of African-Americans.

NATIONAL ARCHIVES DOCUMENT

AMENDMENT XIII

Section 1.
Neither slavery nor involuntary servitude, except as a punishment for crime whereof the party shall have been duly convicted, shall exist within the United States, or any place subject to their jurisdiction.

Section 2.
Congress shall have power to enforce this article by appropriate legislation.

Passed by Congress January 31, 1865. Ratified December 6, 1865. ✳

$20 REWARD.

Ranaway from the Subscriber, on the 22nd December last, his negro man MARTIN, aged about 23 years. He has a pleasing countenance, round face, is quick spoken, and can tell a very plausible story; he is a shining black, stout built, with large limbs, short fingers, and small feet; the toe next to his great toe has been mashed off.

The above reward will be paid on his delivery to me, or at any Jail in North Carolina.

JAMES R. WOOD.
Wadesboro', Feb. 5, 1844.

Above: The Thirteenth Amendment abolished slavery in America and put an end to posters such as the one above.

Critical Thinking

Analyze Cause and Effect

In 1860 fewer than one-fourth of all white Southerners owned slaves. For those who did, half owned fewer than five slaves, with only one percent of slaveholders owning more than 100 enslaved African-Americans. Why then was there such overwhelming opposition to the abolition of slavery among southern states?

Determine Point of View

In Lincoln's Second Inaugural Address he stated,

> If we shall suppose that American slavery is one of those offenses which, in the providence of God, must needs come, but which, having continued through His appointed time, He now wills to remove, and that He gives to both North and South this terrible war as the woe due to those by whom the offense came, shall we discern therein any

departure from those divine attributes which the believers in a living God always ascribe to Him? Fondly do we hope, fervently do we pray, that this mighty scourge of war may speedily pass away.

What was Lincoln's point of view on slavery? How do you think the country received his view?

Assess Significance

Reread Jefferson's quote on page 211. Jefferson owned about 200 slaves who worked his tobacco and wheat plantation in Virginia, making him not only a slaveholder, but a large-scale one by southern standards at the time. Yet, Jefferson's words reflect an antislave stance, placing his words and lifestyle in opposition. Is it possible to rectify this contradiction? If so, how? If not, why not?

Research and Writing

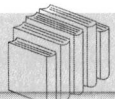

Historical Interpretation

Slavery was the antithesis of liberty, a system built on prejudice and inhumanity, all occurring in "the land of the free." Laws across the South ensured its survival. For example, in *State v. Mann* (1829), North Carolina Chief Justice Thomas Ruffin wrote, "The power of the master must be absolute, to render the submission of the slave perfect." Research the practice of slavery in the United States as the country entered the Civil War years. Write an essay explaining its human toll.

Analysis

The paradox of a country fighting for its liberty while participating in the trade and enslavement of a race of people did not escape those striving to make America free in the late eighteenth century. Between 1776 and 1786, eleven states heavily taxed those who imported slaves. In 1780 Pennsylvania law allowed for the gradual freeing of all slaves. In 1783 the high court in Massachusetts ruled that slavery was illegal based on the words found in its state constitution—"all men are born free and equal." Within a short time, other northern states abolished slavery within their borders. Research the history of abolition in America. Why did

abolition occur in the North, while the slave system remained entrenched in the South? What role did women play? Was the question of the abolition of slavery ultimately one of economics, politics, state's rights, or principle?

Relating Events

In an effort to escape southern retribution and the oppression imposed by sharecropping, thousands of African-American "Exodusters" migrated to Kansas in the 1870s with the desire to stake out a parcel of land, farm, and live in peace. It was the "Great Exodus"—the migration of a hopeful people in search of a free and promising land. Upon arriving in Kansas, former slave John Soloman Lewis wrote to relatives,

> When I landed on the soil [of Kansas] I looked on the ground and I says this is free ground. Then I looked on the heavens and I says them is free and beautiful heavens. Then I looked within my heart and I says to myself, I wonder why I was never free before?

Research the Exodusters. Who were Henry Adams and Pap Singleton? What role did they play in the migration of blacks to Kansas? Where did the Exodusters settle? What difficulties did they face? Did they find the freedom they so desperately sought?

1868 Treaty of Fort Laramie

"To maintain peace with the Indian,
let the frontier settler treat him with humanity. . ."

—REPORT TO THE PRESIDENT BY THE INDIAN PEACE COMMISSION, JANUARY 7, 1868

HISTORICAL BACKGROUND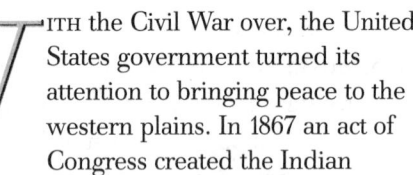

WITH the Civil War over, the United States government turned its attention to bringing peace to the western plains. In 1867 an act of Congress created the Indian Peace Commission. Its mission was "to call together the chiefs and headmen of such bands of Indians as were then waging war, for the purpose of ascertaining their reasons for hostility, and, if thought advisable, to make treaties with them." The commission's lengthy report chronicled its peace efforts. It also attempted to establish a sympathetic perspective on the plight of Native Americans. One section of the report made reference to both the provisions and violations of the 1851 Treaty of Fort Laramie.

> In 1851, a short time after the discovery of gold in California, when a vast stream of emigration was flowing over the western plains, which up to that period had been admitted by treaty and by law to be Indian territory. . . . A council was convened at Fort Laramie on the 17th day of September of that year, at which the Cheyennes, Araphahoes, Crows, Assinaboines, Gros-Ventres, Mandans, and Arickarees were represented. To each of these tribes boundaries were assigned. . . . The Indians granted us the right to establish roads and military and other posts within their respective territories, in consideration of which we agreed to pay the Indians $50,000 per annum for 50 years. . . . When this treaty reached the Senate, "50 years" was stricken out and "ten years" substituted. . . . Some years after this gold and silver were discovered in the mountains of Colorado, and thousands of fortune-seekers, who possessed nothing more than the right of transit over these lands, took possession of them for the purpose of mining, and, against the protests of the Indians, founded cities, established farms, and opened roads.

The recommendation of the Peace Commission was to institute a reservation system that protected the hunting rights of Native Americans and established firm boundaries where the tribes could live unharmed and unaffected by white settlement. On April 29, 1868, representatives of the U.S. government and many leaders of the Sioux Nation (Lakota peoples) signed a second Treaty of Fort Laramie. The treaty set aside a large tract of land, including the Black Hills, for exclusive use by the Lakota. The treaty was a covenant of peace between the Lakota peoples and the United States, a promise of mutual respect, and a hope that the conflicts and mistakes of the past could be set aside and replaced with mutual trust. It was a fragile treaty, based on good faith and a vision that two cultures in opposition could coexist. And, though those in attendance held the treaty with the utmost integrity, its success depended on others to respect its provisions with equal integrity. To truly keep the peace, the treaty had to prove itself to be more than just an inventory of good intentions.

The 1868 Treaty of Fort Laramie prohibited whites from moving onto reservation land. In return, the Lakota peoples agreed to end hostilities against those traveling on westward trails and against workers building the westward-expanding railroad lines. Though the Black Hills were protected as the sacred grounds of the Sioux by the treaty, in 1874 Lt. Col. George A. Custer accompanied a group of miners in search of gold onto Sioux land. The discovery of gold in the Black Hills soon compromised the promises inherent in the 1868 Treaty of Fort Laramie. The federal government rebuked the intrusion of whites onto Sioux land; yet, miners crossing into the Black Hills demanded protection from the U.S. Army. Violations of the treaty provoked the "Indian Wars," a series of bloody battles between Native Americans and the U.S. Army, ending with the massacre of more than 300 Lakota at Wounded Knee on the Pine Ridge Reservation in South Dakota in 1890.

NATIONAL ARCHIVES DOCUMENT

ARTICLE I.

From this day forward all war between the parties to this agreement shall for ever cease. . . .

If bad men among the whites, or among other people subject to the authority of the United States, shall commit any wrong upon the person or property of the Indians, the United States will, upon proof made to the agent, and forwarded to the Commissioner of Indian Affairs at Washington city, proceed at once to cause the offender to be arrested and punished according to the laws of the United States, and also reimburse the injured person for the loss sustained.

If bad men among the Indians shall commit a wrong or depredation upon the person or property of nay one, white, black, or Indian, subject to the authority of the United States, and at peace therewith, the Indians herein named solemnly agree that they will, upon proof made to their agent, and notice by him, deliver up the wrongdoer to the United States, to be tried and punished according to its laws. . . .

ARTICLE XI.

. . . the tribes who are parties to this agreement hereby stipulate that they will relinquish all right to occupy permanently the territory outside their reservations as herein defined, but yet reserve the right to hunt on any lands north of North Platte, and on the Republican Fork of the Smoky Hill river, so long as the buffalo may range thereon in such numbers as to justify the chase. And they, the said Indians, further expressly agree:

1st. That they will withdraw all opposition to the construction of the railroads now being built on the plains. . . .

Below: Peace commissioners meet with the Lakota in 1868 to negotiate the Fort Laramie Treaty. Seated are General William S. Harney (white beard) and General William Tecumseh Sherman (to Harney's left).

ARTICLE XVI.

The United States hereby agrees and stipulates that the country north of the North Platte river and east of the summits of the Big Horn mountains shall be held and considered to be unceded Indian territory, and also stipulates and agrees that no white person or persons shall be permitted to settle upon or occupy any portion of the same; or without the consent of the Indians, first had and obtained, to pass through the same; and it is further agreed by the United States, that within ninety days after the conclusion of peace with all the bands of the Sioux nation, the military posts now established in the territory in this article named shall be abandoned, and that the road leading to them and by them to the settlements in the Territory of Montana shall be closed.

In testimony of all which, we, the said commissioners, and we, the chiefs and headmen of the Brule band of the Sioux nation, have hereunto set our hands and seals at Fort Laramie, Dakota Territory, this twenty-ninth day of April, in the year one thousand eight hundred and sixty-eight. ✳

Critical Thinking

Determine Point of View

The 1867 Peace Commission report to the president, quoted on page 214, noted that "These Indians saw their former homes and hunting grounds overrun by a greedy population, thirsting for gold. They saw their game driven east to the plains, and soon found themselves the objects of jealousy and hatred." What was the position taken by the 1867 Peace Commission?

Compare and Contrast

Compare the recommendations of the 1867 Peace Commission with the provisions of the 1887 Dawes Act (pages 27–29).

Assess Significance

Why do you think the 1868 Fort Laramie Treaty (unlike the 1851 treaty) did not provide for the building of railroads, roads, or military forts on reservation land?

Research and Writing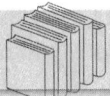

Historical Interpretation

After gold was discovered in the Black Hills, the federal government attempted to purchase the land from the Sioux. Sitting Bull, one of the signatories of the 1868 Treaty of Fort Laramie, responded by stating he was not willing to sell even a pinch of dust. The resulting conflict culminated in the Battle of the Little Bighorn. On June 25–26, 1876, Lt Col. George Armstrong Custer and 262 soldiers attacked the combined forces of Sitting Bull and Crazy Horse. Custer hoped for the glory of a victorious battle. He had, however, seriously underestimated the strength and number of the enemy. Research the events that led to the Battle of the Little Bighorn. What retaliation occurred following this battle? What was the end result? What other significant battles occurred during the Indian Wars, as conflict between Native Americans and the U.S. Army spread west and southwest?

Analysis

Access and read the entire 1868 Treaty of Fort Laramie. Create a list of its provisions. Which provisions benefited Native Americans affected by the treaty? Which provisions were for the benefit of whites? Do you believe the treaty respected Native American culture? Explain using examples from the treaty.

Link to the Present

Two modern U.S. Supreme Court decisions illustrate the disagreements that exist yet today over the sovereignty of land that was once part of the 1868 Treaty of Fort Laramie. In each case, the Court referred to the language in the treaty to support its decision. In *Montana v. United States* (1981), the Crow Tribe of Montana wanted to prohibit hunting and fishing on reservation land by anyone who was not a member. The tribe believed that it had the power to restrict hunting and fishing based on 1868 Treaty of Fort Laramie, as well as what the tribe understood to be its ownership of the riverbed of the Big Horn River. In *South Dakota v. Bourland* (1993), the restriction of hunting rights of nonwhites was again in question. The ruling in this case was based on the 1868 Treaty of Fort Laramie, the Flood Control Act of 1944 and the Cheyenne River Act. At the heart of the question was 104,420 acres of reservation land ceded to the United States for the Oahe Dam and Reservoir Project. Research both of these U.S. Supreme Court rulings. How did language in the 1868 Fort Laramie Treaty affect each case? How did the ruling in each case impact the sovereignty of the Tribe? Draw a comparison between the two cases and their rulings.

1868 Fourteenth Amendment

"All persons born or naturalized in the United States, and subject to the jurisdiction thereof, are citizens of the United States."

—FOURTEENTH AMENDMENT

HISTORICAL BACKGROUND

IN 1866 Congress passed legislation designed to undo southern Black Codes. Termed the Civil Rights Act, the legislation stipulated:

All persons born in the United States and not subject to any foreign power, excluding Indians not taxed, are hereby declared to be citizens of the United States; and such citizens, of every race and color, without regard to any previous condition of slavery or involuntary servitude . . . shall have the same right, in every State and Territory in the United States, to make and enforce contracts, to sue, be parties, and give evidence, to inherit, purchase, lease, sell, hold, and convey real and personal property, and to full and equal benefit of all laws . . . as is enjoyed by white citizens, and shall be subject to like punishment, pains, and penalties.

The 1866 Civil Rights Act placed power within "the land or naval forces of the United States, or of the militia" to enforce the law. It packed the political punch sought by Radical Republicans in Congress. However, proponents of the law knew its continuance was dependent upon political winds. The legislation had originally been the victim of a presidential veto, countered by a congressional override. President Andrew Johnson was a firm believer in limited national power. As such, his veto of the controversial legislation rested on the principle that the federal government had no business intruding into the affairs of the states. Johnson's veto also was bolstered by the fact that he was an ardent racist. He simply believed that African-Americans were not equal to whites and thus not deserving of governmental policies designed to promote equality. His pro-Union Civil War stance, in fact, was supported less by a desire to end slavery than by his wish to dismantle the South's planter aristocracy, of which, as a Tennessee tailor, he had never been a member.

In the spring of 1866, a Joint Committee on Reconstruction worked on a draft of the Fourteenth Amendment. The intent was to permanently guarantee the rights granted by the Civil Rights Act of 1866, rights that then could not be altered by legislative action or presidential whim. By mid-June the amendment had received the necessary two-thirds majority approval from both houses of Congress. It was subsequently sent to the states for ratification.

The Fourteenth Amendment became the cornerstone of the Republican Party platform during the 1866 congressional elections. Meanwhile, racial violence permeated areas of the country. The following excerpt from an 1866 news article by E.L. Godkin describes the violence that resulted in the deaths of forty-six African-Americans in Memphis, Tennessee:

The row which followed was taken up by the citizens at large, and when renewed in the afternoon, after a short pause, it took the form of a general massacre of such of the colored population as showed themselves in the streets. This part of the tragedy appears to have been inconceivably brutal, but its brutality was, after all, not the most remarkable thing about it. Its most novel and most striking incident was, that the *police* headed the butchery.

Ironically, Tennessee, Johnson's home state, was the third state to ratify the Fourteenth Amendment. On July 28, 1868, the amendment became the law of the land. The legislatures of southern states responded to the federal government's imposition of its will with a series of insidious "Jim Crow" segregation laws that perverted the very meaning of equality. Such laws required separate railroad cars, circus ticket booths, hospital entrances, prison facilities, drinking fountains, restaurant seating, and more. It would take another hundred years of strife before the equality of African-Americans was truly recognized by the courts.

NATIONAL ARCHIVES DOCUMENT

AMENDMENT XIV

Section 1.
All persons born or naturalized in the United States, and subject to the jurisdiction thereof, are citizens of the United States and of the State wherein they reside. No State shall make or enforce any law which shall abridge the privileges or immunities of citizens of the United States; nor shall any State deprive any person of life, liberty, or property, without due process of law; nor deny to any person within its jurisdiction the equal protection of the laws.

Section 2.
Representatives shall be apportioned among the several States according to their respective numbers, counting the whole number of persons in each State, excluding Indians not taxed. . . .

Section 3.
No person shall be a Senator or Representative in Congress, or elector of President and Vice-President, or hold any office, civil or military, under the United States, or under any State, who, having previously taken an oath, as a member of Congress, or as an officer of the United States, or as a member of any State legislature, or as an executive or judicial officer of any State, to support the Constitution of the United States, shall have engaged in insurrection or rebellion against the same, or given aid or comfort to the enemies thereof. But Congress may by a vote of two-thirds of each House, remove such disability.

Above: With citizenship came the right to vote. Scenes like the one depicted above, however, were an exception.

Section 4.
The validity of the public debt of the United States, authorized by law, including debts incurred for payment of pensions and bounties for services in suppressing insurrection or rebellion, shall not be questioned. But neither the United States nor any State shall assume or pay any debt or obligation incurred in aid of insurrection or rebellion against the United States, or any claim for the loss or emancipation of any slave; but all such debts, obligations and claims shall be held illegal and void.

Section 5.
The Congress shall have the power to enforce, by appropriate legislation, the provisions of this article. ✳

Critical Thinking

Analyze Cause and Effect

Reread Section 1 of the Fourteenth Amendment. What impact did Section 1 have on the Dred Scott decision? How does this section ensure equality before the law?

Compare and Contrast

Compare the Constitution's Three-Fifths Compromise with Section 2 of the Fourteenth Amendment. Why was this provision important?

Assess Significance

In what way did Sections 3 and 4 uphold the power of the federal government over the actions of the former Confederacy?

Research and Writing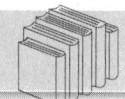

Relating Events

The Republican Party began as a political rally in February 1854 in Ripon, Wisconsin, largely in opposition to the spread of slavery to the western territories. At its inception, the party was a combination of Whigs, Free-Soilers, Know-Nothings, and abolitionists. The Republican Party officially met in July 1854 in Jackson, Michigan. Research the early years of the Republican Party. What was the political stance of the Whigs, the Free-Soilers, and the Know-Nothings? What was the common thread that brought these fractured political groups together?

Counterpoint

The Civil Rights Act of 1875 was passed to ensure equal treatment among the races in the private sector. In that regard, the legislation assured

> That all persons within the jurisdiction of the United States shall be entitled to the full and equal enjoyment of the accommodations, advantages, facilities, and privileges of inns, public conveyances on land or water, theaters, and other places of public amusement; subject only to the conditions and limitations established by law, and applicable alike to citizens of every race and color, regardless of any previous condition of servitude.

The Civil Rights Cases (1883) challenged the constitutionality of the 1875 Civil Rights Act. In each of the five cases, grouped together as the Civil Rights Cases, an African-American was denied accommodations equal to that afforded whites. At the heart of each case was the "equal protection of the laws" clause found in the Fourteenth Amendment. Research the Civil Rights cases argued before the U.S. Supreme Court in 1883. What were the specifics in each case? What was the ruling in each case? How did the Court interpret the scope of the Fourteenth Amendment? Read the dissent written by Justice John Harlan. What was Justice Harlan's counterpoint? In what way was the Fourteenth Amendment used to support both the majority and dissenting opinions?

Link to the Present

The "due process" clause found in Section 1 of the Fourteenth Amendment was of critical importance during the Civil Rights Movement of the 1960s. This important language was cited in case after case where the constitutional rights of African-Americans were subjugated. *Haynes v. Washington* (1963) is an example of one such decision.

> In a Washington State Court, petitioner was tried on a charge of robbery, convicted and sentenced to imprisonment. Over his timely objection, there was admitted in evidence a written confession obtained after he had been held incommunicado for 16 hours and had been told that he could not call his wife until he had signed it. In accordance with local practice, the question as to the voluntariness of the confession was left for determination by the jury, and it brought in a general verdict of guilty. Held: On the record in this case, the confession was not voluntary, and its admission in evidence violated the Due Process Clause of the Fourteenth Amendment."

Research the case of *Haynes v. Washington, Escobedo v. Illinois* (1964), or *Miranda v. Arizona* (1966). What were the specifics of the case? In what way did the Court use the due process clause of the Fourteenth Amendment to support its decision?

1870 Fifteenth Amendment

"The right of citizens of the United States to vote shall not be denied."

–FIFTEENTH AMENDMENT

HISTORICAL BACKGROUND

I
N an 1867 speech before the U.S. House of Representatives, Thaddeus Stevens stated, "I am for Negro suffrage in every rebel State. If it be just, it should not be denied; if it is necessary, it should be adopted; if it be a punishment to traitors, they deserve it." Stevens was a leader of the Radical Republicans in Congress who believed the southern states had engaged in treasonous acts against the federal government, and thus deserved not only punishment but required strict oversight. Therefore, as a precondition for re-entry into the Union, southern states had first to accept the Fourteenth Amendment. However, as Frederick Douglass emphasized, the Fourteenth Amendment was but a first step in granting African-Americans full citizenship. More would be needed.

The legislative journey taken by the Fifteenth Amendment began when all reference to voting was eliminated from language originally proposed for the Fourteenth Amendment. The exclusion of suffrage in the Fourteenth Amendment left voting rights for African-Americans to the whim of the states. To encourage black suffrage, Congress passed legislation that granted voting rights to African-Americans in the District of Columbia and in the territories. It was also at this point that Congress established voting rights for all citizens as a precondition for readmission of states to the Union. In the following session, with former Union general Ulysses S. Grant now president, Congress passed the Fifteenth Amendment. The battle, even at the federal level, was intense. Some members of Congress opposed any federal constitutional guarantee of suffrage for African-Americans. Others were content with the language as prescribed by the amendment. Still others wanted far more stringent language,

including the elimination of all voting contingencies, such as educational tests or property-ownership requirements. In the end, the middle ground won the day.

The Fifteenth Amendment passed Congress on February 26, 1869. Its ratification by the states would mimic debates held in Congress, and fall along partisan lines. At one point, seventeen Republican-dominated states had ratified the amendment, while four Democratic states had rejected it. Yet, with Congress dictating ratification of the Fifteenth Amendment as a condition for readmission to the Union, the southern states were left with little choice. On March 30, 1870, the Fifteenth Amendment became the law of the land. To many, it was the culmination of a life-long struggle. Abolitionist William Lloyd Garrison stated,

> Citizenship is yours, with political enfranchisement whereby you are to help decide what shall be the laws for the common defence [sic] and the general welfare, and ultimately to obtain a fair share of the honors and emoluments of public life. . . . Indeed in view of your liberated and enfranchised condition it may be truly affirmed that since the Declaration of Independence was published to the world, never has our country been so powerful as now, never so reputable and influential as now in the eyes of the world. Hence, we have all reason to be glad as to the present, and hopeful as to the future, for the interests of the North are as the interests of the South, and the institutions of one section of the country essentially like those of every other.

With ratification of the Fifteenth Amendment, African-Americans, many of whom had withstood the oppression of the slave system and were now in their elder years, stood in line for the first time in their lives to cast a vote. While some African-Americans were elected to public office, before long the celebration of black enfranchisement would be replaced by devious efforts at the state level to undo what Congress and the Constitution had done. Poll taxes, grandfather clauses, literacy tests, confused election procedures, and sheer intimidation were used to prohibit African-Americans from exercising their constitutional right to vote. Gerrymandering, or the redrawing of voting district boundaries to dilute votes cast by minorities, ensured that political power in the South would remain in white hands. Moreover, white supremacist vigilante groups, in particular the Ku Klux Klan, employed violence as a means to subjugate the rights of African-Americans. Ratification of the Fifteenth Amendment could well have been the realization of complete citizenship for African-Americans. Instead, by the late 1800s, it appeared that the struggle had just begun. It would remain to the courts to determine and implement the full meaning of the Fifteenth Amendment.

NATIONAL ARCHIVES DOCUMENT

A Resolution Proposing an amendment to the Constitution of the United States.

Resolved by the Senate and House of Representatives of the United States of America in Congress assembled, (two-thirds of both Houses concurring) that the following article be proposed to the legislature of the several States as an amendment to the Constitution of the United States which, when ratified by three-fourths of said legislatures shall be valid as part of the Constitution, namely:

Article XV.

Section 1. The right of citizens of the United States to vote shall not be denied or abridged by the United States or by any State on account of race, color, or previous condition of servitude—

Section 2. The Congress shall have the power to enforce this article by appropriate legislation. ✳

Above: The Fifteenth Amendment granted African-Americans full and undeniable voting rights.

Critical Thinking

Analyze Cause and Effect

In 1870–1871 Congress passed three Enforcement Acts to ensure the right of African-Americans to vote. The First Enforcement Act stipulated that:

> If any person, by force, bribery, threats, intimidation, or other unlawful means, shall hinder, delay, prevent, or obstruct, or shall combine and confederate with others to hinder, delay, prevent, or obstruct any citizen from doing any act required to be done to qualify him to vote or from voting at any election as aforesaid, such person shall for every such offence forfeit and pay the sum of five hundred dollars to the person aggrieved thereby.

In what way did this law strengthen the Fifteenth Amendment?

Compare and Contrast

Compare the Thirteenth, Fourteenth, and Fifteenth Amendments. In what way do they relate? Why did it take three amendments to grant full citizenship to African Amendments? Could the same result have succeeded as one amendment?

Determine Point of View

In 1886, on the twenty-fourth anniversary of emancipation, Frederick Douglass stated, "Where justice is denied, where poverty is enforced, where ignorance prevails, and where any one class is made to feel that society is in an organized conspiracy to oppress, rob, and degrade them, neither persons nor property will be safe." What wisdom is Douglass imparting? How can his words be applied across time?

Research and Writing

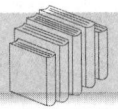

Relating Events

In a letter written in 1868, Thaddeus Stevens noted,

> I have never insisted that the franchise should be unjustly regulated so as to secure a Republican ascendancy; but I have insisted, and do insist, that there can be no unjust regulation of that franchise which will give to any other party the power if the Republicans are true to themselves....

At a Republican gathering in Maryland following ratification of the Fifteenth Amendment it was decreed "That we pledge the newly enfranchised vote in Maryland to the Republican party." Research the change in political leadership following passage of the Fifteenth Amendment. Did the Republican Party retain dominance in the federal government? Why were white southern Republicans called *scalawags*? What impact did the 1872 Amnesty Act have on the political process? Was Stevens ultimately correct in his 1868 assertion? Explain your reasoning.

Analysis

Though Tennessee was the only southern state to ratify the Fourteenth Amendment, it has never ratified the Fifteenth Amendment. Some states ratified the Fifteenth Amendment years after it became the law of the land. California, for example, ratified it in 1962, having rejected it in 1870. Kentucky ratified it in 1976. Though Maryland rejected the amendment in 1870, it was finally approved by the governor of Maryland over one hundred years later. Research the history of the ratification of the Fifteenth Amendment. What arguments were posed for and against the Fifteenth Amendment? What role did northern-imposed governments in the South play in the amendment's ratification?

Link to the Present

In 1932 the Democratic state convention in Texas adopted the following resolution:

> Be it resolved, that all white citizens of the State of Texas who are qualified to vote under the Constitution and laws of the state shall be eligible to membership in the Democratic Party and as such entitled to participate in its deliberations.

The constitutionality of the Texas Democratic Party's denial of voting rights to blacks in primary elections was tested in *Grovey v. Townsend* (1935), *Smith v. Allright* (1944), and again in *Terry v. Adams* (1953). Research these three Texas cases. What were the circumstances of each case? What was the Court's ruling in each? What was the significance of Justice Sherman Minton's dissenting opinion in *Terry v. Adams* when he stated, "this Court has power to redress a wrong under that Amendment only if the wrong is done by the *State*"?

1882 Chinese Exclusion Act

"The superior whites had to exclude the inferior Asiatics, by law, or, if necessary, by force of arms."

–SAMUEL GOMPERS, IN RESPONSE TO THE CHINESE EXCLUSION ACT

HISTORICAL BACKGROUND

"**I** reached my hand down and picked it up; it made my heart thump, for I was certain it was gold. The piece was about half the size and shape of a pea. Then I saw another." The 1848 discovery of gold by John Marshall as he was building a sawmill on John Sutter's land would change the course of history. By 1850 gold mining was big business in California. Thousands of "Forty-niners" had arrived the year before to stake a claim and mine the land for riches. Still others had traveled the long distance to California as entrepreneurs, coveting sums of money to be made from the sale of goods and services needed by the would-be miners. The lack of regulation at the onset of the California Gold Rush allowed anyone to stake a claim, buy a metal pan whose price had escalated from twenty cents to fifteen dollars virtually overnight, grab a pick, and call himself a miner.

Among the thousands seeking their fortunes in gold in the California hills were foreigners from Australia, New Zealand, Peru, Mexico, and China. By 1852, some 25,000 Chinese had come to California, settling in a place called *Gum Shan*–" Gold Mountain." Immigrants from China assumed the responsibilities of cooks, laundry workers, farmers, and servants. They became indispensable workers who, without much choice, worked for low wages. Some Chinese became miners, seeking their own fortunes in gold yet to be found in old claims abandoned by white miners. Soon, however, the surface gold was gone, along with the dreams of white miners hoping to strike it rich. Foreign miners became an instant threat to dwindling hopes of prosperity. In short order, California sought to regulate and profit from foreign miners.

In 1850 the Foreign Miners' Tax became law. The tax required all miners who were not citizens to purchase a mining license for $20 per month. The result was an exodus of penniless Chinese, who left the mining fields to find solace in the city of San Francisco. Realizing its miscalculation for tax revenue, the California legislature repealed the law within the year. However, the Foreign Miners' Tax was reinstituted in 1852 at the rate of a more manageable $3 per month. Provisions in the law gave tax collectors the authority to confiscate and sell a miner's property in lieu of the tax payment, or simply expel Chinese miners from the minefields. Though California had its share of seedy opportunists, who soon found employment impersonating tax collectors, the state profited well from the tax on foreign miners. By 1870 nearly one-fourth of the state's tax revenues were attributable to the Foreign Miners' Tax.

The 1862 Pacific Railway Act resulted in the large-scale employment of Chinese workers. Faced with dwindling mining opportunities, Chinese immigrants joined other displaced miners to build America's railroads. At one point the Central Pacific Railroad employed approximately 10,000 Chinese workers. They were paid $25–$35 per month to work in some of the most hazardous areas. Faced with a labor shortage in 1866, the Central Pacific Railroad recruited even more Chinese workers from Kwantung Province in China. Known as "Celestials" because they originated from the Celestial (Chinese) Empire, the Chinese were lowered on ropes down the cliff faces of the Sierra Nevada Mountains. There they drilled holes, packed them with powder, and lit the fuse. They had precious little time to climb to safety. Chinese workers laid rock bed, blasted tunnels, and shoveled and drilled through the worst of weather and the deepest of snow. Hundreds died in the process.

Through it all, the California legislature continued to press for immigration restriction. In 1862 it passed *An Act to Protect Free White Labor Against*

Competition with Chinese Coolie Labor, and to Discourage the Immigration of the Chinese into the State of California. The law stipulated a $2.50 per month police tax on "Mongolian" workers. Tax-collection procedures were similar to the 1850 Foreign Miners' Act. When the California state constitution was rewritten in 1879, Article 19 forbade the hiring of Asian workers and declared that "foreigners ineligible to become citizens of the United States [are] declared to be dangerous to the well-being of the State." Then, in 1882, Congress passed the Chinese Exclusion Act. It placed a ten-year moratorium on the immigration of Chinese workers. Additionally, it barred all Chinese from becoming naturalized citizens. In 1888 the act was revised to ban the immigration of almost all Chinese. Extended in 1892, Congress did not repeal the ban until 1943. Even with its repeal, the annual quota for Chinese immigrants was set at a mere 105 people, though the legislation did allow for naturalization and citizenship.

NATIONAL ARCHIVES DOCUMENT

An Act to execute certain treaty stipulations relating to Chinese.

Whereas in the opinion of the Government of the United States the coming of Chinese laborers to this country endangers the good order of certain localities within the territory thereof: Therefore,

Be it enacted by the Senate and House of Representatives of the United States of America in Congress assembled, That from and after the expiration of ninety days next after the passage of this act, and until the expiration of ten years next after the passage of this act, the coming of Chinese laborers to the United States be, and the same is hereby, suspended; and during such suspension it shall not be lawful for any Chinese laborer to come, or having so come after the expiration of said ninety days to remain within the United States.

SEC.13. That this act shall not apply to diplomatic and other officers of the Chinese Government traveling upon the business of that government, whose credentials shall be taken as equivalent to the certificate in this act mentioned, and shall exempt them and their body and house- hold servants from the provisions of this act as to other Chinese persons.

SEC.10. That every vessel whose master shall knowingly violate any of the provisions of this act shall be deemed forfeited to the United States, and shall be liable to seizure and condemnation in any district of the United States into which such vessel may enter or in which she may be found.

SEC. 14. That hereafter no State court or court of the United States shall admit Chinese to citizenship; and all laws in conflict with this act are hereby repealed.

SEC.15. That the words "Chinese laborers," wherever used in this act, shall be construed to mean both skilled and unskilled laborers and Chinese employed in mining. ✳

Below: A nineteenth-century political cartoon depicting the perils of the Chinese Exclusion Act.

Critical Thinking

Analyze Cause and Effect

In 1880 the Unites States and China signed a treaty limiting Chinese immigration. In part it stated,

> Whenever in the opinion of the Government of the United States, the coming of Chinese laborers to the United States, . . . affects or threatens to affect the interests of that country, . . . the Government of China agrees that the Government of the United States may regulate, limit, or suspend . . . Chinese who may go to the United States as laborers, other classes not being included in the limitations.

In what way was this treaty a precursor to the Chinese Exclusion Act of 1882?

Compare and Contrast

The Chinese Exclusion Act allowed for the entry of Chinese teachers, officials, students, merchants, and travelers. Why do you think these individuals were allowed to immigrate while laborers were not?

Assess Significance

Of what importance was the provision in the Chinese Exclusion Act which prohibited Chinese immigrants from becoming naturalized citizens?

Research and Writing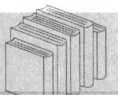

Related Events

From 1910 to 1940, the federal government operated the Angel Island Immigration Station. Angel Island was the Ellis Island of the West Coast. Located six miles offshore from San Francisco, it served as a processing center for thousands of Chinese immigrants who hoped to enter the United States based on being a "paper" son or daughter. These individuals claimed to be the children of naturalized U. S. citizens whose records has been destroyed in the fires that followed the 1906 San Francisco earthquake. A thriving "paper sons" trade evolved where, for a fee, would-be immigrants were provided with fictitious names and documents. Paper sons was an attempt to circumvent Chinese exclusion laws. The result was the detention of prospective Chinese immigrants for days into months. Research Angel Island. What impact did paper sons have on the workings of Angel Island?

Analysis

The term *coolie* originally referred to skilled and unskilled Chinese laborers. The term eventually was used as a derogatory reference to all workers from Asia. In a 1906 edition of *Organized Labor*, reference was made to the perceived threat of Asian workers.

> Thousands of fair minded and well meaning people who were biased and ignorant on the question of Japanese immigration have during the last year, entirely changed their views on the subject. They have learned the truth that the Japanese coolie is even a greater menace to the existence of the white race, to the progress and prosperity of our country than is the Chinese coolie. But if there has been danger from Asiatic immigration to our state before, that danger has not lessened now.

In what way did use of the term "coolies" encourage the discrimination of Asians? What role did organized labor play in the discrimination of Asian workers? To what other groups did organized labor want exclusion laws applied?

Link to the Present

In 1892 the Geary Act extended the provisions of the Chinese Exclusion Act. Immigration laws in 1917 and 1924 further limited immigration by imposing quotas and rigorous stipulations for entry into the country. Other federal legislation in 1943, 1965, 1968, and 1990 created parameters under which immigration could occur. Research the history of U. S. immigration laws beginning with the 1882 Chinese Exclusion Act. What was the purpose of each law? What parameters did it place on immigration?

1896 Plessy v. Ferguson

"Success is to be measured not so much by the position that one has reached in life as by the obstacles which he has overcome."

–Booker T. Washington

Historical Background

It was designed as a test. In 1890 Louisiana had passed the Separate Car Act. The law required all rail companies carrying passengers in Louisiana to provide separate but equal accommodations for white and nonwhite passengers. An individual bold enough to sit in the wrong car or section of a car was subject to a fine of $25 or twenty days in jail. In 1892 the Citizens' Committee to Test the Constitutionality of the Separate Car Law decided to challenge the constitutionality of the Louisiana statute. The plan was to have an individual of "mixed blood" violate the law, proving its arbitrariness. The committee enlisted the aid of Homer Plessy, a shoemaker living in southern Louisiana who was one-eighth African-American, but could "pass" as white. Under Louisiana law, Plessy was considered "colored" because of his "one-eighth" status, and thus required to sit in the colored rail car. Accordingly, Plessy boarded the train with the intent of sitting in the car designated for white passengers. The committee had previously arranged with both the railroad conductor and a private detective to detain Plessy when, as planned, he refused to move to the colored car.

The test seemed to be working perfectly. Plessy was arrested, jailed, and charged with violation of the Separate Car Act. Plessy's lawyer, Albion Tourgée, had already successfully argued before Judge Howard Ferguson in the state's district court that forced segregation in railway cars running between Louisiana and another state was unconstitutional. In Plessy's case, Tourgée planned to argue the unconstitutionality of segregated rail cars *within* the state of Louisiana. It was to be the next step in striking down the Jim Crow laws that pervaded Louisiana. In appearing once again before Judge Ferguson, Tourgée based his argument on the premise that the Separate Car Act violated the Thirteenth and Fourteenth Amendments.

In an unexpected turn of events, Plessy filed a petition asking Louisiana's state supreme court to stop Ferguson from rendering a decision on the case. Plessy argued that he should have been treated at the time of his arrest as a white man because of his seven-eighths Caucasian ancestry. The Louisiana Supreme Court directed Judge Ferguson to answer Plessy's petition. First, Ferguson ruled that railroad cars within the state were under the purview of state laws, thus the Separate Car Act was constitutional. Secondly, Ferguson determined that Plessy simply refused to admit he was a black man. With that, Plessy was convicted of violating the Separate Car Act. Upon appeal, the Louisiana Supreme Court agreed with the lower court ruling. The next step was an appeal to the United States Supreme Court. The case was a golden opportunity to strike down every Jim Crow law in the nation, should the U.S. Supreme Court rule in Plessy's favor.

In presenting the case before the country's highest court, Tourgée argued that the Separate Car Act perpetuated the essential features of slavery, thus it was in violation of the Thirteenth Amendment. In response, the Court opined:

> A statute which implies merely a legal distinction between the white and colored races—a distinction which is founded in the color of the two races, and which must always exist so long as white men are distinguished from the other race by color—has no tendency to destroy the legal equality of the two races, or re-establish a state of involuntary servitude. Indeed, we do not understand that the thirteenth amendment is strenuously relied upon by the plaintiff in error in this connection.

Tourgée also argued that Plessy's Fourteenth Amendment rights had been violated based on the

Equal Protection Clause. To that the Court answered:

> While we think the enforced separation of the races, as applied to the internal commerce of the state, neither abridges the privileges or immunities of the colored man, deprives him of his property without due process of law, nor denies him the equal protection of the laws, within the meaning of the fourteenth amendment . . .

The Court also left it to the states to determine the race of an individual, striking down Plessy's argument that he was white and, as such, had not violated the Separate Car Act by sitting in a "whites-only" railroad car.

The ruling in *Plessy v. Ferguson* established the constitutionality of "separate but equal" laws throughout the South. Soon statutory segregation permeated all aspects of southern life. Segregationist activities not governed by law were governed by custom. Ultimately, the ruling perpetuated racism for decades to come. What began as a test and evolved into a golden civil rights opportunity, in the end succumbed to the misguided attempt by the U.S. Supreme Court to explain segregation.

NATIONAL ARCHIVES DOCUMENT

In Error to the Supreme Court of the State of Louisiana . . .

This case turns upon the constitutionality of an act of the general assembly of the state of Louisiana, passed in 1890, providing for separate railway carriages for the white and colored races. . . .

The first section of the statute enacts 'that all railway companies carrying passengers in their coaches in this state, shall provide equal but separate accommodations for the white, and colored races, by providing two or more passenger coaches for each passenger train, or by dividing the passenger coaches by a partition so as to secure separate accommodations: provided, that this section shall not be construed to apply to street railroads. No person or persons shall be permitted to occupy seats in coaches, other than the ones assigned to them, on account of the race they belong to.'

Above: Separate facilities pervaded American society for decades following the 1896 *Plessy v. Ferguson* decision.

By the second section it was enacted 'that the officers of such passenger trains shall have power and are hereby required to assign each passenger to the coach or compartment used for the race to which such passenger belongs; any passenger insisting on going into a coach or compartment to which by race he does not belong, shall be liable to a fine of twenty-five dollars, or in lieu thereof to imprisonment for a period of not more than twenty days in the parish prison. . . .

. . . we cannot say that a law which authorizes or even requires the separation of the two races in public conveyances is unreasonable, or more obnoxious to the fourteenth amendment than the acts of congress requiring separate schools for colored children in the District of Columbia, the constitutionality of which does not seem to have been questioned, or the corresponding acts of state legislatures.

We consider the underlying fallacy of the plaintiff's argument to consist in the assumption that the enforced separation of the two races stamps the colored race with a badge of inferiority. If this be so, it is not by reason of anything found in the act, but solely because the colored race chooses to put that construction upon it. . . . The argument also assumes that social prejudices may be overcome by legislation, and that equal rights cannot be secured to the negro except by an enforced commingling of the two races. We cannot accept this proposition. . . .

The judgment of the court below is therefore affirmed. ※

Critical Thinking

Analyze Cause and Effect

In explaining the intent of the Fourteenth Amendment, the U.S. Supreme Court reasoned that "the power to assign to a particular coach obviously implies the power to determine to which race the passenger belongs, as well as the power to determine who, under the laws of the particular state, is to be deemed a white, and who a colored, person." In your opinion, does this language in the ruling extend or restrict the arbitrariness of the Separate Car Act?

Make Predictions

In *Plessy v. Ferguson*, the Court stated,

> Laws permitting, and even requiring, their separation, in places where they are liable to be brought into contact, do not necessarily imply the inferiority of either race to the other, and have been generally, if not universally, recognized as within the competency of the state legislatures in the exercise of their police power.

In what way did the language of this ruling perpetuate Jim Crow Laws?

Assess Significance

In the *Plessy v. Ferguson* ruling, the Court stated, "Laws forbidding the intermarriage of the two races may be said in a technical sense to interfere with the freedom of contract, and yet have been universally recognized as within the police power of the state." What importance did the Court give to the word "universally"? In what way were Jim Crow laws designed to interfere with the possibility of intermarriage?

Research and Writing

Analysis

The Supreme Court in part based its ruling in *Plessy v. Ferguson* on the "Slaughterhouse Cases" (1873). In writing for the majority, Justice Samuel Miller stated, "It is quite clear, then, that there is a citizenship of the United States, and a citizenship of a State, which are distinct from each other, and which depend upon different characteristics or circumstances in the individual." Research the Slaughterhouse Cases. What did they involve? How did the Court rule? In what way did the Slaughterhouse Cases lend support to discriminatory laws within the states?

Counterpoint

In his dissenting opinion, Justice John Marshall Harlan characterized the majority ruling in the *Plessy* case as "pernicious as the decision made by this tribunal in the Dred Scott Case." Read Justice Harlan's dissent in *Plessy v. Ferguson*. Summarize Harlan's point-by-point counter to the majority opinion in this case.

Biography

Two strong but conflicting advocates for African-American civil rights were Booker T. Washington and W.E.B. Du Bois. In what has become known as his Atlanta Compromise, Washington stated,

> No race can prosper till it learns that there is as much dignity in tilling a field as in writing a poem. It is at the bottom of life we must begin, and not at the top. Nor should we permit our grievances to overshadow our opportunities.... In all things that are purely social we can be as separate as the fingers, yet one as the hand in all things essential to mutual progress.

Du Bois strongly disagreed with Washington's approach toward obtaining social and political equality for African-Americans. In his Niagara Movement Speech, Du Bois countered Washington's views when he fervently declared, "We claim for ourselves every single right that belongs to a freeborn American, political, civil and social; and until we get these rights we will never cease to protest and assail the ears of America." Research the lives of Washington and Du Bois. How were their social and political philosophies in opposition? What did each see as the ultimate goal? How would you characterize the civil rights approaches of Washington and Du Bois? With which approach do you most agree? Why?

"I hope you voted too."

—SUSAN B. ANTHONY IN AN 1872 LETTER TO ELIZABETH CADY STANTON

HISTORICAL BACKGROUND

VOTES *for women* was a banner cry that had been heard for decades across America. Following adoption of the Fourteenth Amendment in 1868, activist Susan B. Anthony demanded equal rights for women based on the language of the amendment—"all persons born . . . in the United States . . . are citizens of the United States." As a citizen, in 1871 Anthony exercised her right to vote in the local Rochester, New York, election. In the 1872 federal election, Anthony voted again. Though the election officials agreed to accept her vote, other authorities would have none of it. Shortly after the election, she was arrested and charged with voting illegally. A feisty and determined Anthony went on the offensive. In an exhaustive speaking tour in which she delivered a speech titled "Is it a Crime for a Citizen of the United States to Vote?" Anthony chastised all who questioned a woman's right to vote.

> Surely, the right of the whole people to vote is here clearly implied. For however destructive in their happiness this government might become, a disfranchised class could neither alter nor abolish it, nor institute a new one, except by the old brute force method of insurrection and rebellion. One-half of the people of this nation to-day are utterly powerless to blot from the statute books an unjust law, or to write there a new and a just one. The women, dissatisfied as they are with this form of government, that enforces taxation without representation,—that compels them to obey laws to which they have never given their consent, —that imprisons and hangs them without a trial by a jury of their peers, that robs them, in marriage, of the custody of their own persons, wages and children,—are this half of the people left wholly at the mercy of the other half, in direct violation of the spirit and letter of the declarations of the framers of this government.

In June 1873 Anthony was tried, convicted, and ordered to pay a fine of $100 plus the cost of prosecution. She refused stating, "May it please your honor, I will never pay a dollar of your unjust penalty."

The saga of the woman's movement began in 1848, when Lucretia Mott and Elizabeth Cady Stanton produced the "Declaration of Sentiments," a document patterned after the Declaration of Independence. In part it read, "We hold these truths to be self-evident; that all men and women are created equal." Four years later Susan B. Anthony joined Mott, Stanton, and other women activists at the Woman's Rights Convention in Syracuse, New York. As the movement grew, annual meetings were held. In 1866 woman activists presented Congress with 10,000 signatures in favor of universal suffrage. In 1869 the woman's movement split into two factions and the movement lost much of its collective energy. Nevertheless, in that same year the Wyoming Territory granted full suffrage to women, a status retained once it gained statehood in 1890. With the passage of the Fourteenth and Fifteenth Amendments, the opportunity for universal suffrage seemed obvious to the suffragettes. To that end, in 1878 a Woman Suffrage Amendment was introduced into Congress by Senator A. A. Sargent of California. It would continue to be introduced into Congress every year for the next forty-one years.

By 1900, Utah, Colorado, and Idaho had granted full citizenship to women. Women in other states were allowed to vote in municipal and school board elections, yet no other state legislatures seemed inclined to grant women the right to vote. The movement, however, was by no means at a standstill. Energized by such young, educated women as Carrie Chapman Catt, Charlotte Perkins Gilman, S. Josephine Baker, and Harriet Stanton

Blatch, the concept of "feminism" was born. Women sought equality not only in the vote, but also advocated civil and social equality as well. Slowly the tide toward equality was turning, evidenced in part by Theodore Roosevelt's 1912 presidential platform, which supported enfranchising women.

In 1915 the National American Woman Suffrage Association joined others in promoting the adoption of a constitutional amendment, the very amendment first proposed in 1878. An intensive grassroots campaign followed, which included picketing in front of the White House and a parade of 40,000 suffragettes down Fifth Avenue in New York City. In 1917 New York became the first state east of the Mississippi River to grant female suffrage. Yet, it took a world war to turn the tide in favor of an amendment to grant women the right to vote nationwide. Women took on the jobs of men who had gone off to fight in World War I, establishing the proving ground of a woman's worth.

In May 1919 Congress mustered the necessary two-thirds vote needed to advance the Nineteenth Amendment to the states. Wisconsin, Michigan, and Illinois were the first states to ratify the amendment, followed by thirty-two other states. Southern states, however, represented a geographical void in the ratification process. In the end it was left to Tennessee to lead the way. Though the vote appeared deadlocked in the state legislature, a final vote cast by twenty-four-year-old Harry Burn placed Tennessee on the side of ratification. In his pocket was a note from his mother encouraging votes for women. "Don't forget to be a good boy," it said, "vote for suffrage." On August 26, 1920, the Nineteenth Amendment was certified and became the law of the land.

NATIONAL ARCHIVES DOCUMENT

Sixty-sixth Congress of the United States of America; At the First Session,

Begun and held at the City of Washington on Monday, the nineteenth day of May, one thousand nine hundred and nineteen.

JOINT RESOLUTION

Proposing an amendment to the Constitution extending the right of suffrage to women.

Below: Women participate in a suffrage parade in New York City on May 6, 1912.

Resolved by the Senate and House of Representatives of the United States of America in Congress assembled (two-thirds of each House concurring therein), That the following article is proposed as an amendment to the Constitution, which shall be valid to all intents and purposes as part of the Constitution when ratified by the legislature of three-fourths of the several States.

"The right of citizens of the United States to vote shall not be denied or abridged by the United States or by any State on account of sex.

Congress shall have power to enforce this article by appropriate legislation." ※

Critical Thinking

Draw Conclusions

As a school child, Susan B. Anthony questioned her teacher about why he taught division to the boys, but not to the girls. He answered, "A girl needs to know how to read her Bible and count her egg money, nothing more." Anthony responded by situating herself in class so that she would learn long division whether the teacher liked it or not. Given all the barriers faced in gaining the vote, how would you describe the character of the nineteenth-century suffragettes?

Determine Point of View

The prevailing belief during the nineteenth century was that women were most suited for domestic work and raising children. In *Bradwell v. Illinois* (1873), U.S. Supreme Court Justice Joseph Bradley wrote for the majority,

It is true that many women are unmarried and not affected by any of the duties, complications, and incapacities arising out of the married state, but these are exceptions to the general rule. The paramount destiny and mission of woman are to fulfill the noble and benign offices of wife and mother. This is the law of the Creator. And the rules of civil society must be adapted to the general constitution.

Women in the nineteenth century were barred from serving on juries, generally could not own property, had virtually no marital rights and little educational opportunity, and of course, could not vote. Why do you think there was such resistance to woman's suffrage?

Compare and Contrast

Compare the suffrage movement for women with the movement to gain voting rights for African-Americans.

Research and Writing

Analysis

The 1872 presidential election created similar challenges for Virginia Minor in Missouri as it did for Susan B. Anthony in New York. Minor, however, sought redress through the court system. In *Minor v. Happersett* (1874) the U.S. Supreme Court ruled as follows:

If the right of suffrage is one of the necessary privileges of a citizen of the United States, then the constitution and laws of Missouri confining it to men are in violation of the Constitution of the United States, …

Research *Minor v. Happersett*. On what grounds was the Court's decision based? Were there any dissenting opinions? What impact did this case have on the suffrage laws of other states? In what way did the Court use the concept of "original intent" to endorse the practices of the time?

Biography

Though ardent suffragettes, neither Susan B. Anthony nor Elizabeth Cady Stanton would live to see universal suffrage; Anthony died in 1906 and Stanton in 1902. Both women dedicated years of their lives to promoting political and social equality for women. Research the lives of these two forthright and tenacious women. Compare their lives, goals, and achievements. In your opinion, what do you feel was their greatest achievement? How would you define their legacy?

Relating Events

An article in *The New York Times* described passage of the proposed Nineteenth Amendment in Congress:

The friends of woman suffrage in both parties have carried out their word. In the result we can turn our backs upon the end of a long and arduous struggle, needlessly darkened and embittered by the stubbornness of a few at the expense of the many. 'Eyes front,' is the watchword as we turn upon the struggle for ratification by the States.

Research the history of the ratification of the Nineteenth Amendment. Which states resisted ratification? Why? Why do you think Senator Oscar Underwood of Alabama attempted to amend the Nineteenth Amendment to allow for ratification by constitutional conventions rather than state legislatures? What influence did President Woodrow Wilson have in the ratification debate? What do you think finally tipped the balance in favor of ratification of the Nineteenth Amendment?

1941 Executive Order 8802

"For it is only within the framework of democracy that labor and minorities can achieve freedom, equality, and justice."

–A. Philip Randolph

Historical Background

On June 25, 1941, President Roosevelt signed Executive Order 8802. It banned discriminatory employment practices by unions or businesses engaged in defense-related work. To ensure fair labor practices in the defense industry, Executive Order 8802 also created the Fair Employment Practices Committee (FEPC). This committee was charged with the power to investigate employment complaints. It also had the ability to offer redress to victims of employment discrimination.

Roosevelt's support for Executive Order 8802 was lukewarm at best. His consideration for its provisions only came after being confronted with the possibility of a planned march on Washington, D.C., by some 100,000 African-Americans, the purpose of which was to protest rampant discriminatory practices found both on federal defense jobs and within the military. The leader of the proposed March on Washington was black union leader A. Philip Randolph, president of the Brotherhood of Sleeping Car Porters. After learning of the impending march, Roosevelt sent delegates to meet with Randolph in an attempt to forestall it. They returned with an adamant reply from Randolph—prohibit discriminatory practices or face the political embarrassment of thousands of African-Americans on the Capitol's doorstep. Roosevelt reluctantly agreed to target unfair hiring practices among defense contractors, as well as create an oversight committee—the FEPC—to ensure enforcement. Yet, he refused to address one of Randolph's prime objectives—an executive order ending the military's policy of segregating black and white soldiers.

The possibility of well-paying wartime jobs lured thousands of African-Americans from the South to the country's shipyards and weapons plants. Yet, discrimination followed past segregation policies, as most African-American job-seekers were hired for low-end jobs rather than offered employment building planes and other military hardware, as their white co-workers were. Though migrating blacks continued to be encouraged by the possibility of war-related employment, companies holding defense-related government contracts were not always willing to comply. To strengthen the oversight capabilities of the FEPC, as well as increase the committee's ability to deal with violations of Executive Order 8802, in 1943 Congress increased the FEPC's budget. By 1945 a full 200,000 African-Americans were employed by the defense industry, a threefold increase over four years earlier.

Though the quality of employment was still in dispute, the increase in employment opportunities within the defense industry was certainly significant. Since the onset of unionized labor, African-Americans had met resistance from unions and employers. For years, African-Americans who attempted to organize black laborers were met with violence. One of the most appalling examples was the violence that occurred in Phillips County, Arkansas, in 1919. In late September of that year, sharecroppers and tenant farmers had gathered at a local church to organize the black Progressive Farmers and Household Union of America. Two white officers came to the church, ostensibly looking for a bootlegger. Confusion ensued. Before it was over, one officer lay dead from gunshots and the other was wounded. The next day over two hundred armed white men from Mississippi flooded Phillips County, intent on vengeance. The violence continued unabated for three days, resulting in the shooting deaths of possibly two hundred African-Americans. Eventually, the military restored order. Whites justified the bloodshed by charging that the unionizing effort of blacks was in actuality a ploy to dispossess white farmers.

In stark contrast, under the leadership of A. Philip Randolph, the Brotherhood of Sleeping Car Porters was officially recognized in 1934 as the bargaining agent for black porters. It became the first all-black labor union recognized by a U.S. corporation. However, the struggle had been uphill, as Randolph battled the discriminatory practices of the powerful American Federation of Labor (AFL). Executive Order 8802, thus, was the first inroad on the long journey of equal employment.

In 1948 President Harry Truman recommended a civil rights package that included the establishment of a permanent FEPC, a federal antilynching law, and the abolishment of the poll tax—legislation not welcomed by southern members of Congress. Filibustering in Congress ended hope of the bill's success and brought a halt to the work of the FEPC. Though the provisions of Executive Order 8802 were short-lived, its impact was far-reaching. Prior to its inception, twenty-six American Federation of Labor unions barred African-Americans. By the end of World War II, over 600,000 blacks were members of AFL unions. In 1955 Randolph became the first black vice-president of the newly merged AFL-CIO. In 1963 the Brotherhood of Locomotive Firemen and Enginemen was the only remaining union that banned the membership of blacks.

National Archives Document

WHEREAS it is the policy of the United States to encourage full participation in the national defense program by all citizens of the United States, regardless of race, creed, color, or national origin, in the firm belief that the democratic way of life within the Nation can be defended successfully only with the help and support of all groups within its borders; and

WHEREAS there is evidence that available and needed workers have been barred from employment in industries engaged in defense production solely because of considerations of race, creed, color, or national origin, to the detriment of workers' morale and of national unity:

NOW, THEREFORE, by virtue of the authority vested in me by the Constitution and the statutes, and as a prerequisite to the successful conduct of our national defense production effort, I do hereby reaffirm the policy of the United States that there shall be no discrimination in the employment of workers in defense industries or government because of race, creed, color, or national origin, and I do hereby declare that it is the duty of employers and of labor organizations, in furtherance of said policy and of this order, to provide for the full and equitable participation of all workers in defense industries, without discrimination because of race, creed, color, or national origin;

And it is hereby ordered as follows:

There is established in the Office of Production Management a Committee on Fair Employment Practice. . . .

Franklin D. Roosevelt
The White House,
June 25, 1941. ✳

Below: Executive Order 8802 provided African-Americans with never-before opportunities for employment in the defense industry.

Critical Thinking

Analyze Cause and Effect

Why do you think Roosevelt finally agreed to issue Executive Order 8802?

Draw Conclusions

In what way was Executive Order 8802 in conflict with the Jim Crow laws that characterized the times?

Assess Significance

In 1947 Jackie Robinson of the Brooklyn Dodgers became the first African-American to play professional baseball since the late nineteenth century. Robinson had garnered a great deal of attention while playing in the segregated "Negro leagues." Nevertheless, as an African-American now playing baseball in what had been an all-white National League, Jackson suffered extreme acts of bigotry and racial hatred. Base runners spiked him, spectators booed and spat on him, pitchers intentionally threw at him, and baseball fans spared few words in hate mail sent to Robinson. Yet, his outstanding performance earned him the 1947 Rookie of the Year Award. With civil rights stalled at the federal level in the late 1940s, why was Robinson's contribution so pivotal?

Research and Writing

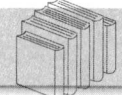

Relating Events

The history of black labor unions has its beginnings in the early nineteenth century, when the New York African Society for Mutual Relief formed in 1806. Touting membership by carpenters, bootmakers, porters, and ministers, the society functioned as a fraternal insurance group for African-Americans, providing both sick and death benefits. Research the history of black labor unions. Who were the leaders? What were the major issues? What great challenges did the black unions face? What impact did the Great Migration in the first half of the twentieth century have on the movement? How did increased black advocacy for equal rights result in horrific acts of violence targeted against African-Americans?

Biography

Mary McLeod Bethune was a tireless civil rights advocate. Research the life of Mary McLeod Bethune. What were Bethune's early accomplishments? What was her role and influence in Roosevelt's administration? What was the National Youth Administration? Explain how Bethune helped to break racial and gender barriers in the civil, social, and political realms.

Link to the Present

In 1931 Congress passed the Davis-Bacon Act. In explaining the bill's intent, Pennsylvania Senator James Davis described what happened when black construction workers were brought north by an Alabama contractor who had won the bid on a 1927 federal contract to build a Veterans Bureau Hospital in New York:

> [Black construction workers] were herded onto this job, they were housed in shacks, they were paid a very low wage, and ... it seems to me that the federal government should not engage in construction work in any state and undermine the labor conditions and the labor wages paid in that state.

The act was amended in 1935, when union members complained that the law did not go far enough to protect members' jobs. In 1941 the Davis-Bacon Act was extended to military construction projects. Today the Davis Bacon Act continues to govern federally funded contracts. Research the 1931 Davis-Bacon Act. What impact did it have on Executive Order 8802? Did the law assist in breaking down the color barrier in federal construction jobs? How is it applied today? To what does the law owe its resiliency?

1942 Japanese Relocation Order

*They've sunk the posts deep into the ground
They've strung out wires all the way around.
With machine gun nests just over there,
And sentries and soldiers everywhere.*

—ANONYMOUS POEM
POSTON CAMP, ARIZONA, 1942–1946

HISTORICAL BACKGROUND

ON February 19, 1942 President Franklin D. Roosevelt issued Executive Order 9066. It directed the secretary of war to create military districts in the United States, which essentially restricted the rights of individuals to "enter, remain in, or leave" the zone. Areas along the East Coast, West Coast, Gulf Coast, and Great Lakes were all subject to this order. The order followed the December 1941 attack on Pearl Harbor and subsequent declaration of war on Japan. At that time approximately 127,000 Japanese Americans lived in the United States, most along the West Coast. Beginning in early 1942 some 112,000 individuals of Japanese descent were ordered to sell their homes and businesses, often at great financial loss, take only what they could carry, and relocate to designated military areas—all in the interest of national security. Internment camps were created throughout western states for Japanese resettlement. In large barrack-type buildings, families were given one small room in which to live. In a report explaining the rationale behind relocation, Lt. Gen. J.L. DeWitt wrote the following to the Chief of Staff, U.S. Army on June 5, 1943:

> The evacuation was impelled by military necessity. The security of the Pacific Coast continues to require the exclusion of Japanese from the area now prohibited to them and will so continue as long as that military necessity exists. . . . More than 115,000 persons of Japanese ancestry resided along the coast and were significantly concentrated near many highly sensitive installations essential to the war effort. Intelligence services records reflected the existence of hundreds of Japanese organizations in California, Washington, Oregon and Arizona which, prior to December 7, 1941, were actively engaged in advancing Japanese war aims. These records also disclosed that thousands of American-born Japanese had gone to Japan to receive their education and indoctrination there and had become rabidly pro-Japanese and then had returned to the United States. Emperor-worshipping ceremonies were commonly held and millions of dollars had flowed into the Japanese imperial war chest from the contributions freely made by Japanese here. The continued presence of a large, unassimilated, tightly knit and racial group, bound to an enemy nation by strong ties of race, culture, custom and religion along a frontier vulnerable to attack constituted a menace which had to be dealt with. Their loyalties were unknown and time was of the essence. The evident aspirations of the enemy emboldened by his recent successes made it worse than folly to have left any stone unturned in the building up of our defenses. It is better to have had this protection and not to have needed it than to have needed it and not to have had— as we have learned to our sorrow. . . .

> On February 14, 1942, I recommended to the War Department that the military security of the Pacific Coast required the establishment of broad civil control, anti-sabotage and counter-espionage measures, including the evacuation, there from of all persons of Japanese ancestry. In recognition of this situation, the President issued Executive Order No. 9066 on February 19, 1942, authorizing the accomplishment of these and any other necessary security measures.

Thereafter, American citizens of Japanese descent were prohibited from living, working, or traveling along the West Coast. Japanese immigrants also were not allowed to become American citizens. The prohibition against returning to their former homes and occupations was not lifted until December 1944. Of course, for most, all had been lost as the result of the relocation order.

On February 19, 1976, President Gerald Ford formally rescinded Executive Order 9066. In 1980 President Jimmy Carter established the Commission on Wartime Relocation and Internment of Civilians. The commission's research into government documents was extensive. It also conducted "20 days of hearings in cities across the country . . . hearing testimony from more than 750 witnesses." In 1982 the commission issued its report entitled *Personal Justice Denied*. The report concluded that Executive Order 9066 was not justified by national security, but rather inspired by racial prejudice, war hysteria, and a failure in leadership.

NATIONAL ARCHIVES DOCUMENT

Authorizing the Secretary of War to Prescribe Military Areas

Whereas the successful prosecution of the war requires every possible protection against espionage and against sabotage to national-defense material, national-defense premises, and national-defense utilities . . .

Now, therefore, by virtue of the authority vested in me as President of the United States, and Commander in Chief of the Army and Navy, I hereby authorize and direct the Secretary of War, and the Military Commanders whom he may from time to time designate, whenever he or any designated Commander deems such action necessary or desirable, to prescribe military areas in such places and of such extent as he or the appropriate Military Commander may determine, from which any or all persons may be excluded, and with respect to which, the right of any person to enter, remain in, or leave shall be subject to whatever restrictions the Secretary of War or the appropriate Military Commander may impose in his discretion. . . .

I hereby further authorize and direct the Secretary of War and the said Military Commanders to take such other steps as he or the appropriate Military Commander may deem advisable to enforce compliance with the restrictions applicable to each Military area hereinabove authorized to be designated, including the use of Federal troops and other Federal Agencies, with authority to accept assistance of state and local agencies. ✳

Below: The Japanese Relocation Order affected some 112,000 Japanese Americans, including thousands of children.

Critical Thinking

Determine Point of View

In its 1982 report, the Commission on Wartime Relocation and Internment of Civilians concluded:

> The only justification for exclusion here, beyond DeWitt's belief that ethnicity ultimately determines loyalty, is the unsupported conclusion that 'indications' show that the Japanese 'are organized and ready for concerted action.' The General's best argument for the truth of this was the fact that it hadn't happened yet. It would be hard to concoct a more vicious, less professional piece of military reasoning.

Reread the excerpt from De Witt's report. Would you agree with the commission's conclusion? Explain why or why not.

Assess Significance

Following the attack on Pearl Harbor, the FBI arrested some 2,300 Japanese nationals and Japanese Americans suspected of subversive activity against the United States. The FBI and U.S. Justice Department felt law enforcement efforts had removed any threat by the Japanese community to national security. Why, then, do you think Roosevelt still issued Executive Order 9066?

Draw Conclusions

In 1988 President Ronald Reagan signed into law Civil Liberties Act of 1988. In part it said, "these actions were carried out without adequate security reasons and without any acts of espionage or sabotage documented by the Commission, and were motivated largely by racial prejudice, wartime hysteria, and a failure of political leadership." Each surviving victim of Executive Order 9066 was given a reparation payment of $20,000. Of what importance was the reparation payment?

Research and Writing

Analysis

Research the history of the Japanese internment camps. What was life like at the camps? What did former internees say about their experience? Describe the poignancy of the camps. Explain their aftermath.

Counterpoint

In *Korematsu v. United States* (1944), Justice Hugo Black, in writing for the majority, began his opinion with a caveat,

> All legal restrictions which curtail the civil rights of a single racial group are immediately suspect. That is not to say that all such restrictions are unconstitutional.... Pressing public necessity may sometimes justify the existence of such restrictions; racial antagonism never can.

In this landmark case, the U.S. Supreme Court was asked to determine if the constitutional rights of Toyosaburo Korematsu had been abridged when he refused to leave his home in San Leandro, California. Research this landmark case. In what way did it question the constitutionality of the relocation order?

Of what significance was Korematsu's citizenship and loyalty to the U.S. government? On what basis did Justices Roberts, Murphy, and Jackson base their dissenting opinions? Why was this not a clear-cut case challenging the expulsion order?

Biography

During World War II some 33,000 Japanese Americans served in the U.S. Army. Most of them volunteered for service, since Japanese Americans were draft ineligible beginning with the attack on Pearl Harbor in December 1941 and lasting until January 1944. During World War II Japanese Americans served as linguists, interrogators, and front-line soldiers. The all-Japanese American 442nd Regiment became the most decorated unit in all of military history during the unit's service in World War II. Research the 442nd Regiment. Who were these soldiers? Where did they serve? Why did they serve? Why were members of the 100th Battalion/442nd Regiment called "the Purple Heart Battalion"?

"If we are fighting for the same thing, if we are to die for our country, then why does the Government allow such things to go on?"

–Corp. Rupert Trimmingham

Historical Background

"The policy of the War Department is not to intermingle colored and white enlisted personnel." Thus stated an October 1940 memo from President Franklin D. Roosevelt. Although Roosevelt would soon ban discriminatory hiring practices in the defense industry, racism would remain entrenched in the backbone of the nation's defense—its military. As America entered World War II, some 1.2 million African-American men were inducted into the military. Yet, a color line divided America's armed forces, with Jim Crow "whites only" policies permeating military bases. Though the Selective Service Act of 1940 banned discrimination in recruitment and training, it did not ban segregation. In basic training units, where new soldiers represented a multitude of dialects, religions, community backgrounds, and economics, the one thing that separated recruits was not skill, loyalty, or desire to serve, but the color of the person's skin. Segregationist practices in the military extended from recruitment and training to base theaters, post exchanges, canteens, and advancement in rank.

The military's reasoning for perpetuating Jim Crow was couched in the disingenuous belief that segregation reduced racial tension within the enlisted ranks. Thus, with few exceptions, African-Americans served in lower level service jobs in maintenance, logistics, and supply. They waited tables, loaded ammunition, and cleaned. The few blacks who were permitted to fight served with distinction in combat, such as the all-black 761st Tank Battalion which served under General George Patton in the Battle of the Bulge. However, not a single Medal of Honor was awarded to an African-American during World War II. The hypocrisy of fighting tyranny in Europe but denying rights to African-Americans at home appeared lost on a large segment of American society that turned a blind eye to racial equality and justice.

The hypocrisy, however, was not lost on an array of civil rights activists. In 1947, A. Philip Randolph and Grant Reynolds formed the Committee against Jim Crow in Military Service and Training in hopes of influencing congressional legislation to mandate universal military training. Randolph and Reynolds were aware of a plan by President Harry Truman to require a year's military service for all able young men between the ages of eighteen and twenty. Randolph and Reynolds knew they had an ally in the White House. Truman had already incensed southern legislators by publicly condemning the lynching of blacks and calling for federal legislation to protect African-Americans' right to vote by eliminating poll taxes. In writing to a friend, Truman stated, "The main difficulty with the South is that they are living eighty years behind the times and the sooner they come out of it the better it will be for the country and themselves."

In a memo to Truman on March 22, 1948, Randolph's committee suggested a course of action for the president, to break the color barrier in the military once and for all. Among other recommendations, the committee requested the following of Truman:

- Antisegregation legislation "pertaining to travel by men in uniform on public carriers, to use public facilities, to attacks by police, mob and vigilante troops as well as to the military training program itself."
- An end by "Executive Order, [of] all racial discrimination and segregation in the already existing armed services."

- The assignment of "Negro enlistees, on an unsegregated basis, in the experimental UMT [Universal Military Service] at Fort Knox, Ky."

The Military Selective Service Act became law on June 24, 1948. Subsequently, Randolph informed Truman that African-American youth would resist conscription unless the president issued an executive order ending segregation in the military. Soon after, on July 26, 1948, Truman signed Executive Order 9981 desegregating the armed forces. In response to a comment by Secretary of the Army Kenneth Royall that it would take time to fully desegregate the Army, Truman created the Committee on Equality of Treatment and Opportunity in the Armed Services. Appeased, Randolph called off plans for a draft boycott. By March 18, 1951, all basic training had been integrated. By 1953, ninety-five percent of all military units were integrated.

NATIONAL ARCHIVES DOCUMENT

WHEREAS it is essential that there be maintained in the armed services of the United States the highest standards of democracy, with equality of treatment and opportunity for all those who serve in our country's defense:

NOW THEREFORE, by virtue of the authority vested in me as President of the United States, by the Constitution and the statutes of the United States, and as Commander in Chief of the armed services, it is hereby ordered as follows:

1. It is hereby declared to be the policy of the President that there shall be equality of treatment and opportunity for all persons in the armed services without regard to race, color, religion or national origin. . . .

2. There shall be created in the National Military Establishment an advisory committee to be known as the President's Committee on Equality of Treatment and Opportunity in the Armed Services. . . .

Below: Famed journalist Edward R. Morrow holds a microphone during an interview of an African-American soldier.

3. The Committee is authorized on behalf of the President to examine into the rules, procedures and practices of the Armed Services in order to determine in what respect such rules, procedures and practices may be altered or improved with a view to carrying out the policy of this order. . . .

4. All executive departments and agencies of the Federal Government are authorized and directed to cooperate with the Committee in its work. . . .

5. When requested by the Committee to do so, persons in the armed services or in any of the executive departments and agencies of the Federal Government shall testify before the Committee. . . .

6. The Committee shall continue to exist until such time as the President shall terminate its existence by Executive order. ✷

Critical Thinking

Assess Significance

In 1944 Rupert Trimmingham recounted what happened when he and other African-American GIs traveled in uniform to an Army hospital in Arizona. Local restaurants would not serve them. The lunchroom manager at the railroad depot told the black GIs to go around back to the kitchen for a sandwich and coffee. As they did, Trimmingham recalled,

> About two dozen German prisoners of war, with two American guards, came to the station. They entered the lunchroom, sat at the tables, had their meals served, talked, smoked, in fact had quite a swell time. I stood on the outside looking on, and I could not help but ask myself why are they treated better than we are? Why are we pushed around like cattle? If we are fighting for the same thing, if we are to die for our country, then why does the Government allow such things to go on?

Following publication of Trimmingham's story in the military publication, *Yank*, many soldiers wrote in support of the integration of the armed forces. Why was it easier for frontline soldiers to accept integration than for communities across America?

Analyze Cause and Effect

In speaking before Congress, A. Phillip Randolph said, "I personally pledge myself to openly counsel, aid and abet youth, both white and Negro, to quarantine any Jim Crow conscription system." When reminded that such action would result in charges of treason against him, Randolph replied,

> We would be willing to … face the music and to take whatever comes, and we, as a matter of fact, consider that we are more loyal to our country than the people who perpetrate segregation and discrimination upon Negroes because of color or race.

Yet, Congress was slow to respond. Why?

Draw Conclusions

Do you feel the time it took to implement Executive Order 9981 was reasonable? Why or why not?

Research and Writing

Biography

> A couple of our fighters rescued a crippled bomber and brought them back to base. The bomber's flight crew came over to look us up and when the pilot discovered there was nothing but black faces, he turned around and walked away. The pilot did not realize that the P-51 pilots flying cover for him were African-American. He was heard to say under his breath, 'It ain't so.' We shared the sky with white pilots, but that's all we shared.… We were fighting two battles. I flew for my parents, for my race, for our battle for first-class citizenship and for my country. We were fighting for the 14 million black Americans back home. We were there to break down barriers, open a few doors, and do a job … But we're all Americans. That's why we chose to fight. I'm as American as anybody. My black ancestors were brought over here, perhaps against their will, to help build America. My German ancestors came over to build a new life. And my Cherokee ancestors were here to greet all the boats.

So spoke Tuskegee Airman Joseph P. Gomer. Research the history of the Tuskegee Airmen. Who were they? What barriers did the face? Summarize their distinguished service during World War II.

Relating Events

From 1942 to 1945 some four hundred Navajo Code Talkers served in every U.S. Marine division fighting in the Pacific. Transmitting telephone and radio messages in their native language, the Navaho Code Talkers thwarted Japanese intelligence efforts to intercept U.S. wartime communications. On September 17, 1992, Navajo Code Talkers from World War II were honored in a ceremony at the Pentagon in Washington, D.C. Research the history of minorities serving in the military during World War II. How many served? In what capacity did they serve? In what ways did they distinguish themselves? How did their service help to break down long-held racial prejudices in the armed forces?

Link to the Past

Every individual entering the U.S. military must complete some three months of basic training. A look at any basic training graduating class will show diversity in ethnicity, race, and gender. Research today's military. Are there yet unresolved barriers faced by minorities serving in the United States Armed Forces?

1954 Brown v. Board of Education

*"In the field of public education, the doctrine
of 'separate but equal' has no place."*

–CHIEF JUSTICE EARL WARREN

HISTORICAL BACKGROUND

PLESSY *v. Ferguson* provided the rationale and legal basis for the segregation of races, whether by statute or custom, for more than fifty years. Relegated to an inferior status, blacks saw their civil rights at the ballot box, in restaurants, in public transportation, in hospitals, in education—essentially in every aspect of society—denied them solely on the basis of race. The legal status of "separate but equal" in reality was "separate and anything but equal," as standards for public facilities for "coloreds" fell far below those for whites. However, the U.S. Supreme Court ruling in *Brown v. Board of Education of Topeka, Kansas* produced a huge crack in a racially biased system that had seemed rock solid. Interestingly, the landmark ruling was based not on the fairness of "separate but equal," nor on the equality of public services offered, but instead fell on the psychological ramifications of segregation within an educational setting. In the Court's 1954 ruling, Chief Justice Earl Warren wrote:

> Segregation of white and colored children in public schools has a detrimental effect upon the colored children. The impact is greater when it has the sanction of the law, for the policy of separating the races is usually interpreted as denoting the inferiority of the negro group. A sense of inferiority affects the motivation of a child to learn. Segregation with the sanction of law, therefore, has a tendency to [retard] the educational and mental development of negro children and to deprive them of some of the benefits they would receive in a racial[ly] integrated school system. . . . Any language in Plessy v. Ferguson contrary to this finding is rejected.

Brown v. Board of Education was one of five cases the U.S. Supreme Court agreed to hear on appeal in 1951. Originally argued before the Court in 1952, the justices decided to schedule a second

hearing on the cases, in particular because of dissent among the justices. There was a consensus among them that the cases were so far-reaching, and so potentially volatile, that a unanimous decision by the Court was of absolute necessity. Thus a second hearing was scheduled for 1953. Because of their similarity, the Court dispensed collectively with all five cases under the title *Brown v. Board of Education*. The five cases had been initiated and organized by the NAACP, whose team of attorneys was led by Thurgood Marshall. The *Brown* ruling collapsed the ability of states to lawfully maintain segregation in publicly funded schools. It was a huge legal victory in the NAACP's larger effort to end the socially restrictive and injurious Jim Crow practice of "separate but equal."

The *Brown* ruling, issued on May 17, 1954, ignited reaction across the country that resembled none of the consensus seen on the Court. Although the *Atlanta Constitution* called for cool heads to prevail over "hasty or ill-considered" actions as a result of the decision, the angry response of the Jackson, Mississippi, *Daily News* was clearly ominous:

> Human blood may stain Southern soil in many places because of this decision but the dark red stains of that blood will be on the marble steps of the United States Supreme Court building. . . . White and Negro children in the same schools will lead to miscegenation. Miscegenation leads to mixed marriages and mixed marriages lead to mongrelization of the human race.

Although not all southern newspapers were as inflammatory as the *Daily News*, most were equally unwilling to endorse the Court's ruling. The University of Virginia's *Cavalier Daily* wrote,

> It is too early to tell what effect the Supreme Court decision to abolish segregated schools will have on the

South. . . . Although it is hard from a strict legal point of view to justify any action contrary to law, we feel that the people of the South are justified in their bitterness concerning this decision. To many people this decision is contrary to a way of life and violates the way in which they have thought since 1619.

Many northern newspapers, however, viewed the ruling differently. *The New York Times* editorialized, "The highest court in the land, the guardian of our national conscience, has reaffirmed its faith—and the undying American faith—in the equality of all men and all children before the law." The *Chicago Tribune* added,

> Neither the atom bomb nor the hydrogen bomb will ever be as meaningful to our democracy as the unanimous decision of the Supreme Court of the United States that racial segregation violates the spirit and letter of our Constitution. This means the beginning of the end of the dual society in American life and the . . . segregation which supported it.

NATIONAL ARCHIVES DOCUMENT

These cases come to us from the States of Kansas, South Carolina, Virginia, and Delaware. They are premised on different facts and different local conditions, but a common legal question justifies their consideration together in this consolidated opinion.

In each of the cases, minors of the Negro race, through their legal representatives, seek the aid of the courts in obtaining admission to the public schools of their community on a nonsegregated [sic] basis. In each instance, they had been denied admission to schools attended by white children under laws requiring or permitting segregation according to race. This segregation was alleged to deprive the plaintiffs of the equal protection of the laws under the Fourteenth Amendment. In each of the cases other than the Delaware case, a three-judge federal district court denied relief to the plaintiffs on the so-called "separate but equal" doctrine announced by this Court in Plessy v. Ferguson. . . .

. . . there are findings below that the Negro and white schools involved have been equalized, or are being equalized, with respect to buildings, curricula, qualifications and salaries of teachers, and other "tangible" factors. Our decision, therefore, cannot turn on merely a comparison of these tangible factors in the Negro and white schools involved in each of the cases. We must look instead to the effect of segregation itself on public education.

In approaching this problem, we cannot turn the clock back to 1868, when the Amendment was adopted, or even to 1896, when Plessy v. Ferguson was written. We must consider public education in the light of its full development and its present place in American life throughout the Nation. Only in this way can it be determined if segregation in public schools deprives these plaintiffs of the equal protection of the laws. . . .

We conclude that, in the field of public education, the doctrine of "separate but equal" has no place. Separate educational facilities are inherently unequal. . . . ✳

Below: *Brown v. Board of Education* struck down *Plessy v. Ferguson.* No longer could public schools be an avenue for the segregation of children based on race.

Critical Thinking

Make Predictions

Beginning in 1955 the U.S. Supreme Court required states to formulate plans for the integration of public schools "with all deliberate speed." How quickly do you think this happened? Explain your reasoning.

Draw Conclusions

Why do you think the Supreme Court decided to base its *Brown* ruling on the negative psychological effects of separate-but-equal educational facilities rather than on the constitutionality of separate-but-equal facilities?

Analyze Cause and Effect

What impact did the Court's ruling in *Brown v. Board of Education* have on Jim Crow laws?

Research and Writing

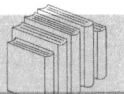

Analysis

Thurgood Marshall was the first African-American justice on the United States Supreme Court. Prior to his Court service, Marshall served as legal counsel for the NAACP. Research the following three segregation-related U.S. Supreme Court cases: *Smith v. Allwright* (1944), *Sweatt v. Painter* (1950), and *McLaurin v. Oklahoma State Regents* (1950), each successfully argued by Thurgood Marshall prior to his U.S. Supreme Court appointment. What issues were addressed in each case? What was its outcome? How did each case successfully eliminate a barrier to racial equality? What common theme runs through all three cases? In what way do the cases support Marshall's contention that "Equal means getting the same thing, at the same time, and in the same place"?

Relating Events

In *Gong Lum v. Rice* (1927), the U.S. Supreme Court was asked to determine if the constitutional rights of Martha Lum, a nine-year-old Chinese-American, had been abridged when she was denied the opportunity to attend an all-white school in Mississippi. In reviewing the lower court rulings, the Court stated,

The case then reduces itself to the question whether a state can be said to afford to a child of Chinese ancestry, born in this country and a citizen of the United States, the equal protection of the laws, by giving her the opportunity for a common school education in a school which receives only colored children of the brown, yellow or black races.

Research *Gong Lum v. Rice.* Review the opinion of the Court rendered by Chief Justice William Howard Taft (former U.S. President Taft). What major points did Chief Justice Taft make in support of the Court's ruling? How did the court rule? Explain the significance of this case.

Counterpoint

In *Missouri v. Jenkins* (1995) Justice Clarence Thomas, in adding to the Court's majority opinion, wrote,

It never ceases to amaze me that the courts are so willing to assume that anything that is predominantly black must be inferior.

Research this important ruling. Read the entire opinion rendered by Justice Thomas. Read the entire *Brown v. Board of Education* decision. Are the two decisions in conflict? How might Thurgood Marshall have viewed the Court's decision in *Missouri v. Jenkins*? What is your opinion?

1957 Desegregation of Central High School

"Two, four, six, eight, we ain't gonna integrate."

–CROWD OUTSIDE CENTRAL HIGH SCHOOL, SEPTEMBER, 1957

HISTORICAL BACKGROUND

IN 1955 the U.S. Supreme Court rendered the second half of its *Brown v. Board of Education* decision. Known as *Brown II*, the unanimous ruling required "a prompt and reasonable start toward full compliance with our May 17, 1954 ruling." Nevertheless, the stipulations enumerated in *Brown II* allowed that states "may find that additional time is necessary to carry out the ruling in an effective manner." The Court's language provided unwilling states the means, perhaps not to bolt the door on integration, but certainly to forestall opening it for a while.

Arkansas was in no hurry to integrate its schools. The city of Little Rock's plan called for integration to be a phased-in process, with the senior high schools integrated for the 1957 school year, followed by integration of the junior high schools (grades 7–9) once successful integration of the high schools had occurred. Thereafter, the elementary schools would be integrated. The Little Rock school board planned to continue operating Horace Mann as an all-black high school. All-white Central High would admit seventeen African-American students who had volunteered to attend that school. As the start of school approached, however, the number of volunteers dwindled to nine.

On August 27, 1957, Mrs. Clyde Thomason, representing the Mothers League of Little Rock Central High School, filed suit to halt the integration plan based on a rumor she had heard "that white and Negro youths were forming gangs and some of them were armed with guns and knives." To prevent such rumored violence, Judge Murray O. Reed granted an injunction to halt the integration of Central High School. Undeterred, federal judge Ronald N. Davies overruled the injunction and ordered the school board to proceed with its integration plans. Yet, just before school began, Governor Orville Faubus announced that integration was simply an impossibility. He instructed 270 National Guard troops to surround Central High to prevent the black students from enrolling in the school. On the first day of school, all nine African-American students stayed home. On the second day, black student Elizabeth Eckford was greeted by an angry mob that threatened, among other things, to lynch her. The National Guard prevented Eckford and the other eight students from entering the school.

Though President Dwight D. Eisenhower was not necessarily supportive of school integration, he did believe in the need to uphold the law. On September 14, he met with Governor Faubus to discuss the volatile situation. Eisenhower later recalled, "I got definitely the understanding that he [Faubus] was going back to Arkansas to act within a matter of hours to revoke his orders to the Guard to prevent re-entry of the Negro children into the school." It didn't happen. Thus, on September 20, Judge Davies granted NAACP attorneys Thurgood Marshall and Wiley Branton an injunction prohibiting Governor Faubus from using the National Guard to deny black students admittance to Central High.

On September 23, the "Little Rock Nine" entered the school through a delivery entrance. As word spread that the nine black students were inside Central High, chaos erupted. The African-American students were quickly removed from the school. Outside, a large white mob attacked the students on the street. By September 24, the mayor of Little Rock was appealing to President Eisenhower for federal troops to restore order. Eisenhower responded with Executive Order 10730, directing the secretary of defense "to order into the active military service of the United States as he may deem appropriate all of the units of the National Guard . . . within the state of Arkansas," thus placing the Guard under federal control. He also authorized the Secretary of Defense to "use such of the armed forces of the United States as he may deem necessary." With that, some 1,100 soldiers of the 101st Airborne descended on Little Rock, Arkansas.

NATIONAL ARCHIVES DOCUMENT

EXECUTIVE ORDER 10730

PROVIDING ASSISTANCE FOR THE REMOVAL OF AN OBSTRUCTION OF JUSTICE WITHIN THE STATE OF ARKANSAS

"WHEREAS certain persons in the state of Arkansas, individually and in unlawful assemblages, combinations, and conspiracies, have willfully obstructed the enforcement of orders of the United States District Court for the Eastern District of Arkansas with respect to matters relating to enrollment and attendance at public schools, particularly at Central High School, located in Little Rock School District, Little Rock, Arkansas. . . .

"WHEREAS such obstruction of justice constitutes a denial of the equal protection of the laws secured by the Constitution of the United States and impedes the course of justice under those laws:

"NOW, THEREFORE, I, DWIGHT D. EISENHOWER, President of the United States, under and by virtue of the authority vested in me by the Constitution and Statutes of the United States. . . .

do command all persons engaged in such obstruction of justice to cease and desist there from, and to disperse forthwith;" and

WHEREAS the command contained in that Proclamation has not been obeyed and willful obstruction of enforcement of said court orders still exists and threatens to continue. . . .

I hereby authorize and direct the Secretary of Defense to order into the active military service of the United States as he may deem appropriate to carry out the purposes of this Order, any or all of the units of the National Guard of the United States and of the Air National Guard of the United States within the State of Arkansas to serve in the active military service of the United States for an indefinite period and until relieved by appropriate orders. . . . ✳

Below: Hazel Bryant yelling at Elizabeth Eckford in 1957 at Central High School.

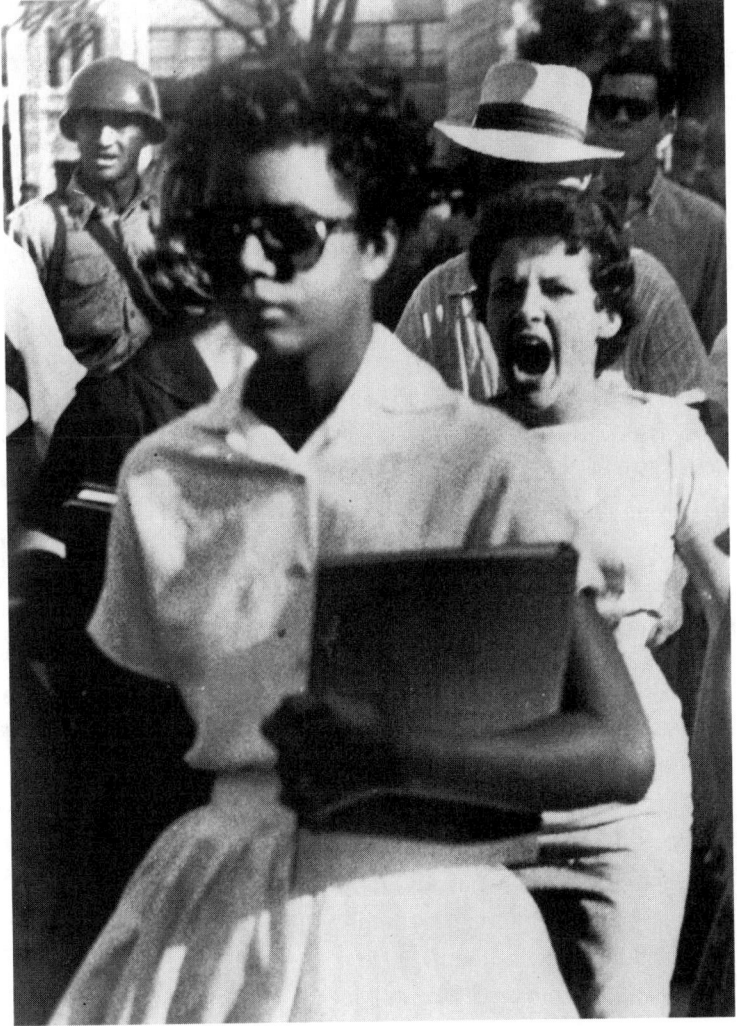

Critical Thinking

Draw Conclusions

Do you think Mothers League of Little Rock Central High School was a pro-integration or an anti-integration group? Why? Do you think Judge Reed was justified in granting an injunction halting the integration plan for Central High?

Assess Significance

On September 23, 1957, the mayor of Little Rock, Arkansas, sent a telegram to President Eisenhower. In it he wrote,

> The city police, together with the state police, made a valiant effort to control the mob today at Central High School....The manner in which the mob was formed and its action ...leads to the inevitable conclusion that Governor Faubus at least was cognizant of what was going to take place....If the Justice Department desires to enforce the orders of the Federal Court in regard to integration in this city, the city police will be available to lend such support as you may require.

Based on this information, do you think Eisenhower acted appropriately by sending federal troops to Little Rock?

Cause and Effect

Federal soldiers stayed in Little Rock until the end of November. However, National Guardsmen, under federal authority, stayed for one year. In a CNN interview in 2004, Elizabeth Eckford recalled, "We were assaulted every day. The principal's rule was that, no matter what was reported, he wouldn't act on any reports if a teacher didn't corroborate what we said happened." With the situation so difficult at Central High, why do you think the "Little Rock Nine" chose to continue the school year there?

Research and Writing

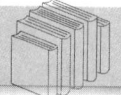

Analysis

Following the graduation of Ernest Green from Central High, segregationists once again appealed to the state courts to delay integration in Little Rock schools until 1961. Once again an injunction was granted, only to be overturned by a federal court. Governor Faubus then signed a package of bills granting him the power to close schools at will in the state. He thereafter closed Little Rock's four high schools for the upcoming school year. The law granting Faubus this power was subsequently declared unconstitutional. In a 1957 letter to Arkansas Congressman Oren Harris, Eisenhower noted,

> Acquiescence in State use of force to block the implementation of Federal court orders, and acquiescence in the use of violence to thwart the Federal judiciary, would be acceding first, to anarchy, and second, to the reversion of our Federal system to the impotent confederacy of 200 years ago from which our Union sprang.

Research Eisenhower's decision to send federal troops to Little Rock, Arkansas. What was his primary motivation? Why was he not comfortable with the notion of sending troops under federal authority to Little Rock? What was Eisenhower's record on civil rights issues?

Relating Events

Arkansas was by no means the only state that resisted integration of its public schools. In 1956, twenty-two U.S. Senators and eighty-two U.S. Representatives from southern states signed the "Southern Manifesto." What was this document? What was its importance? What was its impact? How were efforts to integrate public schools thwarted in other states? How successful was the directive given in *Brown II*?

Counterpoint

In *Cooper v. Aaron* (1958) the state of Arkansas argued that a governor, as well as the U.S. Supreme Court, had the power to interpret the U.S. Constitution. Thus, argued the state, since the governor disagreed with the *Brown v. Board of Education* ruling, the state of Arkansas was not bound by the court's decision. Research the case of *Cooper v. Aaron*. What were the specifics of the case? What was the Court's ruling? Why was it important for the ruling to be unanimous? In what way did this ruling reaffirm the decision in *Brown v. Board of Education*? What was the Court's response to Arkansas's contention that a governor was equal to the Court in the power to interpret the U.S. Constitution? What impact did this decision have on education in the United States?

1963 The March on Washington Official Program

"And so even though we face the difficulties of today and tomorrow, I still have a dream."

—MARTIN LUTHER KING JR.

HISTORICAL BACKGROUND

ON August 28, 1963, A. Philip Randolph stood in front of the Lincoln Memorial. He gazed out over a huge crowd of 250,000 civil rights demonstrators who had come to Washington, D.C., determined to end the injustices of racial segregation and discrimination. Randolph paused and then spoke these words:

> Fellow Americans, we are gathered here in the largest demonstration in the history of this nation. Let the nation and the world know the meaning of our numbers. We are not a pressure group, we are not an organization or a group of organizations, we are not a mob. We are the advance guard of a massive moral revolution for jobs and freedom.

The 1963 March on Washington was the culmination of over twenty years of efforts by A. Philip Randolph, an undertaking supported by the civil rights organization CORE (Congress of Racial Equality). It marked a pivotal point in the civil rights movement. Demands for justice had moved from nonviolent demonstrations to a call for federal legislation that would truly balance the scales by granting equal rights to all Americans. The March on Washington jolted the conscience of America to correct the wrongs of a society entrenched in racial segregation. Its success, borne on the backs of the many African-Americans who had challenged discrimination, ultimately changed America's social landscape.

The March on Washington took a mere two months to organize. Thousands of people headed to the nation's capital via some thirty special trains and two thousand chartered buses. They scraped together the price of the fare, packed their lunches, and became a part of history that forever changed the nation for the better. Impassioned speeches by the most active of civil rights leaders at the time

served not to incite, but to unite the crowd. John Lewis, Chairman of the Student Nonviolent Coordinating Committee (SNCC), put the nation on notice when he stated, "By the force of our demands, our determination and our numbers, we shall splinter the segregated South into a thousand pieces, and put them back together in the image of God and Democracy." NAACP Executive Secretary, Roy Wilkins urged the crowd to "stay in the streets of every city in the country until this fight is won." Yet it was the speech by Martin Luther King Jr. that most captivated the crowd—and the nation. "I have a dream," King said, "that my four little children will one day live in a nation where they will not be judged by the color of their skin but by the content of their character."

Perhaps most gratified by the words spoken on the steps of the Lincoln Memorial that day were the women given tribute as "Fighters for Freedom." December 1, 1955, had been a fateful day for one of those honored, for this was when Rosa Parks decided to make her stand as an African-American no longer willing to be considered a second class citizen. In 1955 Parks was a member of both the NAACP and the Women's Political Council in Montgomery, Alabama. As a political statement, Parks was more than willing to test the limits of Montgomery's law requiring segregated seating on city buses. Thus, when Parks was asked by a bus driver to move to allow a white man to sit down, she simply refused and, quite predictably, was arrested. Her arrest sparked the beginning of a well-orchestrated bus boycott by African-Americans in Montgomery that lasted for 381 days. The issue was finally resolved in November 1956 when the U.S. Supreme Court upheld a lower federal court ruling that declared segregation on buses unconstitutional. The boycott, however, continued until the court order requiring the integration of public buses was served on officials in Montgomery. The Court's ruling also did not end the violence perpetuated against African-Americans, including the bombing of the home of the bus boycott's leader, Martin Luther King Jr.

The Montgomery bus boycott brought to light the power of organized protest. It gave birth to a civil rights movement that led over 250,000 people to converge on Washington, D.C., some seven years later. Though the original plan for the March on Washington called for a sit-in to last until Congress passed pending civil rights legislation, the idea was rejected instead for a full day's activities held on the steps of the Lincoln Memorial. The day ended, not with the violence predicted by law enforcement, but instead with a national awareness that the days of segregation were coming to an end.

NATIONAL ARCHIVES DOCUMENT

MARCH ON WASHINGTON FOR JOBS AND FREEDOM
AUGUST 28, 1963
LINCOLN MEMORIAL PROGRAM

1. **The National Anthem** *Led by* Marian Anderson.
2. **Invocation** The Very Rev. Patrick O'Boyle, *Archbishop of Washington.*
3. **Opening Remarks** A. Philip Randolph, *Director, March on Washington for Jobs and Freedom.*
4. **Remarks** Dr. Eugene Carson Blake, *Stated Clerk, United Presbyterian Church of the U.S.A.; Vice Chairman, Commission on Race Relations of the National Council of Churches of Christ in America.*
5. **Tribute to Negro Women Fighters for Freedom** Daisy Bates, Diane Nash Bevel, Mrs. Medgar Evers, Mrs. Herbert Lee, Rosa Parks, Gloria Richardson.
6. **Remarks** John Lewis, *National Chairman, Student Nonviolent Coordinating Committee.*
7. **Remarks** Walter Reuther, *President, United Automobile, Aerospace and Agricultural Implement Workers of America, AFL-CIO; Chairman, Industrial Union Department, AFL-CIO.*
8. **Remarks** James Farmer, *National Director, Congress of Racial Equality.*
9. **Selection** Eva Jessye *Choir*
10. **Prayer** Rabbi Uri Miller, *President, Synagogue Council of America.*
11. **Remarks** Whitney M. Young, Jr., *Executive Director, National Urban League.*
12. **Remarks** Matthew Ahmann, *Executive Director, National Catholic Conference for Interracial Justice.*
13. **Remarks** Roy Wilkins, *Executive Secretary, National Association for the Advancement of Colored People.*
14. **Selection** Miss Mahalia Jackson
15. **Remarks** Rabbi Joachim Prinz, *President, American Jewish Congress.*
16. **Remarks** The Rev. Dr. Martin Luther King Jr., *President, Southern Christian Leadership Conference.*
17. **The Pledge** A. Philip Randolph
18. **Benediction** Dr. Benjamin E. Mays, *President, Morehouse College.*

"WE SHALL OVERCOME" ✳

Below: Over 250,000 people participated in the 1963 March on Washington.

Critical Thinking

Assess Significance

The idea for the March on Washington was first envisioned by long-time civil rights advocate A. Philip Randolph. In what way did Randolph's stature in the civil rights movement help to forge a consensus among civil rights activists to proceed with plans for the March on Washington?

Make Predictions

The March on Washington was an historic moment that unified several factions of the Civil Rights Movement. The gathering crossed both generational and racial lines as blacks and whites, young and old, stood united in the quest for equal rights for all. What impact do you think this nonviolent gathering of more than 250,000 civil rights demonstrators had on the nation?

Cause and Effect

How effective do you think a staged sit-in would have been, had it been a part of the March on Washington? Why do you think the organizers of the March on Washington decided not to include a sit-in as part of the organized demonstration?

Research and Writing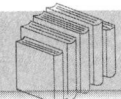

Analysis

Read the entire transcript of Martin Luther King Jr.'s "I Have a Dream" speech, delivered on the steps of the Lincoln Memorial in Washington, D.C. Extract references from his speech that refer to events occurring in individual states. Research those events. Write an essay explaining the poignancy of King's speech.

Relating Events

CORE was founded in 1942 by an interracial group of students in Chicago, Illinois. Influenced by the teachings of India's Mohandas Gandhi, CORE's founders began its nonviolent approach to desegregating American society by organizing sit-ins against segregated public facilities in the North. In 1947 CORE decided to test the constitutionality of segregated interstate travel by sending black and white "freedom riders" on buses across the South. This led to the arrest and conviction in North Carolina of several CORE activists, and their assignment to a prison labor chain gang. CORE also provided the impetus behind the 1955 Montgomery bus boycott. In 1960, four African-American college students, prompted by information in CORE leaflets, sat at an all-white lunch counter in a Woolworth's store in Greensboro, North Carolina, and demanded to be served. When they were asked to leave, they determinedly waited to be served. Rather than serve the four black students, the store closed. The event marked the beginning of sit-ins at "white's only" lunch counters across the South, culminating in the U.S. Supreme Court case *Peterson v. City of Greenville* (1963). Research *Peterson v. City of Greenville*. What were the specifics in the case? In what way did the Court's ruling impact Jim Crow laws? Why is *Peterson v. Greenville* considered a landmark case?

Biography

Martin Luther King Jr., like many other African-Americans, became a victim of violent, abject racism. Research the life of Martin Luther King Jr. How did he rise from being a minister in Montgomery, Alabama, to become one of the most powerful civil rights leaders of the time? What was his approach to achieving full civil rights for African-Americans? What role did he play in the Civil Rights Movement? What was his legacy?

1964 Civil Rights Act

> *"The heart of the question is . . . Whether we are going to treat our fellow Americans as we want to be treated."*
>
> –PRESIDENT JOHN F. KENNEDY

HISTORICAL BACKGROUND

PRESIDENT John F. Kennedy entered office in 1961. As a senator, Kennedy's record on civil rights was far from stellar, including his vote against the 1957 Civil Rights Act. This law established the Commission on Civil Rights. It also protected the rights of all individuals to vote in federal elections. Once he became president, Kennedy often chose to distance himself as much as possible from civil rights issues, preferring instead to address critical needs in foreign affairs–though domestic issues certainly couldn't be ignored. Kennedy was, above all else, a politician. To maintain the support of Southern Democrats necessary for re-election, Kennedy appointed staunch segregationists to the federal judiciary. Yet, to ensure equality of justice under federal law, he appointed his brother and civil rights advocate, Robert (Bobby) Kennedy, as the nation's Attorney General. It was a delicate balance hinged on politics and faith in the judicial system, a balance undone by a Civil Rights Movement so strong and so just that the issue of civil rights could no longer be relegated to incidental politics.

In September 1962 James Meredith, an African-American, applied to the doctoral program at the University of Mississippi. Though Meredith was qualified, and had even served for ten years in the U.S. Air Force, his application was denied. With the support of the NAACP, Meredith sought redress in the courts. He received it when the U.S. Supreme Court enjoined the university to admit him. To ensure the university's compliance with the law, and to protect Meredith against rumors of a possible lynching, Robert Kennedy sent 500 U.S. marshals to the University of Mississippi. In an ensuing riot, almost 200 marshals were injured and two bystanders were shot. To maintain law and order, President Kennedy federalized 5,000 Mississippi National Guard soldiers. In a nationally televised address, he said,

> Our Nation is founded on the principle that observance of the law is the eternal safeguard of liberty and defiance of the law is the surest road to tyranny. . . . Americans are free, in short, to disagree with the law but not to disobey it. For in a government of laws and not of men, no man, however prominent or powerful, and no mob however unruly or boisterous, is entitled to defy a court of law.

By the summer of 1963, the country appeared gripped by the volatility of racial violence. Perhaps it was the Freedom Riders who had been beaten with pipes and bats, or the lynchings that occurred in the North as well as the South. Possibly it was the 5,000 troops required to enforce the integration of the University of Mississippi that finally spurred Kennedy's resolve for fairness and justice. In any event, on June 11, 1963, in a televised address to the nation, the President explained the reasoning behind the controversial civil rights legislation he planned to send Congress.

> If an American, because his skin is dark, cannot eat lunch in a restaurant open to the public, if he cannot send his children to the best public school available, if he cannot vote for the public officials who represent him, if, in short, he cannot enjoy the full and free life which all of us want, then who among us would be content to have the color of his skin changed and stand in his place? Who among us would then be content with the counsels of patience and delay?

Then came the August 1963 March on Washington. Initially rejected by President Kennedy because he felt such a demonstration might cause Congress to discard any civil rights legislation, he ultimately gave his nod of approval. Although

Kennedy met with leaders of the March on Washington, he made little commitment to their demands, including the immediate passage of "meaningful" civil rights legislation, the immediate elimination of all racial segregation in public schools, and a federal law prohibiting racial discrimination in employment—public and private.

Kennedy's resolve on civil rights legislation was tested again on September 15, 1963, when a bomb tore through the basement of the Sixteenth Street Bethel Baptist Church in Birmingham, Alabama, killing four young African-American girls. Home to the powerful Ku Klux Klan (KKK), the city had been the site of dozens of bombings over the years, earning it the name "Bombingham." Homes and businesses of any African-American who dared to challenge the white supremecy beliefs of the KKK were targeted for deadly reprisal.

President Kennedy was assassinated on November 22, 1963. The fate of the Civil Rights Bill fell to newly installed President Lyndon Baines Johnson. Following considerable pressure by the White House, the Civil Rights Act finally passed the House by a vote of 290 to 130, and the Senate by a vote of 73 to 27. The bill was signed into law on July 2, 1964. It was legislation that was a long time in coming. Almost one hundred years after passage of the Thirteenth, Fourteenth, and Fifteenth Amendments to the U.S. Constitution, the country had civil rights legislation that finally put Jim Crow to rest. What had taken so long? Was it fear, greed, sheer ignorance, the unwillingness to change a social and political structure that had given power to a few at the expense of many? Or, was it simply "the illusion of differences," as Robert Kennedy so eloquently observed? Whatever the root of segregation, the Civil Rights Act of 1964 ended legally sanctioned segregation once and for all. It was the federal legislation hoped for by those who had participated in the March on Washington. For some in Congress, it was the ultimate compromise. But for most, the Civil Rights Act of 1964 was legislation that touched the conscience of America and provided an opportunity to right the wrongs of so many years past.

NATIONAL ARCHIVES DOCUMENT

To enforce the constitutional right to vote, to confer jurisdiction upon the district courts of the United States to provide injunctive relief against discrimination in public accommodations, to authorize the Attorney General to institute suits to protect constitutional rights in public facilities and public education, to extend the Commission on Civil Rights, to prevent discrimination in federally assisted programs, to establish a Commission on Equal Employment Opportunity, and for other purposes.

Be it enacted by the Senate and House of Representatives of the United States of America in Congress assembled, That this Act may be cited as the "Civil Rights Act of 1964." ✳

Below: President Lyndon Baines Johnson signed the Civil Rights Act on July 2, 1964.

Critical Thinking

Assess Significance

In a 1966 speech at the University of Capetown, in South Africa, Robert Kennedy addressed the imposition of apartheid in that country.

> Few will have the greatness to bend history; but each of us can work to change a small portion of the events, and in the total of all these acts will be written the history of this generation … Each time a man stands up for an ideal, or acts to improve the lot of others, or strikes out against injustice, he sends forth a tiny ripple of hope, and crossing each other from a million different centers of energy and daring those ripples build a current which can sweep down the mightiest walls of oppression and resistance.

In what way was Kennedy also addressing the history of civil rights in the United States?

Compare and Contrast

The 1875 Civil Rights Act stated,

> That all persons within the jurisdiction of the United States shall be entitled to the full and equal enjoyment of the accommodations, advantages, facilities, and privileges of inns, public conveyances on land or water, theaters, and other places of public amusement; subject only to the conditions and limitations established by law, and applicable alike to citizens of every race and color, regardless of any previous condition of servitude.

How are the 1875 and 1964 Civil Rights Acts similar in intent? Were the laws social and political equals?

Draw Conclusions

What is the state of racial relations in the country today?

Research and Writing

Historical Interpretation

Research John F. Kennedy's record on civil rights during his tenure as president of the United States. What civil rights events took place? What was his response? What influence did Robert Kennedy have on his brother's stance on civil rights issues? Why did the president decide to support the Civil Rights Act? In sum, how would you characterize President Kennedy's record on civil rights?

Relating Events

During the 1950s and 1960s, Birmingham was a city enveloped by fear. Violence against blacks had become commonplace, and for the most part was overlooked by a police department with ties to the Ku Klux Klan. Throughout the latter half of the nineteenth century, and for much of the twentieth, the influence of the KKK permeated every aspect of government in the South, from local governments such as that in Birmingham, through the state courts, state legislatures, and into the executive branch of several states. Research the history of the KKK in the South. Where and why did it first form? What are examples of how it perpetuated racial hatred and violence? Why was it allowed to exist? In what way was the judicial process complicit in its actions? What influence did the KKK have in northern states? Why didn't the federal judicial system simply shut down the Ku Klux Klan? Does the KKK continue to be active today?

Analysis

Access the entire Civil Rights Act of 1964. Note that this lengthy and comprehensive legislation is divided into separate titles as follows:

- Title I –Voting Rights.
- Title II – Discrimination in Places of Public Accommodation
- Title III – Desegregation of Public Facilities
- Title IV – Desegregation of Public Education
- Title V – Commission on Civil Rights
- Title VI – Nondiscrimination in Federally Assisted Programs
- Title VII – Equal Employment Opportunity
- Title VIII – Registration and Voting Statistics
- Title IX – Intervention and Procedure after Removal in Civil Rights Cases
- Title X – Establishment of Community Relations Service
- Title XI – Miscellaneous (in regard to criminal proceedings)

Choose one title of the Civil Rights Act of 1964 to research. What does the legislation mandate? Why was legislation in this area necessary? In what way does the legislation prohibit Jim Crow laws? In what way does it ensure the civil rights of all Americans?

"It is all of us, who must overcome the crippling legacy of bigotry and injustice. And we shall overcome."

—President Lyndon Baines Johnson

Historical Background

On June 20, 1964, three civil rights workers set off from Ohio destined for Mississippi. They were Mickey Schwerner, a native of New York; James Chaney, an African-American from Meridian, Mississippi; and Andrew Goodman from the Upper West Side of Manhattan in New York City. All three were members of the Congress of Racial Equality or CORE. Mickey Schwerner had previously been targeted by white supremacists in Mississippi as a troublemaker for organizing a boycott by African-Americans of a store in Meridian. Though the store depended on its black customers, it had refused to employ African-Americans. Schwerner was known as "Jew-Boy" by the white supremacists. The Ku Klux Klan in Mississippi in 1964 had as little regard for individuals of the Jewish faith as it did for African-Americans.

Schwerner, Chaney, and Goodman traveled into Mississippi in 1964 as part of the Freedom Summer Project. They were among some six hundred students affiliated with the Student Non-Violent Coordinating Committee (SNCC) and CORE, who were sent to all parts of Mississippi. The project's intent was to register black voters. It was a dangerous undertaking. Several African-American churches where activists had come to organize had been bombed. So it was with trepidation that the three entered Mississippi. After stopping in Meridian, they left to investigate a possible church bombing to the northwest. They were never heard from again. In response to their disappearance, the Justice Department dispatched some 200 FBI agents to Neshoba County to search for the students. In August they were found buried in an earthen dam. All three had been executed.

In January 1965 Martin Luther King, Jr. joined SNCC members in Selma, Alabama, to organize a mass demonstration in support of federal legislation ensuring voting rights for all. Though African-Americans made up some 50 percent of all eligible voters in the South, only about 1 percent of those who could vote were actually registered. Intimidation tactics included beatings, church bombings, arson of businesses and homes, lynchings, and drive-by shootings. Such insidious strategies kept African-Americans who dreamed of voting far from the voting booth. Those who attempted to register to vote were challenged by registrars. The registrars then turned over their names to the local White Citizens Council. This group of businessmen would subsequently deny bank loans, impose foreclosures or evictions, or fire an African-American employee who dared to try to vote.

On March 7, 1965, as King and some 600 other demonstrators, both black and white, attempted to march from Selma to Montgomery, Alabama, they were stopped by state troopers armed with teargas, horsewhips, and clubs. They had made it to the Edmund Pettus Bridge six blocks from where they had started. The state troopers attacked and drove the demonstrators back to Selma. The resulting melee became known as "Bloody Sunday." Two weeks later, on March 21, some 3,200 demonstrators began a renewed march to Montgomery. Covering about twelve miles per day, and gathering additional recruits along the way, by the time they reached Montgomery on March 25, the protestors numbered 25,000.

On March 15, President Johnson introduced the Voting Rights Bill to Congress. In doing so, he stated,

At times history and fate meet at a single time in a single place to shape a turning point in man's unending search for freedom. . . . So it was last week in Selma, Alabama. . . . Many of the issues of civil rights are very complex and most difficult. But about this there can and should be no argument. Every American citizen must have the right to vote.

President Johnson signed the Voting Rights Act on August 6, 1965. Within months, voter registration among African-Americans in the South rose to 70 percent or more in states like Mississippi, Tennessee, Arkansas, and Texas. Prior to passage of the Voting Rights Act, barely 100 African-Americans held elective office. By 1989 some 4,500 African-Americans had been elected to public office in the South alone. It had been a long and costly struggle. Embodied in the words of Martin Luther King, Jr. was the heart of the Civil Rights Movement,

We must all learn to live together as brothers or we will all perish together as fools. We are tied together in the single garment of destiny, caught in an inescapable network of mutuality. And whatever affects one directly affects all indirectly. For some strange reason I can never be what I ought to be until you are what you ought to be. And you can never be what you ought to be until I am what I ought to be.

NATIONAL ARCHIVES DOCUMENT

AN ACT To enforce the fifteenth amendment to the Constitution of the United States. . . .

SEC. 2. No voting qualification or prerequisite to voting, or standard, practice, or procedure shall be imposed or applied by any State or political subdivision to deny or abridge the right of any citizen of the United States to vote on account of race or color. . . .

(b) If in a proceeding instituted by the Attorney General . . . finds that a test or device has been used for the purpose or with the effect of denying or abridging the right of any citizen of the United States to vote on account of race or color, it shall suspend the use of tests and devices. . . .

SEC. 4. . . . (c) The phrase "test or device" shall mean any requirement that a person as a prerequisite for voting or registration for voting (1) demonstrate the ability to read, write, understand, or interpret any matter, (2) demonstrate any educational achievement or his knowledge of any particular subject, (3) possess good moral character, or (4) prove his qualifications by the voucher of registered voters or members of any other class.

SEC. 11. (a) No person acting under color of law shall fail or refuse to permit any person to vote who is entitled to vote under any provision of this Act or is otherwise qualified to vote, or willfully fail or refuse to tabulate, count, and report such person's vote. ✳

Below: African-Americans wait in line to register to vote. Voter registration among African-Americans rose significantly following passage of the Voting Rights Act.

Critical Thinking

Determine Point of View

In 1963 President Kennedy told the nation, "It is not enough to pin the blame on others, to say this is a problem of one section of the country or another,… A great change is at hand, and our task, our obligation, is to make that revolution, that change, peaceful and constructive for all." What do you think Kennedy was attempting to accomplish with these words?

Assess Significance

In 1964, the Lowell, Mississippi, *Liberator* reported the following:

> A thousand college students from the North are reported to be invading Mississippi this summer in order to engage in a Negro voter registration drive. It is unbelievable that a thousand college students would do this of their own volition. Those who know the ways of propaganda, especially of a Communist nature, probably correctly suspect that the idealism of some college youngsters has been taken advantage of by some very hard boiled left wingers and Communists who know exactly what they want to do—stir up trouble in the South.

In what way had the Freedom Summer Project become politicized?

Draw Conclusions

Beginning in the late 1800s, southern states imposed poll taxes as a means to disenfranchise poor whites and, in particular, African-Americans. In 1964 the Twenty-Fourth Amendment to the U.S. Constitution was ratified. The amendment abolished poll taxes in federal elections. In 1966 the U.S. Supreme Court abolished poll taxes in all elections held in the United States. Its ruling was based on the "equal protection clause" of the Fourteenth Amendment. Of what significance were the amendment and Court's ruling?

Research and Writing

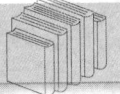

Analysis

Literacy tests had long been used in the South as a means to disenfranchise African-Americans. Literacy tests were purposefully written to confuse the test-taker. In Alabama, for example, one question asked, "In what year did the Congress gain the right to prohibit the migration of persons to the states?" Literacy tests included detailed questions on the Constitution and local political practices. Additionally, some states required a lengthy registration process, which required a follow-up interview before one gained acceptance as a duly registered voter. Research literacy tests used in the South. What type of questions did they have? How were they given? Which states utilized literacy tests? How were literacy tests used in conjunction with the "grandfather clause" to exempt African-Americans from voting? What does the 1965 Voting Rights Act say in regard to literacy tests? What impact did the Voting Rights Act have on the practice of imposing literacy tests as a condition of voting?

Relating Events

In October 1964, seven of the eighteen individuals indicted on conspiracy to commit murder were found guilty in the deaths of Michael Schwerner, Andrew Goodman, and James Chaney. The maximum sentence possible was ten years in prison. The end result was the U.S. Supreme Court case *United States v. Price*. Research the events of the trial surrounding the deaths of Schwerner, Goodman, and Chaney. How was the trial conducted? What issues were addressed of *United States v. Price*? What was the Court's ruling? Why was this ruling significant?

Link to the Past

The Voting Rights Act of 1965 was extended in 1970, 1975, and 1982. Access and read the entire 1965 act. What provisions were extended in later years? Why was this necessary? What current efforts are in place to protect voting rights?

Domestic Policy

"This Nation asks for action, and action now."

—FRANKLIN DELANO ROOSEVELT (1882–1945)

Prologue

T he extent of government involvement in the lives of its citizens is the core of a country's prevailing domestic policy. In 1937 President Franklin Delano Roosevelt consoled and encouraged a nation still suffering the economic perils of the Great Depression. "We recognized . . . the need to find through government the instrument of our united purpose to solve for the individual the ever-rising problems of a complex civilization. Repeated attempts at their solution without the aid of government had left us baffled and bewildered." In 1961 a newly elected President John Kennedy told Americans: "Ask not what your country can do for you—ask what you can do for your country." Twenty years later, President Ronald Reagan told the nation, "We are a nation that has a government—not the other way around. . . . Our government has no power except that granted it by the people. It is time to check and reverse the growth of government which shows signs of having grown beyond the consent of the governed." Different times, different presidents, different solutions to the nation's ever-changing needs. Does government protect or provide? Should it do both? Can it afford to do both? Where is the balance? In this final unit, you will learn how the domestic policy of government has changed over the years.

"Before sunset the flag of the Confederate States floated over the ramparts of Fort Sumter."

—GENERAL P.G.T. BEAUREGARD,
COMMANDER PROVISIONAL ARMY OF THE CONFEDERATE STATES

HISTORICAL BACKGROUND

WHEN the votes were counted on November 6, 1860, the fate of the nation teetered on the passions of an electorate determined to define the power of the national government. Should states, as so many southerners ardently believed, hold the reigns of power, with the capability to maintain the institution of slavery as they wished? Or, should the sovereignty of the federal government be unconditional in its authority to forever ban slavery? Views touting the absolute sovereignty of the federal government were considered audacious in the South, and incensed many southerners. Accordingly, when the votes were counted that fateful November day, a worrisome sectional split was all too evident. Abraham Lincoln carried every free state. He received three of New Jersey's seven electoral votes and seven votes from California and Oregon. South of the Mason-Dixon Line, however, Lincoln's electoral vote tallied an ill-omened zero. Even so, with 180 electoral votes, Lincoln captured the presidency. It didn't take the South long to respond to his election.

On December 3, lame-duck President James Buchanan attempted to cajole a discordant Congress, appease the South, and quiet the clamor for secession. In his Fourth Annual Message, Buchanan reasoned,

> How easy it would be for the American people to settle the slavery question forever and to restore peace and harmony to this distracted country! . . . All that is necessary to accomplish the object, and all for which the slave States have ever contended, is to be let alone and permitted to manage their domestic institutions in their own way. As sovereign States, they, and they

alone, are responsible before God and the world for slavery existing among them. For this the people of the North are not more responsible and have no more right to interfere than with similar institutions in Russia or in Brazil.

It didn't work. On December 20, South Carolina approved an ordinance of secession. It would be the first of eleven states that ultimately became the Confederate States of America—tearing the country in two.

Meanwhile, more trouble was brewing in South Carolina. Major Robert Anderson commanded three U.S. forts located in Charleston Harbor: Moultrie, Sumter, and Castle Pinckney. With secession from the Union firmly in place, South Carolina's governor, Francis W. Pickens, demanded that President Buchanan surrender all three forts to the state. Buchanan refused, telling Pickens, "if South Carolina should attack any of these forts, she will then become the assailant in a war against the United States." Under the cover of darkness, on December 26 Anderson quietly transferred his men and arms from a more vulnerable Fort Moultrie to Fort Sumter, located on an island three miles from Charlestown. Anderson and his ten officers, sixty-eight soldiers, and fifty-one civilians were now isolated on an island that South Carolina considered to be in the hands of a foreign power. By February 1, Mississippi, Florida, Alabama, Georgia, Louisiana, and Texas had joined South Carolina in seceding from the Union. On February 18, Jefferson Davis took the oath of office as president of the Confederate States of America.

On March 4, 1861, Abraham Lincoln was sworn in as the sixteenth president of the United States. In his Inaugural Address he stated, "The power confided to me will be used to hold, occupy, and possess the property and places belonging to the Government." Back at Fort Sumter, Anderson was rapidly running out of provisions for his men. He requested that Lincoln quickly send both troops and provisions. Without relief, Anderson estimated that his troops would be starved out in six weeks. Though advised to abandon Fort Sumter by both the army and his secretary of state, Lincoln instead decided to hold to his Inaugural Address promise. To that end, on April 4, 1861, he gave the order to send a fleet of warships to Charlestown Harbor, with instructions for smaller boats to be used to transfer supplies to the fort. The South, however, would have none of the plan.

On April 10, 1860, General P.G.T. Beauregard was given the command to force the immediate evacuation of Fort Sumter. To that end, he already had surrounded the island fort with some 6,000 troops. On April 12, Beauregard presented Anderson with conditions for the fort's surrender. When Anderson refused, Beauregard opened fire. Following thirty-three hours of bombardment, and some 3,300 projectiles later, with the fort on fire, Anderson capitulated. On April 14, he lowered the United States flag, complete with a fifty-gun salute—an honor afforded him by Beauregard. The answer to the difficulties between the North and the South was now at hand. There would be no more diplomacy, no gentlemen concessions to settle disagreements. It was war.

National Archives Document

S.S. BALTIC. OFF SANDY HOOK APR. EIGHTEENTH. TEN THIRTY A.M. .VIA
NEW YORK. . HON. S. CAMERON. SECY. WAR. WASHN. HAVING DEFENDED
FORT SUMTER FOR THIRTY FOUR HOURS. UNTIL THE QUARTERS WERE EN
TIRELY BURNED THE MAIN GATES DESTROYED BY FIRE. THE GORGE WALLS
SERIOUSLY INJURED. THE MAGAZINE SURROUNDED BY FLAMES AND ITS
DOOR CLOSED FROM THE EFFECTS OF HEAT. FOUR BARRELLS AND THREE
CARTRIDGES OF POWDER ONLY BEING AVAILABLE AND NO PROVISIONS
REMAINING BUT PORK. I ACCEPTED TERMS OF EVACUATION OFFERED BY
GENERAL BEAUREGARD BEING ON SAME OFFERED BY HIM ON THE ELEV
ENTH INST. PRIOR TO THE COMMENCEMENT OF HOSTILITIES AND MARCHED
OUT OF THE FORT SUNDAY AFTERNOON THE FOURTEENTH INST. WITH
COLORS FLYING AND DRUMS BEATING. BRINGING AWAY COMPANY AND
PRIVATE PROPERTY AND SALUTING MY FLAG WITH FIFTY GUNS. ROBERT
ANDERSON. MAJOR FIRST ARTILLERY. COMMANDING.

Left: On April 18, 1861, Major Robert Anderson sent this telegram to Secretary of War Simon Cameron announcing the withdrawal of federal troops from Fort Sumter.

Critical Thinking

Determine Point of View

In his February 18, 1861, Inaugural Address, Jefferson Davis, Provisional President of the Confederacy, stated,

> The declared purpose of the compact of Union from which we have withdrawn was "to establish justice, insure domestic tranquility, provide for the common defense, promote the general welfare, and secure the blessings of liberty to ourselves and our posterity;" and when, in the judgment of the sovereign States now composing this Confederacy, it had been perverted from the purposes for which it was ordained, and had ceased to answer the ends for which it was established, a peaceful appeal to the ballot-box declared that so far as they were concerned, the government created by that compact should cease to exist. In this they merely asserted a right which the Declaration of Independence of 1776 had defined to be inalienable.

To what was Jefferson Davis referring? How does he explain the choice to form a new government?

Draw Conclusions

On December 18, 1860, Kentucky's Senator John J. Crittenden offered legislation—a compromise—to save the Union. He proposed to restore the Missouri Compromise line all the way to California. Slavery would be allowed in all areas below this line and in all states where it already existed. In the end the legislation failed on a 25 to 23 vote. Do you think this compromise would have been enough to save the nation from civil war? Explain.

Assess Significance

In February 1861 delegates from twenty-one states met in Washington, D.C., to attempt to save the nation from the possibility of war. One proposal met with success— a constitutional amendment that would have guaranteed slavery where it currently existed. The proposed amendment passed in both the House of Representatives and in the Senate. However, it was never ratified by the states. Instead, a different Thirteenth Amendment was added to the Constitution. What is different in the intent of the amendment that almost became the Thirteenth Amendment and the one that actually was ratified by the states?

Research and Writing

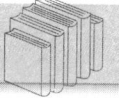

Analysis

In Abraham Lincoln's First Inaugural Address he expressed his belief in the sovereign rights of states in regard to the issue of slavery.

> I have no purpose, directly or indirectly, to interfere with the institution of slavery in the States where it exists. I believe I have no lawful right to do so, and I have no inclination to do so. . . .

Lincoln also promised to enforce the Fugitive Slave Act. Following his speech, southerners such as Emma Holmes of Charlestown pronounced the "stupid, ambiguous, vulgar and insolent [speech] is everywhere considered a virtual declaration of war." Access and read Lincoln's First Inaugural Address. What concessions did he make to the South? What domestic issue did he feel warranted the greatest effort? What did he mean when he stated, "Perpetuity is implied, if not expressed, in the fundamental law of all national governments"? What did he promise, given his authority as president of the United States?

Historical Interpretation

On April 15, Lincoln issued a proclamation calling for the states to supply 75,000 militiamen to put down the rebellion in the South. Both the North and the South felt the ensuing war would be short-lived. Both felt confident of their ability to squelch any attack. The North, especially, felt its resources and manpower could easily overwhelm the rebellious South. Much, however, was overlooked or downplayed as the opposing forces readied for war. Research the initial battles of the Civil War. What advantages did each side have? Who had the upper hand? Why? What indications early on dispelled the naïve belief of a short-lived war?

Relating Events

Research the states that were part of the Confederacy. Compare the declarations of secession of at least two states. What reasons were given for secession? What was the status of Kentucky and Missouri? Why did Delaware, a slave state, remain in the Union? What measures did Lincoln take to diminish the threat of Maryland becoming a Confederate state? How and why did the state of West Virginia originate?

1862 Morrill Act

"Other reforms are remedial; education is preventative."

—Horace Mann

Historical Background

Justin Smith Morrill was born in Vermont in 1810. Morrill worked as a clerk, a merchant, and a farmer before being elected to the House of Representatives in 1854. Ever mindful of the need a sound education, in 1857 Morrill introduced a bill into the House "to establish at least one college in every state." The bill called for the federal government to donate public land to states and territories, which would then be sold. Proceeds from the sale of the land would thereafter be used to establish "colleges for the benefit of agriculture and the mechanic arts." After much debate, the bill was passed by both houses of Congress and in 1859 forwarded to President James Buchanan for his signature. Buchanan, however, was not enamored by the bill's provisions. He vetoed Morrill's bill on the belief that it would open the door to fraudulent land speculation, would cause friction between the states, and would be injurious to existing colleges. Moreover, he considered the legislation unconstitutional.

Undeterred, in 1861 Morrill reintroduced his bill, which was once again passed by Congress. This time, President Abraham Lincoln signed it into law. The intent of the new legislation was "to promote the liberal and practical education of the industrial classes in the several pursuits and professions in life." The Morrill Act, more commonly known as the Land-Grant College Act, provided for a grant of federal land to each state proportional to its representation in Congress. At 30,000 acres per senator and representative, even the smallest states received at least 90,000 acres of land. States with insufficient federal acreage within their borders were given land on the western frontier. The act stipulated that all revenue from the sale of the newly granted land would be invested in stocks. Money earned on the investments would thereafter become part of a perpetual endowment fund to establish at least one college in every state. Each

land-grant college would have "studies" focused on agriculture, engineering, and military science, fully accessible to a broad segment of the population interested in a liberal and practical education.

The 1862 Morrill Act ultimately granted over 17 million acres of federal land to the states, proceeds from which totaled some $7 million. By 1880 it had provided the means for the establishment of more than seventy institutions of higher learning throughout the Midwest and West, including the University of Wisconsin, University of Nebraska, Iowa State University, and Michigan State University. Though the act prohibited land grants to states "in a condition of rebellion or insurrection," after the Civil War southern states also took advantage of the Morrill Act to establish land grant colleges. The University of Mississippi, for example, was established as a land grant college in 1878.

By 1890 Morrill was an octogenarian who had represented Vermont in Congress for thirty-six years, thirteen in the House of Representatives and twenty-three in the Senate. Yet, he continued to tirelessly work for advancements in education. That year he introduced into Congress what has become known as the Second Morrill Act. It provided for an annual federal allocation of $50,000 to each state and territory, with the money then applied to instruction at each land-grant college. To prevent discrimination, the act also stipulated "That no money shall be paid out under this act to any State or Territory for the support and maintenance of a college where a distinction of race or color is made in the admission of students." Nevertheless, recognizing the reality of nineteenth-century segregation practices, the Second Morrill Act provided that "the establishment and maintenance of such colleges separately for white and colored students shall be held to be a compliance with the provisions of this act if the funds received in such

State or Territory be equitably divided." And to ensure observance with this provision, the act stipulated,

> That if any portion of the moneys received by the designated officer of the State or Territory for the further and more complete endowment, support, and maintenance of colleges, or of institutions for colored students . . . shall . . . be diminished or lost, or be misapplied, it shall be replaced by the State or Territory to which it belongs, and until so replaced no subsequent appropriation shall be apportioned or paid to such State or Territory.

The Morrill Acts of 1862 and 1890 were both visionary and ambitious. In a country fractured by war and subsequently enveloped by the turmoil of rapid change, the Morrill Acts provided focus and direction through the establishment of state institutions of higher learning.

National Archives Document

Be it enacted by the Senate and House of Representatives of the United States of America in Congress assembled, That there be granted to the several States, for the purposes hereinafter mentioned, an amount of federal land, to be apportioned to each State a quantity equal to thirty thousand acres for each senator and representative in Congress to which the States are respectively entitled by the apportionment under the census of eighteen hundred and sixty. . . .

SEC. 4. And be it further enacted, That all moneys derived from the sale of the lands aforesaid by the States to which the lands are apportioned, and from the sales of land scrip hereinbefore provided for, shall be invested in stocks . . . and that the moneys so invested shall constitute a perpetual fund, the capital of which shall remain forever undiminished . . . and the interest of which shall be inviolably appropriated . . . to the endowment, support, and maintenance of at least one college where the leading object shall be, without excluding other scientific and classical studies, and including military tactics, to teach such branches of learning as are related to agriculture and the mechanic arts. . . .

Provided, That when any Territory shall become a State and be admitted into the Union, such new State shall be entitled to the benefits of the said act. . . . ❈

Left: The Morrill Act helped to established land-grant colleges across the country, such as the University of Wisconsin, in Madison, Wisconsin, shown here.

Critical Thinking

Assess Significance

The 1862 Morrill Act required studies in "military tactics." This eventually led to the establishment of Reserve Officers Training Corps (ROTC) programs within land-grant state colleges and universities. Why do you think Morrill included this component in his legislation?

Determine Point of View

The 1862 Morrill Act was part of a nineteenth-century reform movement intent on improving society. At the forefront of educational reform was Horace Mann, a proponent of free, nonsectarian education. In speaking for the times, Mann stated that "slavery would abolish education, if it should invade a free state; education would abolish slavery, if it could invade a slave state." What did Mann mean?

Draw Conclusions

Over the years, several other pieces of legislation augmented the Morrill Acts. The Hatch Act of 1887 established agricultural experiment stations. The Nelson Amendment in 1907 extended the annual funding of $50,000 to each state and territory for land-grant colleges. The Smith-Lever Act of 1914 set up the Cooperative Extension System, which still today brings the expertise found at land-grant colleges into communities to assist with solving problems. In 1994 legislation conferred land-grant status on twenty-nine Native American tribal colleges. Why do you think the tenets of the 1862 Morrill Act have remained intact for well over one hundred years?

Research and Writing

Analysis

Though industrial growth was paramount in the United States during the latter nineteenth century, agriculture was in the midst of its own revolution. As people moved west and settled on the land, the number of farms increased from two million in 1860 to five-and-three-quarter million in 1890. Acres farmed increased almost fourfold during the same time period. The thirty-two million people engaged in farming produced rice, cotton, sugarcane, potatoes, pork, beef, and other commodities needed for their own survival and for thriving city markets. Recognizing this, the Second Morrill Act provided federal dollars for agricultural and "mechanical arts," whose curriculums gave "special reference to their applications in the industries of life." Research the growth in industry during the latter half of the nineteenth century. Why was a need seen for studies in engineering in colleges across the country? How did advances in industry benefit agriculture? What impact did industrial growth have on the country?

Historical Interpretation

Major changes occurred in education during the nineteenth century, much of it due to the efforts of Horace Mann. Research the history of education in America. What influence did Horace Mann exert on education? Why did he feel it needed reform? What were common schools? What were normal schools? What were country schools? What educational opportunities were afforded African-Americans? How did education evolve during the 1800s?

Link to the Past

As a result of the 1862 and 1890 Morrill Acts, every state and territory of the United States has at least one land-grant college. In 1907 the Department of Interior delineated a list of approved studies for land-grant colleges. They included instruction in agriculture, engineering, the English language, mathematics, the natural and physical sciences, economics, and preparation of teachers for the industrial fields, home economics, and agriculture. Research the institutions of high learning in your state. Which began as a land-grant college? What was its original academic purpose? What is the core curriculum of the land-grant institution today? How closely does the current curriculum compare with its original purpose, as well as the studies stipulated by the secretary of the interior for land-grant colleges in 1907? In your opinion, does the school meet the original intent of the 1862 and 1890 Morrill Acts?

1864 Wade-Davis Bill

"That every person who shall hereafter hold or exercise any office . . . in the rebel service, state or confederate, is hereby declared not to be a citizen of the United States."

—WADE-DAVIS BILL

HISTORICAL BACKGROUND

THE Civil War was a long and bloody conflict that tore apart the social and political fabric of the nation. It raged from one bloody, shattered battlefield to the next. The battles of Bull Run, Shiloh, Antietam, Gettysburg, Vicksburg, and many others on land and at sea hardened the resolve of both the North and the South. Through the heat of the summer and the cold winds of winter, the Civil War continued. What was once believed to be a short-lived rebellion became a war of monumental proportions, where a sense of nationality and brotherhood was replaced by anger, vengeance, and the firm desire to punish to the fullest extent all who were responsible for the mayhem.

President Abraham Lincoln hoped a rational and generous postwar peace plan would prompt Southern consideration to end the war. Hence, in December 1863, Lincoln issued his Proclamation of Amnesty and Reconstruction. In it he asserted his role as president of the United States to formulate a reconstruction plan that would allow rebellious states to rejoin the Union. To bolster his position, Lincoln cited his constitutional power to "grant reprieves and pardons for offences against the United States." With that in place, Lincoln continued,

> I, Abraham Lincoln, President of the United States, do proclaim, declare, and make known to all persons who have, directly or by implication, participated in the existing rebellion . . . that a full pardon is hereby granted to them and each of them, with restoration of all rights of property, except as to slaves.

Lincoln's only requirement to receive a full presidential pardon and regain confiscated property (except for former slaves) was for an

individual to take a loyalty oath and accept the abolition of slavery. Excluded from Lincoln's pardon were officers in the Confederate forces, individuals who left federal offices to fight for the Confederacy, or those who had mistreated prisoners of war. Lincoln also proclaimed that once ten percent of the qualified electorate had taken the citizenship oath, the state would be allowed to rejoin the Union. Additionally, a re-admitted state could once again be represented in Congress after it established a plan that provided for the abolition of slavery and for the education of African-Americans.

Though some in Congress supported Lincoln's plan, an influential group of Radical Republicans sought harsh punishment of the South. In February 1864 Senator Benjamin Wade and Representative Henry Davis introduced the Wade-Davis Bill into Congress. Along with requiring a majority of white males to swear an oath to the federal government, the bill also stipulated that each rebel state ban slavery and repudiate all Confederate debts. Moreover, the Wade-Davis Bill stipulated that "no person who has held or exercised any office, civil or military, state or confederate, under the rebel usurpation, or who has voluntarily borne arms against the United States, shall vote."

Congress passed the Wade-Davis Bill in the closing days of the 1864 legislative session. Lincoln, however, refused to sign it and instead let the legislation die through a "pocket veto." On July 8, 1864, he proclaimed, "I am . . . unprepared, by a formal approval of this Bill, to be inflexibly committed to any single plan of restoration." Lincoln's dismissal of the bill infuriated Radical Republicans. On August 4 the bill's sponsors published the Wade-Davis Manifesto in the *New York Tribune.* First, Wade and Davis accused the president of vetoing the bill for the sole purpose of re-election. "The President, by preventing this bill from becoming a law, holds the electoral votes of the Rebel States at the dictation of his personal ambition," they argued. They also accused Lincoln of usurping the power of Congress. "But he must understand," wrote Wade and Davis, "that the authority of Congress is paramount and must be respected . . . (H)e must confine himself to his executive duties-to obey and execute, not make the laws."

National Archives Document

SEC. 2. And be it further enacted, That so soon as the military resistance to the United States shall have been suppressed in any such state, and the people thereof shall have sufficiently returned to their obedience to the constitution and the laws of the United States, the provisional governor shall direct the marshal of the United States . . . to enroll all white male citizens of the United States, resident in the state in their respective counties, and to request each one to take the oath to support the constitution of the United States . . . and if the persons taking that oath shall amount to a majority of the persons enrolled in the state, he shall, by proclamation, invite the loyal people of the state to elect delegates to a convention charged to declare the will of the people of the state relative to the reestablishment of a state government subject to, and in conformity with, the constitution of the United States.

SEC. 7. And be it further enacted, That the convention shall declare, on behalf of the people of the state, their submission to the constitution and laws of the United States, and shall adopt the following provisions. . . .

First. No person who has held or exercised any office, civil or military, except offices merely ministerial, and military offices below the grade of colonel, state or confederate, under the usurping power, shall vote for or be a member of the legislature, or governor.

Second. Involuntary servitude is forever prohibited, and the freedom of all persons is guaranteed in said state.

Third. No debt, state or confederate, created by or under the sanction of the usurping power, shall be recognized or paid by the state.

SEC. 12. And be it further enacted, that all persons held to involuntary servitude or labor in the states aforesaid are hereby emancipated . . . and they and their posterity shall be forever free. . . . ✳

Below: Handwritten copy of the Wade-Davis Bill.

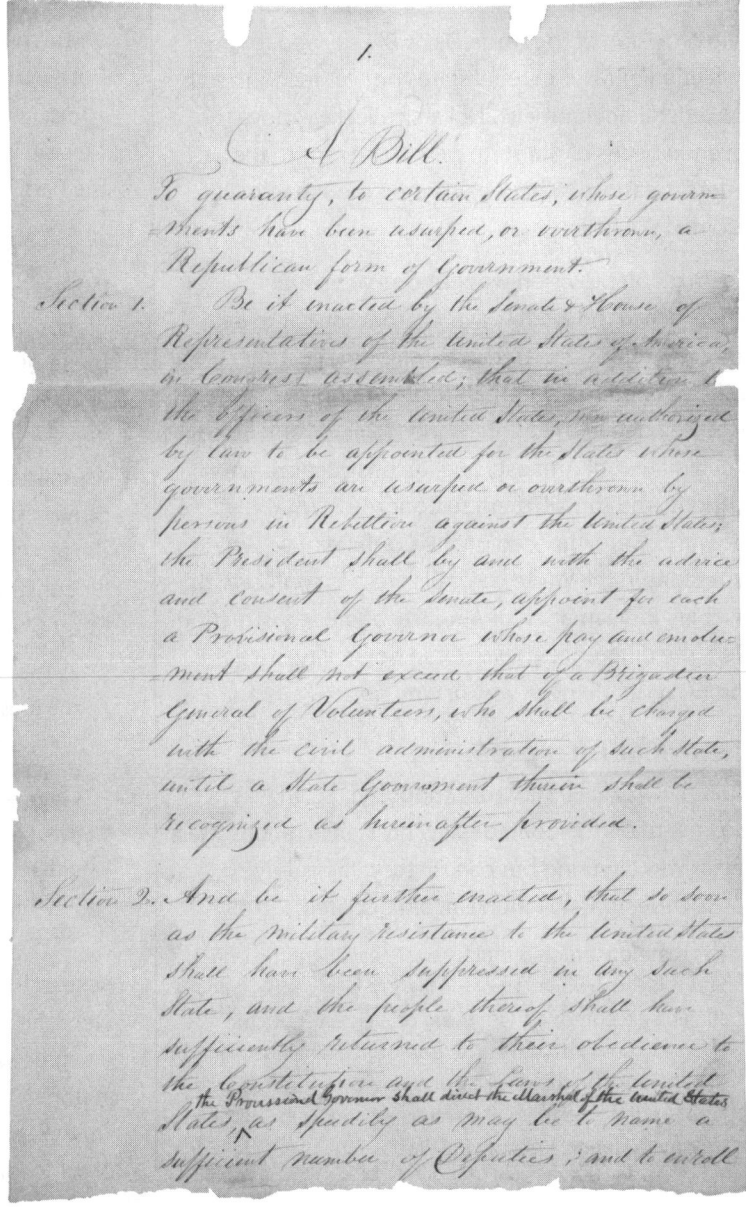

Critical Thinking

Classify Information

Reread the quote on page 264. Why do you think this provision was included in the Wade-Davis Bill?

Draw Conclusions

The conflict over whether the president or Congress held authority over Reconstruction was complicated by the fact that no language exists in the Constitution granting authority to either the president or to Congress in the case of secession. With all the forethought shown by the framers of the Constitution, why do you think this language is absent?

Determine Point of View

Do you feel the provisions of the Wade-Davis Bill were politically extreme? Explain.

Research and Writing

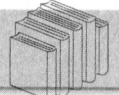

Analysis

One provision of the Wade-Davis Bill allowed for the collection of taxes in rebel states not yet recognized by the federal government. Dollars collected above the revenue needs of the state were to be sent to the federal treasury, to be repaid when the state finally rejoined the Union.

The taxation provision was just one of several provisions in the Wade-Davis Bill that sought to deal with "the states declared in rebellion against the United States" in a paternalistic and punitive manner. Access and read the entire Wade-Davis Bill and Lincoln's Proclamation of Amnesty and Reconstruction. What authority did the bill grant to Congress? What measures were imposed on the Confederacy? What provisions in the Wade-Davis Bill were in conflict with Lincoln's Proclamation of Amnesty and Reconstruction? Were the differences beyond the possibility of compromise? Explain why or why not.

Historical Interpretation

Though Radical Republicans thought Lincoln was far too lenient on the Confederacy, his stance on prisoners of war was anything but conciliatory. In his July 30, 1863, Order of Retaliation Lincoln declared:

> It is therefore ordered that for every soldier of the United States killed in violation of the laws of war, a rebel soldier shall be executed; and for every one enslaved by the enemy or sold into slavery, a rebel soldier shall be placed at hard labor on the public works and continued at such labor until the other shall be released and received the treatment due to a prisoner of war.

Access and Read Lincoln's Order of Retaliation. Then research the conditions of the prisoner of war camps both in the South and in the North. How did they compare? Why did conditions in Southern prison camps fuel the ire of Radical Republicans? How do you think the Radical Republicans responded to Lincoln's order?

Counterpoint

Wade and Davis believed President Lincoln overstepped his constitutional authority when he established the parameters by which a state could rejoin the Union in his December 1863 Proclamation of Amnesty and Reconstruction: "He has already exercised this dictatorial usurpation in Louisiana, and he defeated the bill to prevent its limitation," charged Wade and Davis. It wasn't the first time Lincoln had been accused of overstepping his constitutional limits. In *Ex parte Merryman*, Supreme Court Chief Justice Roger B. Taney wrote:

> As the case comes before me, therefore, I understand that the president not only claims the right to suspend the writ of habeas corpus himself, at his discretion, but to delegate that discretionary power to a military officer ... I had supposed it [habeas corpus] to be one of those points of constitutional law upon which there was no difference of opinion, and that it was admitted on all hands, that the privilege of the writ could not be suspended, except by act of congress.

Research the case of *Ex parte Merryman* (1861). What were the specifics of the case? Would you agree or disagree with Justice Taney's assessment of Lincoln's actions? Why? What was Lincoln's response to Justice Taney's order? Was his response unconstitutional? Why or why not?

1865 Lincoln's Second Inaugural Address

"A second term would be a great honor and a great labor, which together, perhaps I would not decline, if tendered."

—President Lincoln
IN A LETTER TO ILLINOIS CONGRESSMAN ELIHU WASHBURNE

HISTORICAL BACKGROUND

IN August 1864 Republican leader Thurlow Weed informed Secretary of State William Seward he had written to the president, "I have told Mr. Lincoln that his re-election was an impossibility," Weed conveyed. Indeed, Lincoln's prospects for a second term looked grim. Not only had widespread criticism of Lincoln's handing of the Civil War dimmed his prospects for re-election, no president had won a second term in thirty-two years. Additionally, not all in the North shared Lincoln's determination to free the slaves. Sensing political defeat, in late August Lincoln wrote the following memorandum:

> This morning, as for some days past, it seems exceedingly probably that this Administration will not be re-elected. Then it will be my duty to so cooperate with the President-elect, as to save the Union between the election and the inauguration; as he will have secured his election on such ground that he can not possibly save it afterwards.

On the Democratic ticket was George B. McClellan. The Democratic platform called for a cease-fire, along with a negotiated settlement with the South. McClellan, however, quickly dispensed with the Democratic position. In its place he pledged to wage war far more effectively than Lincoln.

On September 1, 1864, General William T. Sherman wired the president, "Atlanta is ours and fairly won." The fall of Atlanta became a military and political boon for Lincoln. When the November votes were counted, Lincoln proved the victor. Despite the fact that McClellan captured forty-five percent of the popular vote, his electoral vote tallied a meager twenty-one. Lincoln, however, won every Union state, with the exception of Delaware, his birth state of Kentucky, and New Jersey. With 55 percent of the popular vote and 212 electoral votes, the president had managed a landslide victory. Republicans also captured every governorship and state legislature in the North, along with three-fourths of all Congressional elections. The 1864 vote proved to be an election extraordinaire for the Republicans and a mandate for Lincoln to continue his war plans.

On March 4, 1865, Lincoln delivered his Second Inaugural Address. After four years of horrific war, he had become convinced that the war had a higher purpose beyond the disputed right of a state to determine its own social and political destiny. Lincoln spoke of the Civil War as a war directed by God to end slavery—the great sin of the South.

> If we shall suppose that American slavery is one of those offenses which, in the providence of God, must needs come, but which, having continued through His appointed time, He now wills to remove, and that He gives to both North and South this terrible war as the woe due to those by whom the offense came. . . . Fondly do we hope, fervently do we pray, that this mighty scourge of war may speedily pass away. Yet, if God wills that it continue until all the wealth piled by the bondsman's two hundred and fifty years of unrequited toil shall be sunk, and until every drop of blood drawn with the lash shall be paid by another drawn with the sword.

In his address, Lincoln extended the hand of reconciliation to the South and provided an example of gracious humility for the North: "With malice toward none, with charity for all." Lincoln's great hope was for a nation that could put aside the strife and passions of war and "do all which may achieve and cherish a just, and a lasting peace among ourselves." It was a tall order. The South lay ravaged by an uncompromising Union army. With a Northern victory in the offing, Radical Republicans in Congress were intent on waging legislative vengeance on the South. Yet, in his Second Inaugural Address, Lincoln asked the country to place forgiveness above revenge. His eloquence sought conciliation and the hope of a reunited nation.

National Archives Document

On the occasion corresponding to this four years ago, all thoughts were anxiously directed to an impending civil-war. All dreaded it—all sought to avert it. . . . Both parties deprecated war; but one of them would make war rather than let the nation survive; and the other would accept war rather than let it perish. And the war came.

One-eighth of the whole population were colored slaves, not distributed generally over the Union, but localized in the southern part of it. These slaves constituted a peculiar and powerful interest. All knew that this interest was somehow the cause of the war. To strengthen, perpetuate, and extend this interest was the object for which the insurgents would rend the Union even by war, while the Government claimed no right to do more than to restrict the territorial enlargement of it. Neither party expected for the war the magnitude or the duration which it has already attained. Neither anticipated that the cause of the conflict might cease with or even before the conflict itself should cease. Each looked for an easier triumph, and a result less fundamental and astounding. . . .

With malice toward none, with charity for all, with firmness in the right as God gives us to see the right, let us strive on to finish the work we are in, to bind up the nation's wounds, to care for him who shall have borne the battle and for his widow and his orphan, to do all which may achieve and cherish a just and lasting peace among ourselves and with all nations. ✳

Below: A depiction of Abraham Lincoln taking the oath of office for the second time at the U.S. Capitol on March 4, 1865.

LINCOLN TAKING THE OATH AT HIS SECOND INAUGURATION, MARCH 4, 1865.—PHOTOGRAPHED BY GARDNER, WASHINGTON.—[SE

Critical Thinking

Analyze Cause and Effect

In speaking to the 148th Ohio Regiment, Lincoln campaigned, "We are striving to maintain the government and institutions of our fathers, to enjoy them ourselves, and transmit them to our children and our children's children forever." Lincoln was presented as the candidate who would continue the fight until full victory was at hand. A vote for McClellan, according to Lincoln's supporters, might bring a rapid end to the conflict, yet result in a country permanently divided. Although the soldiers' vote amounted to only four percent of the total vote, the vast majority were cast for Lincoln. As one soldier commented, "I can not vote for one thing and fight for another." Why didn't most soldiers vote for McClellan, since such a vote offered the hope of a swift return home?

Draw Conclusions

Lincoln wrote of the great importance of the 1864 presidential election.

We can not have free government without elections; and if the rebellion could force us to forego, or postpone a national election it might fairly claim to have already conquered and ruined us.… The election … has demonstrated that a people's government can sustain a national election, in the midst of a great civil war. Until now it has not been known to the world that this was a possibility.

How was the 1864 election a test of democracy?

Determine Point of View

The Confederate states observed the 1864 election with profound interest. "We are fighting for existence; and by fighting alone can independence be gained," Jefferson Davis told the Confederate Congress following the Union election. "Nothing has changed in the purpose of its Government, in the indomitable valor of its troops, or in the unquenchable spirit of its people." Why do you think the South hoped for a McClellan victory? In what way was Davis attempting to build morale following Lincoln's re-election as President of the United States?

Research and Writing

Analysis

Research the 1864 presidential election. Why did the Republicans choose Lincoln as the presidential candidate even though public sentiment for him was lukewarm? Why did the Republican Party use the name National Unity Party? Who were the "Copperheads"? What role did they play in the election? Why was McClellan's position that he could wage a more strategic and effective war than Lincoln ironic? Why did John C. Frémont eventually withdraw from the campaign? What do you think won the election for Lincoln?

Biography

In 1876 Frederick Douglass said of Lincoln,

He [Lincoln] was assailed by Abolitionists; he was assailed by slave-holders; he was assailed by the men who were for peace at any price; he was assailed by those who were for a more vigorous prosecution of the war; he was assailed for not making the war an abolition war; and he was bitterly assailed for making the war an abolition war.…

Research the writings of Abraham Lincoln, including Lincoln's Second Inaugural Address. Based on his words, would you consider Lincoln proslavery, antislavery, or ambivalent? Did his position change over the course of the war? What do you think he hoped to achieve during his second term in office?

Relating Events

In January 1865 John Wilkes Booth met with a group of conspirators to make plans for Lincoln's demise. Booth blamed Lincoln for all the ills that had befallen the South. Together, Booth and his co-conspirators contrived to kill President Lincoln, Vice President Andrew Johnson, Secretary of State William Seward, and General Grant. Research the assassination of President Lincoln. What was John Wilkes Booth's background? Who were his co-conspirators? What justice befell them? What happened to Johnson and Seward? What did Booth hope to accomplish by Lincoln's assassination? How did the nation respond to Lincoln's death?

1865 Surrender of the Army of Northern Virginia

"We lost near everything but honor."

—GENERAL JUBAL A. EARLY
IN A LETTER TO GENERAL ROBERT E. LEE

HISTORICAL BACKGROUND

THE fall of Atlanta in 1864 was a disaster for the Confederate cause. Union forces had struck deep in the heart of the South, conquering its second-largest city. In a futile effort to save Atlanta, General John Hood had ordered the Army of the Tennessee to stall General William Tecumseh Sherman's Union army as it advanced toward the city. Subsequent Confederate defeats at the Battles of Peachtree Creek (July 20), Atlanta (July 22), and Ezra Church (July 28) further reduced Hood's troops by 15,000 men. Inevitably, a victorious Sherman forced the evacuation of all Confederate troops from Atlanta. A letter from Sherman to the mayor of Atlanta presaged the cataclysm of the coming months: "War is cruelty, and you cannot refine it, and those who brought war into our country deserve all the curses and maledictions a people can pour out."

The loss of Atlanta deepened the pallor of gloom already engulfing the Confederacy. For months, General Robert E. Lee's once imposing Army of Northern Virginia had been in retreat, pursued by General Ulysses S. Grant, a military mind the rival of Lee. Grant's strategy was unremitting—wear down the enemy until the simple attrition of soldiers caused the eventual collapse of the Confederate army. To that end, a determined Grant relentlessly sent his troops against Lee's resilient and spirited forces. The losses on both sides were great. When the gunsmoke cleared over the Battle of Spotsylvania (May 8–12, 1864), over 27,000 Confederate and Union soldiers lay dead or wounded. At Cold Harbor, Grant's troops suffered 7,000 casualties in twenty minutes of hellish fighting. An entry in a diary found on the body of a Union soldier captured the hopelessness of the

moment with its grim forecast, "June 3, 1864, Cold Harbor, Virginia. I was killed." Grant's offensive continued as he pursued Lee to Petersburg on the outskirts of Richmond. For seven long weeks, Confederate and Union had been embroiled in intense and deadly fighting. Confederate casualties, numbering 35,000 to that point, had cut the size of Lee's army in half. Grant's Army of the Potomac suffered even greater losses—65,000 struck down in battle. Stalemated for the next ten months in trenches near Petersburg, Lee's besieged army suffered further from cold, hunger, and desertion.

The circumstances were just as dire for other Confederate forces. In an effort to destroy another Union army before it reached Nashville, and against the advice of his commanders, General Hood attacked at the Battle of Franklin (November 30, 1864). The results were grisly. In the ensuing five-hour battle, the Army of Tennessee lost over 6,000 soldiers, bodies falling upon bodies. In one of the numerous ironies of the Civil War, Theodrick Carter, seeing his homestead for the first time in three years, died in the fighting. Meanwhile, General Sherman was making good on his promise to "march to the sea." On November 15, he burned the city of Atlanta. Moving on toward Savannah, Sherman's army looted and destroyed crops, livestock, and property at will, cutting a path of destruction 250 miles long. On December 24, Sherman offered the city of Savannah as a Christmas present to Lincoln. Moving north into South Carolina, the Union army unleashed brutal vengeance against the state that had championed the cause of secession. Sherman's troops set fire to town after town. On February 14, his forces moved into Columbia, burning the state's capitol building to the ground.

On April 2, 1865, Grant launched a final attack against Lee's forces, capturing Petersburg. Recognizing defeat at hand, Jefferson Davis gathered what he could carry and escaped from Richmond by train, only to be captured on May 10 at Irwinville, Georgia. On April 4, Lincoln walked the streets of a burned-out Richmond—torched this time by the Confederates to destroy anything of military or industrial value—and sat at the desk of Jefferson Davis. After several futile attempts to break through Union lines, and against the shouts of his soldiers pledging their willingness to continue the fight, on April 9 Lee chose to surrender what remained of his battle-worn army in the village of Appomattox Court House. Grant honored Lee's request for his soldiers to keep their side arms, horses, and mules. The formal surrender ceremony of the Army of Northern Virginia took place three days later. Afterward, each Confederate soldier received his parole papers, guaranteeing him safe return to his home. It was the unofficial end to a Civil War that had cost over 600,000 lives.

NATIONAL ARCHIVES DOCUMENT

Appomattox Court House Virginia

April 10, 1865

Agreement entered into this day in regard to the surrender of the Army of Northern Virginia to the United States Authorities.

1st The troops shall march by Brigades and Detachments to a designated point, stock their Arms, deposit their flags, Sabers, Pistols, etc. and from thence march to their homes under charge of their Officers, superintended by their respective Division and Corps Commanders, Officers, retaining their side arms, and the authorized number of private horses.

2. All public horses and public property of all kinds to be turned over to Staff Officers designated by the United States Authorities.

3. Such transportation as may be agreed upon as necessary for the transportation of the Private baggage of Officers will be allowed to accompany the Officers, to be turned over at the end of the trip to the nearest U.S. Quarter Masters, receipts being taken for the same.

4. Couriers and Wounded men of the artillery and Cavalry whose horses are their own private property will be allowed to retain them.

Below: A depiction of General Robert E. Lee signing the Articles of Agreement, surrendering the Army of Northern Virginia.

5. The surrender of the Army of Northern Virginia shall be construed to include all the forces operating with that Army on the 8th inst., the date of commencement of negotiation for surrender, except such bodies of Cavalry as actually made their escape previous to the surrender, and except also such forces of Artillery as were more than Twenty (20) miles from Appomattox Court House at the time of Surrender on the 9th inst. ❋

Critical Thinking

Analyze Cause and Effect

What effect do you think the surrender of the Army of Northern Virginia had on the morale of other Confederate troops and armies?

Draw Conclusions

Following Lee's official surrender, General Joshua Chamberlain ordered his Union troops to offer the Confederate soldiers an honorary salute as they filed past. The Confederate soldiers returned the act of respect. Chamberlain recalled later that the Confederate soldiers passed in complete silence, without the usual military fanfare of drums and trumpets. No cheers were uttered. No comments made. Given this final blow to the Confederacy, why were the proceedings so solemn?

Determine Point of View

Though originally not part of the surrender agreement, Grant acquiesced to Lee's request for his men to keep their horses and mules once Grant learned that the animals belonged to each man. Why was this final provision a significant concession on the part of Grant? What is your assessment of the articles of surrender?

Research and Writing

Analysis

In Grant's reports chronicling the surrender of Lee's troops at Appomattox, he notes that he was jubilant when first informed of Lee's offer of surrender. However, upon meeting Lee, Grant commented that he,

> felt like anything rather than rejoicing at the downfall of a foe who had fought so long and valiantly, and had suffered so much for a cause, though that cause was, I believe, one of the worst for which a people ever fought, and one for which there was the least excuse. I do not question, however, the sincerity of the great mass of those who were opposed to us.

After surrendering, Lee informed Grant that "his army was in a very bad condition for want of food, and that they were without forage; that his men had been living for some days on parched corn," Grant arranged for Lee to have "all the provisions wanted" for his remaining 25,000 troops. Access and read Grant's notes describing the days surrounding the surrender of Lee's army. What is discussed? How do the discussions concerning surrender proceed? Why, after four years of harsh warfare, was there a distinct absence of overt hostility at the surrender proceedings? What happened to Lee following the surrender of his troops? What happened to Grant?

Relating Events

On April 11, from the balcony of the White House, Lincoln stated,

> We all agree that the seceded States, so called, are out of their proper practical relation with the Union; and that the sole object of the government, civil and military, in regard to those States is to again get them into that proper practical relation. I believe it is not only possible, but in fact, easier, to do this, without deciding, or even considering, whether these states have even been out of the Union, than with it.... Let us all join in doing the acts necessary to restoring the proper practical relations between these states and the Union.

Three days later the president lay dead, the victim of an assassin's bullet. Lincoln's death elevated Andrew Johnson to the presidency. Research Johnson's Reconstruction plans. How closely did Johnson follow Lincoln's plans for Reconstruction? How did plans proceed for the re-entry of rebel states into the Union? What barriers resulted? What was the reaction of the Radical Republicans? How long did Reconstruction last? How would you define the Reconstruction of the South?

Historical Interpretation

The Civil War was incredibly costly in lives and in property. Its social, economic, and political impact would last for decades. Research the costs of the Civil War. What was its effect on the North and on the South? Did the war produce any benefits? In what way did the war transform the South? How would you characterize the war's impact on the North? Did the dissolution of the Confederacy end regional disunity?

1872 Act Establishing Yellowstone National Park

"Standing there . . . I thought how utterly impossible it would be to describe to another the sensations inspired by such a presence."

—NATHANIEL PITT LANGFORD

HISTORICAL BACKGROUND

IT was a wonderment beyond their imaginings. In 1870 Nathaniel Pitt Langford and his fellow geologists overlooked the Midway Geyer Basin on the Firehole River. They gazed in awe as boiling water, trailed by rolling plumes of steam, erupted from Earth. At times flowing and graceful, and at other times energized and spirited, the steam from the mighty geysers seemed to dance in the air as it rose over the majestic landscape. Langford marveled, "As I took in the scene, I realized my own littleness, my helplessness, my dread exposure to destruction, my inability to cope with or even comprehend the mighty architecture of nature."

Almost seventy years earlier, explorer and trapper John Colter had been captivated by similar mysteries of nature stumbled upon while trapping beaver along the Gardner River in present-day Montana. Colter's vivid descriptions of pots of heated mud bubbling from Earth were dismissed by many as figments of an overly zealous imagination. Yet, Colter had been a member of the famed Corps of Discovery, the 1803 expedition led by Lewis and Clark. That group had meticulously documented the richness and diversity in fauna, plant life, and landscape to be found in the West. Perhaps, some reasoned, Colter's wanderlust had led him to an area of the most astonishing and most improbable spectacles of nature. At a time when the vast West held the thrill of a large present waiting to be unwrapped, anything seemed possible.

Known to the Minnetaree tribe as *Mi-tsi-a-da-zi*, or "river of the yellow rocks," the area that became Yellowstone National Park was once traversed by the Shoshone, Bannock, Blackfoot, Flathead, Nez Perce, Ute, Crow, Piegan, and Paiute Indians as they followed herds of bison. Archeological studies indicate that Native Americans inhabited Yellowstone for some ten thousand years before Colter happened upon the mysterious thermal area.

In the early 1800s, Yellowstone's pristine land was populated by the Shoshone and the Nez Perce, as well as by their adversary—the Blackfoot. They lived as their ancestors had—free and independent. However, the marvels of Yellowstone would soon bring other white explorers and trappers into the region. Before long, survey expeditions guided by the U.S. Army Corps of Topographical Engineers began to map the area in order to facilitate westward expansion. Momentous change was in the offing—all happening within the span of one human lifetime.

By the time of the Civil War, covered wagons loaded with the belongings of westward-bound pioneers moved along trails cutting through the western frontier. Mining had brought great waves of migrants to scour the western hills in search of gold and silver. Small towns grew into such bustling cities as Denver, San Francisco, and Dodge City. Yet, much of Yellowstone's geology remained uncharted. Its potential for mineral extraction, however, had not gone unnoticed. With industrial growth at full speed, the country's need for natural resources was paramount. Accordingly, on March 2, 1867, Congress authorized the first of what became known as the Four Great Surveys of the West. The object of the expedition was to study the geological and natural resources found along the Fortieth Parallel, the route of the planned transcontinental railroad. Placed in charge of the survey was Clarence King. In 1880 King reflected on the importance of the expedition, "Eighteen sixty-seven marks, in the history of national geological work, a turning point, when the science ceased to be dragged in the dust of rapid exploration and took a commanding position in the professional work of the country."

By 1871 drawings and photographs produced by Ferdinand Hayden's geological survey team, were presented to Congress. Concern was expressed that the marvels of Yellowstone urgently required protection from those who sought to exploit its mineral resources. Convinced, a majority in Congress voted to preserve the Yellowstone region as a national treasure. On March 1, 1872, President Ulysses S. Grant signed the Act Establishing Yellowstone National Park into law. With Nathaniel Pitt Langford assigned as its first superintendent, the new park included some 2,142,720 acres of land in the Wyoming and Montana territories. The legislation launched the establishment of a system of national parks. In 1890 Congress established Yosemite, Sequoia, and General Grant National Parks. That same year Congress also passed legislation establishing the Chickamauga-Chattanooga National Military Park, the first of several future parks commemorating the battles of the Civil War.

By 1916 the U.S. Department of Interior supervised fourteen national parks. United States soldiers were put to work developing park roads and buildings, as well as enforcing regulations against overuse of the land. However, with legislative opinions clashing over the regulation of natural resources versus their preservation, the country lacked a clear policy for protecting the country's heritage and beauty. The answer was found in the economic benefits of tourism. After an exhaustive public relations campaign, in August 1916 President Woodrow Wilson established the National Park Service as an agency within the Department of Interior.

NATIONAL ARCHIVES DOCUMENT

Be it enacted by the Senate and House of Representatives of the United States of America in Congress assembled, That the tract of land in the Territories of Montana and Wyoming, lying near the headwaters of the Yellowstone River, and described as follows, to wit, commencing at the junction of Gardiner's river with the Yellowstone river, and running east to the meridian passing ten miles to the eastward of the most eastern point of Yellowstone lake; thence south along said meridian to the parallel of latitude passing ten miles south of the most southern point of Yellowstone lake; thence west along said parallel to the meridian passing fifteen miles west of the most western point of Madison lake; thence north along said meridian to the latitude of the junction of Yellowstone and Gardiner's rivers; thence east to the place of beginning, is hereby reserved and withdrawn from settlement, occupancy, or sale under the laws of the United States, and dedicated and set apart as a public park or pleasuring-ground for the benefit and enjoyment of the people; and all persons who shall locate or settle upon or occupy the same, or any part thereof, except as hereinafter provided, shall be considered trespassers and removed therefrom. ✳

Below: A waterfall at Yellowstone National Park.

Critical Thinking

Assess Significance

The Organic Act of March 3, 1879, established the U.S. Geological Survey within the Department of Interior. Among other provisions, the legislation "directed [the Geological Survey] to classify the public lands and examine the geological structure, mineral resources, and products within and outside the national domain." Why was this legislation significant?

Draw Conclusions

The National Park Service Organic Act of 1916 directed the newly established agency to

promote and regulate the use of the Federal areas known as national parks, monuments, and … to conserve the scenery and the natural and historic objects and the wildlife therein and to provide for the enjoyment of the same in such manner and by such means as will leave them unimpaired for the enjoyment of future generations.

In what way did the establishment of the National Park Service help to direct a policy of preservation rather than the exploitation of America's resources and heritage?

Classify Information

Why was the 1872 Act Establishing Yellowstone National Park visionary?

Research and Writing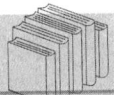

Analysis

Choose two of the 388 parks supervised today by the National Park Service. Research the history of each park. Compare and contrast each park's purpose and scope. Evaluate the park's development over the years against the 1916 legislative mandate issued to the National Park Service by Congress.

Relating Events

The Geological Exploration of the Fortieth Parallel, led by Clarence King in 1867, was followed by surveys of Nebraska, Wyoming, and Colorado. Each of the Great Four Surveys were approved by Congress and functioned under the supervision of the Interior Department. Research the Four Great Surveys. Who led the surveys? What area was surveyed? How long did they take? What did they document? How significant were their discoveries? How did the advent of photography bolster preservation efforts? In what way did the Four Great Surveys help to establish a domestic policy focused on the preservation of America's unique landforms, plants, and animals?

Link to the Past

One provision of the Act Establishing Yellowstone National Park charged that the secretary of interior "provide against the wanton destruction of the fish and game found within said park, and against their capture or destruction for the purposes of merchandise or profit." In 1872 wolves were indigenous to Yellowstone. Considered a dangerous predator, deliberate federal extermination programs led to the near extinction of wolves. Between 1914 and 1926, some 136 wolves were intentionally killed at Yellowstone National Park. They were the last wolves seen at Yellowstone for years to come. Later years brought a greater awareness of the necessity of the wolf as a part of a functioning ecosystem. To that end, beginning in 1987 the U.S. Fish and Wildlife Service established the Northern Rocky Mountain Wolf Recovery Plan, the goal of which was to reintroduce breeding pairs of wolves into Greater Yellowstone. The plan was not without controversy. Research the Northern Rocky Mountain Wolf Recovery Plan. What were the specifics of the plan? Why was it controversial? What has been the result?

1883 The Pendleton Act

> *"History has tried hard to teach us that we can't have good government under politicians. Now, to go and stick one at the very head of the government couldn't be wise."*
>
> —MARK TWAIN

HISTORICAL BACKGROUND

GOVERNMENT seemed to mushroom following the Civil War. By 1876 some 127,000 persons were on the federal payroll. Many of those employed were part of a long-established hiring system whereby individuals were rewarded with jobs in government as payment for their support of the reigning political party. Under what was termed the "spoils system," the capabilities of government employees often came second to their party affiliation. Consequently, with each newly elected president, people who had jobs in government often lost them, replaced by a new group of political cronies. According to President Andrew Jackson, who had fostered the spoils system some fifty years earlier, such rotation in office made for good government. Jackson reasoned,

> No man has any more intrinsic right to official station than another. . . . The duties of all public officers are, or at least admit of being made, so plain and simple that men of intelligence may readily qualify themselves for their performance.

There it was. Anybody, according to Jackson, could learn to be capable in public office, given time and opportunity.

Though revered by Jackson and others, the spoils system did little for continuity in the administration of government policies. Each time a new senator or congressman was elected, people holding federal government jobs in his state or district scrambled to find new work. The turnover of employees caused a series of starts and stops that confounded well-intended legislation. With job tenure short, and loyalty to the position fleeting, government functioned in a series of gasps. Moreover, persons hired for managing the nation's policies were often untrained and indifferent to their duties. Significant

time was spent managing the system. President Benjamin Harrison, for example, estimated that he spent, on average, five hours each day responding to requests for employment in the federal government.

Perhaps the most pernicious aspect of the spoils system was its potential to foster corruption in government, as those who achieved employment through political favor contrived to gain financially from their position. The spoils system's propensity for corruption, for example, characterized the scandals that peppered the patronage-laden administration of President Grant, in particular the Whiskey Ring scandal.

The election of 1880 sparked a new round of presidential hopefuls, along with calls from both Democrats and Republicans for reform in government. Republican James A. Garfield handily won the election. As president, Garfield quickly tired of incessant patronage requests from what he called "disciplined office hunters" who, prior to his inauguration, had been "lying in wait like vultures for a wounded bison." Charles Guiteau, a disgruntled attorney who had unsuccessfully sought public employment, and who believed he had been called upon to save the Republican Party, gunned down Garfield on July 2, 1881. With Garfield's death, Vice-President Chester A. Arthur rose to the presidency. As a former administrator of the customs house in New York City, Arthur was well versed on government payrolls embellished by patronage.

Much to the dismay of advocates of the spoils system, President Arthur proved to be a reform-minded president. A public clamoring for civil service reform, along with the assassination of Garfield, lent a sense of urgency for legislative action. After much congressional wrangling, President Arthur signed the Civil Service Reform Act of 1883 into law. Commonly known as the Pendleton Act for one of its most ardent supporters, Representative George Hunt Pendleton of Ohio, the new law promised an end to employment through political favor. The main provision of the bill established a bipartisan Civil Service Commission charged with administering employment based on merit rather than political affiliation.

The Pendleton Act quickly impacted federal employment. In 1883 the Civil Service Commission had authority over fewer than 15,000 jobs, or about 14 percent of all government employees. By 1887 some 86,000 federal employees, almost half the federal payroll, were in positions classified for oversight by the Civil Service Commission. By 1920, some 80 percent of all federal employees were subject to the provisions of the Pendleton Act. Today, civil service exams are required by most individuals seeking government employment. Exemptions to the law are only allowed for jobs found at the highest policy-making levels in government.

NATIONAL ARCHIVES DOCUMENT

An act to regulate and improve the civil service of the United States.

Be it enacted by the Senate and House of Representatives of the United States of America in Congress assembled, That the president is authorized to appoint, by and with the advice and consent of the Senate, three persons, not more than two of whom shall be adherents of the same party, as Civil Service Commissioners, and said three commissioners shall constitute the United States Civil Service Commission. Said commissioners shall hold no other official place under the United States.

SECOND. And, among other things, said rules shall provide and declare, as nearly as the conditions of good administration will warrant, as follows:

First, for open, competitive examinations for testing the fitness of applicants for the public service. . . .

Second, that all the offices, places, and employments so arranged or to be arranged in classes shall be filled by selections according to grade from among those graded highest as the results of such competitive examinations.

Third, appointments to the public service aforesaid in the departments at Washington shall be apportioned among the several States and Territories and the District of Columbia upon the basis of population as ascertained at the last preceding census. . . .

Fourth, that there shall be a period of probation before any absolute appointment or employment aforesaid.

Fifth, that no person in the public service is for that reason under any obligations to contribute to any political fund, or to render any political service, and that he will not be removed or otherwise prejudiced for refusing to do so.

Below: The Pendleton Act undid the spoils system fostered by President Andrew Jackson.

CIVIL SERVICE REFORM.
OFFICE-SEEKER. "St. Jackson, can't you save us? Can't you give us something?"

Sixth, that no person in said service has any right to use his official authority or influence to coerce the political action of any person or body.

Seventh, there shall be non-competitive examinations in all proper cases before the commission, when competent persons do not compete, after notice has been given of the existence of the vacancy, under such rules as may be prescribed by the commissioners as to the manner of giving notice.

Eighth, that notice shall be given in writing by the appointing power to said commission of the persons selected for appointment or employment from among those who have been examined. . . . ✳

Critical Thinking

Draw Conclusions

Why do you think the Pendleton Act was initially limited to about fourteen percent of all government jobs?

Analyze Cause and Effect

Despite the scandals that had rocked his presidency, in 1880 former President Ulysses S. Grant seemed the strongest candidate for the Republican nomination. However, after thirty-four ballots, the Republican National Convention couldn't decide if Grant, James Blaine, or John Sherman should get the nomination. In a surprise move, on the thirty-fifth ballot, delegates from Wisconsin cast sixteen votes for James A. Garfield of Ohio. Garfield, who was Sherman's campaign manager, rose to protest but was ruled out of order. On the next ballot Garfield received the Republican nomination for president. Why do you think the Republicans chose a "dark horse" as its candidate for the country's highest office in 1880?

Compare and Contrast

The Hatch Act, passed by Congress in 1939, imposed significant restrictions on the ability of government employees to participate in political activities. The law pertained specifically to federal employees, District of Columbia (D.C.) government employees, and certain state and local government employees. In 1993, Congress amended the Hatch Act in order to allow federal employees to take an active role in political campaigns. Greater restrictions, however, apply to individuals serving in the military. In what way do the Pendleton Act of 1883 and the Hatch Act of 1939 compare? How do they contrast? In what way do they work together to achieve political reform?

Research and Writing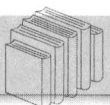

Analysis

Access and read the entire Pendleton Act. Analyze its provisions. What parameters did it set for employment? How did it structure the Civil Service Commission? What fail-safes against patronage were included in the act? Why was the act constructed to be independent of federal cabinet positions?

Counterpoint

A December 2, 2004, online article in the *Boston Globe* presented a stinging critique of the civil service system.

> The Boston Police Department could hire more strategically, promote from within more intelligently, and maintain better internal discipline if it were freed from the restrictions of civil service. Once a protection against vindictive managers and cronyism in hiring, the civil service system is now an impediment to progress.... Boston's Police Commissioner ... rightly sees the combination of the civil service examination and veterans' preference rules as a barrier to hiring minority officers or candidates with foreign language skills.... The basic civil service examination measures a candidate's reading and math abilities, important for tasks associated with police work. But it doesn't measure communication skills and judgment.

Research three occupations in your area that require passage of a civil service exam for employment. Support or refute the position presented in the *Boston Globe* article.

Link to the Past

Today, almost three million people are employed by the federal government in every type of job from those who work directly with elected officials to those who manage federal programs in states and territories far from Washington, D.C. Research the Civil Service Commission. What types of jobs are under the Civil Service Commission's oversight and control? What types of jobs are not? Through what process does an individual gain civil service employment? What restrictions are placed on such employees? What are the advantages of holding such jobs?

1887 The Interstate Commerce Act

> *"No country can be well governed unless its citizens as a body keep religiously before their minds that they are the guardians of the law."*
>
> —Mark Twain and Dudley Warner, *The Gilded Age*

HISTORICAL BACKGROUND

In 1874 Jay Gould acquired controlling stock in the Union Pacific Railroad. It was a fortune in the making. Gould had already established himself as a master of fraudulent business practices as the architect of the 1869 gold-for-profit scheme known as Black Friday. Following acquisition of the Union Pacific, Gould continued to purchase smaller western rail companies until he controlled some 16,000 miles of track, including half the mileage southwest of St. Louis and Kansas City. Besides the Union Pacific, his railroad holdings included the Erie, Missouri Pacific, Colorado Central, St. Louis Southwestern, Texas & Pacific, and several others. Gould also had controlling interests in several telegraph companies, including Western Union. Rivaling Gould for control of the rail lines was Cornelius Vanderbilt. Having secured control of the railroads leading into New York City, in 1873 Vanderbilt linked rail lines leading from New York to Chicago.

The United States had entered the Gilded Age, a time of dynamic change as new technologies redefined the political, social, and economic landscape of the country. Changes in laws governing corporations allowed for large-scale speculation in land and industry—and for large-scale corruption in business and politics. Fortunes were made and lost overnight, as cunning investors found ways to manipulate the stock market to their advantage. Attention centered on the building of America's infrastructure—its communication and transportation lines. Those who controlled both held the key to the country's economic future, and to their own fortunes. Politicians, who at times were willing partners in schemes to reap huge profits in shady corporate deals, played a significant role in the rapid expansion of America's transportation systems.

The power to build railroads linking the country's financial and agricultural centers became concentrated in a few corporations led by men collectively called railroad barons. However, the railroad barons, who controlled the transit of goods and people, exacerbated farmers' problems by charging more to ship their crops than they charged manufactures to ship goods. By controlling the markets in several geographic areas, railroad monopolies were able to set prices and exclude the competition by simply buying a competing rail line. In response to such schemes, in 1867 incensed farmers turned to the Patrons of Husbandry (the Grange) to obtain political action favoring farmers over the railroads. Allying with the Mugwumps, politicians intent on establishing more efficient and rational government, in 1871 the Grange succeeded in obtaining railroad regulatory legislation in Illinois. Other Midwestern states soon followed. Laws regulating their business practices within a state, collectively known as Granger Laws, were battled by the railroads, and inevitably ended at the door of the U.S. Supreme Court.

In a series of decisions known as the Granger Cases, the Supreme Court wrestled with these state laws. In *Peik v. Chicago & N. W. R. Co* (1876), for example, the Court held that "until Congress acts in reference to the relations of . . . interstate commerce, it is certainly within the power of Wisconsin to regulate its fares, &c., so far as they are of domestic concern." However, in *Wabash, St. Louis Pacific Railway Company v. State of Illinois* (1886) the Court further stated, "It is not, and never has been, the deliberate opinion of a majority of this court that a statute of a state which attempts to regulate the fares and charges by railroad companies within its limits, for a transportation which constitutes a part of commerce among the states, is a valid law."

Recognizing the need for federal legislation, on February 4, 1887, Congress approved the Interstate Commerce Act. This momentous legislation created the Interstate Commerce Commission. The bill required that shipping rates be "reasonable and just," that rates had to be published, and that secret rebates for preferred customers were in violation of the law.

It also prohibited price discrimination in small markets. The White House at the time was occupied by Grover Cleveland. Though President Cleveland had a distinct disdain for big government, he believed the sovereign power of the federal government over railroads was of necessity. In the spirit of the public good, Cleveland signed the bill into law.

NATIONAL ARCHIVES DOCUMENT

An Act to regulate Commerce.

Be it enacted by the Senate and House of Representatives of the United States of America in Congress assembled, That the provisions of this act shall apply to any common carrier or carriers engaged in the transportation of passengers or property wholly by railroad, or partly by railroad and partly by water when both are used. . . . *however*, That the provisions of this act shall not apply to the transportation of passengers or property, or to the receiving, delivering, storage, or handling of property, wholly within one State, and not shipped to or from a foreign country from or to any State or Territory as aforesaid.

Sec. 2. That if any common carrier . . . shall, directly or indirectly, by any special rate, rebate, drawback, or other device, charge, demand, collect, or receive from any person or persons a greater or less compensation for any service rendered, or to be rendered, . . . than it charges, demands, collects, or receives from any other person or persons for doing for him or them a like and contemporaneous service in the transportation of a like kind of traffic under substantially similar circumstances and conditions, such common carrier shall be deemed guilty of unjust discrimination, which is hereby prohibited and declared to be unlawful.

Sec. 3. That it shall be unlawful for any common carrier subject to the provisions of this act to make or give any undue or unreasonable preference or advantage to any particular person, company, firm, corporation, or locality, or any particular description of traffic. . . .

Sec. 4. That it shall be unlawful for any common carrier subject to the provisions of this act to charge or receive any greater compensation in the aggregate for the transportation of passengers or of like kind of property, under substantially similar circumstances and conditions, . . . ✳

Below: By the mid-1880s, railroads had gained control over the marketing of goods across the United States, with pricing power concentrated in a few "railroad barons."

Critical Thinking

Analyze Cause and Effect

How did the Interstate Commerce Act of 1887 serve to check and balance the power of the U.S. Supreme Court in *Wabash, St. Louis Pacific Railway Company v. State of Illinois* (1886)?

Draw Conclusions

In writing for the majority in *Wabash, St. Louis Pacific Railway Company v. State of Illinois* (1886), Justice Samuel Miller rested the decision of the court on the Commerce Clause found in Article 1, Section 8, Clause 3 of the U.S. Constitution.

> [The Commerce Clause] would be a very feeble and almost useless provision … if, at every stage of the transportation of goods and chattels through the country, the state … could impose regulations concerning the price.

In what way did the Court consider the framers' original intent in its decision? Do you think use of the doctrine of "original intent" is valid for situations that arise decades after the Constitution was written?

Assess Significance

In 1873 Mark Twain and Dudley Warner wrote *The Gilded Age*. This fictional work was a commentary on the political corruption and arrogant affluence of such extraordinarily wealthy barons as Vanderbilt and Gould. Over the years the book's title came to identify the era. In *The Gilded Age* one character laments,

> Wait till the railroads come, and the steamboats! We'll never see the day, Nancy—never in the world—never, never, never, child. We've got to drag along, drag along, and eat crusts in toil and poverty, all hopeless and forlorn—but they'll ride in coaches, Nancy! They'll live like the princes of the earth; they'll be courted and worshiped; their names will be known from ocean to ocean!

It is reported that when Abraham Lincoln met Harriet Beecher Stowe in 1862, author of the anti-slavery novel *Uncle Tom's Cabin*, he said to her, "So you're the little woman who wrote the book that started this Great War!" In what way can works of fiction such as *Uncle Tom's Cabin* and *The Gilded Age* promote changes in domestic policy?

Research and Writing

Analysis

In *Munn v. Illinois* (1876) the Supreme Court ruled that the state could set limits on what fees grain storage facility operators imposed on farmers. With its decision, the Court sent a clear message that "when private property is devoted to a public use, it is subject to public regulation." In *Wabash, St. Louis Pacific Railway Company v. State of Illinois* (1886), however, the Court ruled against the regulatory power of the states. In enumerating the Court's reasoning, Justice Samuel Miller cited *Munn v. Illinois*. Research these two cases. What were the specifics of each? Were their rulings contradictory? Why did Justice Miller cite the *Munn v. Illinois* decision in *Wabash, St. Louis Pacific Railway Company v. State of Illinois*? How was the latter ruling instrumental in passage of the Interstate Commerce Act of 1887?

Historical Perspective

Research the Patrons of Husbandry (the Grange) and the Farmers' Alliances? What was the position of the Alliances in regard to the railroads? How significant was the lobbying power of farmers in passage of the Interstate Commerce Act of 1887? How effective was the Hepburn Act of 1906 and the Mann-Elkins Act of 1910 in strengthening the regulatory power of the Interstate Commerce Commission?

Link to the Past

Section 101 of the ICC Termination Act of 1995 simply states, "The Interstate Commerce Commission is abolished." What was the reasoning behind this legislation? Access and read both the Interstate Commerce Act of 1887 and the ICC Termination Act of 1995. In what way did legislation in 1995 undo well-intended legislation passed in 1887? In your opinion, did the ICC Termination Act of 1995 promote the pubic good? Explain why or why not.

1890 Sherman Anti-Trust Act

"Corporations, which should be the carefully restrained creatures of the law and the servants of the people, are fast becoming the people's masters."

—GROVER CLEVELAND

HISTORICAL BACKGROUND

FROM 1880 to 1890, nine million immigrants settled on American soil, almost one-third of them in New York City. It was the largest wave of immigration in any ten-year span in American history. In the early 1800s, most came from Ireland, England, and Germany. As the twentieth century approached, immigrants from Italy, Russia, Poland, Greece, and other countries, even more foreign in traditions and religion, stepped onto America's shore. All the immigrants were yearning for a better life. Some came to America thinking its streets were paved with gold. Most joined the ever-increasing labor force, intent to work where they could for any wage possible. America was rapidly changing from an agrarian to an urban society. In 1880 twenty-eight percent of Americans lived in thriving urban communities. By 1900 that figure had climbed to forty percent.

The late nineteenth century was also a time of unprecedented wealth propelled by two business structures: the corporation and the trust. Corporations, where individuals act as shareholders of a company, assisted in America's expansion and growth. Railroads were the first businesses to form corporations. Manufacturing soon followed. Trusts were formed when the stock of several smaller companies was placed in a "trust" and managed by one board. This arrangement gave the trust wide control over the many different facets that made up a particular market, from raw materials to finished product. With control of specific markets, money flowed into the trusts as they met the country's needs in transportation, communications, food processing, and the means to power it all—oil.

America's insatiable quest for oil began in the 1850s when individuals noticed a black, oily substance seeping from the ground in Pennsylvania.

It was soon discovered that the oil could be burned for heat and light and used to lubricate machinery. Realizing a fortune in the making, in 1859 an entrepreneur named Edwin L. Drake drilled a hole in the ground in Titusville, Pennsylvania, in hopes of finding an abundance of profit-laden petroleum. Soon Drake was pumping out fifteen barrels of oil a day. Word spread and the oil rush was born. In 1865 John D. Rockefeller and four partners established an oil refinery in Cleveland, Ohio. Five years later Rockefeller organized the Standard Oil Company. A shrewd and aggressive tycoon, Rockefeller gradually acquired competing refineries, combining them into one corporation and creating a monopoly.

Rockefeller didn't stop with the ownership of refineries, however. He bought forests to produce the wood that made the oil barrels. He produced and owned the pipelines through which the oil flowed. In 1882 Standard Oil formed a trust and became a corporate empire. Beginning in 1889, New Jersey and other states passed laws that made it easier for companies to merge. Such mergers allowed economic power to be concentrated in a few corporations and individuals. By 1900 one-third of all manufacturing in the United States was controlled by just one percent of American corporations. Power, wealth, and the nation's economic strength became concentrated in what some critics called the "robber-barons"—men like Rockefeller in the oil industry and Andrew Carnegie in steel.

The vast financial empires built by big business came at the expense of small businesses. Because of their size and scope, large corporations such as Standard Oil and the Carnegie Steel Company could set prices lower than competing companies, ultimately leading to the financial ruin of their smaller competitors. Once their competition was eliminated, the oil, steel, sugar, railroad, meat, and other trusts that controlled the marketplace had little incentive to keep prices low. Moreover, as employment opportunities in competing companies dwindled, workers were left to accept whatever wages and working conditions the corporate giants chose to offer. It was a setting that inevitably led to clashes between management and labor. In response to growing pressure to loosen the grip

trusts held on American business, in 1890 Congress passed the Sherman Anti-Trust Act. The law sought to "protect trade and commerce against unlawful restraint and monopoly." Because the law neglected to clearly define such terms as "trust" and "monopoly," it lacked the strength needed for true reform. However, in its attempt to place restraints on big business, the Sherman Anti-Trust Act ultimately served as the basis for future constraints by the government on corporate giants.

National Archives Document

An act to protect trade and commerce against unlawful restraints and monopolies.

Be it enacted by the Senate and House of Representatives of the United States of America in Congress assembled,

Sec. 1. Every contract, combination in the form of trust or other wise, or conspiracy, in restraint of trade or commerce among the several States, or with foreign nations, is hereby declared to be illegal. Every person who shall make any such contract or engage in any such combination or conspiracy, shall be deemed guilty of a misdemeanor, and, on conviction thereof, shall be punished by fine not exceeding five thousand dollars, or by imprisonment not exceeding one year, or by both said punishments, at the discretion of the court.

Sec. 2. Every person who shall monopolize, or attempt to monopolize, or combine or conspire with any other person or persons, to monopolize any part of the trade or commerce among the several States, or with foreign nations, shall be deemed guilty of a misdemeanor, and, on conviction thereof; shall be punished by fine not exceeding five thousand dollars, or by imprisonment not exceeding one year, or by both said punishments, in the discretion of the court.

Sec. 7. Any person who shall be injured in his business or property by any other person or corporation by reason of anything forbidden or declared to be unlawful by this act, may sue therefore in any circuit court of the United States in the district in which the defendant resides or is found, without respect to the amount in controversy, and shall recover three fold the damages by him sustained, and the costs of suit, including a reasonable attorney's fee.

Sec. 8. That the word "person," or " persons," wherever used in this act shall be deemed to include corporations and associations existing under or authorized by the laws of either the United States, the laws of any of the Territories, the laws of any State, or the laws of any foreign country. ✳

Below: This nineteenth-century cartoon characterizes the controlling power of trusts during the late 1800s.

Critical Thinking

Analyze Cause and Effect

Why didn't Section 1 of the Sherman Anti-trust Act immediately negate the trust agreements of such giant corporations as Standard Oil and Carnegie Steel?

Assess Significance

Andrew Carnegie was an astute businessman who controlled every aspect of steel making—from the coal fields, to the ore ships, to the plants that made the steel. He also was among the philanthropists of the time who believed that personal wealth should be shared. In 1889 he wrote in *The Gospel of Wealth* that personal wealth beyond what was required to care for the needs of one's family should be returned to the community. To that end, Carnegie spent $59 million (the equivalent of over $700 million today) to build 2,509 libraries in communities throughout the country, from New York City to small, rural towns in states like Wisconsin and Illinois. Carnegie also contributed to adult education and to the fine arts. Did the philanthropic efforts of America's "robber barons" at the dawn of the twentieth century help to improve the image of the trusts in the eyes of the public? Explain why or why not.

Determine Point of View

John D. Rockefeller once said, "Singleness of purpose is one of the chief essentials for success in life, no matter what may be one's aim." Do you agree? Why or why not? How did Rockefeller put his philosophy into practice?

Research and Writing

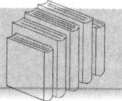

Analysis

In the early 1900s, President Theodore Roosevelt sought to regulate corporations through a series of trust-busting lawsuits aimed, in particular, at trusts in beef, tobacco, oil, and investment banking. Research the trust-busting efforts of the Roosevelt administration. What was the impact of the Court's ruling in *Northern Securities Company v. U.S.*? How effective was Roosevelt in breaking the strength of the trusts?

Historical Perspective

Between 1880 and 1884, George M. Pullman built the town of Pullman on 4,000 acres of land near Chicago. It was America's first model industrial town, with everything from the homes, to the schools, to the parks, to stores meticulously planned by Pullman. People lived in Pullman homes, played in Pullman parks, and bought what they needed at Pullman stores. At the center of town was the Pullman Palace Car Company, where many of Pullman's residents worked making luxury railroad passenger cars. In 1893 Pullman laid off 3,000 of his 5,800 employees and cut wages 25–40 percent. However, rent for those living in Pullman's homes and the cost of food in Pullman's store remained the same. This situation prompted a strike that eventually impacted railroad operations in twenty-eight states. In the case of *In re Debs* (1895), the American Railway Union was alleged to have "entered into a combination and conspiracy to prevent the railroad companies … from performing their duties as common carriers of interstate commerce." Justice David Josiah Brewer wrote, "The strong arm of the national government may be put forth to brush away all obstructions to the freedom of interstate commerce." Research the Pullman Strike and *In re Debs*. How did the two relate? In what way did the Pullman Strike become intertwined with interstate commerce? How did the Court use the language of the Sherman Anti-trust Act as a means to regulate labor as opposed to business?

Link to the Past

In 2001, software giant Microsoft settled a series of class-action, antitrust lawsuits filed against it by eighteen states and the federal government. In commenting on the settlement, Attorney General John Ashcroft stated, "This historic settlement will bring effective relief to the market and ensure that consumers will have more choices in meeting their computer needs." Research the case against Microsoft. Why did the government believe Microsoft held a monopoly? What were the provisions of the court settlement? Did every state agree to the settlement? Would you agree with Attorney General Ashcroft's assessment of the settlement? Explain.

> *"The income tax has made more liars
> out of the American people than golf has."*
>
> —WILL ROGERS, HUMORIST

HISTORICAL BACKGROUND

THE question of how to pay for the workings of government was an issue even before the United States became an independent nation. Great Britain imposed excise taxes on tea, sugar, paper, and other commodities used by the colonists as a source of income for the British crown. The cry of "no taxation without representation" fueled the call for liberty. Following the American Revolution, the United States turned to tariffs as a source of revenue. While trade flourished, placing a fee on goods entering the country provided a means to fund the government without placing a financial burden on the citizenry. To support its war effort in 1812, the federal government imposed an emergency tax on property. It was a direct tax based on ownership. By 1817 the country returned to reliance on tariffs as its primary revenue source. The financial burden of the Civil War, however, forced Congress to seek a greater and more consistent source of income.

In 1861 Congress levied the country's first tax on the individual incomes of citizens. The plan imposed a three-percent tax on all annual income over $800, a figure that exempted most wage earners of the time. With the 1861 income taxes as yet uncollected, and a raging war costing some $2 million each day, money flowing into the national treasury was of critical importance. To that end, Congress replaced the 1861 law with the Internal Revenue Act of 1862. The new law created a graduated tax structure. It imposed a three-percent rate on incomes between $600 and $10,000 and a five-percent rate on incomes over $10,000. Taxes were automatically withheld from the salaries of government employees and on the dividends paid to stockholders. Moreover, consumption-oriented "sin" taxes were levied on liquor, tobacco, playing cards, billiard tables,

newspaper advertisements, yachts, and carriages— items used by the more affluent. To manage the collection of taxes, the act created the Commissioner of Internal Revenue.

Though the income tax proved a flexible and consistent source of income, there was little support for it in Congress. In the wake of a budget surplus and a seemingly healthy economy, the tax was repealed in 1872. Additionally, Congress enacted a 10-percent reduction in tariffs and eliminated duties on coffee and tea. Severe economic problems were just around the corner, however. A combination of high transportation costs, declining farm prices, and mounting debt placed many western and southern farmers in dire economic straits. Yet, tariffs continued to protect manufacturers against foreign competition. The result was a general increase in prices for goods needed by farmers. To make matters worse, farmers were forced to sell their products to foreign countries at substantially lowered prices. In 1886 drought struck Texas. Out west the blizzards of 1886–1887 descended on the homesteads scattered across America's breadbasket killing herds of cattle. A lack of available currency exacerbated the worsening economic picture. In 1893 the Philadelphia and Reading Railroad declared bankruptcy. It set off a panic on Wall Street. By the fall of 1893 over six hundred banks had closed. By 1894 the country was in severe economic trouble.

In 1894 a reform-minded Congress enacted a 2 percent tax on personal incomes above $4,000 as part of the Wilson-Gorman tariff act. Soon after, in *Pollock v. Farmers' Loan and Trust Company* (1895) the U.S. Supreme Court struck down the tax, ruling it a direct tax in violation of Article 1, Section 9 of the Constitution. With that, the United States was once again forced to rely on tariff revenue to fund the government. In 1909 a controversial income tax provision was attached to the Payne-Aldrich tariff bill. In an effort to eliminate the possibility of Congress enacting an income tax, opponents cleverly proposed enactment of an income tax amendment to the Constitution. Much to their dismay, Congress gravitated to the idea and passed the amendment in July 1909, later ratified in 1913. The tax that Congress soon levied focused on the wealthy, imposing a 1-percent tax rate on annual incomes above $3,000 and a 6-percent rate on those over $500,000. In 1913 approximately 1 percent of the population paid some amount in income taxes. Today, with a graduated rate structure, the federal income tax is the largest single source of federal receipts.

NATIONAL ARCHIVES DOCUMENT

Sixty-first Congress of the United States of America, At the First Session,

Begun and held at the City of Washington on Monday, the fifteenth day of March, one thousand nine hundred and nine.

JOINT RESOLUTION

Proposing an amendment to the Constitution of the United States.

Resolved by the Senate and House of Representatives of the United States of America in Congress assembled (two-thirds of each House concurring therein), That the following article is proposed as an amendment to the Constitution of the United States, which, when ratified by the legislature of three-fourths of the several States, shall be valid to all intents and purposes as a part of the Constitution:

"**ARTICLE XVI.** The Congress shall have power to lay and collect taxes on incomes, from whatever source derived, without apportionment among the several States, and without regard to any census or enumeration." ✳

Below: Most Americans are required to report their incomes and pay their income taxes by April 15 of every year.

Critical Thinking

Analyze Cause and Effect

In what way did language in the Sixteenth Amendment alter Article 1, Section 9 of the U.S. Constitution?

Assess Significance

How did the Sixteenth Amendment serve to check the power of the U.S. Supreme Court?

Determine Point of View

In *McCulloch v. Maryland* (1819) Chief Justice John Marshall wrote, "the power to tax involves the power to destroy." Because the federal income tax relies on taxation rates based on a graduated system, do you think the federal income tax is a disincentive for individuals or business to make more money? Why or why not? Do you agree with Will Rogers that the system is a disincentive to honesty? Why or why not? How do you think Chief Justice Marshall would have viewed the Sixteenth Amendment?

Research and Writing

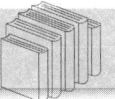

Analysis

Today more than 99,000 people work for the Internal Revenue Service (IRS), helping individual taxpayers, small businesses, and large corporations meet their income tax obligations. With an annual budget that tops $10 billion, the IRS processes some 230 million tax returns each year. Research the effectiveness of income taxes as a revenue source for the federal government. What are the government's tax receipts? What other taxes fund the workings of government? How are the receipts distributed? With taxes flowing annually into the federal treasury, why is the country in debt? How extensive is the nation's public debt? Should taxes be increased? Explain your position.

Counterpoint

In commenting on the Internal Revenue Act of 1862, Representative Thaddeus Stevens stated,

> While the rich and the thrifty will be obliged to contribute largely from the abundance of their means ... no burdens have been imposed on the industrious laborer and mechanic ... The food of the poor is untaxed; and no one will be affected by the provisions of this bill whose living depends solely on his manual labor.

The 1862 Internal Revenue Act was based on the philosophical concept of one's ability to pay. Some critics believe the current system of taxation unfairly places the greatest income tax burden on the working middle class. Would you agree? Who is exempt from income taxes? Who pays the most?

Research the Internal Revenue Act of 1862. Compare the current graduated system with that created in 1862. Could the comment made by Stevens in 1862 still apply today? Explain.

Link to the Past

By April 15 of each year most people have gathered together the necessary documentation, filled out the appropriate forms, and filed their income tax returns with the IRS. As a bureau within the U.S. Treasury Department, the mission of the IRS is to "provide America's taxpayers top quality service by helping them understand and meet their tax responsibilities and by applying the tax law with integrity and fairness to all." The monies paid into the Treasury to fund the workings of the United States government are determined by a highly complex series of tax codes that span some 2,000 pages. An industry of accountants, corporate lawyers, and tax specialists has developed over the years to apply those laws in ways that minimize the tax burdens on their respective clients. Some suggest that fundamental tax reform is needed, replacing the current graduated tax system with a flat-rate tax. Others also suggest eliminating the current system of taxing income, replacing it instead with a national sales tax. Research the concept of a flat-tax system and a national sales tax. Compare the graduated system of today with the two other systems. In your estimation, which is the most fair and efficient system of taxation? Explain your position.

1916 The Keating-Owen Child Labor Act

"Yes, I want to learn, but can't when I work all the time."

—FURMAN OWENS, AGE 12

HISTORICAL BACKGROUND

As the United States moved into the twentieth century, the clang and crash of machinery echoed through the mills and factories that filled the nation's expanding industrial centers. The sounds were the heartbeat of a society enthralled with the possibilities of the modern machine. It was the rapid industrialization of America, a time when dust-filled, noisy buildings became a refuge for immigrants hungry for work and for young farm boys seeking the sights and sounds of the city. Employment was framed by long hours, far-from-safe working conditions, and the ever-present threat of job loss should an injury occur. Inside, adults and children often worked together as the machinery chugged and churned, turning out spools of thread, fabric, and items of all kinds.

In 1908 almost two million children stood before such machinery instead of occupying a seat near a coal or wood stove in a neighborhood school. They were cheap labor, easily replaced, and did as they were told. At age twelve, Furman Owens had already worked in the mills of South Carolina for four years when photojournalist Lewis Hine happened upon him, took his picture, and jotted down his story. Hine noted that young Furman couldn't read—didn't even know his ABCs. The boy would be one of many children Hine interviewed. He had been hired by the National Child Labor Committee to create a visual record of children working in sweatshops and other industries across the nation. They were not hard to find. Using whatever pretext he could, Hine gained entrance into the factories of America, then interviewed children who labored at machines, secretly noting their stories. He talked to spinners not yet five feet tall, working days—and sometimes nights—for forty-eight cents a day. He talked with Newsies, street-smart New York City boys as young as five, who sold newspapers by day for a penny each.

And he spoke with young boys working in mines and glass-blowing factories, clothes covered with soot. Perhaps the lucky ones were the youngsters he found doing licensed "homework" with their families in New York City tenement houses six days a week, stitching clothes from early morning to late at night. Hine's photographs chronicled a part of American society that favored the turn of a profit over the worth of a child. And to many Americans, it was appalling.

Though several states had laws on the books between 1908 and 1912, the years Hines spent documenting child labor in America, they were often ignored or ineffective. In response to reformers' demands for federal intervention, in 1916 President Woodrow Wilson signed the Keating-Owen bill into law. The new legislation utilized the federal government's constitutional power to regulate interstate commerce as its legal foundation. It banned the sale of products outside a state's borders from shops, factories, or canneries that employed children under the age of fourteen, from mines that employed children under the age of sixteen, or from sweatshops where children worked for more than eight hours a day or at night. The U.S. Supreme Court, however, disagreed. In *Hammer v. Dagenhart* (1918) Justice William R. Day wrote,

> If Congress can thus regulate matters entrusted to local authority by prohibition of the movement of commodities in interstate commerce, all freedom of commerce will be at an end, and the power of the states over local matters may be eliminated, and thus our system of government be practically destroyed. . . . For these reasons we hold that this law exceeds the constitutional authority of Congress.

In 1924 Congress approved an amendment to the Constitution granting it the power to regulate child labor. In part, it read, "Congress shall have power to limit, regulate, and prohibit the labor of persons under eighteen years of age. . . . [T]he operation of State laws shall be suspended to the extent necessary to give effect to legislation enacted by the Congress." However, the amendment failed to receive ratification by the required number of states. Some state legislators charged the amendment subverted the right of states to govern labor within their borders. Others claimed it was part of a communist plot to undermine the Constitution. Responding to the amendment's failure, in 1938 Congress passed the Fair Labor Standards Act. This time the Supreme Court upheld the law's constitutionality. In writing for the majority in *U. S. v. Darby* (1941)., Justice Harlan Stone stated,

The Fair Labor Standards Act set up a comprehensive legislative scheme for preventing the shipment in interstate commerce of certain products and commodities produced in the United States under labor conditions as respects wages and hours which fail to conform to standards set up by the Act. . . . The Act is sufficiently definite to meet constitutional demands. One who employs persons, without conforming to the prescribed wage and hour conditions, to work on goods which he ships or expects to ship across . . . is warned that he may be subject to the criminal penalties of the Act.

National Archives Document

AN ACT To prevent interstate commerce in the products of child labor, and for other purposes.

Be it enacted by the Senate and House of Representatives of the United States of America in Congress assembled, That no producer, manufacturer, or dealer shall ship or deliver for shipment in interstate or foreign commerce, any article or commodity the product of any mine or quarry situated in the United States, in which within thirty days prior to the time of the removal of such product therefrom children under the age of sixteen years have been employed or permitted to work, or any article or commodity the product of any mill, cannery, workshop, factory, or manufacturing establishment, situated in the United States, in which within thirty days prior to the time of the removal of such product therefrom children under the age of fourteen years have been employed or permitted to work, or children between the ages of fourteen years and sixteen years have been employed or permitted to work more than eight hours in any day, or more than six days in any week, or after the hour of seven o'clock postmeridian, or before the hour of six o'clock antemeridian: *Provided,* That a prosecution and conviction of a defendant for the shipment or delivery for shipment of any article or commodity under the conditions herein prohibited shall be a bar to any further prosecution against the same defendant for shipments or deliveries for shipment of any such article or commodity before the beginning of said prosecution. ❋

Below: Some two million children worked long days in dangerous conditions in America's factories during the early 1900s, earning less than their adult counterparts.

Critical Thinking

Determine Point of View

In addressing the issue of states' rights, Edward Keating of Colorado sent a message to each state when lobbying Congress for passage of his bill. Keating said, "If you wish to tolerate this immoral, this pestilential thing—child labor—you may do so, but you shall not spread the contagion." What federal power was Keating hoping to use to stop the "spread of the contagion"?

Analyze Cause and Effect

How did the Supreme Court's decision in *Hammer v. Dagenhart* (1918) place states' rights at the heart of the child labor issue?

Assess Significance

In referring to the *Hammer v. Dagenhart* (1918) decision, the U.S. Supreme Court in *U.S. v Darby* (1941) stated,

> It was held by a bare majority of the Court ... that Congress was without power to exclude the products of child labor from interstate commerce. The reasoning and conclusion of the Court's opinion there cannot be reconciled with the conclusion which we have reached.

With the U.S. Constitution serving as the basis for both Supreme Court decisions, how was it possible for the two decisions to be in opposition?

Research and Writing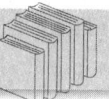

Analysis

> One day Durham advertised in the paper for two hundred men to cut ice; and all that day the homeless and starving of the city came trudging through the snow from all over its two hundred square miles. That night forty score of them crowded into the station house of the stockyards district—they filled the rooms, sleeping in each other's laps, toboggan fashion, and they piled on top of each other in the corridors, till the police shut the doors and left some to freeze outside. On the morrow, before daybreak, there were three thousand at Durham's, and the police reserves had to be sent for to quell the riot. Then Durham's bosses picked out twenty of the biggest; the "two hundred" proved to have been a printer's error.

This excerpt from the 1906 novel *The Jungle* by Upton Sinclair is an example of the changing style of journalism in the early twentieth century, a style that emphasized reform by exposing injustice, corruption, and political favors. In *The Jungle* Sinclair wrote of the horrors of the Chicago meatpacking industry. Sinclair was one of a group of journalists, nicknamed *muckrakers* by President Teddy Roosevelt, whose exposés shocked society. Research the muckrakers. Who were the most prominent? What did they expose? How effective were the muckrakers in affecting social change?

Historical Interpretation

In 1893 nurse Lillian Wald established a medical aid station on the top floor of a run-down tenement building on New York City's Lower Eastside. By 1913 she had ninety-two staff members dispensing medical aid to the city's poor. She brought her nursing services to city schools, which led to the establishment of the first public nursing program. Lillian Wald, Jane Addams, Mother Cabrini, and Mary Church Terrell were among the growing number of educated women intent on social reform. They established settlement houses and orphanages for the poor, founded hospitals, and championed woman's suffrage. They were social activists who determinedly worked to remedy the plight of the poor. Research the social activism of women in the early 1900s. Where did they work? What did they accomplish? What barriers did they face? What impact did they have? How did their social activism contribute to the changing role of women in the early 1900s?

Link to the Past

Today the Fair Labor Standards Act continues to regulate the employment of minors. Research the act's provisions specific to the regulation of child labor. What is allowed? What is restricted? What penalties are stipulated for employers who violate the law? Are laws governing child labor in your state more restrictive or less restrictive than the provisions of the Fair Labor Standards Act? How do both the federal laws and the laws of your state impact the employment of minors in your area?

1933 National Industrial Recovery Act

"This Nation asks for action, and action now."

—Franklin Delano Roosevelt

Historical Background

In his 1929 Inaugural Address, President Herbert Hoover boasted, "I have no fears for the future of our country. It is bright with hope." By 1933, thirteen million people were out of work. Within those four years, factories and banks had closed. Farms had gone bankrupt. With twenty-five percent of workers unemployed and many others working less than full time, private charities found it hard to feed those who lined up at neighborhood soup kitchens. Groups of make-shift shelters of tar paper and old packing boxes sprung up on the outskirts of cities. Within these "Hoovervilles" people wrapped themselves in newspapers—"Hoover blankets"—to keep warm, their out-turned, empty pockets called "Hoover flags." It was sarcasm aimed at a president who appeared to be stymied by the seething economic crisis precipitated by the crash of the stock market just seven short months after his inauguration.

Hoover's initial answer to the looming economic depression was to encourage Americans to remain confident in the country's ability to weather the crisis. "While the crash only took place six months ago, I am convinced we have now passed the worst and with continued unity of effort we shall rapidly recover." he told an anxious U.S. Chamber of Commerce on May 1, 1930. Yet, as months passed, it became obvious to Hoover that government intervention was needed. To that end he signed the Glass-Steagall Act of 1932. Alongside the Federal Home Loan Bank Act of 1932, the legislation provided a series of banking measures meant to ease the acquisition of loans by the public. "Trickle-down" his critics complained. "Is there any reason why we should not likewise extend a helping hand to that forlorn American, in every village and every city of the United States, who has been without wages since 1929?" asked an outraged Senator Robert G. Wagner of New York. In an October 1932 speech in Detroit,

Michigan, Hoover declared, "It can be demonstrated that the tide has turned and that the gigantic forces of depression are today in retreat. Our measures and policies have demonstrated their effectiveness. They have preserved the American people from certain chaos." A crowd of several hundred met him at the Detroit train station holding signs that read "Hoover—baloney and applesauce."

Hoover's 1932 re-election efforts met with defeat. In his place stood Franklin Delano Roosevelt. At his presidential nomination months before, Roosevelt emphatically stated, "I pledge you. I pledge myself to a new deal for the American people." In his second day as president, Roosevelt shut down the nation's banks and called a special session of Congress. Its members quickly passed the Emergency Banking Relief Act of 1933. In reopening the banks Roosevelt told the nation, in the first of a series of radio messages known as "fire-side chats," that keeping money in banks was safer than keeping it "under the mattress." American citizens, yearning for confidence in their leaders and government, responded. Deposits soon exceeded withdrawals in banks across the country. In other, belt-tightening measures, Roosevelt cut the government payroll. He also urged Congress to pass the Twenty-first Amendment repealing the Eighteenth Amendment and putting an end to Prohibition.

During his first hundred days in office in 1933, Roosevelt also signed into law the National Industrial Recovery Act (NIRA). It was sweeping legislation that directed the country away from a free-market economy and imposed in its place a set of government regulations designed to stimulate production. The law suspended antitrust monitoring, allowing the leaders of industry instead to cooperatively fix prices while dividing markets to each one's advantage. In an effort to appease labor, provisions in the act addressed minimum wages and maximum hours, as well as the right of workers to form unions and bargain collectively. The resulting "codes of practice" were subsequently approved by a government-appointed National Recovery Administration (NRA), already established through an executive order.

By the end of Roosevelt's first hundred days, his New Deal policies had ended a banking crisis, established programs to assist the country's unemployed, addressed the issue of home and farm foreclosures, and forged an alliance between industry and government while offering an olive branch to labor unions. His second hundred days lay ahead.

NATIONAL ARCHIVES DOCUMENT

AN ACT

To encourage national industrial recovery, to foster fair competition, and to provide for the construction of certain useful public works, and for other purposes.

SECTION 1. A national emergency productive of widespread unemployment and disorganization of industry, which burdens interstate and foreign commerce, affects the public welfare, and undermines the standards of living of the American people, is hereby declared to exist. It is hereby declared to be the policy of Congress to remove obstructions to the free flow of interstate and foreign commerce which tend to diminish the amount thereof; and to provide for the general welfare by promoting the organization of industry for the purpose of cooperative action among trade groups, to induce and maintain united action of labor and management under adequate governmental sanctions and supervision, to eliminate unfair competitive practices, to promote the fullest possible utilization of the present productive capacity of industries, to avoid undue restriction of production (except as may be temporarily required), to increase the consumption of Industrial and agricultural products by increasing purchasing power, to reduce and relieve unemployment, to improve standards of labor, and otherwise to rehabilitate industry and to conserve natural resources.

To effectuate the policy of this title, the President is hereby authorized to establish such agencies, to accept and utilize such voluntary and uncompensated services to appoint without regard to the provisions of the civil service laws. . . . ✳

Below: This political cartoon shows the policies of the National Recovery Administration as being advantageous for both workers and business owners.

Critical Thinking

Draw Conclusions

One provision in the National Industrial Recovery Act provided a means to finance Roosevelt's New Deal. The provision stipulated that "for each year ending June 30 there is hereby imposed upon every domestic corporation with respect to carrying on or doing business for any part of such year an excise tax of $1 for each $1,000 of the adjusted declared value of its capital stock." Was this a fair way to help finance the New Deal? Explain.

Analyze Cause and Effect

In the spring of 1932 some 15,000 unemployed World War I veterans held a vigil outside Washington, D.C., to obtain immediate payment of a cash bonus approved by Congress in 1924, but not payable until 1945. They called themselves the "Bonus Expeditionary Force." As the veterans camped within sight of the Capitol, events turned sour. Led by General Douglas MacArthur and assisted by Dwight D. Eisenhower and George S. Patton, seven hundred soldiers descended on the vets, razing their makeshift camp, burning their shacks, and scattering those who remained. What effect do you think this event had on Hoover's reputation? Why?

Assess Significance

Why did Roosevelt move so quickly to establish his reforms?

Research and Writing

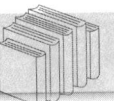

Relating Events

Research the factors that led to the Great Stock Market Crash of 1929. Could the pitfalls have been avoided? Why didn't the government make the necessary corrections to avert the crisis? What occurred on Black Thursday, Black Monday, and Black Tuesday? What were the immediate effects of the stock market crash?

Historical Interpretation

In *The Grapes of Wrath*, published in 1939, author John Steinbeck depicted the plight of a fictional Oklahoma farming family who traveled in a ramshackle car across the Arizona desert to reach California. Throughout the precarious trip they embraced the hope of finding work in California's thriving farm fields. Drought, bank foreclosures, and the consequences of sharecropping found many farm families drawn to California by false advertisements of grand employment opportunities at a time when the Agricultural Adjustment Act of 1933 paid subsidies to farmers to *cut back* production. Research the Agricultural Adjustment Act. What exactly did it stipulate? Why was it a stark departure from traditional agricultural and economic policy? What was the impact of the AAA on the farmers? Did it help or exacerbate their plight? Why was it struck down by the U.S. Supreme Court in *United States v. Butler* (1936)? What legislation replaced the AAA?

Counterpoint

In *Schechter Poultry Corporation v. United States* (1935) the U.S. Supreme Court struck down Section 3 of the National Industrial Recovery Act. In writing for the majority, Chief Justice Charles Evans Hughes stated,

> Section 3 of the Recovery Act … is without precedent.… Instead of prescribing rules of conduct, it authorizes the making of codes to prescribe them.… In view of the scope of that broad declaration and of the nature of the few restrictions that are imposed, the discretion of the President in approving or prescribing codes, and thus enacting laws for the government of trade and industry throughout the country, is virtually unfettered. We think that the code-making authority thus conferred is an unconstitutional delegation of legislative power.

Access and read Section 3 of the National Industrial Recovery Act and the majority opinion in *Schechter Poultry Corporation v. United States*. What broad powers did the National Industrial Recovery Act give the president? Do you agree with the Court's decision in *Schechter Poultry Corporation v. United States*? Support your position with excerpts from each document.

1935 National Labor Relations Act

"It shall be an unfair labor practice for an employer . . . [to] interfere with the formation or administration of any labor organization."

—SECTION 8, NLRA

HISTORICAL BACKGROUND

IN the early 1930s, many workers refrained from any action that might jeopardize their jobs. The country was in the midst of the Great Depression, and most who had jobs counted themselves among the fortunate. However, the picture changed with passage of the National Industrial Recovery Act (NIRA) in 1933. John L. Lewis, the head of the miners' union, considered the legislation a declaration of rights for labor.

> Organized labor is a single unit in its approval of the objectives of the National Industrial Recovery Act. . . . From the standpoint of human welfare and economic freedom, we are convinced that there has been no legal instrument comparable with it since President Lincoln's Emancipation Proclamation of seventy years ago.

Despite high unemployment, beginning in 1934 thousands of workers in cities across the country engaged in labor actions, some of which turned militant. On May 15, 1934, in a well-orchestrated job action, six thousand truckers in Minnesota voted to strike all trucking employers, demanding union recognition and wage increases. The group had enlisted the support of the Minnesota Farmer-Labor Party. As in so many strike actions of the past, events turned violent. However, three months later, the truckers' demands were met. In the summer of 1934, longshoremen in Seattle, Washington, demanded coast-wide contracts and improved wage and hour agreements. Waiting out an eighty-three day strike, which included a confrontation with 300 Seattle policemen and the death of one striker, the longshoremen won on every point. Said one union member, "We had a new sense of our worth, of our power as workers." In contrast were the results of a strike by textile workers in the fall of 1934. Beginning on Labor Day, some 450,000 United Textile

Workers of America, from Massachusetts to Alabama, walked off their jobs. It was the largest strike in the nation's history. The strike turned violent when Georgia's governor used National Guard troops against the striking workers. Several workers died in the ensuing violence. When the strike collapsed twenty-two days later, few striking workers were rehired.

Labor encountered another setback with the derailing of the NIRA by the Supreme Court in *Schechter Poultry Corporation v. United States* (1935). The Court's action spurred passage of the National Labor Relations Act (NLRA), also called the Wagner Act, later that same year. This legislation protected the right of workers to form unions and engage in collective bargaining. It also created a National Labor Relations Board to investigate labor complaints and enforce workers' rights. In addition, the NLRA barred unfair labor practices, such as firing workers for union affiliation, discrimination against members of labor unions, and the creation of company-controlled labor organizations. Cognizant of the political strength of union members, Roosevelt signed the legislation into law.

With the strength of the NLRA behind it, in 1936 the Congress of Industrial Organizations (CIO) was founded to organize and unite workers in the nation's steel, auto, textile, and other major industries. The steel industry, which employed some 800,000 workers, offered the potential for an especially powerful union. To curtail these efforts, United States Steel Corporation, the leader in the steel industry, granted a wage increase to its employees. Yet, despite this concession, membership in the Steel Workers Organizing Committee (SWOC) grew. In 1937, a strike in Chicago turned deadly when police, wielding tear gas, clubs, and guns, attacked marchers, who police believed were attempting to drive nonunion workers from a steel plant. The SWOC turned to the National Labor Relations Board (NLRB) to mediate the conflict between steel workers and management. In a victory for organized labor, in 1941 the Board helped establish the bargaining rights of what became the United Steel Workers of America (USWA). Other unions, like the United Auto Workers (UAW), founded in 1935, also owe much of their success to the NLRA. The NLRA continues to be the cornerstone of federal labor law today. It remains a tribute to fallen union members whose courage in standing up for workers' rights paved the way for a federal response to unfair labor practices.

NATIONAL ARCHIVES DOCUMENT

AN ACT To diminish the causes of labor disputes burdening or obstructing interstate and foreign commerce, to create a National Labor Relations Board, and for other purposes.

It is declared to be the policy of the United States to eliminate the causes of certain substantial obstructions to the free flow of commerce and to mitigate and eliminate these obstructions when they have occurred by encouraging the practice and procedure of collective bargaining and by protecting the exercise by workers of full freedom of association, self-organization, and designation of representatives of their own choosing, for the purpose of negotiating the terms and conditions of their employment or other mutual aid or protection.

Sec. 7. Employees shall have the right to self-organization, to form, join, or assist labor organizations, to bargain collectively through representatives of their own choosing, and to engage in other concerted activities for the purpose of collective bargaining or other mutual aid or protection, and shall also have the right to refrain from any or all such activities except to the extent that such right may be affected by an agreement requiring membership in a labor organization as a condition of employment. . . . ✳

Below: The American Federation of Labor (AFL) and the Congress of Industrial Organizations (CIO) merged in 1955. Here workers take an oath of membership.

Critical Thinking

Analyze Cause and Effect

The Norris-La Guardia Act of 1932 barred the use of "yellow-dog" contracts in which workers were forced to promise they would not join a union as a condition of employment. The legislation acted as a counter to the Supreme Court's decision in *Adair v. The United States* (1908), which struck down a provision in the Erdman Act of 1898 prohibiting the use of yellow-dog contracts. In 1908 the Court believed such a restriction represented an infringement on the contract process. As legislation passed during the depths of the Great Depression, why do you think public sentiment in 1932 shifted in favor of the Norris-LaGuardia Act?

Draw Conclusions

Why was it necessary for the NLRA to not only specify the rights of employees under the new legislation, but to also delineate unfair labor practices?

Assess Significance

How significant was the National Labor Relations Act as a domestic policy? Explain your reasoning.

Research and Writing

Analysis

With over 700,000 members in the United States, Canada, and Puerto Rico, today the United Auto Workers (UAW) is one of the largest unions in North America. Officially the United Automobile, Aerospace, and Agricultural Implement Workers of America International Union, the UAW was founded in 1935 in Detroit, Michigan. Originally part of the powerful American Federation of Labor (AFL), the union subsequently became affiliated with the Congress of Industrial Organizations (CIO) headed by John L. Lewis. The success of the UAW's sit-down strikes in 1936 marked the beginning of its strength among automotive industry workers. Research the difference between those unions organized by the AFL and those by the CIO. When did the AFL and the CIO form? Why did industrial unions such as the Steel Workers Organizing Committee (SWOC) and the UAW organize under the umbrella of the CIO? When did the AFL and CIO combine? What prompted them to join forces?

Historical Interpretation

In 1947 Congress overrode President Harry Truman's veto to pass the Labor-Management Relations Act (also called the Taft-Hartley Act). Though the legislation strengthened the National Labor Relations Act, it also included provisions interpreted as antilabor. Over the years, presidents have invoked the Taft-Hartley Act more than thirty times as a means to halt work stoppages in labor disputes. Access and read the National Labor Relations Act of 1935. Then, research the Taft-Hartley Act. How did this later legislation augment the NLRA? Why are some of its provisions considered antilabor? What are three examples of its use by presidents seeking to control the arbitration of labor disputes? What was the result?

Link to the Past

Today the AFL-CIO boasts thirteen million members. Research the AFL-CIO. Who are its members? What are its current issues? What problems does it face? How powerful is it as a labor organization?

1935 Social Security Act

"A law that will take care of human needs."

—FRANKLIN DELANO ROOSEVELT

HISTORICAL BACKGROUND

THE years of the Great Depression cast a pall of resignation and aching humility over some thirteen to fifteen million unemployed breadwinners. The effects of unemployment enveloped forty million men, women, and children—the young and the old—in abject poverty. For many, being poor became a way of life—a seemingly endless misery framed by hunger, homelessness, and despondency. Perhaps worse than the poverty was the shame felt by those Americans who were forced to accept charity. Even in the most difficult of times, Americans had lived on a foundation of self-reliance—a take care of yourself attitude. They had settled the West, constructed the railroads that crisscrossed the land, and filled the factories that industrialized the country at a startling pace. They built America on sheer willpower and on the belief that an individual's success came from hard work. To be without work, to consider oneself a slacker unable to care for family, was for many an unbearable disgrace. Yet, having to accept a handout was far worse. Dependency tore at the fabric of the independent American. It was a grave insult to a nation filled with pride. As one migrant farmer put it, "This is a hard life to swallow, but I just couldn't sit back there and look to someone to feed us." In the end, people relied on their resilience and ingenuity to cope with immense hardships. For some, it was all they had.

Life in the 1930s was a paradox. The motion picture industry was in full swing. Shirley Temple, James Cagney, Mickey Rooney, and the like turned out movies where good always triumphed over evil. Hollywood was glitzy and alive with song and dance. In contrast were those who stood on the streets of New York hoping to sell apples for five cents each to some compassionate passersby. Extended families, where homes included the young and the old, were the norm during the first half of the twentieth century. The elderly contributed to the family in whatever way possible. They sewed, helped to farm, took care of children, and provided guidance and stability. With money scarce, any member who was at a loss to contribute to the financial well-being of the family became a burden. This included the elderly and children with medical problems. The expense of caring for the elderly, the ill, and the disabled was overwhelming for penniless families.

Against this backdrop President Franklin Delano Roosevelt proposed the Social Security Act of 1935. In signing the legislation, Roosevelt commented,

> This Social Security measure gives at least some protection to thirty million of our citizens who will reap direct benefits through unemployment compensation, thorough old-age pensions, and though increased services for the protection of children and the prevention of ill-health. . . . We can never ensure 100 percent of the population against 100 percent of the hazards and vicissitudes of life, but we have tried to frame a law which will give some measure of protection to the average citizen and to his family against the loss of a job and against poverty-ridden old age.

The Social Security Act of 1935 included three major provisions. First, it set up a pension fund for retirees over the age of sixty-five, funded through a payroll tax beginning in 1937. Second, it set up a system of unemployment insurance, financed by a tax on employers, to financially assist those who had lost their jobs. Third, it provided public assistance grants to the states in order to provide relief for elderly poor, fatherless children, the blind, and the handicapped. The system was not without its critics. However, with pension and unemployment benefits funded through a system of taxation, Congress rallied behind the legislation to pass what Roosevelt described as "a law to flatten out the peaks and valleys of deflation and of inflation—in other words, a law that will take care of human needs."

National Archives Document

AN ACT to provide for the general welfare by establishing a system of Federal old-age benefits, and by enabling the several States to make more adequate provision for aged persons, blind persons, dependent and crippled children, maternal and child welfare, public health, and the administration of their unemployment compensation laws; to establish a Social Security Board; to raise revenue; and for other purposes.

SECTION 1. For the purpose of enabling each State to furnish financial assistance, as far as practicable under the conditions in such State, to aged needy individuals. . . .

SECTION 301. For the purpose of assisting the States in the administration of their unemployment compensation laws. . . .

SECTION 401. For the purpose of enabling each State to furnish financial assistance, as far as practicable under the conditions in such State, to needy dependent children. . . .

SECTION 501. For the purpose of enabling each State to extend and improve, as far as practicable under the conditions in such State, services for promoting the health of mothers and children, especially in rural areas and in areas suffering from severe economic distress. . . .

SEC. 511. For the purpose of enabling each State to extend and improve (especially in rural areas and in areas suffering from severe economic distress), as far as practicable under the conditions in such State, services for locating crippled children and for providing medical, surgical, corrective, and other services and care, and facilities for diagnosis, hospitalization, and aftercare, for children who are crippled or who are suffering from conditions which lead to crippling. . . . ❋

Left: Workers learn about Social Security benefits in this 1939 New York City photo.

Critical Thinking

Draw Conclusions

When referring to the reasoning behind the provisions of the Social Security Act of 1935, President Roosevelt stated,

> The civilization of the past hundred years, with its startling industrial changes, has tended more and more to make life insecure. Young people have come to wonder what would be their lot when they came to old age. The man with a job has wondered how long the job would last.

What new role did government assume through the legislation? Why was the legislation considered by many as radical?

Assess Significance

Distribution of pension benefits established through the Social Security Act of 1935 began in 1940 for individuals age sixty-five and older. They averaged only $22 per month. Roosevelt stressed that the pension fund was designed to supplement an individual's retirement, not sustain it. Even with eggs at 13 cents per dozen and milk selling for 10 cents a quart, $22 still represented a modest monthly income. With this in mind, why is the legislation considered so significant?

Determine Point of View

Given a belief at the time that individuals should make it on their own wherewithal, why did many people eventually accept the assistance provisions of the Social Security Act of 1935?

Research and Writing

Historical Interpretation

One-third of the nation lived below the poverty line during the early 1930s. Yet, sales increased for gasoline and movie tickets as people looked for ways to escape from the shadow of unemployment. In commenting on the Great Depression, humorist Will Rogers quipped, "We are the first nation in the history of the world to go to the poorhouse in an automobile." Research the human toll of the Great Depression. Who was most impacted by its economic realities? How did people survive the difficult years? What part did relief agencies play in helping individuals cope with unemployment and poverty? Do you agree with Will Rogers's assessment of the times? Why or why not?

Related Events

Access and read the Social Security Act of 1935. Then reread the Preamble to the United States Constitution. Do the provisions of the Social Security Act of 1935 agree or conflict with the vision of American government as seen by its framers. Was the Social Security Act of 1935 an expansion of the role of government or simply an extension of its mandate? Would the framers of the Constitution agree with the provisions set forth by the act? Use examples to explain your position.

Link to the Past

Research current concerns with the Social Security System. What is the average monthly pension benefit? Is social security still considered solely as a supplement to an individual's retirement from the workforce? How stable is it as a retirement fund? What concerns are there about its ability to sustain itself? What changes are proposed in the way the government manages an individual's retirement dollars?

Roosevelt's Speech in Defense of the Second New Deal

"You look much better than you did four years ago."

—FRANKLIN DELANO ROOSEVELT

HISTORICAL BACKGROUND

SOON after President Franklin D. Roosevelt took office on March 4, 1933, thousands of letters poured into the White House from impoverished children. Over 300,000 letters were sent to Eleanor Roosevelt in her first year as America's First Lady. The president and Mrs. Roosevelt, in particular, were seen as helpers of the downtrodden, often a child's last hope. And, while their parents may have been too proud to ask for help, the youth of America seized the opportunity. "I hope mother or dad wont [sic] find out I am writing to you because they don't want to let anyone know how hard-up we are," wrote a child from Colorado. Throughout the years of the Great Depression, the letters just kept coming. The youth of America asked Mrs. Roosevelt for a bicycle, a violin, $52 for piano lessons, $10 to finish school, a new sweater, money to pay the rent, and help to "take back their farm" from foreclosure. "We never can have shoe skates and clothes like other boys. I sure would like to have a pair of shoe skates. . . . Mrs. Roosevelt if you could lend me enough money to buy shoe skates I sure would be happy and would pay you back when I get big and can earn money." Hapless children in hapless times wrote of the cold realities of the Depression. Some were particularly blunt: "You are rich and I am poor," or "But I know you are very, very rich. And we have to work hard . . ."— quiet requests to share the wealth. For some, all rested on the 1936 presidential election, "This may sound awful funny to you but our whole future depends on your presidency. If you don't get in I don't know what we will do. My Dad is only a W.P.A. worker and we are certainly thankful for that."

On October 31, 1936, President Franklin Delano Roosevelt stood before a large, welcoming crowd at New York City's Madison Square Garden. Roosevelt was on the campaign trail, seeking re-election for his second term as president of the United States. He well understood the financial woes impacting so many American families. He didn't have to hear it from his advisors; the children of America had said through their letters that there was much to be accomplished to set the country right. In his words to the crowd and to radio listeners across America, Roosevelt answered those letters received at the White House.

> Of course we will continue to seek to improve the working conditions for the workers of America. . . .
>
> Of course we will continue to work for cheaper electricity in the homes and on the farms of America. . . .
>
> Of course we will continue our efforts in behalf of the farmers of America. . . .
>
> Of course we will provide useful work for the needy unemployed: we prefer useful work to the pauperism of the dole. . . .
>
> Of course we will continue our efforts for young men and women so that they may obtain an education and the opportunity to use it. . . .

President Roosevelt had entitled his speech "We Have Only Just Begun." It spoke to the worth of programs established through the Second New Deal. The people listened. When the November votes were counted, Roosevelt had scored a landslide victory, carrying every state except Maine and Vermont. A close look at the votes told the story. Nearly 81 percent of those with annual incomes of under a thousand dollars voted for Roosevelt. A similar result occurred for those earning between one and two thousand dollars a year. It was a vote of hope and confidence answered by Roosevelt in his Second Inaugural Address on January 20, 1937. "The test of our progress is not whether we add more to the abundance of those who have much; it is whether we provide enough for those who have too little."

NATIONAL ARCHIVES DOCUMENT

In 1932 the issue was the restoration of American democracy; and the American people were in a mood to win. They did win. In 1936 the issue is the preservation of their victory. Again they are in a mood to win. Again they will win.

What was our hope in 1932? Above all other things the American people wanted peace. They wanted peace of mind instead of gnawing fear.

First, they sought escape from the personal terror which had stalked them for three years. They wanted the peace that comes from security in their homes: safety for their savings, permanence in their jobs, a fair profit from their enterprise.

Next, they wanted peace in the community, the peace that springs from the ability to meet the needs of community life: schools, playgrounds, parks, sanitation, highways—those things which are expected of solvent local government. . . .

They also sought peace within the Nation: protection of their currency, fairer wages, the ending of long hours of toil, the abolition of child labor, the elimination of wild-cat speculation, the safety of their children from kidnappers.

And, finally, they sought peace with other Nations—peace in a world of unrest. The Nation knows that I hate war, and I know that the Nation hates war.

I submit to you a record of peace; and on that record a well-founded expectation for future peace—peace for the individual, peace for the community, peace for the Nation, and peace with the world.

"Peace on earth, good will toward men"—democracy must cling to that message. For it is my deep conviction that democracy cannot live without that true religion which gives a nation a sense of justice and of moral purpose. . . . That is why the recovery we seek, the recovery we are winning, is more than economic. In it are included justice and love and humility, not for ourselves as individuals alone, but for our Nation. ✳

Left: The Works Progress Administration was created on May 6, 1935. It provided all types of jobs, from building roads to painting murals, for unemployed Americans.

Critical Thinking

Draw Conclusions

According to the 1940 government report "Children in a Democracy," between 1935 and 1936 the per capita income for a family of 3–4 persons was $542. Two-person families fared better, with a per capita income of $774, while a large family of seven or more persons attempted to pay rent, buy clothes and food, and send children to school all on an average per capita of $221. In many of the letters sent to Mrs. Roosevelt, children pleaded for a small sum of money to buy clothes so they could attend school. What impact do you think the Great Depression had on the education of America's youth?

Determine Point of View

Only 46 percent of individuals with annual incomes of over $5000 voted for Roosevelt in 1936. Roosevelt was a man of great wealth. Why, then, did less than half of the country's more fortunate vote for Roosevelt?

Analyze Cause and Effect

The Supreme Court more often than not ruled against New Deal programs. Roosevelt's answer was to change the structure of the federal courts by adding judges and justices. His "pack the court" plans failed in Congress. How does this failure illustrate the system of checks and balances built into the U.S. Constitution?

Research and Writing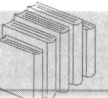

Related Events

In President Roosevelt's Second Inaugural Address, he clearly defined the challenge of the next four years, "I see one-third of a nation ill-housed, ill-clad, ill-nourished." Research one of the following New Deal programs: the Public Works Administration (PWA), the Civilian Conservation Corps (CCC), the Works Progress Administration (WPA), or National Youth Administration (NYA). When was it started? What was the purpose of the program? Who did it help? How successful was it in answering the challenge set forth by Roosevelt in 1936?

Biography

Nine years to the day following Roosevelt's Madison Square Garden campaign speech, Eleanor Roosevelt wrote in her newspaper column My Day:

> Yesterday afternoon I went with some members of the Citizens' Housing Committee to visit an old-law tenement: a house with no hot water and no heat, a house which many families call home—here in the biggest city of the U.S.A.! [New York City] In one place, an old man and woman occupy two rooms, with one stove on the left of a narrow hall as you go in…. The old lady was a pathetic sight—sick, and unable to speak our language very well. I felt guilty as I looked at her, for though she could have been more unhappy in the land from which she came, I realized that our land of promise must be a disappointment to her and many others like her who have come here hoping never again to see the sub-standards which they left…. As I stood in that wretched tenement, I thought of what a place like that meant not just to the people who lived in it, but to the people of our whole city…. I am appalled at the harm this indifference may do us as a nation.

Throughout her years as First Lady, Eleanor Roosevelt was a tireless and passionate spokesperson for the poor. Research the life of Eleanor Roosevelt. Write a brief biography emphasizing her contributions to society before, during, and after her years as the country's First Lady.

Link to the Present

In his October 31, 1936, campaign speech, Roosevelt chastised the arrogance of fortune.

> Here and now I want to make myself clear about those who disparage their fellow citizens on the relief rolls. They say that those on relief are not merely jobless—that they are worthless. Their solution for the relief problem is to end relief—to purge the rolls by starvation. To use the language of the stock broker, our needy unemployed would be cared for when, as, and if some fairy godmother should happen on the scene.

What is the status of federal relief programs today? What programs are available to help those with economic challenges? Who receives help? Are the programs sufficient to meet the financial needs of the unemployed and underemployed? Explain your point of view.

1944 Servicemen's Readjustment Act

"The war changed our whole idea of how we wanted to live when we got back. We set our sights pretty high."

—World War II veteran

Historical Background

"THE great majority of you will be returned to civilian life as soon as the ships and planes can get you here," President Harry Truman assured the troops on August 15, 1945, one day following Japan's surrender ending World War II. Some troops would return to the farm, eager to exchange the sounds and smells of the battlefront for the whir of a tractor chugging through the fields and the sweet smell of freshly cut hay. Most would return to America's cities, hoping to exchange employment by the United States government for a job in one of America's thriving industries.

The wartime economy rejuvenated America. Between 1940 and 1944, unemployment dropped by some 4.6 million people to an unprecedented 1.2 percent. With more than 10 million men drafted over the course of the war, women replaced workers lost to the military in factories across America. They added new earning power to a previously largely unsalaried segment of society. Beginning in 1941, local government agencies asked farmers to increase their production of hogs, milk, and eggs by some 10 to 25 percent, improving the economic outlook in agriculture. In addition, the federal government poured money into contracts that supplied the war effort. The government hired such national contractors as Hercules Powder and Mason and Hanger Construction to build munitions plants and shipyards. It also invested heavily in the aircraft industry—war production that employed six million defense workers, dragging the country out of the economic depths of the Depression years.

V-J Day (Victory in Japan Day) foreshadowed a return to a peacetime economy. It also signaled a dramatic shift in who was employed and what was produced by the nation's factories. "Guns to butter" was a transition that had a difficult start. Factories laid off workers while they retooled to manufacture peacetime goods. In 1947 alone, almost two million working women received employment termination notices. Exacerbating the situation were restrictions the government had placed on building nonmilitary housing during the war. Veterans returning home were eager for a sense of normalcy. However, with jobs difficult to find and housing scarce, many vets initially found themselves dealing with an unanticipated emotional battlefront. The plight of vets was given a light touch in the 1946 Three Stooges comedy spoof *G.I. Wanna Home* and popularized in the 1946 Merle Travis tune *No Vacancy*.

> Not so long ago when the bullets screamed,
> Many was the happy dream I dreamed
> Of a little nest where I could rest when the world was free.
> Now the mighty war over there is won,
> Troubles and trials have just begun
> As I face that terrible enemy sign, "No Vacancy."

To offset postwar unemployment and fend off another widespread economic depression, Congress passed the Servicemen's Readjustment Act of 1944, commonly known as the G.I. Bill of Rights, or simply the GI Bill. Signed into law by President Roosevelt just days following D-Day, the legislation assisted soldiers returning to civilian life with hospitalization, low-interest loans for homes and businesses, and unemployment pay of $20 per week for fifty-two weeks. Returning veterans who could not find work remained in the 52-20 "club" for an average of four months, turning instead to the educational provisions of the GI Bill. The act provided willing GIs with $500 in yearly college tuition, covered the cost of books and fees, and advanced a monthly living allowance of $50, increased to $65 in 1946 and to $75 in 1948. Those with dependents received higher allowances.

Veterans were entitled to one year of full-time college or vocational training plus a period equal to their time in the service, up to forty-eight months.

The effects of the program were immediate. Millions of vets decided to attend school instead of flooding the labor market, dramatically reducing joblessness. In 1947 veterans accounted for 47 percent of all college enrollments. Some fifteen million veterans returned home following World War II. More than half received post-war training through the benefits of the GI Bill. Though the program costs totaled $14.5 billion, as a result of the legislation veterans entered the workforce better prepared to contribute to the support of their families and to strengthening the American economy.

NATIONAL ARCHIVES DOCUMENT

To provide Federal Government aid for the readjustment in civilian life of returning World War II veterans.

Be it enacted by the Senate and House of Representatives of the United States of America in Congress assembled, That this Act may be cited as the "Servicemen's Readjustment Act of 1944".

SEC. 101. The Administrator of Veterans' Affairs and the Federal Board of Hospitalization are hereby authorized and directed to expedite and complete the construction of additional hospital facilities for war veterans. . . .

SEC.103. The Administrator of Veterans' Affairs shall have authority to place officials and employees designated by him in such Army and Navy installations as may be deemed advisable for the purpose of adjudicating disability claims of, and giving aid and advice to, members of the Army and Navy who are about to be discharged or released from active service. . . . ※

Left: The Servicemen's Readjustment Act provided educational benefits for soldiers and sailors returning from World War II.

Critical Thinking

Assess Significance

Most veterans entered World War II lacking a high school diploma. As a result of the Servicemen's Readjustment Act of 1944, some 3.5 million vets finished school or attended agriculture or other job-specific classes, 3.4 million received on-the-job or on-the-farm training, and 2.3 million went on to attend colleges and universities. Why did the GI Bill focus on education as a means to reduce unemployment?

Determine Point of View

Explain the quote at the top of page 303.

Analyze Cause and Effect

It has been estimated that for every $1 spent on veterans via the GI Bill the government received $8 in taxes. How was this possible?

Research and Writing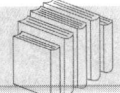

Related Events

In 1947 William Levitt used the principals of the assembly line as a way to address the housing shortage. He purchased 1,200 acres of farmland on Long Island, New York. Utilizing 27 teams, each having a specific task, Levitt built 36 identical houses each day, all exactly sixty feet apart. Eventually Levittown grew to 10,600 homes. The affordable houses were at first only available to veterans, but soon they were sold to nonvets as well. Other housing developments followed. The race for suburbia had begun. Veterans took advantage of the low-income provision in the GI Bill to purchase some 20 percent of all newly constructed homes. Research the growth of suburbs in America after World War II. What part did veterans play in their growth? How did the growth of suburbs change the social landscape of the country? What was their long-term impact on cities? What was their impact on race relations? How did the growth of suburbs alter the American dream?

Analysis

Upon signing the Servicemen's Readjustment Act of 1944, President Roosevelt commented, "With the signing of this bill a well-rounded program of special veterans' benefits is nearly completed. It gives emphatic notice to the men and women in our armed forces that the American people do not intend to let them down." Research the impact of the 1944 GI Bill of Rights on veterans returning to your state. How were they helped? How were your state's colleges and universities affected by the enrollment of veterans? How did the act benefit the veterans and ultimately the economy of your community?

Link to the Present

Since 1956, Congress has passed several other pieces of legislation aimed at extending the benefits of the Servicemen's Readjustment Act of 1944. Today, educational benefits are used as an enlistment incentive for young men and women considering entry in the military. Research current benefits offered to those who enlist in the armed forces. Who is most likely to take advantage of the benefits offered through the current GI Bill?

1961 Eisenhower's Farewell Address

"The potential for the disastrous rise of misplaced power exists and will persist."

—President Dwight D. Eisenhower

Historical Background

PRESIDENT Dwight D. Eisenhower began his military training at West Point. Throughout his fifty years of service to his country Eisenhower viewed the nation's needs and its position in the world through the eyes of a well-trained military officer. In his lifetime Eisenhower experienced two world wars. During World War II, he served as the commander-in-chief of the Allied Expeditionary Force, overseeing one of the most improbable of military missions—the landing of 156,000 troops on the beaches of Normandy on June 6, 1944—D-Day. He went on to serve two terms as president of the United States. He ended the Korean War and helped to bolster the country through growing Cold War fears while restraining the nuclear arms race. Mostly he gave Americans the sense that resolve and experience were in charge of the country. He left the presidency as he had entered it—a general with wisdom to impart.

In preparing his farewell address on January 17, 1961, Eisenhower carefully reread the typed pages—marking points, crossing out handwritten inclusions, and twice underscoring "my countrymen." Like George Washington almost two hundred years earlier, Eisenhower used the last days of his presidency "to share a few final thoughts"—gentle words of warning from another military leader and president who had seen the country through so many difficult years. "America's leadership and prestige depend, not merely upon our unmatched material progress, riches and military strength, but on how we use our power in the interests of world peace and human betterment," cautioned Eisenhower. "Our basic purposes have been to keep the peace; to foster progress in human achievement, and to enhance liberty, dignity and integrity among people and among nations."

Eisenhower recognized that keeping the peace came with a price tag perhaps unrecognized by the American people—an alliance between the military and the huge defense industry that supplied it. "In the councils of government, we must guard against the acquisition of unwarranted influence, whether sought or unsought, by the military-industrial complex," he warned. "The potential for the disastrous rise of misplaced power exists and will persist." The nation's defense had become a business, a double-edged sword where national security depended on up-to-date weapons and equipment that could only be offered by an industry that profited from the sale of war-related technology. The military-industrial complex depended on war, or at least on the preparation for it, to sustain itself. It was the regrettable price of peace. Eisenhower warned that the potential for the industry to lead the country into war for its own sake was a possibility that needed constant vigilance.

> This conjunction of an immense military establishment and a large arms industry is new in the American experience. The total influence—economic, political, even spiritual—is felt in every city, every state house, every office of the Federal government. We recognize the imperative need for this development. Yet we must not fail to comprehend its grave implications. . . . We must never let the weight of this combination endanger our liberties or democratic processes. We should take nothing for granted only an alert and knowledgeable citizenry can compel the proper meshing of huge industrial and military machinery of defense with our peaceful methods and goals, so that security and liberty may prosper together.

NATIONAL ARCHIVES DOCUMENT

This evening I come to you with a message of leave-taking and farewell, and to share a few final thoughts with you, my countrymen. . . .

We now stand ten years past the midpoint of a century that has witnessed four major wars among great nations. Three of these involved our own country. Despite these holocausts America is today the strongest, the most influential and most productive nation in the world. Understandably proud of this pre-eminence, we yet realize that America's leadership and prestige depend, not merely upon our unmatched material progress, riches and military strength, but on how we use our power in the interests of world peace and human betterment. . . .

A vital element in keeping the peace is our military establishment. Our arms must be mighty, ready for instant action, so that no potential aggressor may be tempted to risk his own destruction. . . .

Below: President Eisenhower addressing Congress.

Until the latest of our world conflicts, the United States had no armaments industry. American makers of plowshares could, with time and as required, make swords as well. But now we can no longer risk emergency improvisation of national defense; we have been compelled to create a permanent armaments industry of vast proportions. Added to this, three and a half million men and women are directly engaged in the defense establishment. We annually spend on military security more than the net income of all United State corporations. . . .

In the councils of government, we must guard against the acquisition of unwarranted influence, whether sought or unsought, by the military-industrial complex. The potential for the disastrous rise of misplaced power exists and will persist.

We must never let the weight of this combination endanger our liberties or democratic processes. We should take nothing for granted only an alert and knowledgeable citizenry can compel the proper meshing of huge industrial and military machinery of defense with our peaceful methods and goals, so that security and liberty may prosper together. . . .

We pray that peoples of all faiths, all races, all nations, may have their great human needs satisfied; that those now denied opportunity shall come to enjoy it to the full; that all who yearn for freedom may experience its spiritual blessings; that those who have freedom will understand, also, its heavy responsibilities; that all who are insensitive to the needs of others will learn charity; that the scourges of poverty, disease and ignorance will be made to disappear from the earth, and that, in the goodness of time, all peoples will come to live together in a peace guaranteed by the binding force of mutual respect and love. ❈

Critical Thinking

Assess Significance

Why did Eisenhower choose the format of a farewell address to express his concern about the military-industrial complex rather than just put out a press release?

Determine Point of View

Eisenhower closed his farewell address with what appears to be a concession.

> Disarmament, with mutual honor and confidence, is a continuing imperative. Together we must learn how to compose difference, not with arms, but with intellect and decent purpose. Because this need is so sharp and apparent I confess that I lay down my official responsibilities in this field with a definite sense of disappointment. As one who has witnessed the horror and the lingering sadness of war—as one who knows that another war could utterly destroy this civilization which has been so slowly and painfully built over thousands of years—I wish I could say tonight that a lasting peace is in sight. Happily, I can say that war has been avoided. Steady progress toward our ultimate goal has been made. But, so much remains to be done.

To what is Eisenhower referring? Explain.

Draw Conclusions

"May we be ever unswerving in devotion to principle, confident but humble with power, diligent in pursuit of the Nation's great goals." What did Eisenhower mean?

Research and Writing

Related Events

The 1950s saw a transformation of American society. It was the baby boomer generation. Between 1946 and 1964 the population increased by forty million—a 30 percent increase. Increases in baby food, diaper service, toys, books, and furniture all followed the birth of a record number of American babies. The dramatic increase in home ownership, a whopping 50 percent between 1945 and 1960, spurred a similar increase in the sales of refrigerators, washing machines, vacuum cleaners, and a new American pastime—the television. TV Guide became the fastest growing periodical of the 1950s. Research life in the 1950s. How did advertising affect the consumerism seen in the 1950s? What music identified the times? What TV shows depicted the ideal American family? How did people spend their leisure time? In what way did the baby boomer generation transform American culture?

Analysis

Eisenhower warned the nation of the dangers of close ties between the defense industry and the military—the military-industrial complex. How did ties between military and defense contractors lend to the concern over the growing arms race? How did people deal in their daily lives with the fear of mutually-assured destruction? What domestic policies did the government put into place to help alleviate the anxiety people experienced due to the ever-present threat of a nuclear attack?

Link to the Present

Today the military continues to be tied to specific industries whose profit margins depend on contracts with the U.S. government. Such corporations as Lockheed Martin Corporation, Boeing Corporation, and General Dynamics—three of the largest defense contractors—receive billions of dollars each year in contractual agreements with the United States government. Who are the six largest defense contractors today? What do they manufacture? How important are government contracts to the company's profit margin? Were Eisenhower's warnings of a powerful and influential military-industrial complex prophetic or ill-advised?

Kennedy's Inaugural Address

"We stand today on the edge of a New Frontier."

—JOHN F. KENNEDY

HISTORICAL BACKGROUND

ON July 15, 1960, John F. Kennedy stood before delegates to the National Democratic Convention to accept the nomination as their candidate for president of the United States. He punctuated his speech with an "out with the old, in with the new" theme. "Today our concern must be with that future. For the world is changing. The old era is ending. The old ways will not do." Kennedy spoke of the "technological revolution on the farm," the "peaceful revolution for human rights," the "medical revolution," and the "revolution of automation [that] finds machines replacing men in the mines and mills of America, without replacing their incomes or their training or their needs to pay the family doctor, grocer and landlord." He termed his vision for America the *New Frontier*. Kennedy's appeal was to the young—and if not young in years at least "young in heart." Although his presidential rival was only five years his senior, he placed Vice-President Richard Nixon among those of the old guard—cloaked in complacency and comfort. "I believe the times demand new invention, innovation, imagination, decision," said Kennedy, "I am asking each of you to be pioneers on that New Frontier."

In Kennedy's favor were his eloquence, wealth, looks, and family. Against him were his lack of national prominence and his religion. As a Catholic, to be elected president Kennedy would have to overcome concerns that his religion would unduly influence his decisions. "I hope that no American, considering the really critical issues facing this country, will waste his franchise by voting either for me or against me solely on account of my religious affiliation. It is not relevant," Kennedy told the nation. Richard Nixon had experience, his distinction as the country's vice-president, and his association with domestic policies of the Eisenhower years. Both candidates had served in World War II. Both had

served in the Senate. When the November votes were counted, Kennedy had managed to win the closest presidential election since 1888, capturing the White House with a margin of 118,574 votes out of 68 million cast.

On January 20, 1961 Kennedy took the oath of office as president of the United States. He then turned to speak to the people, uniting the country on the eve of change.

> We dare not forget today that we are the heirs of that first revolution. Let the word go forth from this time and place, to friend and foe alike, that the torch has been passed to a new generation of Americans—born in this century, tempered by war, disciplined by a hard and bitter peace, proud of our ancient heritage—and unwilling to witness or permit the slow undoing of those human rights to which this nation has always been committed, and to which we are committed today at home and around the world.

Kennedy stood before the nation and challenged its citizens to be an active part of their government. "In your hands, my fellow citizens, more than mine, will rest the final success or failure of our course. . . . Ask not what your country can do for you—ask what you can do for your country." Kennedy called Americans to service in their communities and around the world. His appeal was for Americans to be selfless—not the selflessness seen during World War II, but a willingness to serve those less fortunate. It would be people, not government, who came to the aid of those in need—caring people building a caring nation. Yet Kennedy didn't stop with a call to Americans. In the midst of the Cold War, he also challenged world leaders to establish "a beachhead of cooperation [that] may push back the jungle of suspicion;" Kennedy posed the possibility for a "new world of law, where the strong are just and the weak secure and the peace preserved."

We observe today not a victory of party but a celebration of freedom—symbolizing an end as well as a beginning—signifying renewal as well as change. For I have sworn before you and Almighty God the same solemn oath our forbears prescribed nearly a century and three-quarters ago.

The world is very different now. For man holds in his mortal hands the power to abolish all forms of human poverty and all forms of human life. And yet the same revolutionary beliefs for which our forebears fought are still at issue around the globe—the belief that the rights of man come not from the generosity of the state but from the hand of God. . . .

Let every nation know, whether it wishes us well or ill, that we shall pay any price, bear any burden, meet any hardship, support any friend, oppose any foe to assure the survival and the success of liberty.

This much we pledge—and more. . . .

In your hands, my fellow citizens, more than mine, will rest the final success or failure of our course. Since this country was founded, each generation of Americans has been summoned to give testimony to its national loyalty. The graves of young Americans who answered the call to service surround the globe.

Now the trumpet summons us again—not as a call to bear arms, though arms we need—not as a call to battle, though embattled we are—but a call to bear the burden of a long twilight struggle, year in and year out, "rejoicing in hope, patient in tribulation"—a struggle against the common enemies of man: tyranny, poverty, disease and war itself. . . .

In the long history of the world, only a few generations have been granted the role of defending freedom in its hour of maximum danger. I do not shrink from this responsibility—I welcome it. I do not believe that any of us would exchange places with any other people or any other generation. The energy, the faith, the devotion which we bring to this endeavor will light our country and all who serve it—and the glow from that fire can truly light the world.

And so, my fellow Americans: ask not what your country can do for you—ask what you can do for your country.

My fellow citizens of the world: ask not what America will do for you, but what together we can do for the freedom of man. . . . ✳

Below: Chief Justice Earl Warren administering the oath of office to President-elect John F. Kennedy.

Critical Thinking

Compare and Contrast

Which phrase or sentence in Kennedy's speech do you find to be the most inspiring? Why?

Determine Point of View

Kennedy called himself an "idealist without illusions." What do you think he meant?

Draw Conclusion

Poet Robert Frost paid tribute to President Kennedy at his inaugural with a poem written for the occasion entitled *The Gift Outright.* Kennedy returned the homage paid to him by Frost in a tribute following Frost's death in 1963. Kennedy said of Frost,

> The men who create power make an indispensable contribution to the nation's greatness. But the men who question power make a contribution just as indispensable.... For they determine whether we use power or power uses us. Our national strength matters, but the spirit which informs and controls our strength matters just as much.

What comment was Kennedy making on the role of citizens in government?

Research and Writing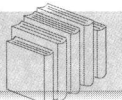

Related Events

On September 26, 1960, John Kennedy and Vice President Richard Nixon participated in the first of four nationally televised debates. It was television's first steps into the political arena of presidential debates. The first debate centered on domestic issues. Nixon at the time was recovering from a recent illness. He looked weary and uneasy. Kennedy, in comparison projected the image of poise and intelligence, a certain charisma—a man perfectly fit for the office of president.

In response to a critical question of why voters should prefer Kennedy over Nixon, Kennedy responded,

> Mr. Nixon comes out of the Republican Party. He was nominated by it. And it is a fact that through most of these last twenty-five years the Republican leadership has opposed Federal aid for education, medical care for the aged, development of the Tennessee Valley, development of our natural resources.... The question before us is: Which point of view and which party do we want to lead the United States?

When asked to comment on Kennedy's criticism of the Republican record, Nixon simply stated, "I have no comment." Some seventy million viewers watched as Kennedy and Nixon exchanged criticisms and promises in that first debate. When it was over, Kennedy's popularity soared. Research the September 26, 1960, debate. Tally the issues covered. Analyze the responses of Kennedy and Nixon. Without the visual impact of two men—one looking ill and the other fit, who do you think won the debate on substance? Who scored points on eloquence? In your opinion, would the results of the debate been different in the absence of a televised image?

Analysis

Access and read Kennedy's entire Inaugural Address of January 20, 1961. Highlight his most significant points. What is most notable about Kennedy's speech? Why do you think Kennedy's Inaugural Address has been identified as among the most influential documents in American history?

Historical Interpretation

Research the accomplishments of Kennedy's administration. What domestic issues were addressed? How successful was he in accomplishing the goals he put before the nation in his Inaugural Address?

1965 Social Security Act Amendments

*"No longer will illness crush and destroy
the savings . . . so carefully put away over a lifetime."*

—LYNDON BAINES JOHNSON

HISTORICAL BACKGROUND

ONE objective President Franklin Delano Roosevelt set aside to assure passage of the Social Security Act of 1935 was his hope for some type of health insurance program for the elderly. Over the years Roosevelt continued to remind Congress that health care for the aged should be of primary importance. In his 1944 State of the Union Address, Roosevelt laid out his "Economic Bill of Rights." "We have come to a clear realization of the fact that true individual freedom cannot exist without economic security and independence," said Roosevelt. Among his list of economic rights was "The right to adequate medical care and the opportunity to achieve and enjoy good health." President Harry Truman continued Roosevelt's quest for health care funding. He called for a national health plan in his 1948 State of the Union Address. Truman said,

> The greatest gap in our social security structure is the lack of adequate provision for the Nation's health. We are rightly proud of the high standards of medical care we know how to provide in the United States. The fact is, however, that most of our people cannot afford to pay for the care they need. I have often and strongly urged that this condition demands a national health program. The heart of the program must be a national system of payment for medical care based on well-tried insurance principles. This great Nation cannot afford to allow its citizens to suffer needlessly from the lack of proper medical care. Our ultimate aim must be a comprehensive insurance system to protect all our people equally against insecurity and ill health.

In 1949 the Wagner-Murray-Dingell Bill was introduced for the fourth time into Congress. Its aim was to establish medical coverage for Americans through Social Security. As had occurred in the past, it failed to gain congressional support. The next year, however, the Social Security Amendments of 1950 established matching funds for state payments to medical providers for those individuals receiving some form of public assistance. Then, after a decade of inaction, the Kerr-Mills Act (Social Security Amendments of 1960) established state-run medical assistance programs for the elderly living on limited incomes. By 1964, thirty-nine states, as well as the District of Columbia, had established medical assistance programs for the needy based on the Kerr-Mills Act of 1960.

In 1960 President-elect John F. Kennedy appointed a "Task Force on Health and Social Security for the American People." In 1961 it recommended "a hospital insurance program for the elderly funded through Social Security. Subsequently, in his 1962 State of the Union Address, Kennedy urged "that its coverage be extended without further delay to provide health insurance for the elderly." Continued efforts in Congress to establish a national plan resulted in passage of the Social Security Amendments of 1965. The long-awaited legislation signed into law by President Lyndon Baines Johnson established two programs: Medicare—a health insurance plan designed for individuals aged 65 and older, and Medicaid—health insurance for low-income individuals and families. Johnson believed the legislation to be of paramount importance.

> No longer will older Americans be denied the healing miracle of modern medicine. No longer will illness crush and destroy the savings that they have so carefully put away over a lifetime so that they might enjoy dignity in their later years. No longer will young families see their own incomes, and their own hopes, eaten away simply because they are carrying out their deep moral obligations to their parents, and to their uncles, and their aunts.

The Social Security Amendments of 1965 established a two-tiered approach to health care for the elderly. Medicare Part A was created as a voluntary and supplementary medical insurance program that covered hospital care for those individuals who paid into the system through payroll taxes. Medicare B set up a means to pay for additional health care costs, funded through a series of monthly premiums. In contrast, Medicaid was established as a joint state-federal program with each state establishing its own eligibility requirements and payment plans. It included three levels of health care maintenance: to low-income families and individuals with disabilities, long-term care for the elderly and individuals with disabilities, and additional coverage for low-income Medicare patients. The Social Security Amendments of 1965 established a system of national health insurance on a limited scale. Today it continues to provide access to medical care for over 30 million Americans.

NATIONAL ARCHIVES DOCUMENT

To provide a hospital insurance program for the aged under the Social Security Act with a supplementary medical benefits program and an extended program of medical assistance, to increase benefits under the Old-Age, Survivors, and Disability Insurance System, to improve the Federal-State public assistance programs, and for other purposes.

TITLE I–HEALTH INSURANCE FOB THE AGED AND MEDICAL ASSISTANCE

PART I–HEALTH INSURANCE BENEFITS FOR THE AGED

TITLE XVIII–HEALTH INSURANCE FOR THE AGED

PART A–HOSPITAL INSURANCE BENEFITS FOR THE AGED

PART B–SUPPLEMENTARY MEDICAL INSURANCE BENEFITS FOR THE AGED

TITLE I–HEALTH INSURANCE FOR THE AGED AND MEDICAL ASSISTANCE ✳

Left: Medicare was established through the Social Security Act Amendments of 1965. Today Medicare continues to help pay for the medical needs of the elderly.

Critical Thinking

Analyze Cause and Effect

Both Medicare and Medicaid are considered entitlement programs, which are available to all who meet eligibility requirements. Their impact on local, state, and federal budgets can be quite volatile. Why do entitlement programs such as Medicare and Medicaid present budgetary difficulties for government?

Determine Point of View

Would you consider President Truman's 1948 comments concerning health care timely? Explain.

Draw Conclusion

Upon signing the Social Security Amendments of 1965, President Johnson said the following:

> Many men can make many proposals. Many men can draft many laws. But few have the piercing and humane eye which can see beyond the words to the people that they touch. Few can see past the speeches and the political battles to the doctor over there that is tending the infirm, and to the hospital that is receiving those in anguish, or feel in their heart painful wrath at the injustice which denies the miracle of healing to the old and to the poor. And fewer still have the courage to stake reputation, and position, and the effort of a lifetime upon such a cause when there are so few that share it.

Would you agree? Why or why not?

Research and Writing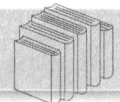

Counterpoint

One of the difficulties with Medicaid is the level of payment for medical services rendered for individuals on the program. Often reimbursement for Medicaid patients is only about half of what a medical provider would receive for the same services billed directly to the individual or to private insurance providers. Research the reimbursement issues of Medicaid. Are Medicaid reimbursement rates a deterrent to quality health care for those of limited financial means?

Analysis

The amendments that created Medicare and Medicaid were not without their critics. Some felt the tenets of social security were becoming far too closely aligned with the tenets of socialism. Even Roosevelt disagreed with the concept of socialized medicine—a system of national health care funded through the government.

However, over the years, few have disagreed with the right of the elderly and of those without the ability to pay to have access to quality medical care. Research the universal health care program established in Canada. How does it work? How is it funded? Would a program like the one in Canada be possible in the United States? Support your position.

Link to the Past

Every state, each territory, and the District of Columbia all have individually administered Medicaid programs. Research how the program functions in your area. What are the eligibility requirements? What type of medical assistance is available? Are other medical assistance programs available for people who do not qualify for Medicaid? Are there programs specifically designed for children? How well do the programs meet the need?

IMAGE CREDITS

Cover image: PhotoDisc/Getty Images; p. i, Courtesy National Archives; p. 1, Leonard de Selva/CORBIS/MAGMA; p. 4, top, North Wind Picture Archives, bottom, Courtesy National Archives; p. 7, North Wind Picture Archives; p. 9, Courtesy National Archives; p. 10, Courtesy National Archives; p. 16, North Wind Picture Archives; p. 25, Kansas Historical Society; p. 31, Courtesy National Archives; p. 33, The Granger Collection, New York; p. 36, Milne Special Collections, University of New Hampshire Library; p. 39, North Wind Picture Archives; p. 42, North Wind Picture Archives; p. 45, North Wind Picture Archives; p. 48, North Wind Picture Archives; p. 51, Bettmann/Corbis; p. 54, Courtesy National Archives; p. 57, Courtesy National Archives; p. 60, MPI/Getty Images; p. 63, North Wind Picture Archives; p. 66, Ed Clark/Time Life Pictures/Getty Images; p. 68, Bettmann/Corbis; p. 71, North Wind Picture Archives; p. 74, Courtesy National Archives; p. 77, North Wind Picture Archives; p. 83, Courtesy Library of Congress; p. 86, Bettmann/Corbis; p. 92, MPI/Getty Images; p. 95, Courtesy National Archives; p. 98, Courtesy National Archives; p. 101, Courtesy Library of Congress; p. 104, Dr. Seuss Collection, Mandeville Special Collections Library, University of California, San Diego; p. 107, Courtesy National Archives; p. 110, Courtesy National Archives; p. 113, Courtesy National Archives; p. 116, UN Photo/Mark Garten; p. 119, Courtesy National Archives; p. 122, Getty Images; p. 125, Courtesy Library of Congress; p. 131, Courtesy National Archives; p. 134, Courtesy National Archives; p. 137, Courtesy National Archives; p. 142, Bettmann/Corbis; p. 154, Wichita State University Libraries, Department of Special Collections; p. 157, Bettmann/Corbis; p. 160, Courtesy National Archives; p. 163, A Celebration of Women Writers; p. 165, Bettmann/Corbis/MAGMA; p. 168, Kean Collection/Getty Images; p. 171, Courtesy National Archives; p. 174, Courtesy National Archives; p. 177, Courtesy Library of Congress; p. 180, Hulton Archive/Getty Images, Courtesy National Archives; p. 183, Courtesy Library of Congress; p. 186, Art Shay/Time Life Pictures/Getty Images; p. 189, Getty Images; p. 191, Hulton Archive/Getty Images; p. 200, North Wind Picture Archives; p. 203, Courtesy Library of Congress; p. 206, Courtesy Library of Congress; p. 209, Courtesy Library of Congress/Getty Images; p. 212, Duke University, Rare Book, Manuscript & Special Collections Library; p. 215, Courtesy National Archives; p. 218, Courtesy Library of Congress; p. 224, MPI/Getty Images; p. 227, Russell Lee/MPI/Getty Images; p. 230, Hulton Archive/Getty Images;

NOTES

NOTES

Contents

ANNE GRAHAM LOTZ

Anne Graham Lotz, founder of AnGeL Ministries, has passionately proclaimed God's Word to people around the world for over 30 years. Her gripping narratives and heart-touching teaching have inspired listeners in arenas and prison cells, stadiums and Bible studies, sanctuaries and seminaries, the United Nations and Amsterdam 2000. The daughter of Dr. and Mrs. Billy Graham, Anne is an award-winning and best-selling author. Her books include *Just Give Me Jesus*, *The Vision of His Glory*, *God's Story*, and *I Saw The LORD*. Anne and her husband, Dr. Dan Lotz, reside in North Carolina and have three children and three grandchildren.

AnGeL Ministries is a non-profit organization that seeks to revive
the hearts of God's people through drawing them into His Word.
Contact AnGeL Ministries,
5115 Hollyridge Drive,
Raleigh, NC 27612
www.AnneGrahamLotz.com

Preface

I flew to my father's side from where I had been speaking. I was responding to an urgent message that said my father thought he was dying and wanted me to come. As I walked into his hospital room my heart was in my throat, tears were in my eyes, and a confused jumble of thoughts and prayers were on my mind. My father looked like a shadow of his handsome, commanding self. His body seemed unhealthily thin, his skin was drawn and gray, and his gorgeous thick hair was partially missing where it had been shaved away on one side. His face, softly radiant, became very emotional as he recognized me. I put my arms gently around him and just held him as I whispered how much I loved him and had come in response to his call.

As the days went on he rallied, and I left. On returning home, I received news that he had undergone another emergency procedure. I boarded a plane and flew back to be with him. It was Father's Day 2000 when I walked into his hospital room again. This time he was sleeping. I took my place in a chair by his bed where he could see me when he opened his eyes.

My emotions overwhelmed me, and the tears began to rush furiously down my cheeks. "God, please, oh please, I know my daddy is ready to go 'Home,' but I'm not ready to let him go. Heal him, restore him, strengthen him. I've had Daddy for 52 years, but it's not enough. I long for more—more time, more conversations, more prayers, more counsel, more walks on the mountain. Please just give me more of my daddy ..." Because when you love someone with all your heart, you just can't ever get enough.

For three years the apostle John, along with the other disciples, had given all he had and all he was to follow Jesus. During that time they had witnessed never-to-be-forgotten, life-changing experiences. John had become convinced that Jesus of Nazareth was indeed the Messiah, the Son of God. Jesus had become John's life, hope, peace, and reason for living. Living one moment without Him or ever being separated from Him was unthinkable.

John was desperate for more of Jesus—more of His time, more of His thoughts, more of His teaching. Like John and the other disciples, I have known Jesus personally. While their knowledge was face-to-face, my knowledge is by faith. Mine is personal, direct, experiential knowledge nonetheless.

Like John, I feel that this time in His presence, this devotion to His service, is just not enough. It will never be enough until I am with Him in glory. Until that day, I find my yearning for Him is ravenous, and it has once again led me to immerse myself in the pages of His Word—in particular, the eyewitness account of His life and ministry recorded by the disciple with whom I most identify: John.

This study is based on the passages from John's Gospel that contain what Jesus taught His disciples at the end of His time with them. I wanted to know what He had to say to those who were desperate for more of Him. As I have pored over the Scriptures, my heart has cried out for more than just enough ...

to escape a fiery hell.

to be saved from God's wrath.

to call myself a Christian.

to manage my guilt.

to get a ticket to heaven.

to squeak through heaven's gate.

I long for more than enough ...

to bend my will!

to awaken my conscience!

to break my heart!

to transform my mind!

to overcome my prejudices!

to soar in my spirit!

to conform me into His glorious image!

to give me an abundant entrance into heaven!

I long to be saturated in Jesus! So, please, dear God, just give me more ...

Dear Participant,

Thank you for choosing this study. I know a great variety of Bible studies are available today, and I am delighted you will be involved in this one. You will receive a three-fold, life-changing benefit.

First, you will benefit from the fellowship of others who join you in this study. As you share your insights with each other, you will meet spiritual "soul mates" who will become close friends.

Second, you will benefit from the content of the material. It is based on selected, familiar passages from John's Gospel that will come to life in personal meaning for you as you study the passage for yourself, discuss it with others, then watch the video teaching.

Third, the tools used for the Bible study portion have been designed to take you directly into God's Word. There is no middle person. There are no blanks to fill in. There is not even any cross-referencing required. This simple format for meditating on Scripture has been developed from my own daily time in God's Word as a means of reading a passage in order to hear Him speaking to me personally through it. Day after day, as I use this method in my own Bible reading, I have "heard" God's voice speaking to my heart.

And this is my prayer: *that your love may abound more and more in knowledge and depth of insight, so that you may be able to discern what is best and may be pure and blameless until the day of Christ, filled with the fruit of righteousness that comes through Jesus Christ—to the glory and praise of God* (Philippians 1:9-11).

Pursuing More of Him,

Anne Graham Lotz

Getting Started in Bible Study

JOHN 16:5-16

This Bible study workshop has a single purpose: to present an approach that will help you know God in a personal relationship and communicate with Him through His Word as you learn to listen to His voice. The following information is introduced in detail in the video presentation. Use this section of the participant's guide as your viewing guide and workshop material. Underline key thoughts and take additional notes as you participate in the workshop. (The passage used as the example in the video workshop is on pp. 12-13.)

THE PREPARATION

Spiritual discipline is an essential part of an individual's ability to grow in one's personal relationship with God through knowledge and understanding of His Word. It is my sincere prayer that whether you use this study and the method you'll learn as part of your own personal devotions or with others in a weekly group Bible study, it will provide you with an easy, meaningful format for this growth to occur.

To stay on track and make this study most effective and meaningful to your life, I offer these specific suggestions:

- Set aside a regular place for your daily Bible study.
- Set aside a regular time for your daily Bible study. Have readily available there your Bible, a pen or pencil, and a notebook.
- Pray before beginning each day's journey, asking God to speak to you through His Word.
- Write out your answers for each step of the worksheets in sequence. Do not skip a step.
- Make the time to be still and listen, reflecting thoughtfully on your responses, especially in step 5.

Step 1
READ GOD'S WORD.
Look at the passage.

Begin by reading the designated passage of Scripture printed in each session, which is divided into days. (If your group meets less frequently than once a week, you may want to extend your study time for each passage). When you have finished reading the daily verses, move to step 2.

Step 2
WHAT DOES GOD'S WORD SAY?
List the facts.

When you have finished reading the passage, make a verse-by-verse list of the outstanding facts. Don't get caught up in the details; just pinpoint the most obvious facts. As you make your list, do not paraphrase, but use actual words from the passage itself.

Step 3

WHAT DOES GOD'S WORD MEAN?

Learn the lessons.

After reading the passage and listing the facts, look for a lesson to learn from each fact. Ask yourself: What are the people in the passage doing that I should be doing? Is there a command I should obey? A promise I should claim? A warning I should heed? An example I should follow? Focus on the spiritual lessons.

Step 4

WHAT DOES GOD'S WORD MEAN TO ME?

Listen to His voice.

Though Step 4 is the most meaningful, you can't do it effectively until you complete the first three steps. In order to complete step 4, rephrase the lessons you found in step 3 and put them in the form of questions you could ask yourself, your spouse, your child, your friend, your neighbor, or your coworker. As you write the questions, listen for God to communicate to you through His Word.

There are some challenging passages in this study. Don't get hung up on what you don't understand. Look for the general principles and lessons that can be learned. Remember, don't rush. It may take you several moments of prayerful meditation to discover meaningful lessons and hear God speaking to you. The object is not to get through it but to develop a vibrant personal relationship with God.

Step 5

HOW WILL I RESPOND TO GOD'S WORD?

Live it out!

Read the assigned Scripture verses prayerfully, objectively, thoughtfully, and attentively as you listen for God to speak. He may not speak to you through every verse, but He will speak. When He does, record in the step 5 section the verse number (if applicable), what He seems to be saying to you, and your response to Him. The last page of each week's homework will challenge you to note which response stood out most to you. You will be asked to hold yourself accountable to follow through in obedience, marking the date and your intended response. God bless you as you seek to learn this simple yet effective method of reading His Word so that you might hear His voice speaking to you personally through it.

LUKE 24:27-31

Step 1
READ GOD'S WORD.
Look at the passage.

Step 2
WHAT DOES GOD'S WORD SAY?
List the facts.

27 And beginning with Moses and all the Prophets, he explained to them what was said in all the Scriptures concerning himself.

28 As they approached the village to which they were going, Jesus acted as if he were going farther.

29 But they urged him strongly, "Stay with us, for it is nearly evening; the day is almost over." So he went in to stay with them.

30 When he was at the table with them, he took bread, gave thanks, broke it and began to give it to them.

31 Then their eyes were opened and they recognized him, and he disappeared from their sight.

v. 27 Beginning with Moses & prophets, He explained the Scriptures concerning Himself.

v. 28 As they approached the village, Jesus acted as if He were going.

v. 29 They urged him, "Stay with us. …" So He went in with them.

v. 30 When at the table, He gave thanks, broke bread, and began to give it to them.

v. 31 Then their eyes were opened, they recognized Him, and He disappeared.

{ EXAMPLE }

Step 3

WHAT DOES GOD'S WORD MEAN?
Learn the lessons.

v. 27 Sometimes we need someone to help explain the Scriptures to us.

v. 28 Jesus will not offer us more of Himself unless we ask.

v. 29 When we ask Jesus for more of Himself, wanting to linger in His presence, He responds and gives us more of Himself.

v. 30 Jesus will break open the Bread of Life for us and give us insights that will feed our hungry spirits.

v. 31 As Jesus breaks the Bread for us as we read our Bibles, He opens our eyes not just to facts and information, but to Himself.

Step 4

WHAT DOES GOD'S WORD MEAN TO ME?
Listen to His voice.

v. 27 Am I willing to listen to this explanation of how to read my Bible? How do I study God's Word? Just for information? Or to see Jesus?

v. 28 Am I longing for more of Jesus and wondering why He seems to have passed me by?

v. 29 When have I asked Jesus for more of Himself?

v. 30 Am I hungry for Jesus? Isn't it time that I asked Him to break the Bread for me?

v. 31 What is keeping me from seeing Jesus in the pages of my Bible?

{ EXAMPLE }

Step 5

HOW WILL I RESPOND TO GOD'S WORD?
Live it out!

Date:_____

I am going to pursue more of Jesus as I read my Bible in this study, asking Him to reveal Himself to me personally in a fresher, deeper way.

JOHN 16:5-16

5 "Now I am going to him who sent me, yet none of you asks me, 'Where are you going?'

6 "Because I have said these things, you are filled with grief.

7 "But I tell you the truth: It is for your good that I am going away. Unless I go away, the Counselor will not come to you; but if I go, I will send him to you.

8 "When he comes, he will convict the world of guilt in regard to sin and righteousness and judgment:

9 in regard to sin, because men do not believe in me;

10 in regard to righteousness, because I am going to the Father, where you can see me no longer;

11 and in regard to judgment, because the prince of this world now stands condemned.

12 "I have much more to say to you, more than you can now bear.

13 "But when he, the Spirit of truth, comes, he will guide you into all truth. He will not speak on his own; he will speak only what he hears, and he will tell you what is yet to come.

14 "He will bring glory to me by taking from what is mine and making it known to you.

15 "All that belongs to the Father is mine. That is why I said the Spirit will take from what is mine and make it known to you.

16 "In a little while you will see me no more, and then after a little while you will see me."

Step 3

WHAT DOES GOD'S WORD MEAN?

Learn the lessons.

Step 4

WHAT DOES GOD'S WORD MEAN TO ME?

Listen to His voice.

Step 5

HOW WILL I RESPOND TO GOD'S WORD?

Live it out!

WORKSHOP ONE: NOTES

More of His Voice

JOHN 10:1-10

Have you been confronted with those who, in essence, have said, "God told me to tell you if you only had more faith, you would be healed," or "If God really loved you, that bad thing would not have happened to you," or "It's God's will that your loved one died"? Such "words of knowledge" spoken by sincere people within our circle of Christian friends can put us in a tailspin of emotional devastation and spiritual doubt. It is especially traumatic and confusing when someone in a position of religious leadership utters those words.

How can you and I know which voice speaks the truth and is therefore authentic?

The Bible tells us that God does speak to His children and that we will hear and know His voice even as sheep hear and know the voice of their shepherd.

JOHN 10:1

Step 1
READ GOD'S WORD.
Look at the passage.

1 "I tell you the truth, the man who does not enter the sheep pen by the gate, but climbs in by some other way, is a thief and a robber."

Step 2
WHAT DOES GOD'S WORD SAY?
List the facts.

Step 3

WHAT DOES GOD'S WORD MEAN?

Learn the lessons.

Step 4

WHAT DOES GOD'S WORD MEAN TO ME?

Listen to His voice.

Step 5

HOW WILL I RESPOND TO GOD'S WORD?

Live it out!

JOHN 10:2-3

Step 1

READ GOD'S WORD.

Look at the passage.

2 "The man who enters by the gate is the shepherd of his sheep.

3 "The watchman opens the gate for him, and the sheep listen to his voice. He calls his own sheep by name and leads them out."

Step 2

WHAT DOES GOD'S WORD SAY?

List the facts.

Step 3

WHAT DOES GOD'S WORD MEAN?

Learn the lessons.

Step 4

WHAT DOES GOD'S WORD MEAN TO ME?

Listen to His voice.

Step 5

HOW WILL I RESPOND TO GOD'S WORD?

Live it out!

JOHN 10:4-5

Step 1

READ GOD'S WORD.

Look at the passage.

4 "When he has brought out all his own, he goes on ahead of them, and his sheep follow him because they know his voice.

5 But they will never follow a stranger; in fact, they will run away from him because they do not recognize a stranger's voice."

Step 2

WHAT DOES GOD'S WORD SAY?

List the facts.

Step 3
WHAT DOES GOD'S WORD MEAN?
Learn the lessons.

Step 4
WHAT DOES GOD'S WORD MEAN TO ME?
Listen to His voice.

Step 5
HOW WILL I RESPOND TO GOD'S WORD?
Live it out!

JOHN 10:6-9

Step 1

READ GOD'S WORD.

Look at the passage.

6 Jesus used this figure of speech, but they did not understand what he was telling them.

7 Therefore Jesus said again, "I tell you the truth, I am the gate for the sheep.

8 "All who ever came before me were thieves and robbers, but the sheep did not listen to them.

9 "I am the gate; whoever enters through me will be saved. He will come in and go out, and find pasture."

Step 2

WHAT DOES GOD'S WORD SAY?

List the facts.

Step 3
WHAT DOES GOD'S WORD MEAN?
Learn the lessons.

Step 4
WHAT DOES GOD'S WORD MEAN TO ME?
Listen to His voice.

Step 5
HOW WILL I RESPOND TO GOD'S WORD?
Live it out!

JOHN 10:10

Step 1
READ GOD'S WORD.

Look at the passage.

10 "The thief comes only to steal and kill and destroy; I have come that they may have life, and have it to the full."

Step 2
WHAT DOES GOD'S WORD SAY?

List the facts.

Step 3
WHAT DOES GOD'S WORD MEAN?
Learn the lessons.

Step 4
WHAT DOES GOD'S WORD MEAN TO ME?
Listen to His voice.

Step 5
HOW WILL I RESPOND TO GOD'S WORD?
Live it out!

JOHN 10:1-10

RESPONDING TO GOD

Focus on what God is saying to you from this section's Scripture verses. As you reflect on your responses from each day's step 5, which was most meaningful to you? Write out that day's response next to the appropriate space below, along with today's date and your statement of how you plan to follow through in obedience.

John 10:1

John 10:2-3

John 10:4-5

John 10:6-9

John 10:10

Talk with God now about what He has said and how you will respond. Ask Him to give you more of His voice in your ear; then, recommit to daily Bible reading using the curriculum to help you stay consistent.

JOHN 10:1-10

More of His Voice

I. The Authentic Voice Is Biblical (John 10:1-2)

II.   The Authentic Voice Is Personal (John 10:3-6)

III.   The Authentic Voice Is Powerful (John 10:7-10)

More of His Courage in My Convictions

JOHN 15:5-16

Dr. John Perkins addressed a room packed with Christian missionaries and workers. With passion resonating in his voice, he boldly articulated what I earnestly believe to be true when he stated "the greatest crisis in America today is a crisis of leadership. And the crisis of leadership," he went on to say, "is rooted in a crisis of courage and a crisis of convictions."

Are you part of the crisis? What are your genuine, personal convictions concerning the Gospel? Are you convinced that Jesus is the only Way to God, the only Truth about how to get to heaven, the only Life that is eternal and abundant? Are you convinced that no one will ever be accepted by God the Father, except they come to Him through Jesus Christ? If these statements, which paraphrase Jesus' own claims, are your convictions, then do you have the courage to state them publicly? Today? To your family, friends, neighbors, and coworkers? Many church members in our pluralistic, tolerant society not only lack the courage to stand up for the truth that faith in Jesus Christ alone is the only way to God, they actually reproach others who do!

In the light of such spiritual anemia, my heart's cry is, "Please, Jesus, give me more of Your courage in my convictions."

JOHN 15:5-7

Step 1
READ GOD'S WORD.
Look at the passage.

5 "I am the vine; you are the branches. If a man remains in me and I in him, he will bear much fruit; apart from me you can do nothing.

6 "If anyone does not remain in me, he is like a branch that is thrown away and withers; such branches are picked up, thrown into the fire and burned.

7 "If you remain in me and my words remain in you, ask whatever you wish, and it will be given you."

Step 2
WHAT DOES GOD'S WORD SAY?
List the facts.

Step 3
WHAT DOES GOD'S WORD MEAN?
Learn the lessons.

Step 4
WHAT DOES GOD'S WORD MEAN TO ME?
Listen to His voice.

Step 5
HOW WILL I RESPOND TO GOD'S WORD?
Live it out!

JOHN 15:8

Step 1

READ GOD'S WORD.

Look at the passage.

8 "This is to my Father's glory, that you bear much fruit, showing yourselves to be my disciples."

Step 2

WHAT DOES GOD'S WORD SAY?

List the facts.

Step 3

WHAT DOES GOD'S WORD MEAN?

Learn the lessons.

Step 4

WHAT DOES GOD'S WORD MEAN TO ME?

Listen to His voice.

Step 5

HOW WILL I RESPOND TO GOD'S WORD?

Live it out!

JOHN 15:9-11

Step 1
READ GOD'S WORD.
Look at the passage.

9 "As the Father has loved me, so have I loved you. Now remain in my love.

10 "If you obey my commands, you will remain in my love, just as I have obeyed my Father's commands and remain in his love.

11 "I have told you this so that my joy may be in you and that your joy may be complete."

Step 2
WHAT DOES GOD'S WORD SAY?
List the facts.

Step 3

WHAT DOES GOD'S WORD MEAN?

Learn the lessons.

Step 4

WHAT DOES GOD'S WORD MEAN TO ME?

Listen to His voice.

Step 5

HOW WILL I RESPOND TO GOD'S WORD?

Live it out!

JOHN 15:12-13

Step 1

READ GOD'S WORD.

Look at the passage.

12 "My command is this: Love each other as I have loved you.

13 "Greater love has no one than this, that he lay down his life for his friends."

Step 2

WHAT DOES GOD'S WORD SAY?

List the facts.

Step 3

WHAT DOES GOD'S WORD MEAN?

Learn the lessons.

Step 4

WHAT DOES GOD'S WORD MEAN TO ME?

Listen to His voice.

Step 5

HOW WILL I RESPOND TO GOD'S WORD?

Live it out!

JOHN 15:14-16

Step 1
READ GOD'S WORD.
Look at the passage.

Step 2
WHAT DOES GOD'S WORD SAY?
List the facts.

14 "You are my friends if you do what I command.

15 "I no longer call you servants, because a servant does not know his master's business. Instead, I have called you friends, for everything that I learned from my Father I have made known to you.

16 "You did not choose me, but I chose you and appointed you to go and bear fruit—fruit that will last. Then the Father will give you whatever you ask in my name."

Step 3
WHAT DOES GOD'S WORD MEAN?
Learn the lessons.

Step 4
WHAT DOES GOD'S WORD MEAN TO ME?
Listen to His voice.

Step 5
HOW WILL I RESPOND TO GOD'S WORD?
Live it out!

JOHN 15:5-16

RESPONDING TO GOD

Focus on what God is saying to you from this section's Scripture verses. As you reflect on your responses from each day's step 5, which was most meaningful to you? Write out that day's response next to the appropriate space below, along with today's date and your statement of how you plan to follow through in obedience.

John 15:5-7

John 15:8

John 15:9-11

John 15:12-13

John 15:14-16

Talk with God now about what He has said and how you will respond. Ask Him to give you more of His courage in your convictions; then, recommit to daily Bible reading using the curriculum to help you stay consistent.

JOHN 15:17-27

More of His Courage in My Convictions

I. Courage to Stand Out (John 15:17-25)

II.   Courage to Speak Up (John 15:26-27)

More of His Spirit

JOHN 14:15-27

Because John 16 was studied in the workshop we covered in our very first session, this week's homework will still be about the Holy Spirit, but from John 14, which took place within the upper room. The quiet stillness was broken only by the sound of the beloved Master's voice.

Within the upper room, the quiet stillness was broken only by the sound of the beloved Master's voice. Jesus continued to pour out His heart in words that sought to prepare His disciples for what was coming. And the disciples were beginning to understand—even if vaguely—that the One who was ...

> their Lord,
>> their Master,
>>> their Teacher,
>>>> their best Friend,
>>> the One to whom they had given their lives,
>>> the One who was Life itself to them . . .

He was going away! The loneliness of His pending absence was already beginning to engulf their emotions and sorrow was filling their hearts. So Jesus told them that although He would be leaving them physically and at times they might feel lonely, they would never be alone again! On that quiet Thursday evening before all hell broke loose, He began to unveil the Third Person of the triune God: the Holy Spirit, who would be Jesus—not just with them—but in them.

JOHN 14:15

Step 1

READ GOD'S WORD.

Look at the passage.

15 "If you love me, you will obey what I command."

Step 2

WHAT DOES GOD'S WORD SAY?

List the facts.

Step 3
WHAT DOES GOD'S WORD MEAN?
Learn the lessons.

Step 4
WHAT DOES GOD'S WORD MEAN TO ME?
Listen to His voice.

Step 5
HOW WILL I RESPOND TO GOD'S WORD?
Live it out!

JOHN 14:16-19

Step 1
READ GOD'S WORD.
Look at the passage.

16 "And I will ask the Father, and he will give you another Counselor to be with you forever—

17 the Spirit of truth. The world cannot accept him, because it neither sees him nor knows him. But you know him, for he lives with you and will be in you.

18 "I will not leave you as orphans; I will come to you.

19 "Before long, the world will not see me anymore, but you will see me. Because I live, you also will live."

Step 2
WHAT DOES GOD'S WORD SAY?
List the facts.

Step 3

WHAT DOES GOD'S WORD MEAN?

Learn the lessons.

Step 4

WHAT DOES GOD'S WORD MEAN TO ME?

Listen to His voice.

Step 5

HOW WILL I RESPOND TO GOD'S WORD?

Live it out!

JOHN 14:20-21

Step 1
READ GOD'S WORD.
Look at the passage.

20 "On that day you will realize that I am in my Father, and you are in me, and I am in you.

21 "Whoever has my commands and obeys them, he is the one who loves me. He who loves me will be loved by my Father, and I too will love him and show myself to him."

Step 2
WHAT DOES GOD'S WORD SAY?
List the facts.

Step 3

WHAT DOES GOD'S WORD MEAN?

Learn the lessons.

Step 4

WHAT DOES GOD'S WORD MEAN TO ME?

Listen to His voice.

Step 5

HOW WILL I RESPOND TO GOD'S WORD?

Live it out!

JOHN 14:22-24

Step 1

READ GOD'S WORD.

Look at the passage.

Step 2

WHAT DOES GOD'S WORD SAY?

List the facts.

22 Then Judas (not Judas Iscariot) said, "But, Lord, why do you intend to show yourself to us and not to the world?"

23 Jesus replied, "If anyone loves me, he will obey my teaching. My Father will love him, and we will come to him and make our home with him.

24 "He who does not love me will not obey my teaching. These words you hear are not my own; they belong to the Father who sent me."

Step 3

WHAT DOES GOD'S WORD MEAN?

Learn the lessons.

Step 4

WHAT DOES GOD'S WORD MEAN TO ME?

Listen to His voice.

Step 5

HOW WILL I RESPOND TO GOD'S WORD?

Live it out!

JOHN 14:25-27

Step 1

READ GOD'S WORD.

Look at the passage.

25 "All this I have spoken while still with you.

26 "But the Counselor, the Holy Spirit, whom the Father will send in my name, will teach you all things and will remind you of everything I have said to you.

27 "Peace I leave with you; my peace I give you. I do not give to you as the world gives. Do not let your hearts be troubled and do not be afraid."

Step 2

WHAT DOES GOD'S WORD SAY?

List the facts.

Step 3

WHAT DOES GOD'S WORD MEAN?

Learn the lessons.

Step 4

WHAT DOES GOD'S WORD MEAN TO ME?

Listen to His voice.

Step 5

HOW WILL I RESPOND TO GOD'S WORD?

Live it out!

JOHN 14:15-27

RESPONDING TO GOD

Focus on what God is saying to you from this section's Scripture verses. As you reflect on your responses from each day's step 5, which was most meaningful to you? Write out that day's response next to the appropriate space below, along with today's date and your statement of how you plan to follow through in obedience.

John 14:15

John 14:16-19

John 14:20-21

John 14:22-24

John 14:25-27

Talk with God now about what He has said and how you will respond. Ask Him to give you more of His Spirit; then, recommit to daily Bible reading using the curriculum to help you stay consistent.

JOHN 16:5-15

More of His Spirit

I. More of His Person (John 16:5-7)

II. More of His Power (John 16:8-11)

III. More of His Priority (John 16:12-15)

More of His Glory

JOHN 17:1-26

It was springtime in Jerusalem. The city would have been teeming with pilgrims who had come for Passover. I wonder if the warm evening breeze fluttered through the open windows, causing candle flames to flicker and cast dancing shadows on the walls and ceiling of the upper room. Through the open windows would have come not only the fragrance of the olive blossoms but also the sounds of a city bedding down for the night.

Jesus Himself must have been tired. For the past week, He had taught every day on the temple grounds, slipping back to Bethany in the evenings to spend the night with friends. On this Thursday evening, He had arranged to have a last meal with His beloved disciples—and then had washed twelve pairs of dirty feet. Later He had dismissed Judas, whom He knew even at that moment was betraying Him to the religious authorities.

After pouring His life into these eleven men (Judas was now gone), after teaching them all they would need to know before He left them for the cross, after preparing them for the life-jolting trauma they were about to experience—"After Jesus said this, he looked toward heaven and prayed" (John 17:1). Jesus—the Son of God, the Creator of the universe, the Jehovah of the Old Covenant, the Messiah, the Lord of glory—Jesus prayed!

What kind of a week have you had? If Jesus found it necessary to maintain a continual, active prayer life, what is your excuse for not praying?

JOHN 17:1-5

Step 1

READ GOD'S WORD.

Look at the passage.

Step 2

WHAT DOES GOD'S WORD SAY?

List the facts.

1 After Jesus said this, he looked toward heaven and prayed: "Father, the time has come. Glorify your Son, that your Son may glorify you.

2 "For you granted him authority over all people that he might give eternal life to all those you have given him.

3 "Now this is eternal life: that they may know you, the only true God, and Jesus Christ, whom you have sent.

4 "I have brought you glory on earth by completing the work you gave me to do.

5 "And now, Father, glorify me in your presence with the glory I had with you before the world began."

Step 3

WHAT DOES GOD'S WORD MEAN?

Learn the lessons.

Step 4

WHAT DOES GOD'S WORD MEAN TO ME?

Listen to His voice.

Step 5

HOW WILL I RESPOND TO GOD'S WORD?

Live it out!

JOHN 17:6-12

6 "I have revealed you to those whom you gave me out of the world. They were yours; you gave them to me and they have obeyed your word.

7 "Now they know that everything you have given me comes from you.

8 "For I gave them the words you gave me and they accepted them. They knew with certainty that I came from you, and they believed that you sent me.

9 "I pray for them. I am not praying for the world, but for those you have given me, for they are yours.

10 "All I have is yours, and all you have is mine. And glory has come to me through them.

11 "I will remain in the world no longer, but they are still in the world, and I am coming to you. Holy Father, protect them by the power of your name—the name you gave me—so that they may be one as we are one.

12 "While I was with them, I protected them and kept them safe by that name you gave me. None has been lost except the one doomed to destruction so that Scripture would be fulfilled."

Step 3
WHAT DOES GOD'S WORD MEAN?

Learn the lessons.

Step 4
WHAT DOES GOD'S WORD MEAN TO ME?

Listen to His voice.

Step 5
HOW WILL I RESPOND TO GOD'S WORD?

Live it out!

JOHN 17:13-19

13 "I am coming to you now, but I say these things while I am still in the world, so that they may have the full measure of my joy within them.

14 "I have given them your word and the world has hated them, for they are not of the world any more than I am of the world.

15 "My prayer is not that you take them out of the world but that you protect them from the evil one.

16 "They are not of the world, even as I am not of it.

17 "Sanctify them by the truth; your word is truth.

18 "As you sent me into the world, I have sent them into the world.

19 "For them I sanctify myself, that they too may be truly sanctified."

Step 3
WHAT DOES GOD'S WORD MEAN?
Learn the lessons.

Step 4
WHAT DOES GOD'S WORD MEAN TO ME?
Listen to His voice.

Step 5
HOW WILL I RESPOND TO GOD'S WORD?
Live it out!

JOHN 17:20-23

Step 1
READ GOD'S WORD.
Look at the passage.

20 "My prayer is not for them alone. I pray also for those who will believe in me through their message,

21 that all of them may be one, Father, just as you are in me and I am in you. May they also be in us so that the world may believe that you have sent me.

22 "I have given them the glory that you gave me, that they may be one as we are one:

23 "I in them and you in me. May they be brought to complete unity to let the world know that you sent me and have loved them even as you have loved me."

Step 2
WHAT DOES GOD'S WORD SAY?
List the facts.

Step 3
WHAT DOES GOD'S WORD MEAN?
Learn the lessons.

Step 4
WHAT DOES GOD'S WORD MEAN TO ME?
Listen to His voice.

Step 5
HOW WILL I RESPOND TO GOD'S WORD?
Live it out!

JOHN 17:24-26

Step 1
READ GOD'S WORD.

Look at the passage.

24 "Father, I want those you have given me to be with me where I am, and to see my glory, the glory you have given me because you loved me before the creation of the world.

25 "Righteous Father, though the world does not know you, I know you, and they know that you have sent me.

26 "I have made you known to them, and will continue to make you known in order that the love you have for me may be in them and that I myself may be in them."

Step 2
WHAT DOES GOD'S WORD SAY?

List the facts.

Step 3
WHAT DOES GOD'S WORD MEAN?
Learn the lessons.

Step 4
WHAT DOES GOD'S WORD MEAN TO ME?
Listen to His voice.

Step 5
HOW WILL I RESPOND TO GOD'S WORD?
Live it out!

JOHN 17:1-26

RESPONDING TO GOD

Focus on what God is saying to you from this section's Scripture verses. As you reflect on your responses from each day's step 5, which was most meaningful to you? Write out that day's response next to the appropriate space below, along with today's date and your statement of how you plan to follow through in obedience.

John 17:1-5

John 17:6-12

John 17:13-19

John 17:20-23

John 17:24-26

Talk with God now about what He has said and how you will respond. Ask Him to give you more of His glory; then, recommit to daily Bible reading using the curriculum to help you stay consistent.

JOHN 17:1-5

More of His Glory

I. Enter His Presence (John 17:1)

II. Exalt His Person (John 17:1)

III. Embrace His Purpose (John 17:2-5)

Digging Deeper

Fellow pursuer,

I pray that you have been greatly enriched by your participation in this study and that you have had a fresh encounter with Jesus. But there is more!

The Bible is a very rich book that has layer after layer of treasure. In our first workshop, I shared simple tools that enable you to spend time in the first layer by reading your Bible meditatively so that you can hear God speaking to you through it. I hope that every day for the rest of your life you will listen to His voice ... with your eyes on the pages of your Bible ... and that you will begin to hear Him speaking to you.

As you read your Bible, you will become aware that there is more truth and treasure underneath the surface. It's similar to going into a gold mine, seeing the veins of ore crisscrossing the rock, yet being unable to access it. To go for the gold, you would need a pick, a shovel, and the extra time and energy required to dig it out.

The same is true of Scripture. Psalm 19:10 confirms that God's Word is more precious than gold, than much pure gold. There is "gold" running through the pages, but it is inaccessible without the proper tools to dig it out. The purpose of Workshop Two is to give you those tools. They are tools that work, and if you are willing to put the time and effort into using them, they will enable you to access the treasure that is underneath a surface reading.

I challenge you to be genuinely on a passionate pursuit for more and pray that you will not be satisfied with what you have received so far but will make the extra effort to dig deeper. The treasure is there waiting for you to discover it. And the Treasure is Jesus!

So ... go for the Gold!

Anne Graham Lotz

JOHN 16:5-16

Step 1
READ GOD'S WORD.
Look at the passage.

Step 2
WHAT DOES GOD'S WORD SAY?
Re-list the facts from Workshop 1 (p. 12).

5 "Now I am going to him who sent me, yet none of you asks me, 'Where are you going?'

6 "Because I have said these things, you are filled with grief.

7 "But I tell you the truth: It is for your good that I am going away. Unless I go away, the Counselor will not come to you; but if I go, I will send him to you.

8 "When he comes, he will convict the world of guilt in regard to sin and righteousness and judgment:

9 in regard to sin, because men do not believe in me;

10 in regard to righteousness, because I am going to the Father, where you can see me no longer;

11 and in regard to judgment, because the prince of this world now stands condemned.

12 "I have much more to say to you, more than you can now bear.

13 "But when he, the Spirit of truth, comes, he will guide you into all truth. He will not speak on his own; he will speak only what he hears, and he will tell you what is yet to come.

14 "He will bring glory to me by taking from what is mine and making it known to you.

15 "All that belongs to the Father is mine. That is why I said the Spirit will take from what is mine and make it known to you.

16 "In a little while you will see me no more, and then after a little while you will see me."

Step 2-A
DIVIDE THE FACTS.

- Re-read the list of the facts from step 2.
- Bracket the main facts, keeping the verses in sequence, which share the same event, place, conversations, people, thought and subject.
- Continue bracketing the brackets until you have not more than four, not fewer than two.
- Label each bracket with a Roman numeral, an explanatory sentence that summarizes the facts in the brackets, and verses that are included in the brackets.
- If possible, keep the subject the same in each label.
- Your brackets are now divisions.

Step 2-B
WRITE OUT YOUR SUMMARY SENTENCE.

- Summarize the outstanding facts of the passage in a specific sentence including key words and/or obvious facts that identify the passages from any other.
- The sentence should be complete with subject and verb.
- The sentence should not be more than ten words.

JOHN 16:5-16

Step 2-C
WRITE OUT YOUR AIM.

- Re-read the lessons from each division, seeking a common thread.
- Look for a specific command, which may be the thrust of the entire passage.
- Write out one, overall lesson as an aim, using an action verb.

Begin your aim with the words, "To cause myself to..." then insert an action verb and the rest of the lesson.

Step 2-D
WRITE OUT YOUR APPLICATIONS.

- Keeping in mind your overall aim from Step 5 of each week's lesson, write out a lesson from each division and put it in the form of a question to ask yourself or another.
- Questions should vary from the type requiring a "yes or no" to "when or how," and so forth.
- You should have at least one question for each division that builds up and reinforces your overall aim.

Digging Deeper On Your Own

JOHN 12:1-8

The following worksheet pages have been prepared for you to find the gold that lies beneath John 12:1-8. These worksheets follow the same format you learned in Workshop Two and will serve as your guide as you do this week's homework.

As there is not a teaching video for this passage, upon completing your study, you may choose to read the commentary shared in the book by the same title as this Bible Study, *Pursuing More of Jesus*, Chapter 2.

Remember that there are multiple ways to break down John 12:1-8. On pages 104-105 you will find Anne's examples of various ways she would treat the passage. But, we encourage you to not look ahead to Anne's answers until you have completed the exercise on pages 86-89.

JOHN 12:1-8

Step 1

READ GOD'S WORD.

Look at the passage.

1 Six days before the Passover, Jesus arrived at Bethany, where Lazarus lived, whom Jesus had raised from the dead.

2 Here a dinner was given in Jesus' honor. Martha served, while Lazarus was among those reclining at the table with him.

3 Then Mary took about a pint of pure nard, an expensive perfume; she poured it on Jesus' feet and wiped his feet with her hair. And the house was filled with the fragrance of the perfume.

4 But one of his disciples, Judas Iscariot, who was later to betray him, objected,

5 "Why wasn't this perfume sold and the money given to the poor? It was worth a year's wages."

6 He did not say this because he cared about the poor but because he was a thief; as keeper of the money bag, he used to help himself to what was put into it.

7 "Leave her alone," Jesus replied. "It was intended that she should save this perfume for the day of my burial.

8 "You will always have the poor among you, but you will not always have me."

Step 2

WHAT DOES GOD'S WORD SAY?

List the facts.

Step 3
WHAT DOES GOD'S WORD MEAN?

Learn the lessons.

Step 4
WHAT DOES GOD'S WORD MEAN TO ME?

Listen to His voice.

Step 5
HOW WILL I RESPOND TO GOD'S WORD?

Live it out!

JOHN 12:1-8

Step 2-A
DIVIDE THE FACTS.

Step 2-B
WRITE OUT YOUR SUMMARY SENTENCE.

Step 2-C
WRITE OUT YOUR AIM.

Step 2-D
WRITE OUT YOUR APPLICATION.

Step 1
READ GOD'S WORD.
Look at the passage.

Step 2
WHAT DOES GOD'S WORD SAY?
List the facts.

Step 3
WHAT DOES GOD'S WORD MEAN?
Learn the lessons.

Step 4
WHAT DOES GOD'S WORD MEAN TO ME?
Listen to His voice.

Step 5
HOW WILL I RESPOND TO GOD'S WORD?
Live it out!

Step 2-A
DIVIDE THE FACTS.

Step 2-B
WRITE OUT YOUR SUMMARY SENTENCE.

Step 2-C
WRITE OUT YOUR AIM.

Step 2-D
WRITE OUT YOUR APPLICATION.

Step 1
READ GOD'S WORD.
Look at the passage.

Step 2
WHAT DOES GOD'S WORD SAY?
List the facts.

Step 3
WHAT DOES GOD'S WORD MEAN?
Learn the lessons.

Step 4
WHAT DOES GOD'S WORD MEAN TO ME?
Listen to His voice.

Step 5
HOW WILL I RESPOND TO GOD'S WORD?
Live it out!

Step 2-A

DIVIDE THE FACTS.

Step 2-B

WRITE OUT YOUR SUMMARY SENTENCE.

Step 2-C
WRITE OUT YOUR AIM.

Step 2-D
WRITE OUT YOUR APPLICATION.

Step 5
HOW WILL I RESPOND TO GOD'S WORD?

Live it out!

15 One day the world that was made by the Lord at Creation and bought by Him at Calvary, will be reigned by Him.

THE FOLLOWING
GROUP LEADER GUIDE
INCLUDES:
Group Leader Ideas
Bible Study Workshop Plans
Group Session Plans

Group Leader Guide

A group study of *Pursuing More of Jesus* is appropriate for home and neighborhood groups, Bible study classes, accountability groups, discipleship and prayer groups, and one-on-one discipleship. The study will benefit adults of all ages. Promote the study by showing the promotional segment on DVD 1. Use the short version as an outreach tool on local TV and cable. You can order a broadcast quality version by calling (615) 251-5926.

Meet at a time appropriate for your participants. Sessions can be conducted weekly, monthly, or any interval in between. Group sessions are designed for 90 minutes each, but allow the Holy Spirit to determine your schedule. For example, your group may decide to spend two group sessions on each seminar. Group plans in this section serve as a framework; your goal should be to meet the needs of your group.

Participants can meet at a church or in a home or business. Anywhere that will accommodate a DVD set-up and is conducive for discussion and prayer is appropriate.

Use the following group ideas. As facilitator, you should:

- Pray for group members before each session.
- Complete Bible study material for the session.
- Prepare material for the session; this includes securing equipment to show the video presentations.
- Encourage group members.
- After each session, contact participants who were absent.

WORKSHOP ONE

The Bible Study Workshop is a time of gathering and introducing group members, distributing and overviewing study materials, and participating in the workshop.

1. Begin on time. Ask participants to introduce themselves by giving their names and one expectation they have of the study. Have name tags available if members do not know one another well.

2. Tell participants that prayer will be an important part of this study. Ask for prayer concerns and praises. Pray for the concerns shared and ask God to guide the group during the study.

3. Give each participant a copy of the workbook. Briefly overview the contents page and explain the progression of the study. Invite participants to turn to Workshop 1 on page 9. Call attention to the two major sections in each seminar: individual study (p. 18) and the video listening page (p. 30). Emphasize the importance of completing the Bible study material before each session.

4. Explain the schedule your group will be following during the study. Also cover other logistical issues such as when and where the group will meet, childcare for those who need it, and so on.

5. Say: "We will begin the study with a Bible Study Workshop. During this time Anne Graham Lotz presents an approach that will help us know God in a personal relationship through His Word. The Bible study approach introduced in the workshop helps us communicate with God through His Word."

6. Explain that this Bible study approach is introduced in detail through the video presentation. Invite participants to use the workshop pages as a viewing guide to underline key thoughts and take additional notes as they participate.

7. View the video presentation on the Bible Study Workshop (viewing time: 44 min., does not include stopping the DVD for the activities). Stop the DVD as directed during the

presentation. Allow the time recommended for participants to complete their work. The following is suggested during the presentation for each group activity.

> FIRST ACTIVITY (20 MIN.): What does the passage say? *(10 min.)* Complete individually. Participants share their facts. *(10 min.)*
>
> SECOND ACTIVITY (20 MIN.): What does the passage mean? *(10 min.)* Complete in small groups (three or four in a group). Groups share their answers. *(10 min.)*
>
> THIRD ACTIVITY (20 MIN.): What does the passage mean to me? *(10 min.)* Complete individually. Groups share their answers. *(10 min.)*

Anne debriefs each of these activities with her group. Observe the examples and comments made on the DVD; you will want to do the same before you restart the DVD.

8. Inform participants about the audio downloads and how they can be used to review Anne's video presentation or to catch up with the group if they miss a session. These can be purchased for individual use at either *www.LifeWay.com* or *www.AnneGrahamLotz.com.*

9. Instruct participants to complete the Bible study material for Seminar 1; it begins on page 17. Remind them to bring their workbooks, Bibles, and a pen or pencil with them to every group session. Announce the day, time, and place for the next session.

During the weeks to come you will see God at work in the lives of your group members as you study His Word. This is a thrilling process that needs much prayer. Watch with expectancy and look to God to reap the harvest. Remember that in the Lord, your work is never in vain!

> *Therefore, my beloved brethren, be steadfast, immovable,*
> *always abounding in the work of the Lord,*
> *knowing that your labor is not in vain in the Lord.*
>
> 1 CORINTHIANS 15:58 (NKJ)

LEADER GUIDE

SEMINAR ONE
More of His Voice

JOHN 10:1-10

1. Begin on time. Welcome latecomers with as little interruption as possible. Provide name tags again if necessary.

2. Say: As we continue to study John's Gospel, we will learn more about Jesus and how He speaks to us. We will also learn the Bible study method Anne is teaching us to guide us in God's Word. Have there been times when you have had difficulty distinguishing God's voice from the many voices in your life?

3. Begin each session with prayer and then enter into a time of discussion as you work your way through the three questions. Begin by reading the Scripture portion. Have one person share the entire lesson's facts, allowing more time for the subsequent sections.

4. Next, work through the question, "What does the passage mean?" Ask for participation. Ask: "Would someone like to give a lesson they found in this passage?"

5. Finally, ask for responses to the last question, "What does the passage mean to me?" Ask: "Who would like to share a lesson they put in the form of a question?"

6. View the video presentation of Seminar 1: More of His Voice (viewing time: 53:30).

7. Ask for prayer concerns and needs facing group members. Close with prayer.

8. Be sure to end on time.

9. The following suggestions will help you facilitate the group discussions:

     · Do not answer irrelevant questions; refocus discussion to the issue at hand.

     · Do not share your responses unless contained in a brief comment.

     · Do not bring in outside resources to add to the study.

     · Avoid controversial issues if possible.

     · Do not "grade" answers, but thank the participant and proceed with the discussion.

10. After each session, contact participants who were absent.

SEMINAR TWO
More of His Courage in My Convictions

John 15:17-27

1. Honor each participant's commitment by starting on time.

2. Say: The following is an excerpt from *Pursuing More of Jesus* by Anne Graham Lotz, on which this study is based. In it she shares this story: "Dr. John Perkins recently addressed a group of Christian missionaries and workers. With passion resonating in his voice, he boldly articulated what I earnestly believe to be true when he stated that 'the greatest crisis in America today is a crisis of leadership. And the crisis of leadership,' he went on to say, 'is rooted in a crisis of courage and a crisis of convictions.'" Ask the group for comments on this story.

3. Begin each session with prayer and then enter into a time of discussion as you work your way through the three questions. Begin by reading the Scripture portion. Have one person share the entire lesson's facts, allowing more time for the subsequent sections.

4. Next, work through the question, "What does the passage mean?" Ask for participation. Ask: "Would someone like to give a lesson they found in this passage?"

5. Finally, ask for responses to the last question, "What does the passage mean to me?" Ask: "Who would like to share a lesson they put in the form of a question?"

6. View the video presentation of Seminar 2: More of His Courage in My Convictions (viewing time: 51:30).

7. Ask for prayer concerns and needs facing group members. Close with prayer.

8. Be sure to end on time.

9. After each session, contact participants who were absent.

SEMINAR THREE
More of His Spirit

JOHN 16:5-15

1. As participants arrive, give each person an encouraging word. Begin on time.

2. Begin each session with prayer and then enter into a time of discussion as you work your way through the three questions. Begin by reading the Scripture portion. Have one person share the entire lesson's facts, allowing more time for the subsequent sections.

3. Next, work through the question, "What does the passage mean?" Ask for participation. Ask: "Would someone like to give a lesson they found in this passage?"

4. Finally, ask for responses to the last question, "What does the passage mean to me?" Ask: "Who would like to share a lesson they put in the form of a question?"

5. View the video presentation of Seminar 3: More of His Spirit (viewing time: 59:00).

6. Ask for prayer concerns and needs facing group members. Close with prayer.

7. Be sure to end on time.

8. After each session, contact participants who were absent.

LEADER GUIDE

SEMINAR FOUR
More of His Glory

JOHN 17:1-5

1. Begin on time.

2. Say: This is our last session together. I hope you have learned more tools to study God's Word. I also hope you have learned more about Jesus and your passionate pursuit of Him and relationship with Him.

3. Next, work through the question, "What does the passage mean?" Ask for participation. Ask: "Would someone like to give a lesson they found in this passage?"

4. Finally, ask for responses to the last question, "What does the passage mean to me?" Ask: "Who would like to share a lesson they put in the form of a question?"

5. View the video presentation of Seminar 4: More of His Glory (viewing time: 55:30). Encourage participants to open their Bibles to John 17:1-5 and to take careful notes during the presentation on the Video Listening Page on page 78.

6. In the video presentation, Anne looks at an abbreviated passage from John 17:1-5. She also wraps up the first phase of the *Pursuing More of Jesus* study. Anne challenges members to continue in their Bible study and to look for ways to share what you've learned with others.

7. Ask members to share how the Bible study and the Bible study method have helped them in their pursuit of knowing Jesus more intimately and how they have heard God speak to them through His Word.

8. At this time, present the opportunity for any who want to dig deeper into their Bible to find the "treasure hidden beneath the surface" to meet with you for two additional weeks. Next week's session would be viewing a second Bible Study Workshop that uses material from Workshop 1 and takes it one step further. There will be no homework

leading up to next week's Workshop 2 viewing. After next week's workshop, there will be one week of homework for participants to practice what they learned. The participants will gather one final week to share answers and to discuss what they've learned.

9. Assess the interest in the Workshop 2 session and make plans with participants who have a desire to proceed with the extended material.

10. Close in a prayer of thanksgiving, asking the Lord to protect each person who is pursuing more of Jesus each day ... in the pages of her Bible.

WORKSHOP TWO

1. Welcome members to this session.

2. Before viewing the video of Workshop 2, ask each woman to locate her Workshop 1 worksheets for use in this session. These are located on pages 9-16 of their workbooks. They will be carrying over their List of Facts from Step 2, page 14.

3. Say: "In this session, we learn more steps to go deeper into God's Word. Listen carefully to the video presentation and take careful notes as Anne takes us further into John 16:5-16."

4. View the video presentation of Workshop 2 (viewing time: 51:30 min.). Encourage participants to open their Bibles to John 16:5-16 and the worksheets for Workshop 2 on pages 82-84.

5. After the video, clarify any questions members might have regarding the new steps. Say: "Now that Anne has given us new tools to mine for the gold that lies beneath the surface of a passage, she has given us a passage to practice on this week. We will meet together next week to discuss what we discovered."

WORKSHOP #2—Digging Deeper Study Notes

The following is my personal study worksheet for John 12:1-8. I am including it with the prayer that it will help to further clarify for you the instructions on how to study the Bible for yourself. But let me once again reassure you that if your worksheet is different, it doesn't mean mine is right and yours is wrong or that mine is better and yours is less. It simply means that we see the passage from two different perspectives, which I think actually enriches our study of the Scriptures.

LIST THE FACTS

Verse 1. Before Passover, Jesus arrived where Lazarus lived.

Verse 2. A dinner was given in Jesus' honor. Martha served while Lazarus reclined at the table.

Verse 3. Mary took expensive perfume, poured it on Jesus' feet; the house was filled with the fragrance.

Verse 4. Judas objected.

Verse 5. Why wasn't this sold and given to the poor?

Verse 6. He didn't care about the poor but was a thief; as keeper of the money, he helped himself to it

Verse 7. Leave her alone, Jesus replied. She saved this perfume for My burial.

Verse 8. You will always have the poor but not Me.

DIVIDE THE FACTS

Dividing the passage with Jesus as the subject of each label:

I. Jesus was honored at a dinner in Bethany (vv. 1-2).

II. Jesus was anointed by Mary. (v. 3).

III. Jesus heard Judas's criticism of Mary (vv. 4-6).

IV. Jesus affirmed Mary's sacrifice. (vv. 7-8).

Switching the subject of each label from Jesus to Mary, these are two other sets of divisions:

I. Mary's Sacrifice Was in Gratitude for What Jesus Had Done (vv. 1-2).

II. Mary's Sacrifice Was an Act of Personal Devotion (v. 3).

III. Mary's Sacrifice Provoked Criticism and Praise (vv. 4-8)

I. Mary poured perfume on Jesus at dinner in Bethany (vv. 1-3).

II. Mary's action was affirmed by Jesus (vv. 4-8).

SUMMARIZE THE FACTS

Combining the labels of the two divisions with Mary as the subject:

Mary poured perfume on Jesus and was affirmed by Him.

AIM

Expressing the thrust of the passage from Mary's point of view...

To cause the audience to give Jesus their most precious possession, and receive His affirmation.

APPLICATIONS

Applying the two divisions with Mary as the subject in the labels:

I. Mary poured perfume on Jesus at a dinner in Bethany (vv. 1-3).

What is my "expensive perfume" ... my most precious possession? Am I willing to "pour" it all on Jesus?

II. Mary's action was affirmed by Jesus. (vv. 4-8).

How has Jesus affirmed my act of service/devotion/sacrifice to Him?

Applying the four divisions with Jesus as the subject in each label:

I. Jesus was honored at a dinner in Bethany (vv. 1-2).

How does Jesus feel in my home and at my table...honored or ignored?

II. Jesus was anointed by Mary (v. 3).

What have I given to Jesus that was costly and involved sacrificial service?

III. Jesus heard Judas's criticism of Mary (vv. 4-6).

What has Jesus heard others saying about me and my sacrificial service to Him?

IV. Jesus affirmed Mary's sacrifice (vv. 7-8).

Why do I care what others say when Jesus is pleased with what I have done? Do I care more about His praise than their criticism?

HAVING MORE OF *Jesus* IN YOUR LIFE LEADS YOU INTO A WORLD OF UNPARALLELED PRIVILEGE.

In *Pursuing More of Jesus* (previously titled *My Heart's Cry*), gifted Bible teacher and acclaimed conference speaker Anne Graham Lotz shows you how saturating your life with more of Jesus is the key to:

- restoring love to your marriage
- finding the antidote to fear
- discovering hope in your grief
- making your service to God more fruitful

Doors open, angels attend, mountains move, doubts disappear, and fears fade if we simply pursue Him.

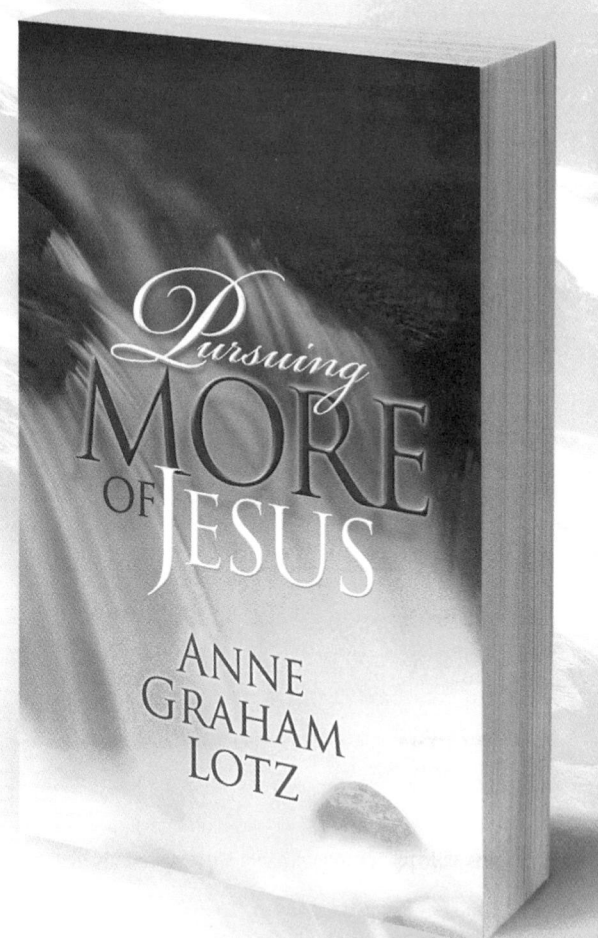

CHRISTIAN GROWTH STUDY PLAN

In the Christian Growth Study Plan (formerly Church Study Course), this book, *PURSUING MORE OF JESUS*, is a resource for course credit in the subject area Person Life of the Christian Growth category of plans. To receive credit, read the book, complete the learning activities, show your work to your pastor, a staff member or church leader, then complete the following information. This page may be duplicated. Send the completed page to:

Christian Growth Study Plan;
One LifeWay Plaza; Nashville, TN 37234-0117
FAX: (615)251-5067; E-mail: cgspnet@lifeway.com
For information about the Christian Growth Plan, refer to the Christian Growth Study Plan Catalog. It is located online at www.lifeway.com/cgsp. If you do not have access to the Internet, contact the Christian Growth Study Plan office (1.800.968.5519) for the specific plan you need for your ministry.

PURSUING MORE OF JESUS
COURSE NUMBER: CG-1444

PARTICIPANT INFORMATION

Social Security Number (USA ONLY-optional)	Personal CGSP Number*	Date of Birth (MONTH, DAY, YEAR)

Name (First, Middle, Last)	Home Phone

Address (Street, Route, or P.O. Box)	City, State, or Province	Zip/Postal Code

Email Address for CGSP use

Please check appropriate box: ☐ Resource purchased by church ☐ Resource purchased by self ☐ Other

CHURCH INFORMATION

Church Name

Address (Street, Route, or P.O. Box)	City, State, or Province	Zip/Postal Code

CHANGE REQUEST ONLY

☐ Former Name

☐ Former Address	City, State, or Province	Zip/Postal Code

☐ Former Church	City, State, or Province	Zip/Postal Code

Signature of Pastor, Conference Leader, or Other Church Leader	Date

*New participants are requested but not required to give SS# and date of birth. Existing participants, please give CGSP# when using SS# for the first time. Thereafter, only one ID# is required. **Mail to:** Christian Growth Study Plan, One LifeWay Plaza, Nashville, TN 37234-0117. Fax: (615)251-5067.

Revised 4-05